Christian Sorcerers on Trial

Christian Sorcerers on Trial

Records of the 1827 Osaka Incident

Translated and with an introduction by Fumiko Miyazaki,
Kate Wildman Nakai, and Mark Teeuwen

COLUMBIA UNIVERSITY PRESS
NEW YORK

Columbia University Press wishes to express its appreciation for assistance given by the Wm. Theodore de Bary Fund in the publication of this book.

Columbia University Press
Publishers Since 1893
New York   Chichester, West Sussex
cup.columbia.edu
Copyright © 2020 Columbia University Press
All rights reserved

Library of Congress Cataloging-in-Publication Data
Names: Miyazaki, Fumiko, translator. | Nakai, Kate Wildman, translator. |
    Teeuwen, Mark, translator.
Title: Christian sorcerers on trial : records of the 1827 Osaka incident / translated
    and with an introduction by Fumiko Miyazaki, Kate Wildman Nakai, and
    Mark Teeuwen.
Description: New York : Columbia University Press, 2020. | Includes bibliographical
    references and index.
Identifiers: LCCN 2019050828 (print) | LCCN 2019050829 (ebook) |
    ISBN 9780231196901 (cloth) | ISBN 9780231196918 (paperback) |
    ISBN 9780231551885 (ebook)
Subjects: LCSH: Osaka (Japan : Prefecture)—Church history—To 1868. |
    Martyrdom—Christianity. | Osaka (Japan : Prefecture)—History—1600–1868.
Classification: LCC BR1310.O7 C47 2020 (print) | LCC BR1310.O7 (ebook) |
    DDC 272/.90952—dc23
LC record available at https://lccn.loc.gov/2019050828
LC ebook record available at https://lccn.loc.gov/2019050829

Columbia University Press books are printed on permanent and durable
acid-free paper.
Printed in the United States of America

Cover design: Milenda Nan Ok Lee
Cover image: Fūryū ningyō no uchi: Watōnai, O-tsuji, Bōtarō. Artist: Utagawa Kuniyoshi. Description: The print depicts a famous scene from a play in which a woman seeking the success of a vendetta performs water austerities with great determination. © The Trustees of the British Museum.

CONTENTS

ACKNOWLEDGMENTS

The idea for this book originated when one of the authors, Fumiko Miyazaki, came across a facsimile manuscript titled "Record of the Case of the Pernicious Sect" at the Historiographical Institute of the University of Tokyo. What immediately drew her attention was the wealth of details that this judicial record dating from 1827–1829 had to offer about the lives of a group of people in Osaka and Kyoto who were accused of engaging in subversive religious activities. The prominent place of women in the incident added to the fascination of this material, and it struck us as a compelling candidate for a new translation project.

This volume is a sequel to *Lust, Commerce, and Corruption: An Account of What I Have Seen and Heard, by an Edo Samurai*, on which the authors collaborated together with Anne Walthall and John Breen (Columbia University Press, 2014; abridged paperback, 2017). That book presented a translation of a comprehensive critique of Japanese society as it appeared to an Edo warrior in 1816. Like the vast majority of Edo-period sources, the critique projects a male and upper-strata perspective on the circumstances of the time. The author undoubtedly would have felt that the 1827 incident confirmed his conclusions about the sorry state of contemporary society, particularly as regards the activities of the marginal floating population of urban residents whom he condemned as "idlers." At the same time, the records of the case offer a view from a quite different angle into the world of such "idlers." This second translation thus complements *Lust, Commerce, and Corruption* while also opening a window into corners of late Edo society rarely visible in a manner this direct.

We have received advice and assistance from numerous people and organizations in preparing this volume. We are indebted to the institutions holding the two manuscript copies of the judicial record on which the translation is based: the Historiographical Institute of the University of Tokyo and the Center for Modern Japanese Legal and Political Documents attached to the University of Tokyo Graduate School for Law and Politics. We would like to express our gratitude especially to Yabuta Yutaka, professor emeritus at Kansai University, who offered his expertise on matters related to the Edo-period administration of Osaka. The maps were produced by Satō Hirotaka of Ritsumeikan University; the Department of Culture Studies and Oriental Languages of Oslo University provided funding for them. The illustrations were edited for this publication by Chiba Azusa. Shimura Kiyoshi kindly allowed us to use his redrawing of the Tobita execution grounds.

KYOTO MAP KEY

PLACES ASSOCIATED WITH GUNKI

1. Samegai, south of Gojō street; where Gunki lived in rental housing owned by his friend Tomitaya Riemon
2. Intersection of Kiyamachi and Matsubara streets; Gunki's final residence

PLACES ASSOCIATED WITH WASA

3. Intersection of Shinbashi and Nawate streets; teahouse operated by Wasa
4. Intersection of Higashi-no-tōin and Nijō streets; residence of Wasa's adoptive daughter Ito

PLACES ASSOCIATED WITH MITSUGI

5. Yasaka Kami-chō; Mitsugi's residence
6. Benten-chō off Shimokawara street; where Mitsugi lived with Iori
7. Nijō Shinchi; the brothel where Mitsugi worked
8. Saiin; where Mitsugi first lived in Kyoto
9. Uchino Nīban-chō; where Mitsugi's brother and mother lived
10. Katagihara; native village of Mitsugi's adoptive son, Kamon

PLACE ASSOCIATED WITH KINU

11. Nushiya-chō, off Shichijō street; where Kinu lived with her husband

PLACES ASSOCIATED WITH SANO

12. Area in front of Kyoto Daibutsu; where Sano lived with her husband
13. Uma-chō; where Sano lived with Kinu
14. Area on Imadegawa street where Sano's grandparents lived

PLACES ASSOCIATED WITH UMON

15. Kami Goryō-mae; where Umon worked as an *Yijing* diviner

16. Sanbongi; where Umon first met Gunki

PLACES ASSOCIATED WITH GUNKI'S FRIENDS

17. Intersection of Akezu and Matsubara streets; residence of Nakamuraya Shintarō
18. Intersection of Akezu and Gojō streets; residence of Kamaya Kyūbei
19. Chion'in Furumonzen Moto-chō; residence of Tsuchiya Shōni
20. Rental horse grounds north of Gionsha; where Shōni first met Gunki
21. Butsuguya-chō on the north side of Kitakōji street; residence of Hōki Masasuke
22. Intersection of Nishi Ishigaki and Shijō streets; residence of Matsusakaya Nihei
23. West side of the Takase River, south of Matsubara street; residence of Minoya Kohachi
24. Intersection of Yanagi-no-banba and Maruta-machi streets; residence of Teradaya Kumazō
25. Shichiken-chō; residence of Minoya Bunsuke

TEMPLES

26. Unseiji, intersection of Samegai and Uonotana streets, south of Gojō street; Gunki's temple
27. Daijōin, Nijō street, on the east side of the Kamo River; Wasa's and Mitsugi's temple

OTHERS

28. Kiyomizu; where Mitsugi and others performed water austerities
29. Nyakuōji; where Mitsugi and others performed water austerities
30. Kyoto Eastern Magistracy
31. Kan'in princely house
32. Nijō house
33. Yamanoi house

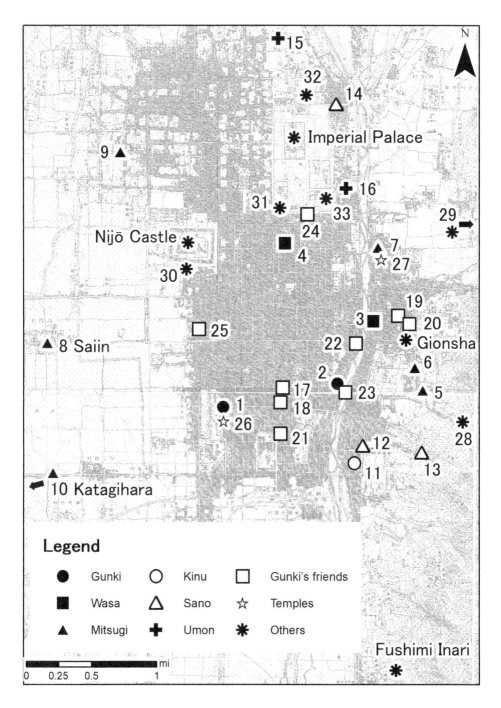

Figure 0.1 Map of Kyoto. Satō Hirotaka. Based on Japanese Imperial Army Survey Corps map of 1887. Ritsumeikan University.

OSAKA MAP KEY

PLACES ASSOCIATED WITH SANO, HER
ACCOMPLICES, AND HER CLIENTS

1. Era-machi in Dōjima; where Sano first
   lived in Osaka
2. Naniwa Bridge; where Sano
   practiced water austerities
3. Shinchi Ura-machi in Dōjima; where
   Sano lived when she met Soyo, Kanzō,
   and Toki
4. Minami Kohata-machi in Tenma;
   where a number of Sano's clients lived
   Kawasaki; village where Sano met Yae
   and where she lived when she was
   arrested
   Kitano; village where Sano had clients
   Shimo Sanba; village where Sano fled
   after returning from Nagasaki

PLACES ASSOCIATED WITH KINU, HER
ACQUAINTANCES, AND HER CLIENTS

5. Tatsuta-machi in Tenma; where Kinu
   and Kahei lived when Kinu was arrested
6. Takama-chō; where Tōzō lived
7. Nōjin-machi in Tenma; where Kinu
   first lived in Osaka
8. Uoya-machi in Tenma; where
   Koto lived with her son, Jōsuke
9. Sunahara Yashiki in Tenma;
   later address of Koto and Jōsuke

PLACES ASSOCIATED WITH UMON

10. Kyōmachibori 4-chōme; where
    Umon initially lived in Osaka
    Sonezaki; village where Umon lived
    when he was arrested

PLACES ASSOCIATED WITH HEIZŌ

11. Matsuyama-machi; where Heizō lived
    when he was arrested

12. Owarizaka-chō; where Heizō
    lived when he met Gunki
13. Sakata-chō; where Heizō lived earlier

PLACES ASSOCIATED WITH KENZŌ

14. Funadaiku-machi in Dōjima;
    where Kenzō lived when he was
    arrested
15. Shinchi 1-chōme in Dōjima; where
    Kenzō lived as the adoptive son-in-law
    of Fujita Kyōan

PLACE ASSOCIATED WITH KINOSHIN

16. Tenma 7-chōme; where
    Kinoshin lived when he was arrested

TEMPLES

17. Enkōji, Kita Miyahara; Sano's temple
18. Jōkōji, Shirokoura-machi; Umon's
    temple
19. Rentakuji, Tenma 1-chōme;
    Kinu's temple
20. Kanzanji, Nishi Tera-machi in
    Tenma; Heizō's temple
21. Enshōji, Aburakake-machi; Kenzō's
    temple

OTHERS

Osaka Castle, headquarters of the Osaka
governor

22. Osaka Eastern Magistracy
23. Osaka Western Magistracy
24. Matsuya-machi Jailhouse
25. Saitō-machi; residence of the
    author of *The State of the
    Floating World*
26. Tenma Tenjin Shrine
27. Tobita execution grounds

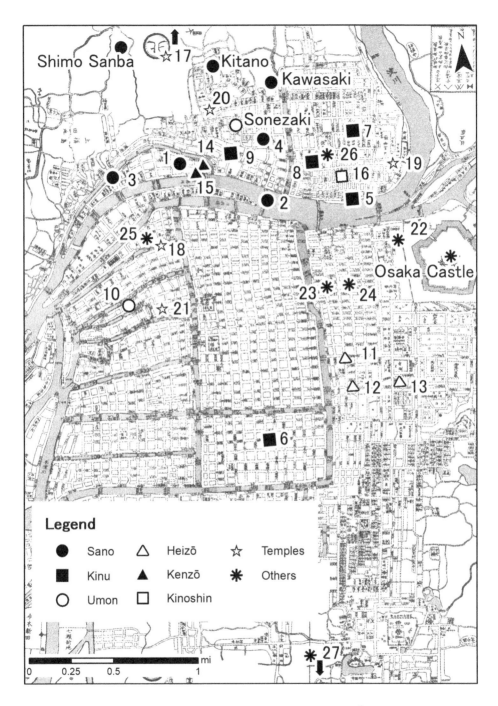

Figure 0.2 Map of Osaka. Satō Hirotaka. Based on *Tenpō shinkai Sesshū Ōsaka zenzu* (1837). International Research Center for Japanese Studies.

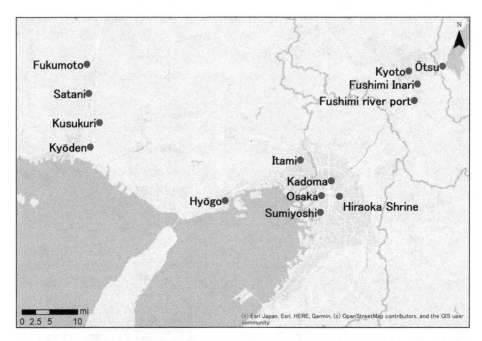

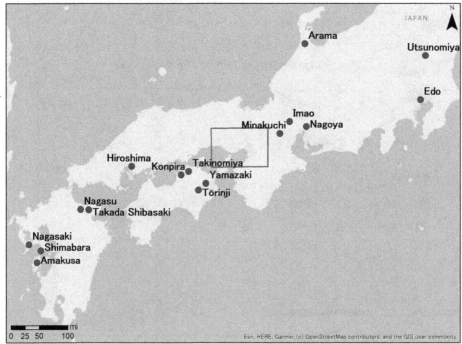

Figure 0.3 Maps of the Kansai area and Japan (partial). Satō Hirotaka.

INTRODUCTION

Late in 1829 word of a startling event spread throughout Japan. In the twelfth month of that year, three women and three men were paraded through Osaka to the Tobita execution grounds, where they were tied to crosses and pierced with spears. Their crime, announced on placards set up at Tobita, was that they had practiced Christianity in defiance of the proscription of that religion. As it so happened, four of the six were already dead. They had died in the Osaka jailhouse, where they had been detained since their arrest in 1827. For the procession to Tobita, their shriveled corpses, which had been kept packed in salt, were propped up in barrels. The four barrels, each slung from a pole carried by two bearers, followed the two survivors, a man and a woman, who were led on horseback through crowds of onlookers. The woman in particular held the viewers' attention. A fifty-six-year-old diviner and medium from Kyoto named Toyoda Mitsugi, she exuded self-control, in striking contrast with the abject appearance and snivels of the other survivor, a forty-eight-year-old man called Heizō.

Executions, even crucifixions, were by no means rare in Edo-period Japan. This event was notable for a number of reasons, nevertheless. Over a century and a half had passed since the mass executions of the 1650s and 1660s, when large numbers of people identified as Christians had been discovered in the central provinces of Mino and Owari as well as in different regions of Kyushu. Subsequently officials had adopted a much more restrained approach. In the decades immediately before the Osaka incident, for example, shogunal and domanial authorities had conducted investigations of villagers in rural parts of northwestern Kyushu whom researchers today assume were "underground Christians" (in Urakami in 1790 and Amakusa in 1805). Circumstantial evidence indicates that the villagers were indeed transmitting practices and perhaps beliefs deriving from the activities of Catholic missionaries in the area in the sixteenth and early seventeenth centuries. The investigators, too, must have contemplated the possibility that these were followers of the proscribed "pernicious sect" (*jashūmon*). Yet they as well as the villagers avoided making Christianity the issue. Both sides instead framed the matter as a question of adherence to an unspecified "deviant creed" (*ishū*), and it was resolved on those terms.[1]

Through this approach the authorities sidestepped taking provocative actions that would have affected large numbers of villagers. They also upheld the premise that measures such as the temple registration system guaranteed the absence of Christians among the populace. Since everyone had to be affiliated with a specific Buddhist temple whose priest was to confirm regularly that none of his parishioners were Christian, any subversive inclinations could in principle be readily identified and dealt with.

The officials of the Osaka Magistracy (*Ōsaka machi bugyō*) who investigated the 1827–1829 incident took an approach very different to that of their Kyushu colleagues. Their handling of the case implied that Christianity was not a past foe, long since defeated; the "pernicious sect" had reared its head once again, and in the heart of the realm. Moreover, the conclusion that Mitsugi and the others had practiced Christianity while observing the conventional requirements of temple registration raised questions about that system's operation. In the incident's wake both government authorities and the Buddhist head temples implicated in the incident would call for tightening surveillance mechanisms.

The subsequent activities of those who conducted the investigation add another dimension to its singular character. The lead investigator was Ōshio Heihachirō (1793–1837), a senior staff official in the eastern division of the Osaka Magistracy. Ōshio, who counted the investigation as one of his three great achievements as an official, resigned in the late summer of 1830 and devoted himself to his private Confucian academy. Seven years later, during a calamitous famine, he sent out a call to action in which he castigated the government's lack of concern for those who were starving and mounted an attack on the magistracy. The fighting ended with much of Osaka in flames. Rumors that circulated in the wake of Ōshio's rebellion linked it to his earlier investigation of the Christians, with some suggesting that Ōshio had been bewitched by Toyoda Mitsugi, or even that he had become a Christian himself. Be that as it may, how Ōshio's personality and convictions may have shaped the investigation's direction remains a pending question.

The incident took on further significance because it occurred at a time when Western nations were once again making their presence known in Japanese waters. Russian traders arrived from the north, British and French warships from the south, and British and American whalers from the east. Some landed to seek provisions and made contact with fishermen. At the forefront of those raising an alarm about this situation were scholars from the influential Mito domain, which had a long Pacific coast and was the site of an encounter with English seamen in 1824, just three years before the Osaka incident.

What worried the Mito scholars above all was their certainty that the Westerners would use the quest for provisions as a pretext for subverting the Japanese populace through the introduction of Christianity.[2] One noted that audacious foreign seamen had presented local people with "sorcerous works" on Christianity written in Chinese; such gifts, he declared, were sure to become "the ground for luring people into that pernicious teaching."[3] The Mito scholars would seize on the 1827–1829 incident as evidence of the need to bolster Japan's defenses against Christianity's seductive dangers. In so doing they also endowed it with an ideological cast.

THE AIMS OF THIS VOLUME

The 1827–1829 incident is well documented. Extant sources include the testimonies of those investigated; exchanges between officials in Osaka and Edo; a detailed consideration of the case's ramifications by the shogunate's main judicial body, the Deliberative Council (hyōjōsho); and multiple accounts of the rumors it engendered. Despite this wealth of information, the incident has not received much attention from historians,

Japanese or otherwise. Perhaps the main reason for this is that it has tended to get caught in the cracks between academic specializations.

Academic research on the incident can be traced to Kōda Shigetomo (1873–1954), who obtained one of the main manuscript copies of the official records of the incident and introduced it in his 1910 biography of Ōshio Heihachirō.[4] Subsequent researchers, however, have not found it easy to incorporate the incident into their accounts of Ōshio's controversial career. Ōshio's unrelenting pursuit of Mitsugi and the others does not sit easily with the popular image of him as a defender of the poor and downtrodden.[5]

The accounts of Toyoda Mitsugi, Heizō, and their fellows have likewise proved difficult to fit into the established narratives of Christianity as it persisted in Edo-period Japan. Those narratives have centered on the experiences of "underground Christian" communities (such as those in Amakusa and Urakami) that covertly held on to some of their ancestors' Christian rites and customs in the face of persecution.[6] Mitsugi and the others, however, were not heirs to that tradition. They had no ascertainable connection to the underground Christian communities that survived in Kyushu, nor to ones that had once existed in central and eastern Japan. The content of their practice, too, was different. A few of them evidently had some familiarity with Christian texts written in Chinese by Matteo Ricci (1552–1610) and other Jesuits active in China, texts that continued to circulate to a certain extent in Japan despite being proscribed. Their devotions, on the other hand, were an amalgam of elements drawn from popular images of Christians as masters of sorcery, along with incantations, spells, and austerities of the sort associated with mountain ascetics and folk mediums who dedicated themselves to the Inari deity.[7]

In 1968, the Christian scholar Ebisawa Arimichi (1910–1992) argued that the "Keihan" (that is, Kyoto–Osaka) group had independently developed a sincere—if distorted—Christian faith.[8] Others, however, have found it more plausible to situate Mitsugi and her fellows within a range of underground traditions that at the time were condemned as subversive, or to link them to the variety of diviners and mediums who were expanding their activities in Kyoto and Osaka in the early nineteenth century.[9]

These approaches shed light on several dimensions of the incident, but inevitably they have tended to focus on one aspect at the expense of others. Through a translation of the pertinent sources, this volume seeks to bring its entire scope into view. The testimonies of the principal figures, presented in part 1, give a picture of what motivated them to knowingly risk death in defying the ban against Christianity. From the questions asked and interpolated comments we can reconstruct how both they and the investigators understood the proscribed creed. At the same time, the investigation extended beyond the six principals to a large number of other people associated with them in one way or another. Apart from information about the practices that were the investigation's main target, the testimonies in toto, of the secondary as well as principal figures, offer a set of remarkable vignettes of late Edo urban life, related by people from a social tier where individual voices are only rarely represented in the historical record.

Part 2, covering exchanges between officials in Osaka and Edo regarding the case, the sentences, and measures taken in its wake, provides a snapshot of the shogunal judicial process. It shows in concrete detail how officials grappled with what they saw as an "unprecedented" situation. Part 3 takes up the broader response to the incident. Three different types of reportage illustrate the nature of the rumors it generated. The ways in which the actual circumstances became distorted in the retelling reveal much about the conceptions of Christians prevalent in the decades immediately before Western Christian nations brought concerted pressure on Japan to open its doors. The reportage also gives a glimpse into how information was obtained and transmitted in an age when the government prohibited open commentary on current events.

What did "Christianity" mean to shogunal officials more than a century after the last confirmed Christians had been caught? Their understanding of what they interchangeably termed "Kirishitan" and "the pernicious sect" owed much to chapbooks, popular tales, and plays that depicted Kirishitan as wily sorcerers and rebels, intent on undermining the social order and taking over the country. This image was painted in vivid colors in such works as *A True Account of the Coming of the Kirishitan Sect to This Country* (*Kirishitan shūmon raichō jikki*), which circulated in manuscript form in multiple versions and under many different titles. Tales of the Shimabara-Amakusa uprising of 1637–1638 reinforced the assumption that Kirishitan were not only sorcerers but also fomenters of rebellion and political subversion. At Shimabara, a motley group of villagers and others had raised banners emblazoned with Christian symbols

and held off a prolonged onslaught by a much larger domanial and shogunal force. Memory of this event left a lasting imprint on the political
elite's perception of the dangers posed by Kirishitan.[10]

Fear of those dangers was exacerbated by a conviction that a mood of
self-interest and greed had taken hold among the commoner population,
making it easy prey for Kirishitan wiles. In 1816, only a few years before
the Keihan incident came to light, a critic of Edo society wrote,

> From what I hear, Kirishitan are greedy. In their yearning for personal
> glory they engage in all sorts of nefarious practices so as to produce
> strange occurrences and thereby deceive the world. The Divine Lord
> [Ieyasu] deeply abhorred their doctrines and . . . promulgated a strict ban
> on this sect. . . . The current popular mood is already one in which peo-
> ple cheat and deceive others, seeking only to achieve their own greedy
> aims, and are attracted to strange occurrences. If this kind of attitude
> continues to grow stronger, heavenly calamities and earthly disasters
> will occur. Taking advantage of those circumstances, the Jesus sect
> might well burst out again. Although it would be quite easy to put down
> a mere fifty or one hundred followers, this sect will be difficult to keep
> under control if the whole world is caught up in it.[11]

Summing up the Keihan incident's significance, the Osaka eastern magistrate used almost identical terms to describe the situation his staff had
uncovered: "It appears . . . that the popular mood here is turning unswervingly toward greed. Those who promote pernicious creeds [jadō] may
well take advantage of this. . . . Should ordinary people secretly become
believers while hiding it even from their parents, children, and siblings,
and should these practices spread throughout the world, the situation will
become irremediable."[12]

Ideas of this sort, along with tales of Kirishitan doings, likely had a
greater influence over the officials' perspective than did any concrete
knowledge of the creed introduced to Japan by Catholic missionaries in
the mid-sixteenth century.[13] The same was true of those whom the officials identified as Kirishitan. Mitsugi and the others do not seem to have
had any inclination toward political subversion, and they presumably did
not share the officials' view of Kirishitan as "pernicious." Nevertheless,
the image perpetuated in popular works also shaped their understanding. They, too, assumed Kirishitan to possess powers to perform

extraordinary deeds. For them, to become a Kirishitan meant to gain access to such powers. To preserve the nuances that had accumulated around the term "Kirishitan" in the eyes of the officials and the Keihan group alike, we adhere as closely as possible to the language they use.[14]

THE BACKGROUND TO THE INCIDENT

The testimonies are our prime source of information about the Keihan Kirishitan and how they became involved in the "pernicious sect." The sequence of the testimonies, however, follows that of the investigation. That is, the first testimonies are those of the first person arrested, a woman named Sano, and her immediate associates. Based on what they learned from Sano, the officials arrested the other principals, including Toyoda Mitsugi, with each phase of the investigation turning up new suspects. As was standard in Tokugawa jurisprudence, the dossier sought to reproduce the stages of the investigation, not to provide a synthetic account of how the incident had evolved. Sano, in fact, was the last of the principals to become a Kirishitan devotee. The report of the investigation recounts events almost in reverse order, suspect by suspect, and it is left to the reader to reconstruct the history of the group as a whole.

Although for convenience we refer to Sano and the others as a "group," this is somewhat of a misnomer. Those investigated did not constitute a close-knit community. To the contrary, none of the principals knew or was in contact with all the others. The primary link was that almost all traced their knowledge of the Kirishitan creed directly or indirectly to a shadowy figure named Mizuno Gunki (d. 1824). Gunki had died three years before Sano came to the attention of the authorities. The investigators thus could not question him directly and had to depend on what they could gather from those they did interrogate. To their frustration (and ours), the officials could obtain only limited information about Gunki's background. Those who knew Gunki directly gave widely different guesses concerning his place of origin, and none could provide an account of how he came by his knowledge of the practices and notions that he transmitted to others.

The testimonies indicate that wherever he had been born, Gunki was living in Kyoto by 1795. There he taught calligraphy and found employment as a scribe successively with two prominent noble houses. Neither period of employment ended well. Gunki became involved in some sort of financial irregularity at the second, the Kan'in princely house, where he had been employed since about 1799.[15] At the end of 1817 he absconded, but was caught and brought back to Kyoto. There he was dismissed, prohibited to take up service with another house of nobility, and subjected to the punitive confiscation of his household possessions. He spent his last years dependent on financial assistance from others and died in impoverished circumstances in Kyoto in the twelfth month of 1824.

During his years of employment as a scribe, Gunki led a double life in which he secretly gathered a number of followers to whom he transmitted what he described as Kirishitan tenets and practices. These included worship of a deity whom he called the Lord of Heaven Buddha (*Tentei nyorai*) and recitation of the mantra *Zensu Maru paraizo* (Jesus, Mary, paradise). The term "Tentei" and the mantra both figure as Kirishitan motifs in popular polemical works such as *A True Account of the Coming of the Kirishitan Sect to This Country*. So do acts of sorcery of the sort that Gunki performed for some of his followers.[16] These parallels suggest that such writings may have been one of his main sources of information about Kirishitan. Popular tales about Kirishitan were not the only source of Gunki's practice, though. He also called on his followers to cultivate an "unwavering mind" by performing austerities such as standing under waterfalls at night. In addition he possessed works of the "Jesus creed" in Chinese, which he expounded to some of his male followers, and an old, faded painting of the Lord of Heaven that evidently showed an image of Mary, holding a child in her left hand and a sword (or, more likely, a scepter) in her right. Gunki occasionally allowed his followers to worship this painting, usually as part of an initiation rite in which they dripped blood on the breast of the Lord of Heaven.

Gunki attracted both male and female followers. His earliest known disciple was a man named Fujii Umon (1767–ca. 1827). Orphaned at a young age, Umon served in temples and shrines as a youth and acquired some familiarity with esoteric rituals. For several years he made a living as an *Yijing* diviner, determining his clients' fortunes by using the hexagrams of the Chinese *Book of Changes* (*Yijing*), but eventually he turned to medicine. He first encountered Gunki in Kyoto in 1801 and was initiated in 1805. He subsequently moved to Osaka but remained in intermittent contact with Gunki.

The other male follower identified as a principal was Heizō (1782–1829). Born the son of a doctor, Heizō became a Zen priest before returning to lay life in his late twenties. He resided largely in Osaka, where he supported himself as an *Yijing* diviner, calligraphy teacher, and storyteller of military tales. He met Gunki through a mutual acquaintance and was initiated in 1818. Gunki explained the writings of Matteo Ricci to both Umon and Heizō, and at Heizō's request, he put on a display of sorcery for him. Neither Umon nor Heizō proved to be committed to the daily practice of water austerities, however. Umon complained that he suffered from diarrhea, and Heizō made the excuse that he was too busy eking out a living. Both hoped for riches and glory, but, according to their testimonies, neither made a concerted effort to put their devotions to the Lord of Heaven to that end. Evidently neither sought to enroll disciples of his own.

Whereas Umon and Heizō apparently did not know one another, the three female principals formed a lineage of sorts. The leader was Mitsugi (1774–1829), who was born in Etchū province and moved to Kyoto with her parents and brother at an early age. She worked first as a maid and then a prostitute, until she met and married a man named Iori when she was in her midtwenties. The son of a Shinto priest, Iori was familiar with *Yijing* divination and techniques for calling down the Inari deity. He taught these skills to Mitsugi, who used them to establish herself as an Inari medium. In 1810, however, some ten years into their marriage, Iori ran away with another woman, leaving Mitsugi consumed with jealous rage. A friend, a woman named Wasa (d. 1818), proposed a solution. Wasa, who operated a teahouse (a place where customers could order female company as well as refreshments), was friends with Mizuno Gunki and quite likely had already been initiated into Kirishitan practice herself. She suggested that Mitsugi seek Gunki's assistance. In a dramatic scene at Wasa's house, Gunki conjured up the wraith of the woman who had stolen Iori's affections, enabling Mitsugi to express and exorcise her anger. After this, Mitsugi decided to become Gunki's disciple. She trained diligently to secure an unwavering mind, and early in 1811 Gunki initiated her into the Kirishitan creed by allowing her to drip blood on the painting of the Lord of Heaven.

Outwardly Mitsugi continued to act as an Inari medium, and she also invested in certification as a yin-yang diviner (*onmyōji*) under the supervision of a retainer of the Tsuchimikado noble house, which exercised a licensing authority over yin-yang diviners.[17] Secretly, however, she performed the mantra and rites to the Lord of Heaven that she had learned from Gunki. As a result, her practice as a medium and diviner thrived. She gained many clients and became known as the clairvoyant of Yasaka, the area in Kyoto where she lived. Mitsugi evidently also had literary talents and developed connections with the Yamanoi noble house as a result of her proficiency in *renga* and *haikai* linked verse. In 1821 she went on a pilgrimage to Konpira, a major shrine-temple complex in Shikoku, as a proxy for the Yamanoi. In Shikoku she got into an altercation with post-station officials. She was arrested upon her return to Kyoto, but the investigation did not alert the officials to her Kirishitan practice.

Prior to meeting Gunki and becoming a Kirishitan devotee, Mitsugi had formed a master-disciple relationship with Kinu (1769–ca. 1827), who had begun to work as an Inari medium after the death of her husband in 1804. Although unaware of the reason, Kinu realized that the manner of Mitsugi's Inari practice changed after her initiation in 1811. Envious of Mitsugi's success, Kinu begged Mitsugi to transmit the secrets of the more effective method to her. At Mitsugi's direction Kinu began ascetic training, and in 1813 Mitsugi arranged for Gunki to initiate Kinu as well.

Meanwhile, Kinu had befriended another woman, Sano (1772–ca. 1827). Sano had a hard time making ends meet after her husband died in 1807, leaving her with a young son. Following her own initiation, Kinu encouraged Sano to become her disciple as an Inari medium. Aware that Kinu's practice was different from that of ordinary Inari mediums, Sano wanted to learn her methods. She began ascetic training, but Kinu did not immediately provide instruction in the secrets of her own techniques. At the end of 1816, Kinu and Sano left Kyoto for Osaka, presumably so as not to infringe on Mitsugi's practice and clientele. Eventually, in late 1819, Kinu recognized that Sano had attained an unwavering mind and initiated her into the mantra and other ways of worshipping the Lord of Heaven.

Since Kinu did not have access to the painting of the Lord of Heaven, Sano's initiation did not involve dripping blood on the painting. Instead Kinu told her that the Kirishitan Lord of Heaven was "a buddha without any shape or form." This only whetted Sano's curiosity. She had heard that at the beginning of each year everyone in Nagasaki, visitors and residents alike, had to tread on a *fumie*, a plate with an image sacred to Kirishitan, so as to prove that they were not adherents of the proscribed creed.[18] She decided to go to Nagasaki with the idea that she would be able to see what the Lord of Heaven looked like if she trod on the image. At the end of 1820, austerities, and Gunki also seems to have abandoned such austerities in his last years. Gunki did not require his male followers to abstain from sexual activity, nor did he himself.[23] He was much stricter with Mitsugi on both counts. He insisted that he would initiate her in the secrets of his practice only if she secured an unwavering mind by practicing austerities and agreed to remain unmarried for the rest of her life. Seki Tamiko, who has examined the incident from the perspective of gender, argues that Gunki made celibacy a condition for female followers because he thought that women would not be able to keep their faith secret from their spouses.[24] This may be the case, but it is also true that Mitsugi and the other women took pride in their ability to keep up a hard regimen of austerities and to "have nothing to do with lust." They saw this ability as setting them apart from others, men as well as women. In their view, their special powers derived as much from this as from devotions to the Lord of Heaven.

Another difference between Gunki's male and female followers was that he lectured on works in Chinese by Matteo Ricci to Umon and Heizō but not to Mitsugi. This may reflect in part a disparity in intellectual background. Both Umon and Heizō were familiar with Buddhist rituals and texts as well as the complexities of *Yijing* divination, which required specialized knowledge. Experience with materials of this sort would have prepared them to follow the theological points made by Ricci and perhaps encouraged an interest in such issues. Mitsugi also engaged in *Yijing* divination, but for her this type of divination was an adjunct to her practice as an Inari medium; she may have picked it up in a more informal manner than did Umon and Heizō.

Intellectual curiosity seems to have been a considerable factor in Umon's and Heizō's involvement in the Kirishitan creed. This bears on their weak commitment to performing austerities. It is also linked to the private nature of their engagement. As noted, neither seems to have attempted to utilize Kirishitan elements in his means of livelihood or to transmit them to others. For Mitsugi, Kinu, and Sano, on the other hand, the Kirishitan creed was foremost a matter of practice. It was also a source of enrichment and power as well as something that they, as devotees, were eager to transmit to others. These differences offered the officials another reason to see the women as more culpable than the men.

Although the testimonies provide a clear view of these differences in motivation and practice, it is difficult to learn much about the specific beliefs of Gunki and his followers. The officials paid close attention to evidence of sorcery and other suspect activities, and they recorded concrete information about conjuring feats, spells, and the use of paper effigies and nails in healing rituals and to spur people to offer donations. The officials likewise put great effort into trying to locate Gunki's painting of the Lord of Heaven and took down detailed descriptions of alternative images that he devised. They did not, however, delve into the ideas of those they questioned. They noted that Kinu told Sano that the Lord of Heaven was "a buddha without any shape or form," but they did not probe further into how the women conceived of the Kirishitan deity. Umon testified that what he heard from Gunki about Ricci's writings led him to realize that the Kirishitan sect "enters into the true by way of the pernicious," but the officials evidently did not ask him to elaborate on this point. Nor did they pursue what underlay Heizō's statement that "the essential points of the teaching of the Lord of Heaven make good sense, and . . . even though this teaching is condemned as the Jesus creed, neither Confucianism nor Buddhism is equal to it."

Even if limited, references to beliefs in combination with the fuller accounts of practices highlight some notable characteristics. Gunki and his followers shared a strong orientation toward benefits to be gained in this world. In transmitting the *Zensu Maru paraizo* mantra to Sano, Kinu told her that it was superior to similar chants calling on Amida or the Lotus Sutra: "Those have to do only with the past and future. Those chants won't bring you any good fortune or prosperity in the present world. If you chant the mantra of the Lord of Heaven, it will give you prosperity in this world." Similarly, although Gunki and his followers impressed on those they initiated that it was essential not to fear death—that was the point of securing an unwavering mind—the testimonies give no evidence of a concern for or interest in the afterlife. Also notable is the absence of any baptismal rite, especially given the fact that it was a central feature of both the sixteenth–seventeenth century encounter with Christianity and the traditions maintained by the underground Kyushu communities.[25] These dimensions of the practices transmitted by Gunki reinforce the question of the sources from which he derived his ideas.

THE INVESTIGATIVE PROCESS

A closer look at the investigative process better alerts us to what we can and cannot expect the testimonies to tell us. The office that oversaw the investigation, the Osaka Magistracy, was one of the main shogunal administrative organs. Second in size after Edo and a major economic center, Osaka in the 1820s had a population of close to four hundred thousand people, most of whom were commoners. The Osaka Magistracy was responsible for overall governance of this commoner population. Judicial matters—both suits brought by one party against another and criminal investigations initiated by the magistracy—made up a large part of its administrative functions. As with many shogunal administrative offices, two divisions shared the responsibilities of the Osaka Magistracy: the Eastern Magistracy and the Western Magistracy. The geographical designation referred to the locations of the two divisions' headquarters, not jurisdiction over different sectors of the city. The two offices were "on duty" alternate months, which meant that the division on duty took charge of whatever cases arose that month. Once either the Eastern or the Western Magistracy assumed responsibility for a case, it saw the matter through to the end, regardless of whether the investigation or adjudication continued into months when it was not on duty.

The two Osaka magistracies were headed by shogunal vassals of bannerman rank who were dispatched to Osaka for limited tours of duty. In 1827 the Osaka eastern magistrate was Takai Sanenori (1763–1834), and the western magistrate was Naitō Noritomo (1766–1841). Both had been posted to Osaka in 1820. Each magistrate had under him thirty senior staff officials (yoriki) and fifty staff officials (dōshin). Unlike the magistrates, who rotated sequentially through a series of shogunal offices, the staff officials served permanently in either the Eastern or Western Magistracy, rising gradually through the hierarchy of specialized positions within the division. In many cases their appointments were effectively hereditary in nature, with a son going through a period of apprenticeship and on-the-job training before succeeding his father. That was true of the senior staff official Ōshio Heihachirō, who had begun his apprenticeship in the Eastern Magistracy around 1806, when he was still in his teens. Ōshio had subsequently risen quite rapidly within the division, and by 1827 he occupied several important positions, including the post responsible for criminal investigations.[26] It was in that capacity that he would take charge of the investigation of the Keihan Kirishitan incident.[27]

Even combined, the staff of the two magistracies was small for administering a city the size of Osaka, and for day-to-day patrol duties and information gathering the officials relied heavily on subordinates drawn from the city's outcast communities (*kaito, hinin*). Such subordinates, known as the magistracy's "hands" (*tesaki*), often took the lead in identifying and arresting wrongdoers. They also handled various matters concerning those remanded to the jailhouse, including executions and disposal of the bodies of those who were sentenced to death or who died while under detention. Mistreatment and unhygienic conditions resulted in high mortality rates among those detained. Apart from the four principals, a large percentage of those investigated in connection with the Keihan Kirishitan incident are recorded as having "fallen ill and died" in the course of the two years before the sentences were handed down.

The preface to the testimonies notes that prior to the first arrests the magistracy had picked up rumors of a noblewoman from Kyoto who was performing rituals that would enable people to prosper. Reports of such rumors probably came from the "hands," and it may well have been a "hand" who arrested Sano in the first month of 1827 when she became engaged in a dispute with one of the supposed noblewoman's clients. Sano's case was presumably handed over to the Eastern Magistracy because it was on duty for the month. In serious or complicated cases, the suspects were remanded to the Matsuya-machi jailhouse for intensive interrogation by staff officials, and that is what happened with Sano. At the order of the eastern magistrate, she was remanded to jail on 1827.1.22.

Ōshio and the others who took charge of the investigation likely started from the assumption that this was a case of fraud and charlatanism. According to the explanation they appended to her testimony, Sano, too, initially claimed that she had simply sought to extort money and goods from her clients. But as the officials probed the nature of Sano's activities, they began to uncover its other dimensions. From their questioning of her landlord and associates, they learned of the rites she avowedly performed to Inari. A search of her house turned up paper effigies, nails, and candles. Suspecting that she might have been engaging in the banned practice of fox witchery, the officials pursued that line of questioning. To throw them off the true situation, she admitted to using fox witchery, but she also evidently changed her story repeatedly. After several months of interrogation, Sano finally led the investigators to her mentor, Kinu, and the Kirishitan dimensions of the case began to come into focus. In the preface to a poem he composed at the time of his resignation as senior staff official, Ōshio noted the fourth month of 1827 as the point when Takai Sanenori, the eastern magistrate, directed him to search out and arrest the members of the pernicious group in Kyoto as well as the Osaka area.[28]

The Osaka Magistracy had substantial powers and autonomy in conducting investigations, but its authority was also circumscribed in important regards. One was the geographical scope of its jurisdiction, which did not extend to people residing in Kyoto. Once the Osaka officials realized that many of the targets of their investigation, including Mitsugi, lived in Kyoto, they had to arrange with their Kyoto counterpart, the Kyoto Magistracy (*Kyōto machi bugyō*), to have them arrested and sent to Osaka. The investigation ultimately required multiple consultations with the Kyoto eastern magistrate, Kan'o Mototaka (dates unknown), and his successor (the Kyoto Magistracy was also divided into eastern and western divisions).[29]

The status-based premises of the shogunal system of governance posed additional challenges. Both the Osaka and Kyoto Magistracies had jurisdiction over only the commoner populations of the two cities. In Kyoto, in particular, the imperial court, despite being under the shogunate's watchful eye, held authority over court nobles. Investigation of matters concerning a noble house by any warrior official required going through layers of liaison, intended to buffer relations between the shogunate and the court. This meant in practice that the noble houses remained off-limits to the Osaka investigators.[30] Mizuno Gunki had been employed by two noble houses and dismissed for malfeasance by one. Mitsugi had contacts with the Yamanoi noble house after she had met Gunki and been initiated by him, and she undertook a proxy pilgrimage on its behalf. The investigators undoubtedly would have been able to gain more information about Gunki and Mitsugi had they questioned representatives of these noble houses. It is also possible that Gunki had followers within the circles connected to the nobility that he frequented. The Osaka investigators' inability to pursue these connections leaves an intriguing aspect of the incident opaque.

In addition to these constraints on the Osaka Magistracy's investigative powers, a distinction between investigative competence and authority to reach a judgment also affected the case's conduct. The magistrate proposed sentences, but he had to consult his immediate superior, the Osaka governor (*Ōsaka jōdai*), before handing them down.[31] For routine cases the Osaka governor had the authority to approve judgments involving even the most severe penalties, but he was expected to refer cases presenting complications or unusual features a further step up the hierarchy to the senior councillors (*rōjū*) in Edo. The senior councillors in turn would often hand the dossier on the case down to the Deliberative Council for more extensive consideration.[32] The materials translated here track this process, from the testimonies compiled in the course of the investigation to the deliberations in Edo regarding the case, followed by the orders handed down by the senior councillors about the sentences and the Osaka eastern magistrate's final reports on the case's conclusion.

THE TESTIMONIES

As can be seen from the preceding description, the testimonies were central to both the investigative process and the ultimate decisions regarding the Keihan Kirishitan incident. They stand as an extraordinary source of information about the incident and how the authorities went about investigating it. They also offer a compelling read, full of vivid details about the lives and doings of the persons providing the testimonies and their interactions with others. Responses to questions from the interrogating officials, often in the form of seemingly near-direct quotes, convey a tone of immediacy.

The reader needs to keep in mind, however, that the testimonies do not tell the whole story. They were composed for a specific judicial purpose, following well-established conventions, and thus are far from a raw and unfiltered account of "what actually happened." Obtaining a formal confession from the accused was a fundamental feature of the system of criminal jurisprudence sketched here. In order to carry a case through to conclusion, or forward it to a higher level for review, the magistrate and his staff had to prepare a written transcript of the testimony provided by the accused in the course of interrogation, describing the details and background of the matter under investigation and acknowledging guilt. This acknowledgment came at the end of the transcript, where the accused affirmed the truth of the preceding account. The transcript was read out in the presence of the magistrate, and the accused had to confirm its validity by affixing a seal, or "nail print" (*tsumein*). This "confirmed testimony" (*ginmi tsumari no kuchigaki*) was the foundation for the process of review and the decision on sentences.

Since a confirmed confession was the sine qua non of Tokugawa criminal jurisprudence, investigating officials did not shrink from using torture when they could not secure a confession otherwise. The testimonies of virtually all the major accused figures note that they were interrogated "severely" (*kibishiku*), which can be interpreted as indicating implicitly that a degree of force was used. An explanation attached to Sano's testimony states explicitly that in the face of her evasiveness and prevarication, the officials repeatedly subjected her to torture (*rōmon*). In this regard, too, the Keihan Kirishitan incident was unusual, as torture was not ordinarily employed on women.[33]

The use of torture on Sano perhaps reflects the officials' exasperation at not being able to crack the case and find a productive lead in the first three months of their investigation. It may be noted that three of Sano's close associates, who must have been interrogated in this same period, died before confirmed testimonies could be obtained from them. These were her son and two people who assisted her with the noblewoman scheme. They undoubtedly were privy to information that the investigators would have found useful, but because whatever evidence the three yielded was not confirmed, it could not be used in building the overall account of the incident, and no reference to it (or to the interrogation of the three) appears in the dossier. As this suggests, a reliance on excessive force could backfire, and to secure effective confirmed testimonies, officials had to maintain a degree of balance in their approach to interrogation.[34]

The circumstances under which the interrogations were conducted is one factor that needs to be kept in mind in weighing the testimonies' validity. Another is that, as mentioned, the investigators' preconceptions undoubtedly shaped the issues they chose to pursue. A third is the testimonies' format. The individual testimonies are organized largely chronologically and read smoothly. Yet as the officials themselves indicate, the process by which the information in the testimonies was extracted was often not smooth at all. Sano, for example, finally let out Kinu's name after three months of interrogation. Once the investigators had found the thread leading to Kinu and arrested her, they could use information gleaned from one to press the other. Nevertheless, it took two more months before the officials learned the name of the third principal figure, Mitsugi; had her arrested in Kyoto and sent under guard to Osaka; and remanded her to jail for interrogation on 1827.6.23. It may not have been until they were well into their interrogation of Mitsugi that the officials could feel that they had clarified the facts of Sano's actions to their satisfaction.

It must have been at that point, we can surmise, that Ōshio or one of his associates sat down with the records of the interrogation up to then to compile Sano's testimony as it appears in the dossier. Sorting through the records' twists and turns, false and fruitful leads, he composed the narrative that we have at present, beginning with Sano's family background and describing the various steps and events leading to her tutelage under Kinu, her initiation into the "pernicious sect," and the activities that resulted in her undoing. In many ways, then, the investigator was as much the author of the testimony as was the person who ultimately confirmed it to be true.

These factors suggest that we should exercise a degree of caution in reading the confessions couched in the voices of Sano and the others, but they do not mean that the testimonies are irretrievably compromised and unreliable. Several standard procedures served to counter outright falsification. Although the accused's confession was a necessary condition to bring a criminal case to conclusion, it was not the sole condition. Jurisprudential norms called for the confession to be checked and corroborated. Such corroboration might come from material evidence, such as the items found in the searches of the houses of Sano and the other principal figures. Most typically, however, it came from the testimony of others—associates, victims, people whose lives had intersected in some fashion with the events described in the confession. Much attention was given to making sure that the multiple testimonies matched (*mōshikuchi fugō*). Where relevant, the officials might cross-examine two parties jointly (*tsukiawase ginmi*), comparing what they said. In compiling the testimonies into a dossier for review by higher-level officials, the investigators added interpolations in red (*shugaki*, translated in the following as "addenda"); in these they described where statements by others corroborated or diverged from the testimony at hand, the material evidence collected, and the further lines of investigation, both successful and not, that had been pursued. Along with providing valuable evidence for today's reader of the investigating officials' perspective on the case and how the investigation proceeded, the addenda back up the main testimonies, as, of course, they were meant to do.

Another feature of the testimonies' format also supports the supposition that they maintain at least some level of truthfulness: the testimonies typically conclude with a statement of what the investigating officials suspected but could not get the accused to confirm. Surmises of this sort were known in Tokugawa jurisprudence as *satto*, "[unverified] suspicion" or "[unverified] accusation." In this instance they bespeak the assumptions that the officials brought to the case. Once the investigators had concluded that they had uncovered a coven of Kirishitan and had found evidence of activities that seemed to fit their preconceptions, they suspected the existence of a larger network linked by seditious motives. The *satto* accusations thus revolve around additional associates, lines of transmission, and pernicious practices to which the persons testifying had not yet admitted, as well as the likelihood that they and their presumed fellows were engaged in unspecified subversive plots. The officials' acknowledgment of the testifiers' refusal to confirm these suspicions has the side effect, from our standpoint, of reinforcing the plausibility of what the accused did affirm to be true. The officials also would have had little reason to fabricate or distort the many incidental details that make the testimonies such a rich source of information about late Edo urban life. It thus seems legitimate to take the testimonies as more or less trustworthy, even if obtained under duress and shaped by the investigating official.

TRANSLATION STRATEGIES

The translation of the dossier on the incident presented in parts 1 and 2 is based on a collation by Fumiko Miyazaki of two manuscript copies (for information about these manuscripts, see appendix 3).[1] In making the translation we have adopted the following strategies for dealing with several of the original's distinctive features.

FORMAT

For readability we have divided the testimonies into chapters and added headings and subheadings.

ADDENDA

As mentioned earlier, the investigators interspersed addenda in red (*shugaki*) in the transcripts of the testimonies. These addenda provide background of different sorts to the testimonies, including statements taken from secondary figures that were used to supplement and cross-check what was said by the main parties. We have added headings to set lengthy addenda off from the testimony in which they are embedded.

Brief addenda have been italicized and put in parentheses. On occasion we have treated similarly passages that clearly are comments by the investigators but are not marked in red.

VOICE

The testimonies are composed in a voice that stands between what would be first and third person in English. We have chosen to render portions where the first-person character predominates as direct statements by the person testifying and to shift to third person where the filtering perspective of the investigators comes to the fore. This means that occasionally those testifying are quoted as referring to themselves or their fellows in terms that they in fact likely did not use (for instance, describing themselves as devotees of "the pernicious sect").

NAMES

People in the Edo period frequently changed their names to reflect shifts in status or living environment. The people figuring in the Keihan Kirishitan incident are no exception. The transcript of the testimonies tracks such name changes, but we have used one name throughout. Because many of the names resemble one another, in choosing which name to adopt we have selected the most distinctive option, which is not necessarily the name that the officials regarded as the main one for the person in question (they favored the name being used at the time of the investigation).[2] People of quasi-warrior or noble status, doctors, and religious practitioners other than Buddhist priests typically used what can be considered a surname (*Mizuno* Gunki, *Toyoda* Mitsugi). Commoners did not have official surnames, but in Kyoto and Osaka, males (and some females operating a business establishment) registered themselves as having a "house name" (*yagō*, a name ending in the suffix -*ya*). We generally have omitted such designations. For officials (Ōshio Heihachirō, Takai Sanenori) we have adopted the forms by which they are commonly listed in standard reference works today.

CURRENCIES, DATES, AGES, AND HOURS OF THE DAY

In the Edo period, gold, silver, and copper cash served as the basic mediums of exchange. Gold and silver were used for larger transactions, copper cash for smaller ones (silver was calculated by weight; coppers and gold by units of coinage). Rates of exchange between the different mediums varied over time. In the 1820s, exchange rates were relatively stable at about 60–65 *monme* in silver or 6,400–6,800 coppers (*zeni*) to 1 *ryō* in gold. The original text also refers to smaller units used for gold, but we have rendered these as fractions of *ryō*. Similarly, we have converted units used to count large amounts of silver and coppers into the equivalent in *monme* and *zeni*.

The original gives dates according to the era name or year in the twelve-year zodiac cycle; we have converted these into the largely equivalent year of the Gregorian calendar. Bunsei 10 (year of the boar) is thus given as 1827. We generally use the format "twenty-second day of the first month, 1827" (the date of Sano's arrest) for lunisolar dates including month and day. At times, however, we adopt the abbreviated format year.month.day: 1827.1.22. Note that 1827.1.22 does not correspond to 22 January 1827 according to the Gregorian calendar; in fact, it fell on 17 February of that year. Gregorian calendar dates, which run one to two months later than lunisolar ones, may even cross into a different year: 1829.12.07, the day the Osaka magistrate reported back to Edo about the sentences carried out two days earlier, corresponds to 1 January 1830.

We have rendered ages and spans of years as in the original. According to the traditional way of reckoning ages, a person was counted as one year old at the time of birth and became a year older at each subsequent New Year's. One to two years should thus be subtracted from each age mentioned to estimate the age by Western count. In the Edo period people used a system for counting time in which the length of hours varied depending on the season. We have translated the times cited by indicating the general time of day—for example, "late in the evening" or "soon after dawn."

MAIN PROTAGONISTS

Mizuno Gunki (calligrapher, onetime court retainer)
    His wife, Soe (also went by the name Suma)
    His concubine, Tomo
    The son of Gunki and Tomo, Makijirō
    Tomo's elder brother, Momijiya Jinbei
Itoya Wasa (teahouse proprietor; introduced Mitsugi to Gunki)
    Her adoptive daughters, Ito and Toki
    Ito's son, Minoya Ichimatsu
Toyoda Mitsugi (as a prostitute used the name Onoe; Inari medium, yin-yang diviner, Gunki's disciple)
    Her elder brother, Kazue
    Her mother, Eshū (known earlier as San)
    Her husband, Iori (later divorced)
    Iori's lover, Katsura
    Her adoptive son, Kamon (son of Mitsugi's clients Iku and Moku-zaemon)

Kinu (also known as Kikue; Inari medium, Mitsugi's disciple)
Sano (Inari medium, Kinu's disciple)
    Her son, Kyōya Shinsuke (called Masajirō as a child)
Fujii Umon (also known as Irakoya Keizō; physician, *Yijing* diviner, Gunki's disciple)
    His wife, Fusa
Takamiya Heizō (nicknamed Kimyō; Zen monk, *Yijing* diviner, calligrapher, storyteller, Gunki's disciple)
    His wife, Mutsu
    A girl whom he intended to adopt on Gunki's advice, Hisae
Fujita Kenzō (physician, book collector)
    His wife, Shū
    Shū's father, Fujita Kyōan (also a physician)
    Shū's mother, Tame
    His adoptive cousin Chūtatsu (also a physician)

MIZUNO GUNKI'S PATRONS AND FOLLOWERS

Nakamuraya Shintarō (merchant; provided Gunki with housing)
    His wife, Wasa
    Wasa's father, Jirobei
    Wasa's nephew, Yazobei (as a child known as Mannosuke)
    His daughter, Mume
    Mume's husband, Shinbei
    His son, Yatarō (known as Shintarō after his father's death)
    Yatarō's wife, Nobu
    The son of Yatarō and Nobu, Sutejirō
    The daughter of Yatarō and Nobu, Kyō
    Yatarō's concubine, Tsugi
    The daughter of Yatarō and Tsugi, Ai
    The shop manager, Tsunehachi
Tomitaya Riemon (merchant; provided Gunki with housing)
    His wife, Kiyo
    His friend, Minoya Bunsuke (arranged to register Gunki's wife falsely as a member of his household)
Kamaya Kyūbei (merchant; helped Gunki after his dismissal)
    His daughter, Moto
    His son, "the present Kyūbei"

MIZUNO GUNKI'S ACQUAINTANCES

Tsuchiya Shōni (also known as Mimura Jōnosuke; onetime court retainer, drum teacher; introduced Gunki to court noble house, took charge of Gunki's papers after his death)

Hōki Masasuke (calligraphy teacher; studied calligraphy with Gunki and looked after Gunki's wife and son)

Teradaya Kumazō (scabbard maker; helped Gunki when he absconded)

Minoya Kohachi (also known as Yōzō; palanquin bearer; did errands for Gunki)

Matsusakaya Nihei (restaurant owner; arranged Gunki's final lodgings and funeral)

MITSUGI'S ACQUAINTANCES

Takeuchi Ōmi (Tsuchimikado retainer, Mitsugi's supervisor as a yin-yang diviner)

Ōmi's father, Chikugo

Harimaya Kinoshin (also known as Kinuya Mitsuemon; used as well the name Tamaki Kurando; failed disciple, Inari medium, Mitsugi's companion on pilgrimage to Konpira)

KINU'S ACQUAINTANCES

Koto (adopted the name Mitsugi; Inari medium; resisted Kinu's efforts to recruit her)

Koto's son, Edoya Jōsuke

Harimaya Kahei (merchant; Kinu's client)

Kahei's infant son, Ichimatsu

Toshimaya Tōzō (Kinu's client; falsely registered by Kahei as Kinu's grandson and household head)

SANO'S ACCOMPLICES AND ACQUAINTANCES

Yae (Sano's neighbor and accomplice)

Her husband, Kenpōya Yoshichi

Iseya Kanzō (masseur; Sano's former neighbor, her accomplice)

Toki (Kanzō's wife; Sano's accomplice)
Kenpōya Yohei (Sano's landlord; investor in the noblewoman's fund)
  His mother, Kiwa
  His wife, Chika
Soyo (Sano's former neighbor)
  Her husband, Harimaya Uhei
  Her hairdresser, Gizō
Yoshidaya Shinshichi and Namariya Kyūbei (pawnbrokers)

OTHER PEOPLE LINKED TO THE PRINCIPALS

Mizuhaya Hida (shrine priest, physician, book collector; mutual acquaintance of Fujii Umon and Fujita Kenzō)
Matsuya Jihei (Osaka merchant; put up Gunki in Osaka, introduced him to Heizō)

PRIESTS

Daizui (priest of Unseiji, where Gunki was registered)
Shōryū (Enkōji, Sano)
Zenshō (Rentakuji, Kinu)
Zekan (Daijōin, Mitsugi and Wasa)
Kanryō (Jōkōji, Umon)
Kōhō (Kanzanji, Heizō)
Ryōnen (Enshōji, Kenzō)

INVESTIGATORS AND OFFICIALS

Ōshio Heihachirō (senior staff official at the Osaka Eastern Magistracy)
Seta Tōshirō (senior staff official at the Osaka Eastern Magistracy)
Takai Sanenori (Osaka eastern magistrate)
Naitō Noritomo (Osaka western magistrate)
Matsudaira Muneakira (Osaka governor until 1828.11.22)
Ōta Suketomo (Osaka governor from 1828.11.22)
Kan'o Mototaka (Kyoto eastern magistrate)
Mizuno Tadaakira (senior councillor, Edo)

Part I

TESTIMONIES

Chapter 1

⁓

Sano and Her Associates

Dossier of the investigation of those who worshipped a buddha image of the proscribed pernicious sect, transmitted its practices and rituals, extorted money and goods, or possessed books of the Jesus creed

Inquiry submitted to the Osaka governor in the ninth month of 1827; sentences pronounced in the twelfth month of 1829

    Osaka eastern magistrate, Takai Sanenori

PREFACE TO THE DOSSIER

Sometime ago we began to receive reports that strange rumors were circulating about a noblewoman from Kyoto living in retirement, of unknown name and domicile, who was staying in the Dōjima area of this city of Osaka. It was said that when people had her perform prayer rituals or divine what fortune or misfortune awaited them, she would be able to foresee everything, and her clients' households would naturally prosper. We were having these rumors looked into when word came of an altercation involving a woman named Sano, resident with her son, Kyōya Shinsuke, in quarters rented from Kenpōya Yohei in Kawasaki village, Settsu province, in the district under the jurisdiction of the intendant Kishimoto Budayū.[1] Sano was said to have plotted together with Shinsuke and a woman named Yae, the wife of Kenpōya Yoshichi, resident in the same village, to persuade Sano's landlord, Yohei, to have prayer rituals performed for his prosperity. Sano had gotten Yohei to put up large amounts of money and goods and subsequently had fled toward Harima. Yohei had pursued her there and brought her back to Osaka. [In the initial investigation of this altercation,] it became clear that the alleged noblewoman of unknown name and domicile from Kyoto who performed prayer rituals was in fact Sano. We arrested her and through repeated interrogation learned the names of others, in addition to Yohei, who had been persuaded to have prayer rituals performed and to put up money and goods. We learned also that this Sano had prayed [to the deity] of the proscribed sect and confounded people by doing so. Thereupon we conducted a thorough investigation and probed the source of these practices. Below is the report of what we have learned about the circumstances of this matter, based on the interrogation of those involved.

TESTIMONY OF SANO

Sano: fifty-six years of age; resident together with her son, Kyōya Shinsuke, in quarters rented from Kenpōya Yohei, village of Kawasaki, Nishinari county, Settsu province, in the district under the jurisdiction of the intendant Kishimoto Budayū

Remanded to jail the twenty-second day of the first month, 1827

Sano's Early Life and Encounter with Kinu

Under interrogation Sano stated as follows:

My forebears came originally from the province of Mino, where my grandparents, who were called Yohei and Shū, were farmers in the village of Imao. I don't recall the county name. According to what I have heard, they were hereditarily adherents of the Ikkō sect.[2] At some point, I don't know exactly when, my grandparents moved to Kyoto, where they rented quarters on Imadegawa street, in the area around the temple of Honpukuji.[3] My grandfather registered himself under the name Iseya Yohei and worked as a day laborer. My grandparents had a daughter named Kino, my birth mother. She married Isogawa Gonzō, who was a retainer of some noble house—I don't know the name. *(Investigators: We looked into the name and residence of Isogawa Gonzō as well as those of this noble house but were unable to find any further information.)*[4]

I was born in Gonzō's house, but the same year my father fell ill and died, and after that my mother went back to my grandfather's house, taking me with her. As my mother was still young, she remarried, and thus I was raised by my grandparents. In 1778, when I was seven, my mother fell ill and died at the house into which she had remarried. I recall hearing about these things from my grandparents later, when I was older. In 1787, when I was sixteen, my grandparents both fell ill and died, one right after the other. Since I had no other blood relatives, I found work here and there as a short-term servant. In 1793, when I was twenty-two, I married a man named Minoya Heibei. He resided in rented quarters located in front of the Kyoto Daibutsu and managed by Shin'edaya Rihei.[5] Heibei made his living as a dealer in secondhand goods. My son, Shinsuke, was born in 1803, when I was thirty-two. As a child he went by the name Masajirō.

Subsequently my husband fell ill and died on the tenth day of the eleventh month of 1807. I was then thirty-six. Being a widow and with Shinsuke, who was still a child, to look after, it was difficult to scrabble together a living, but I had no desire to remarry. Since ancient times, I'd heard, it's been said that humans are the ultimate spiritual being among the myriad things. By concentrating one's mind and undergoing proper training, one can thus acquire miraculous powers and astonish others by doing remarkable things. I wanted to acquire such miraculous powers and hoped to find someone who had mastered arts beyond the ordinary and would teach them to me. But after my husband died, it was hard eking out even a hand-to-mouth existence, and I had to move repeatedly from place to place. In 1813, when I was forty-two, I moved to a rear tenement in Uma-machi owned by Takeya Ihei, where I got by making playing cards for gambling.

While my husband was still alive, I had become friends with a woman named Kinu, the wife of Kyōya Kihei, who rented quarters from Yamatoya Kahei in Nushiya-chō, north of Shichijō street in Kyoto.[6] *(Investigators: This Kinu later took the name Harimaya Kikue and moved to Osaka, where she lived in Tatsuta-machi in the Tenma area.[7] At present she is detained in the jailhouse.)* Kinu's husband had also died a while previously, so she, too, was a widow. She worshipped Inari and called herself an Inari medium, and she made a living [by conducting healing rituals] for the sick and by performing divinations. After I was widowed, Kinu continued to come to visit as before, and I often lamented to her about how hard it was to get through the world while looking after a young child. "You can't begin to

feed yourself by making playing cards," Kinu told me. "Things will surely
not end well if you continue this way. It would be better for your child,
too, if you made up your mind to remarry." But when I explained to her
why I found it distasteful to take another husband, Kinu said she felt the
same way. "I call myself an Inari medium," she said,

> but in fact I've learned mysterious arts from a yin-yang diviner, a
> woman named Toyoda Mitsugi who lives in Yasaka, down the hill
> from Kiyomizu here in Kyoto. I practiced austerities regularly, and lit-
> tle by little I acquired the ability to foresee the future and perform heal-
> ing rituals. I have to pretend that I do these things as an Inari medium
> because otherwise my clients will think it strange, and I would be in
> trouble if the magistracy became suspicious and decided to look into
> the matter. So I act just like ordinary Shinto diviners do when they call
> down Inari to predict the future. I pretend to be possessed by Inari—I
> hold the sacred wand in both hands, shake it, and fall to the ground. I
> put on a show of being in a trance and pronounce what the future holds
> as an oracle from Inari, or if I have an attendant with me, I have that
> person transmit the oracle to the people who have come to learn their
> fortunes.
>
> What ordinary Inari mediums do is in fact little more than a game;
> one can do it without practicing austerities. The method that Mitsugi
> transmitted to me, however, is extremely difficult. If you are indeed
> determined not to take a husband for the rest of your life or to have
> anything to do with lust, I will teach you this method. But it will be
> impossible to master it unless you first rid yourself of any inclination to
> be startled by what you see. And you cannot have the slightest fear for
> your life. So first you must perform austerities to secure an unwaver-
> ing mind. You should go into the mountains at night and you should
> stand every day under a waterfall or douse yourself with well water.

What Kinu told me matched what I had hoped for, and I begged to
become her disciple. She agreed, and we entered into a secret pact to regard
each other as sisters. Kinu gave up her residence in Nushiya-chō and
moved in with me. She began a new business doing the same things as
she had done up to then [in Nushiya-chō]: conduct healing rituals and fore-
tell the future in the guise of an Inari medium. She generally would sense
that people were coming for divination and would make paper effigies of

Figure 1.1 Female medium shaking a wand. *Ehon Raikō ichidaiki*, "Miko" (section). International Research Center for Japanese Studies.

them or something like that beforehand.[8] She didn't explain to me what she was doing, but she seemed to collect a substantial amount of money. I was amazed by Kinu's mysterious powers, so much greater than those of an ordinary Inari medium, and I decided to put all my faith in her.

"If I undergo thorough ascetic training, wouldn't I, too, be able to do all sorts of things?" I asked Kinu. "Of course, it is possible to acquire such powers," she replied,

> but the method for doing so can't be transmitted lightly. First you have to undertake training to secure an unwavering mind by going to the Fushimi Inari mountain at night. If someone sees you, say [that you're doing this to become an Inari medium], since this mountain is connected with Inari.[9] The essential thing is to climb the mountain, seek out terrifying places, close your eyes, and concentrate on securing an unwavering mind, just as in Zen meditation.

Following Kinu's instructions, I secretly doused myself with water at my house during the day, or I went to stand under one of the falls at Nyakuōji in the Higashiyama area, making sure that nobody saw me.[10] At night I climbed the Fushimi Inari mountain, sometimes together with Kinu. For three years I performed these austerities without skipping a single night.

Sano and Kinu Move to Osaka; Kinu Initiates Sano

I was told that the rules of this practice strictly prohibit direct contact with the master of one's master, but I longed to see at least once what Mitsugi looked like, so on one occasion I went with Kinu to Mitsugi's house and was able to catch a glimpse of her. But since it would inconvenience Mitsugi if we continued to engage in these arts in Kyoto, we decided to give up our residence there, and twelve years ago, in the eleventh month of 1816, Kinu and I moved to this city of Osaka. I got an acquaintance, Kagaya Bunjirō (now deceased), who resided in Naga-machi 8-chōme, to act as my guarantor and rented a room from Shioya Heibei in Era-machi in Dōjima.[11] I lived together with my son, Shinsuke, who registered himself under the name of Nakaya Masajirō, and I was listed in the population register as residing with him. Kinu was also eventually able to arrange through an acquaintance to rent quarters from Harimaya Jirobei in Tatsuta-chō in Tenma.

Figure 1.2 Woman performing water austerities. *Katakiuchi buyūden*, vol. 7 (section). National Diet Library Digital Collection.

In the quarters I rented in Osaka, I tried to make a living by pretending to be an Inari medium. Outwardly I performed rites to Inari, wrapping an old piece of silk around a wood scrap to use as the deity body.[12] But I had not yet received transmission of the secret arts, so it was difficult for me to perform effective healing rituals for clients or to make accurate predictions. I consulted Kinu, and we arranged that every afternoon I would send Shinsuke to Kinu. Kinu would perform the rituals and make judgments, and then she would tell Shinsuke the results. Once he had passed these on to me, [I would transmit them to my clients]. More and more people came to me for divinations, and whenever I sent Shinsuke to Kinu, I made sure to write down their names and ages. When I transmitted Kinu's judgments to these clients, she turned out to be right almost every time, and I was also usually able to cure their illnesses. I set aside half the payments I received and every so often had Shinsuke take that portion to Kinu.

My faith in Kinu's powers grew ever stronger, and I wanted above all to master the secret arts myself. It was fruitless, I thought, just to continue dousing myself with water. Since the true deity was not in fact Inari, how could I know to where I should direct my devotions? I repeatedly had Shinsuke ask Kinu to reveal the true deity's name, but all she would say was that I should continue to perform water austerities. Once Kinu was sure that I had come a step closer to acquiring an unwavering mind and would not falter even when confronting death, she would tell me who the deity was. I then reduced my meals to two a day. Saying that my feet hurt, I never went out [during the day]. I doused myself with water from the well three times a day, and late at night, in the wee hours when everyone else was asleep, I would go out, even if it was raining, and perform further water austerities under Naniwa Bridge.

About three years after I moved to Osaka, in the third month of 1819, I decided for financial reasons to move to a tenement owned by Kagiya Heisuke in Shinchi Ura-machi in Dōjima. Having saved a little money, I had Shinsuke work as a greengrocer so as to forestall gossip [about what we were doing]. But I also continued to have him consult Kinu on my behalf. I performed water austerities as before, and I repeatedly sent Kinu pleas to transmit to me the proper practices for invoking the true deity. Finally Shinsuke brought a message that one night I should come myself to see Kinu. Overjoyed that my fervent wish of the past several years would soon be fulfilled, I went to Kinu's room on the night of the second day of the tenth month of 1819.

When I arrived, Kinu began to speak. "However many years may pass without meeting," she said,

> or however distant from one another people may reside, if they sincerely share the same mind, it is as if they are of one family and live together. For the past six or seven years you have diligently pursued the ascetic training necessary to acquire an unwavering mind, not neglecting it for even a day. For certain you have secured an unwavering mind that will not falter even when confronting death. Therefore I will reveal the true deity to you. Whatever punishment you might face, and however severe, you must never speak of your master or the line of transmission but consider it a supreme glory to take the punishment upon yourself alone. On this condition I will reveal the true deity to you.

To this I responded that since I had no husband and had carried out the ascetic training for obtaining an unwavering mind day and night for many years, I would never say anything to others about what was revealed to me, however severe the investigation or punishment I might face. I begged Kinu to tell me about the true deity.

Very late that night, Kinu had me sit facing her, with a large candle between us.[13] She sat there silently for a while, until I felt the hair on my skin stand on end. Finally Kinu spoke. "This secret practice," she said,

> consists of praying to Tentei Buddha, the Lord of Heaven, who is the deity of the Kirishitan sect that is strictly proscribed throughout the realm.[14] This deity is a buddha without any shape or form. You should pray to him day and night with an unwavering mind, constantly reciting the mantra *Zensu Maru paraizo* silently in your heart.[15] Although this is similar to the chant "All hail to Amida Buddha" of the Ikkō sect or the chant "All hail to the Lotus Sutra" of the Nichiren sect, those have to do only with the past and future. Those chants won't bring you any good fortune or prosperity in the present world. If you chant the mantra of the Lord of Heaven, it will give you prosperity in this world.
>
> If someone comes to ask you for prayers to be cured of illness, you should make an effigy out of a clean piece of paper and write the person's house name, name, and age on the front. Fix the effigy to a board, ask the details of the affliction or where the person hurts, and pound large nails into the effigy at the corresponding places. Every

night in the hours after midnight, fill a bowl with fresh water and sprinkle it on the effigy with your hand while praying to the Lord of Heaven with all your heart. Do this until the person recovers. If you do this, the person's illness will be cured through the Lord's grace. Naturally, that person will be filled with gratitude and offer you money in return.

The same method will work not only for curing illness but for other things as well. If you want people to offer up money, you should recite the prayers in the same way, but without pounding nails in an effigy, and money and goods will appear quite miraculously. Similarly, when people ask you to divine good fortune and bad, the answer will well up in your mind, without any doubt at all. But if you forget the Lord of Heaven for even a moment, day or night, this method will lose its marvelous efficacy. More than that, you will receive this buddha's punishment. Be sure not to forget the Lord of Heaven and, apart from your son, tell everyone that these miracles are thanks to Inari. And of course do not teach these things lightly to anyone else or speak of them to others.

Hearing Kinu's words, I understood for the first time that this was what was called Kirishitan and how it was that she had been able to collect money by making paper effigies when we lived together in Kyoto. Although I knew that being Kirishitan is strictly proscribed, a feeling that this was something marvelous and unforgettable rose in me. I promised Kinu that I wouldn't have direct contact with her, just like up to then. To avoid arousing people's suspicions I continued to perform rites to the deity body of Inari at my own house. On the face of it I chanted the universal purification prayer or recited passages from the Lotus Sutra or Kannon Sutra, but in my heart I prayed fervently to the Lord of Heaven.[16]

Sano's Trip to Nagasaki

Although Kinu told me that the Lord of Heaven has no shape or form, I had heard that in Nagasaki there are *fumie* plates with images of the Lord of Heaven and his mother, Santa Maruya, and that every year all men and women in Nagasaki, including travelers who are just visiting, have to tread on one of these *fumie*. If this is the case, I thought, surely the Lord must have a form. I wanted at all costs to go there and see it. But unless I went at the time when people were made to tread on the *fumie* or stayed for some time in Nagasaki, I wouldn't be able to be there at the right moment.

And even if I was there at the right time, unless I trod on the *fumie*, wrong as it is to do so, I wouldn't be able to see the Lord. But, I decided, if I was to tread on the *fumie* as an act of faith, the Lord would realize the depth of my faith and would not send down punishment.[17]

I wanted to set off quickly for Nagasaki, but because Shinsuke was still young, I was afraid he might starve if I left him on his own.[18] Soyo, the wife of Harimaya Uhei, who rented quarters in the same tenement, sometimes asked Shinsuke to do errands for her. She seemed kind, so I thought I might ask her to look after him while I was away, but I worried that she might not pay that close attention to him [unless I found some way to put her in my debt]. I had heard rumors that Soyo had a lover, but I didn't know who the man was. It was beyond my powers of divination to discern this, but Kinu, I was sure, would be able to find it out. I sent Shinsuke to ask Kinu, who replied that it seemed to be a hairdresser who came to Soyo's place to do her hair. But, Kinu said, Soyo had repeatedly refused his advances and had not yet committed adultery with him. Still, if things were left as they were, she might well be forced into an adulterous relationship with this man.

Having learned this, I stopped Soyo one day when she came to buy some vegetables. "Recently something seems to be bothering you," I said ominously. "Since you've been so kind to my son, I secretly consulted Inari about this and received an oracle that a hairdresser is trying to seduce you. According to the oracle, you have not yet yielded, but you are very troubled about the situation. Unless you seek Inari's protection, you may well be forced into an improper relationship." Soyo replied that the hairdresser Gizō had been making repeated improper advances to her. She had refused to listen to him, but since her husband was sick, Gizō paid no heed to her objections. "Please," she said, "perform prayer rituals to save me from disgrace." I promised that I would, and when I prayed to the Lord of Heaven, Gizō suddenly absconded—it was just miraculous. Soyo was overjoyed and showered me with gifts that came altogether to thirty thousand coppers and fifteen articles of clothing. I accepted these, and now that I was certain that Soyo had faith in me, I decided to ask her to look after Shinsuke so I could travel to Nagasaki.[19]

I told Soyo that I wanted to visit my native province of Hizen and pay my respects at my ancestors' graves. I would be gone about half a year, I said, and I wondered if she might be able to look after Shinsuke while I was away. Soyo agreed, so I sent Shinsuke to tell Kinu that I wanted to take a trip to see Nagasaki. I wouldn't be in contact with her for a while, but Shinsuke would continue to call on her in my absence. I didn't say anything about my intent to see the *fumie*. Around the ninth month of 1820 I set off. Since it would be difficult to find places to stay if I traveled on my own, I went first to an acquaintance, Nakaya Shōbei (now deceased), who lived in Naniwa Shinchi 3-chōme. I told him that I wanted to go see the sights in Nagasaki and asked him to help me find a traveling companion. Fortunately, just at that time a troupe of puppeteers was planning to travel to Nagasaki to perform there. I arranged to join them, with the agreement that I would pay for my own expenses.

The same month, we boarded a ship that [followed the route along the coast of the Inland Sea and] reached Kokura in Buzen province in the middle of the tenth month. From that point we traveled by land, stopping off at various points along the way. We reached Nagasaki in the eleventh month. I stayed in the same inn as the puppeteers, and on the seventh day of the first month of the following year, 1821, the local officials brought the *fumie* there. They told the innkeeper and all the members of the household, and also all the guests who were staying in the inn at the time, to tread on the image. I, too, trod on it as if it were nothing special, even though this was not the proper thing to do. It wasn't possible to get a good look at what was on the image, but I could glimpse a female figure. In my heart I apologized for treading on it. I heard from the puppeteers and local people that there was also another kind of *fumie*, showing a person bound to a cross. Having seen a *fumie*, I didn't have any further business in Nagasaki and wanted to return directly to Osaka, but since it might look suspicious if I left immediately, I extended my stay until the second month under the pretext that I was doing some sightseeing. At that point I made up a story that I had used up all my travel money [and so had to return home]. Fortunately, there were some merchants staying in Nagasaki who were planning to return to Osaka, so I arranged to join them and reached Osaka in the middle of the fourth month. Shinsuke was fine, thanks to Soyo's having looked after him, and I expressed my gratitude to Soyo for this.

All the while I had been traveling, I had prayed constantly to the Lord of Heaven day and night, and after returning to Osaka I continued to do so and also put special effort into my water austerities. As a consequence I gained clairvoyance into the things that people asked me about. I wanted to seek out fellows of the same mind, live in prosperity, and find ways to

Figure 1.3 Treading on *fumie* in Nagasaki at New Year's, in what had become a ritualized annual event. At the left, three city officials observe the man in the middle as he steps on the plate. A fourth, in the right foreground, keeps a tally in a ledger. The seated members of the household to the right and the two men chatting at the far right wait their turn. Kawahara Keiga, "Fumie." RV-360-4302. Nationaal Museum van Wereldculturen, Leiden.

spread this secret practice. I explained my wish to Shinsuke, and we left the quarters where we were living, [setting off without saying anything] during the night of the thirteenth day of the ninth month of 1821. Ōmiya Chōemon, a member of the Osaka guild of rental-house guarantors and resident in Suruga-chō, agreed to act as our guarantor,[20] and we arranged to rent a small hut.

Investigators' Questioning of Uhei and Soyo

When we questioned Uhei and his wife, Soyo, their statements matched Sano's. [Soyo stated as follows:][21]

> Sano and Shinsuke lived in the same tenement as we did and sold vegetables. I would buy vegetables from them, and we became friendly in

that way. I used to hire Shinsuke when we had some errand that needed to be done, but he was only available before noon. In the afternoon, he always went out somewhere, rain or shine, and came home only in the evening. Wondering where he went, I asked Sano and Shinsuke, and they told us that since Sano's sister lived by herself in the eastern part of the city, Shinsuke went to check on her every day. Impressed by how thoughtful this was, I felt ever kindlier toward the two.

Calling frequently on Sano, I noticed that she had something like a guardian deity enshrined on the god shelf and saw her offering prayers to it. When I asked Sano about this, she told me it was an Inari in whom she had long had faith. Thanks to this Inari, Sano said, she was able to predict what fortune or misfortune awaited people. I also frequently observed others coming to Sano to get an oracle from Inari. Around this time the hairdresser Gizō, who made the rounds of the town to do people's hair, began to press me to yield to his advances. As Uhei, my husband, was sick, I worried that it might make his illness worse if I said anything openly about this. Then Sano asked me about the matter, hitting it exactly on the mark. *(Investigators: This is as recorded in Sano's written testimony.)* I asked Sano to perform prayer rituals to keep Gizō from making advances to me. Shortly thereafter he absconded in a way that was miraculous. I was overjoyed and was sure this was owing to the prayer rituals Sano had performed.

Uhei began bit by bit to recover, so I told him about the improper advances Gizō had made to me and how as a result of Sano's prayer rituals, he had run away and disappeared. Uhei responded that Gizō would likely come back and that if he made improper advances to me again, I should immediately tell Uhei, who would report the situation and ask the authorities to investigate. If I had been able to escape disgrace thanks to the prayer rituals Sano had performed, Uhei said, she was indeed our benefactor, and we should be ever more solicitous toward her. Thereafter, I gave Sano money or clothes whenever she was short of funds. In all, this amounted to thirty thousand coppers and fifteen articles of clothing.

Then, in the latter part of the ninth month of 1821, Sano suddenly said that she wanted to travel to Hizen province in Kyushu to pay her respects at her ancestors' graves and asked me to look after Shinsuke. After asking Uhei, I agreed. Sano set off in the tenth month. Shinsuke continued to sell vegetables and in the afternoon would go to visit Sano's sister, just as before. Sano came back to Osaka in the fourth month of the following year and thanked me for having looked after Shinsuke all the time she had been away.[22] But then, almost immediately Sano and Shinsuke moved to a hut let out by a rental-house guarantor. We were surprised because it was just as if Sano and Shinsuke had absconded. We couldn't understand at all what had happened. We didn't meet either of them thereafter and assumed they were dead.

Sometime ago we heard that someone from Kyoto living in retirement was staying nearby and propagating a method to increase people's wealth and make them prosper. But we were living quite adequately within our means and had no desire for splendor beyond our station. We thus made no effort to find out more about this person and did not at all put faith in her. We were startled to learn in the course of the current interrogation what Sano had said in her testimony and completely amazed to hear that the person said to be from Kyoto and living in retirement was in fact Sano. Although we gave Sano money and clothes and looked after Shinsuke, it is not at all that we did this out of faith in the strange things Sano did through her Kirishitan practices.

Although Soyo and Uhei declared that this statement was the complete truth, we probed further into the matter. Since Soyo, as she said, was friendly with Sano and often went to her place, had she not seen anything peculiar? When we pressed Soyo on this point, she responded as follows:

I didn't observe anything that was particularly strange, and don't know anything about what Sano did at night. However, for about a year and a half, from the time she moved to the same tenement as us until she went to Hizen,[23] she said she couldn't go out because she was ill, and indeed I never saw her do so. She took only two meals a day, rather than three, and didn't appear to consume much sake or meat. I don't remember when exactly it was, but two or three times I saw Sano dousing herself with water by the tenement well, and the way in which she did this was quite different from the austerities performed by other ascetics. She repeatedly filled a dipper with water, which she threw backward over her head. I secretly watched for a bit, but she soon noticed this and stopped what she was doing or went back into her own quarters, acting as if she hadn't intended [to douse herself]. Apart from this, once some fruit that was set out as an offering on her god shelf suddenly disappeared without a trace while I was watching. I was startled, but I simply assumed, mistakenly, that this showed that people with miraculous powers are able to do things that ordinary people can't. I wasn't aware of Sano going out at night to perform water austerities because this happened only after I was sound asleep.

After hearing from Soyo about the fruit disappearing, we interrogated Sano further about this matter. She replied as follows:

After I had told Soyo that the deity I worshipped was Inari, I wanted to confound her with some kind of miraculous event. I watched for a moment when she wasn't looking and quickly hid the fruit, making it seem as if the deity had miraculously caused it to disappear. Soyo probably believed this was indeed what had happened. You may accuse me of having used sorcery to make the fruit disappear, but in this instance that was not at all the case. You have repeatedly interrogated me severely, and I have confessed the entire matter from beginning to end, so there is nothing further to add.

Sano's testimony thus stands as above.

Sano Embarks on a Scheme for Collecting Contributions in Cooperation with Yae, Toki, and Kanzō

Shinsuke and I absconded from the hut almost immediately after moving there. I went to an acquaintance, a farmer named Yasuemon (now deceased), who was originally from the Kyoto area and lived in the village of Shimo Sanba. I pretended that we were simply drifting from place to place and said that we wanted to find work as masseurs. I asked him to act as a guarantor and to help us find rooms to rent in a village close to the city but not right in the middle of the urban bustle. Yasuemon must have found it difficult to ignore my request, so he agreed. He arranged to have us added to his household's population register and made inquiries about quarters that we might rent. The place where I live now, in quarters rented from Yohei, is located in a village close to the city, so it matched what I was looking for, and we agreed on the rent. I became a parishioner of the Ikkō temple Enkōji in the village of Kita Miyahara in the same province of Settsu, obtained a certificate of affiliation from it, and on the twenty-fifth day of the eighth month of 1822 moved into the quarters rented out by Yohei. I had Shinsuke change his name from Masajirō to Shinsuke, and he registered himself under the new house name Kyōya Shinsuke.

I thought that if I went about freely, my face would become known to others, and that would undermine my plans. I had already saved enough money, and so, with the excuse that I was ill, I refrained from going out. I had Shinsuke work as a day laborer at miscellaneous jobs, and every so often I sent him to Kinu as before. At night I continued to perform water austerities. To draw in people who might become fellow devotees, I wrapped a scrap of wood in a piece of cloth and set it up as Inari, just as I had done previously.

A woman named Yae who was somewhat over fifty years old, the wife of Kenpōya Yoshichi, a resident of the same village, often came by to chat since she lived nearby. She told me about the various difficulties she faced—her husband was deaf and, on top of that, more or less out of his mind, and she had no son or other person to rely on for the future. I tested what lay at the bottom of her heart and found that she was not at all a weak or timorous woman. Her husband being the way he was, it appeared that she hadn't been intimate with him from the time she was forty-two or forty-three. I thought that she might be drawn in as a fellow devotee but decided that it wouldn't be easy to make her my follower unless I first amazed her by performing some sort of miraculous feat. One day when Yae came to chat, I set out what I had deduced about the course of her life from the time she was small until the present, with all the details about her circumstances and experiences. I evidently hit the mark, for she seemed amazed and full of admiration. "How can you know so clearly things that you haven't actually seen?" she asked.

I told her that after my husband died, when I was thirty-six, I had encountered an extraordinary person who transmitted to me the art of communicating with Inari. "I acquired miraculous powers," I said, "and because of my faith in Inari, I'm generally able to know right away the true circumstances of people who come to consult me." Yae seemed to be envious, and she begged to become my disciple. It would be difficult to transmit this method to someone who has a husband, I told her. She replied that since Yoshichi, her husband, was more or less insane, she hadn't been intimate with him for more than ten years. "It's just as if I didn't have a husband," she said, "and if you'll transmit the method to me, I won't go near him from now on." I was sure that my hunch about her was right, but I told Yae that I couldn't transmit the method to her straightaway. First she would have to undergo ascetic training to obtain an unwavering mind, and to that end she should secretly perform water austerities, without letting anyone else know.

Yae did perform water austerities in accordance with my instructions and seemed to be firmly committed, so I told her in confidence that I wanted to find a discreet way to let others know about the miraculous methods of this deity, but it would be difficult to do so unless I first gathered a small pool of money that would enable me to help people overcome their troubles. If I could find a way to collect money and use it to help others, surely they would come to have faith in the deity, and it would be easy to proceed. To get started, I said, I needed someone to put up one or two thousand *monme* in silver. Didn't Yae know of someone who could do this, I asked. Yae was supportive and suggested my landlord, Yohei, who was related to Yae's husband. "Yohei's circumstances are quite comfortable," she said. "But since he's stingy, he won't part with any money unless he gets rent or some other security in return. Since I'm friendly with his mother and wife, it would be best to go through them. But when it comes to money, Yohei is not the sort to listen to anyone, no matter who. So I really don't know what to do."

There was a sure way to get Yohei to hand over the money, I responded. When I lived in Shinchi Ura-machi in Dōjima, I had become friendly with a certain Iseya Kanzō and his wife, Toki, who lived in the same block, and they came to visit after I had moved to the quarters I rented from Yohei. Kanzō is a masseur, so every once in a while I would have him massage me, and I would tell him about the miracles of Inari. As a result, he and Toki had come to have faith in the deity. I thought I could gain more believers if word got around that a woman from a princely house in Kyoto who was living in retirement wanted to propagate a method she had for making people prosper. To that end, she had come to Osaka and was staying with Kanzō. I secretly conferred with Yae, Kanzō, and Toki, as well as my son, and got them to agree to this plan. Under no circumstances, I warned them, were they to divulge my name or situation. If they did, they would be sure to receive divine punishment as severe as decapitation.

Putting this plan into action, I told Yae to go to Yohei and say that a noblewoman from Kyoto living in retirement was staying in the Dōjima area. This woman was deeply compassionate and had mastered a way to save those who are ill or facing other difficulties. If Yohei invested money with her as capital for this purpose, she would see that he prospered, so he should contribute about two thousand *monme* in silver. "Yohei is stingy," Yae replied. "There's no way to get him to hand over money simply by telling him something like that." "He'll put up the money if you do as I say," I told her. "Don't hold to your own reasoning. Just follow my instructions about what to tell him."

Prior to this, I had already made a paper effigy of Yohei and performed the usual rites with it. When Yae went to Yohei and talked with him as I had instructed, he seemed delighted, completely different from his usual stingy self. He said that for the moment he would put up three hundred *monme* in silver and thirty *ryō* in gold.[24] He didn't need any certificate of deposit, but prayed that the noblewoman living in retirement would soon produce evidence of his increased prosperity. Yae took the money and walked aimlessly here and there around the Dōjima area. When night fell, she came back to my place and gave me the money. "I now recognize the deity's extraordinary powers," she exclaimed with astonishment. "That miserly Yohei who would never hand over money without taking rent or security has completely changed! He's tossed out gold as if it were a piece of tile or a stone! Never have there been such miraculous powers—from now on my faith will be even stronger!"

Yae told Kanzō and Toki what had happened, and they were amazed, too. Getting them to agree not to tell anyone else, I had the three go around together to their acquaintances and urge them [to invest money with the noblewoman] like Yohei, or, if someone was ill, to have the noblewoman conduct prayer rites for recovery. I concentrated all my efforts on performing the rites night after night, in the same way as I had [with Yohei].

Investigators' Comments on the Details of the Money and Clothing Collected by Sano

As a result of Sano's scheme, numerous people entrusted money and clothing to the noblewoman living in retirement. They are as follows:

Matsuya Gihei and his wife, Fusa, of Yazaemon-chō in Dōjima: 55 or 56 articles of clothing
Ōmiya Inosuke of Ise-machi in Tenma: 15,200 coppers

Tami, [a woman] residing in the same household as Rihei, who is the legal guardian of [a woman named] Yoshinoya Kō and lives in the same village as Sano: 700 *monme* in silver, 3 *ryō* in gold, and 24,500 coppers, plus 61 or 62 articles of clothing

Tora, mother of Edoya Yahachi and residing in his household, also of the same village: 100,000 coppers and 46 articles of clothing

Han'emon, the father of Nabeya Hanbei and residing in his household, also of the same village: 100 *monme* in silver

Hana, mother of Minoya Sutekichi and residing in his household, also of the same village: 3.75 *ryō* in gold, 3,000 coppers, and 3 articles of clothing

Heishirō, farmer, of the village of Naruo, Settsu province: 11.25 *ryō* in gold, 200 *monme* in silver

Kawachiya Manjirō and his wife, Tora, of Edo-machi: 5 articles of clothing

Toku, wife of Ōshimaya Kiroku of Yazaemon-chō: 7.5 *ryō* in gold, 242.5 *monme* in silver

Kagaya Sanryō, of the village of Kitano, Settsu province: 192,000 coppers

Wataya Zensuke, of the same village: 30,000 coppers and 32 or 33 articles of clothing

Kawachiya Tokubei, of Shinchi Ura-machi in Dōjima: 150 *monme* in silver

Nagaraya Chūbei, of Suzuka-machi in Tenma: 1,000 *monme* in silver

Nagahamaya Kuhei, of Minami Kohata-machi in Tenma: 1,200 *monme* in silver, 17 articles of clothing

Masuya Yasubei, of Kita Kohata-machi in Tenma: 22,650.32 *monme* in silver

Matsuya Kichizō, of Shinchi Ura-machi in Dōjima: 120,000 coppers[25]

In addition to the money that he had contributed previously, Sano's landlord, Yohei, furnished a further 32,000 *monme* or so in silver and 101 articles of clothing. The total of money and clothes collected thus came to more than 59,000 *monme* in silver, 28.25 *ryō* in gold, 720,000 coppers, and 320 articles of clothing.

Sano insists that she did not have anything to do with this money and clothing; she says she left the management of these things up to her son, Shinsuke. Of the clothing, he put 28 articles in pawn with the pawnbroker Yoshidaya Shinshichi of Minami Kohata-chō in Tenma. He did so piece by piece, with himself as the primary depositor; with Yae's help, he used the seal of her husband, Yoshichi, for the joint endorsement. For these he obtained 456.5 *monme* in silver. The remaining items he put in pawn with the pawnbroker Namariya Kyūbei of Oimatsu-chō in Tenma, with himself as the primary depositor and Kanzō as the joint endorser. For these he obtained 3,047.39 *monme* in silver.[26] He converted the gold and coppers that had been collected into silver, and the total, including the silver received for the pawned items, came to more than 72,000 *monme*.[27]

Sano's Statement About How the Money Was Used

In a greedy world, Yohei, Gihei, and Yasubei were known to be particularly avaricious, and as they had put out large sums of money, I knew that if I didn't devise some means for showing them a miraculous increase in wealth, they would start to complain, which would interfere with the plan to spread the creed more widely. I therefore decided to distribute to them some of the money given as contributions or obtained through pawning the clothing. Calling it interest granted by the deity, I had Yae hand this share over to them on several occasions and distributed money in the same fashion to the others as well. Overall I kept twenty-one or twenty-two thousand *monme* in silver, but I left management of the remainder up to Shinsuke, who periodically gave some to Kinu as a token of gratitude to her as my master, and to Yae and Kanzō as payment for their labors. I have no idea exactly how much this came to or how much was used up on household expenses.

Investigators' Comments on the Difficulty of Tracing the Amount of Money Distributed

The approximate overall amount of money Sano appropriated can be ascertained as recorded above. However, as reported in the following addendum, Shinsuke, who was in charge of managing the money, fell ill and died [in the course of interrogation], as did Yae and Kanzō. We consequently have not been able to calculate the amounts sent to Kinu as a token of gratitude, let alone what was distributed to Yae and Kanzō, or the amount used for Sano's household expenses. We repeatedly interrogated Sano on this point, but she held to her testimony as given. Kinu's reception of a share is reported in the record of her interrogation.

Sano's Scheme Falls Through, and She Is Arrested

My plan had been to devise a way to use the money collected by Yae and the others to privately assist people who were impoverished, sick, or disabled. In that way I could lead them to become believers in the deity. But Yohei repeatedly asked Yae to arrange for him to meet with the Kyoto noblewoman, and her various efforts to put him off aroused his suspicions. He followed Yae when she went out, trailing her to Kanzō's place. There he pressed Yae, Kanzō, and Toki to tell him where the Kyoto noblewoman was. They told him that she had gone back to Kyoto, whereupon he went home looking even more suspicious of their story. When Yae told me what had happened, I decided I should go into hiding somewhere, as it would be dangerous if I were found out. I conferred with Yae and Shinsuke, and we decided that Shinsuke should flee to Kyoto, while I would run away to Harima, where Yae has relatives. She and I set out for Harima, but Yohei and some others came after us. We decided that it would be better to go back and put Yohei's doubts to rest once and for all, but when we encountered him, he was astounded. "Isn't the so-called Kyoto noblewoman actually Sano?" he pressed Yae. Keeping up the deception, Yae said that, no, I wasn't the noblewoman. The noblewoman really existed, Yae said, and she promised to arrange for Yohei to meet her. We went back to Kanzō's place and were arguing about the matter there when all of us were arrested.

INVESTIGATORS' REPORT ON THE STATEMENTS TAKEN FROM THOSE WHO MADE DONATIONS TO SANO

We investigated Yae, Kanzō, Toki, and Shinsuke and arrested all of them, but Shinsuke, Yae, and Kanzō fell ill and died in the course of interrogation before a confirmed record of their testimony could be compiled. What was ascertained through the interrogation of Toki is reported below. Yoshichi, Yae's husband, is almost totally deaf and essentially insane. On top of that, he has suffered a stroke and is unable to talk. We thus placed him in the custody of his relatives and did not interrogate him.

Yohei, Shinsuke's [and Sano's] landlord, stated as follows when interrogated:

I rented rooms to Shinsuke and knew that Sano was living with him, but because she was said to be ill and didn't go out, I didn't have any direct contact with her. One day Yae, with whom I'm on friendly terms because she is the wife of my relative Yoshichi, suddenly appeared at my house and began to tell me about a noblewoman from Kyoto living in retirement who was staying in the Dōjima area to spread the practice that she followed. This noblewoman was extremely compassionate and kind, Yae said, and she wanted to assist people who were encountering difficulties. "Won't you contribute two thousand *monme* in silver from your savings?" Yae asked. "If you do, the resulting merit will surely bring you prosperity."

As I looked into Yae's face, somehow a feeling of admiration welled up, and I felt a desire to make a contribution. At complete odds with my usual discretion, I handed over three hundred *monme* in silver and thirty *ryō* in gold to Yae, keeping this hidden from my mother and wife. About ten days later, Yae brought five thousand coppers and said that I should accept it as interest from the prosperity benevolently granted by the deity. I first refused. "Since I made the donation solely out of a sense of reverence, it wouldn't be right to receive money granted by the deity," I told Yae. But she wouldn't listen and said that to refuse [what the deity had granted] would be to invite divine punishment. I thus accepted the money, and about ten days and then twenty days later, she brought more. When she suggested that I make additional donations, the desire to do so welled up even more strongly than before, and so I donated more silver, as well as seventy-two articles of clothing.

From this my mother and wife came to realize what was happening, and they objected. "Yae is deceiving you," they said, "and you should stop giving her money and clothing, or else it will bring the household to ruination." But Yae won them over as well, and they, too, came to feel reverence [for the deity]. Since they don't have money of their own, each of them contributed her own clothes without saying anything about it to me. It got to the point where they were as much as stark naked, whereupon I became aware what was happening. "A while ago you tried to stop me from making donations, so why are you now giving your clothes to the noblewoman?" I asked. "What have you been doing?" we each accused the other. At last, as if we had woken up from a dream, we realized that we were being cheated. When I hurriedly added up the amount of money I had put out, it came to over thirty thousand *monme* in silver. After I subtracted from this what Yae had brought as interest, the total loss came to more than 5,340 *monme*.[28]

This was causing difficulties for my household finances, so I conferred with my mother and wife and decided that I should meet with the Kyoto noblewoman and have her clarify what was happening with the clothes and the money. I went to Yae and asked her to arrange for me to meet with the noblewoman. "The noblewoman has recently returned to Kyoto," she said. "I'll let you know when she comes back to Osaka." Increasingly suspicious, I watched to see when Yae went out and followed her to Kanzō's house, taking care not to let her see me. When I went in, I found Kanzō and Toki deep in consultation with Yae. Announcing myself, I declared that I was sure that the noblewoman from Kyoto must be staying there and demanded that they let me meet with her. To this Kanzō and Toki responded in the same way as Yae. All the more suspicious, I went back to Kanzō and Toki after Yae had left and asked them again about the noblewoman. "The noblewoman living in retirement is not a human being," Toki responded. "It is the deity of the third peak of Fushimi Inari mountain who has miraculously appeared in this world to save people."[29]

I was totally dumbfounded and was now sure that Yae was cheating me. Furious, I decided to drag her to the magistracy to make a complaint. But when I went to her house, she wasn't there. Since Yoshichi, her husband, is as good as insane and also deaf, I couldn't find out anything from him. I made inquiries in various places and learned that someone had seen Yae heading down the road to Harima together with Sano. For the first time I realized that this must be a plot concocted jointly by Yae and Sano. I reckoned that it would be difficult to find them if they succeeded in making an escape to the western provinces, so I hired someone from the neighborhood to help and rushed after them. We caught up with Yae and Sano near the village of Fukumoto in Harima. I demanded to know whether the Kyoto noblewoman existed or not. They continued to insist that she really did exist and that Sano didn't know anything about the matter. The whole situation was so confusing that I decided that it would be best first to return to Osaka and confront them together with Kanzō. At that point Sano and the others were arrested.

When we questioned Yohei's mother, Kiwa, and his wife, Chika, they said the same thing. They had gradually come to realize that Yohei was handing over money and clothes to Yae without any explanation or certificate of deposit and then receiving money from her. Further, this seemed to be happening repeatedly. The items of clothing he gave her came to an immense number. Unable to bear this any longer, Kiwa and Chika pleaded with Yohei to stop. It was strange to hand over an excessive amount of money and goods to a person of little means like Yae, they told him, and it would have a bad effect on their household finances. But, saying one thing and another, he concealed the specifics of the matter from them and insisted that it was a wondrous means of ensuring their greater prosperity. This was so different from his usual character that they began to wonder if he had gone mad, and they decided to talk with Yae about the situation. When Yae came, she said that the noblewoman knew through her clairvoyant powers that Kiwa and Chika, not having faith themselves, were maligning the miraculous method for increasing prosperity in which Yohei had rightly come to believe. The two should instead pray for prosperity. Thereupon Kiwa and Chika suddenly felt a desire to contribute their own possessions. They talked together and eventually donated about thirty articles of clothing.

Yohei, Kiwa, and Chika alike declared that they were astounded to learn through the present interrogation what Sano had said in her testimony. This was the first they had heard of it. They did not have any idea of the creed Sano practiced and did not secretly have faith in it. Nevertheless, they had been extremely foolish and remiss to allow themselves to be confounded and to have given over money and goods so heedlessly. They repent this deeply and are most ashamed. All state that this is the full truth.

When we questioned Gihei and the other eighteen people who had contributed money and clothing, their statements all corroborated those by Yohei, Kiwa, and Chika. Yae and Toki had visited to urge them to contribute, they had experienced a desire to donate money or clothes, and periodically Yae had brought money, saying it was a gift from the deity.

When Yae and Toki first came to urge them to have prayer rituals performed to ensure their prosperity or cure an illness, [the two also gave various sorts of directions]. Those making contributions should never waver in their faith; husband and wife should not quarrel at night over [the noblewoman's instructions]; they should not malign the deity. Yae or Toki would always immediately appear when they did these things. Yae or Toki came if someone broke the strict prohibition against carnal relations, or could not avoid secretly [breaking the prohibition against] allowing a relative with leprosy to stay while prayer rites were being performed to cure a child's illness. If someone felt the stirrings of a desire to offer the deity rice cakes, fruit, or clothing, Yae or Toki would appear. Yae and Toki issued warnings that with her miraculous powers, the noblewoman knew that husband and wife had quarreled. The noblewoman was extremely angry that their faith in the rites was not steadfast, and particularly that they had indulged in carnal relations. When they had been told not to let any unclean person into their house while rites were being performed for them, it was unforgiveable to have secretly allowed someone with a grave illness to stay. Devotion to the deity in wanting to make offerings of rice cakes and such was admirable, but these had to be made at night and brought before dawn, [so as to be sure] the offering was not cursed in some way by an animal.[30] If it was cursed, the noblewoman could not accept it. If they wished to donate clothing, they should offer the deity that patterned or striped garment that they were keeping hidden in their storehouse.

The contributors were struck with awe: how could the noblewoman know these things so precisely, down to the pattern or stripe of a garment? Countless other extraordinary things occurred as well. However much they pondered the matter, they couldn't figure out how the noblewoman could have such clairvoyance into things that were so minute and hidden. With all these strange happenings, they began to think that wealth and prosperity depended on the degree of one's faith, and wanting to donate more, they came to contribute the items and amounts recorded above. After Yae and Sano were arrested, they should have come immediately to the magistracy to report what had happened, but it didn't occur to them that the noblewoman from Kyoto living in retirement must be Sano. In addition, some had given Yae a written pledge addressed to the noblewoman, stating that they wouldn't tell others that they were donating money and clothes and declaring that if they did, they should receive divine punishment as severe as decapitation. With their benighted way of thinking, they feared that the angry deity might indeed wreak retribution, and thus none of them reported the situation. They all insisted that they had not known that this was the Kirishitan creed when they put their faith in the deity, but they acknowledged that they had been extremely foolish and remiss to have allowed themselves to be confounded and to have offered clothes and money in that fashion. They repent this deeply and are most ashamed. All state that this is the full truth.

It was not clear under what circumstances the pawnbrokers Shinshichi and Kyūbei had accepted as security a large number of items of clothing from a person of meager means such as Shinsuke and lent him money in return. We thus questioned Shinshichi and Kyūbei about this. They responded as follows: The person who brought the goods was in most cases Yae, and when the shop clerks saw her face, they felt warmly toward her and lent her the money without paying proper heed. While the arrangements were being made, Shinshichi and Kyūbei, and even the members of their households, realized that [something was irregular and that they should] put a stop to it, but when they saw Yae, they also felt warmly toward her in the same way and came to think that it would be better not to stop the arrangements. In this way, they repeatedly accepted pawned articles without properly realizing that something was suspicious. When in the course of interrogation they heard about Sano's testimony, they were astounded. For the first time they realized that she had used pernicious arts to confound them.

This does not seem to be a usual case [of pawnbrokers] colluding with people pawning [illegally obtained items]. What happened at these pawnshops, and also how various people became confounded and took leave of their senses, heedlessly putting out money and goods, is most strange. There is no way Sano could have caused people to become so foolish simply by making paper effigies, sprinkling them with water, and praying to the Lord of Heaven. Thus, as recorded below, we confronted her with further accusations and repeatedly interrogated her severely under torture.[31] Below is the summation of these accusations and her responses.

INVESTIGATORS' SUMMATION OF SANO'S INTERROGATION

As we noted earlier, Sano entered into a pact of master and disciple with Kinu in which she swore to take all responsibility upon herself alone and never to reveal anything about Kirishitan matters, even if she faced the most severe punishment. She thus initially made up various groundless and false stories. Upon being interrogated severely, she eventually yielded and confessed as we have recorded, but she begged that the others be allowed to escape punishment and that she alone be put to death in their place. Against this we confronted her with the following accusation:

> You received the transmission of the Kirishitan creed and practices from Kinu and engaged in various strange activities under the pretense of performing prayer rites to cure people of illness. You caused people to take leave of their senses and collected large amounts of money and goods from them. Surely you also received the oral transmission of secret scriptures, spells, and practices apart from those you have already described. Despite being a woman, did you not enter into a solemn agreement with Mitsugi and Kinu to engage in wicked deeds? There unquestionably must be many other members of your group [whom you have not yet identified]. Likely you have also received a drawing of the Lord of Heaven and have kept it hidden.[32]

We repeatedly interrogated her severely about these points.
To this Sano responded as follows:

> Apart from the secret practices transmitted to me [by Kinu] that I have already described, I have not received the transmission of any other Kirishitan scriptures, spells, or secret practices. For many years I pursued ascetic training for securing an unwavering mind and prayed constantly day and night to the Lord of Heaven. As a result, I naturally attained the miraculous powers that enabled me to do the things I did. It was because I never received a drawing of the Lord of Heaven from Kinu that, as I described, I went to Nagasaki and trod on the *fumie* plate so as to worship the buddha image on it. Simply to possess the buddha image in itself will not be efficacious.[33] One has to have gone through years of arduous training to obtain an unwavering mind. Lustful or greedy people would never be able to do the things I and my fellows did even if they were initiated into this sect.

The interrogation has fully clarified the circumstances of how Sano, showing not the slightest awe for the shogunal authorities, acted in a manner that was the height of audacity. She states that she has nothing to say in opposition [to what is recorded here] and is filled with remorse.[34]

TESTIMONY OF TOKI

Toki: fifty years of age; wife of Iseya Kanzō (deceased), resident in rented quarters under the management of Izumiya Ihei, Shinchi Ura-machi in Dōjima, Osaka

Remanded to jail the twenty-sixth day of the first month, 1827

Preliminary Comments by the Investigating Officials

Under interrogation Toki stated that Sano had sent her and her husband, Kanzō, out [to recruit believers]. Working with Yae, she and Kanzō urged people to have prayer rituals performed and to contribute money and goods in return. Her testimony concerning how they went about this matches [Sano's]. She stated specifically as follows:

Toki's Testimony

Sano sent word to us that she was living in Kawasaki village, and Kanzō visited her there to provide stomach massage treatment.[35] Yae and Sano urged him to put faith in Inari, saying that this would ensure his prosperity. When he came home he talked with me about this, and I also went to visit Sano every once in a while. At one point we decided to buy some cakes and offer them to the deity. But when we took the cakes, Sano, speaking through Yae, berated us for offering the deity something that was under a spell cast by a filthy animal. This puzzled us since we hadn't done anything to have an animal cast a spell. We went back to the store where we had bought the cakes and found that it had a dog talisman from a Suitengū shrine.[36] How amazing, we thought. For sure Sano must be able to use the deity's powers to perceive everything. We were all the more convinced that she was no ordinary person when we heard that Yae had gone to Yohei, Sano's landlord, and gotten him to readily contribute money. We put our trust in Sano's plan to say that she was a noblewoman from Kyoto living in retirement and currently lodging with Kanzō, and that she had come down to Osaka to spread the benefits of her prayer rituals for curing illness and securing prosperity. We agreed to urge people around us to take advantage of those benefits and pledged that if we ever let Sano's real name or identity be known, we should suffer divine punishment as severe as decapitation.

Dividing up the task with Yae, we went around to the people who are listed as having contributed money and clothes. They were people we knew, and we urged those who had sick household members to have healing rituals performed and those who were greedy to have prayers said for their prosperity. Sano could uncannily tell which of them had failed to behave circumspectly even while asking to have prayer rituals performed, and in which of them faith was budding. When we told these people what Sano had said, almost always she was right on the mark. They, too, were amazed and donated more and more in the way of money and clothes. Kanzō acted as the joint endorser for pawning the clothes. He said he received a portion of the money in return, but since he was the one who received it, I don't know how much it came to.

Then, Sano's landlord, Yohei, began to be suspicious. He followed Yae to our place and demanded to meet the noblewoman from Kyoto living in retirement. Together with Yae we lied and said that the noblewoman had gone back to Kyoto, but Yohei came again and pressed us, so, following Yae's previous instructions, we told him that the noblewoman was not a human being but the deity of the third peak of Fushimi Inari mountain. Startled, Yohei set out to find Sano and Yae, and when he did so, he brought them to our place. We were in the midst of arguing about this and that when we were all arrested. During the interrogation I learned for the first time to my astonishment that the rituals Sano performed were not to Inari but those of the Kirishitan sect.

Investigators' Summation of Toki's Interrogation

In the face of this testimony, we confronted Toki with the following accusations and interrogated her severely: "Surely you knew all along that Sano was a devotee of the pernicious creed, but you were led astray by greed and so went ahead and became her follower. You must have received transmission of the creed and its practices from her. You must know how much money was distributed to you and Kanzō and are simply taking advantage of Kanzō's death to put the blame on him and lie that you don't know the amount involved."

To this Toki responded that such was not at all the case. However, the interrogation having fully clarified the circumstances of her crimes, she states that she has nothing to say in opposition [to what is recorded here].

INVESTIGATORS' CONCLUDING COMMENTS ON THEIR INTERROGATION OF SANO

When Sano was first arrested and interrogated, she insisted that her purpose in presenting herself as a noblewoman from Kyoto living in retirement and using Yae to deceive her landlord, Yohei, and the others had simply been a ruse to extort money and goods. From our questioning of Yohei and the others, however, this did not seem to be an [ordinary] case of extortion. We thought that since Sano worshipped Inari, she might well have used a fox or tanuki [to bewitch people]. We pressed her on this point, whereupon she changed her testimony and said that she had lied when she said she had simply engaged in extortion; in fact she had made use of a fox. We then questioned her about what her fox witchery involved. "Previously, when I lived in Kyoto," she replied, "I happened to get to know a woman from Yamada in Ise province named Nami who had learned fox witchery from someone. I was able to learn it from her in turn and used it to extort money and goods from people as already described."

However, when Sano was arrested and her household possessions investigated, large candles had been found along with paper effigies with nails in them, as mentioned previously. Given this and what we learned about the persons who had contributed money and goods, we began to harbor suspicions about her claim to have used a fox to bewitch people. In particular, it was not clear what had happened to the money. When we interrogated her about this and other points, she appeared firm in her determination. "I swear on my life that what I have said is true," she declared. "Go ahead, I beg you, and punish me!" We found it hard to understand how, as a mere practitioner of fox witchery, she had overcome fear of death and achieved an unwavering mind, but she insisted that she had received the transmission on how to use the effigies and nails from Nami. She also said that Nami had come to Kyoto or Osaka but had no fixed address. We carried out an extensive search for Nami but could find nothing about her. Eventually Sano admitted that Nami was not a real person. She had simply made up that name as her various evil deeds came to light and because we interrogated her about the master who had transmitted the practices to her.

As noted in an earlier addendum, we had learned from our questioning of Soyo, the wife of Harimaya Uhei, that Sano's son, Shinsuke, went out somewhere every day, rain or shine, from afternoon until dark. We pressed Sano for the details of where Shinsuke went, whereupon she responded that she sent him on business to Harimaya Kinu's place in Tatsuta-machi in Tenma. This did not match what we had heard from Soyo, which was, as noted previously, that Sano had sent Shinsuke to look after her sister, who lived in the countryside east [of Osaka]. We pressed Sano further about the nature of the business Shinsuke carried out with Kinu, but she did not give a clear answer. We thus had Kinu arrested, and a search of her house revealed that, just as with Sano, she kept a deity body of Inari made from a scrap of wood and also had paper effigies hidden away. Further, she had concealed gold, silver, and copper coins between the cracks of the ceiling boards and in other places where people would not notice them. It thus appeared that she must be Sano's master, and we cross-examined the two of them together. At this point Sano at last confessed as recorded. The record of Kinu's interrogation follows.

Chapter 2

Kinu and Her Associates

TESTIMONY OF KINU

Kinu, known also as Kikue: fifty-nine years of age; resident together with Harimaya Tōzō in quarters rented from Harimaya Jirobei in Tatsuta-machi in Tenma, Osaka

Remanded to jail the twenty-seventh day of the fourth month, 1827

SUMMARY OF KINU'S ENCOUNTER WITH SANO AND THE CHECKING OF HER TESTIMONY AGAINST SANO'S

Under interrogation, Kinu stated as follows:

I am the daughter of Inaderaya Tahei of the town of Itami Shinchō, Settsu province. My mother was called Tsune. My parents both died years ago, and as I had no other relatives to rely on, I left for Kyoto at the age of six-teen and worked there as a servant in various places. I married Kyōya Kihei, who lived in Nushiya-chō north of Shichijō street, and since Sano's husband, Heibei, lived [nearby] in front of the Kyoto Daibutsu, I became friendly with Heibei and Sano. However, Kihei fell ill and died on the fourteenth day of the fifth month of 1804, leaving me a widow. I then took up the occupation of an Inari medium and subsequently became Toyoda Mitsugi's disciple.

When Sano's husband died, she was left a widow, too, and in straitened circumstances, so I asked her what she intended to do. As she said that she had no desire to remarry, I told her that I had received a transmission from Mitsugi of mysterious arts that little by little enabled me to foresee the future and cure illness through healing rituals. "What ordinary Inari mediums do is a game," I told Sano. "But the secret practices Mitsugi transmitted to me are difficult, and they can't be achieved if one has relations with a man." Since Sano wanted very much to learn this method, I took her as a disciple and the two of us exchanged secret vows to regard each other as sisters. I left the place where I had been living and moved in with Sano. Sano was amazed when she saw what I was able to do in the guise of an Inari medium, curing illness through prayer rituals and performing divinations, and she became all the more committed to learning the method I used. I didn't transmit the secret practices to her, but I taught her how to go into the mountains and perform water austerities so as to acquire an unwavering mind.

After following this ascetic training diligently for three years, Sano said that she wanted to see what Mitsugi looked like. This was quite understandable, but since it was the rule that one shouldn't have direct contact with the master of one's master, I simply took her along casually once when I called on Mitsugi. It would have been inconvenient for Mitsugi [if we had stayed in Kyoto], so I talked about this with Sano, and twelve years ago, in 1816, we decided to move to Osaka. We rented separate quarters, and I continued to use a scrap of wood as the deity body of Inari and called myself an Inari medium. As Sano hadn't yet received the transmission of the secret practices, she sent her son, Shinsuke, to me every afternoon to seek directions whenever someone asked her to perform healing rituals or carry out divinations. We agreed that she would give me half of whatever payment she received.

Sano obtained an unwavering mind by continuing to perform water austerities, so nine years ago in the tenth month of 1819, I summoned her to my house. I gave her strict instructions that she should never say anything about her master or the line of transmission, however severe a punishment she might face, and then I transmitted the creed to her. I explained that the Lord of Heaven has no shape or form and taught her how to chant the mantra *Zensu Maru paraizo*.[1] I also showed her how to make paper effigies, where to pound nails in them when she performed prayers to cure illness, and how to use the effigies just by themselves when she wished to have clients offer money. "The ability to make accurate divinations when people ask for them depends on the rigor of your training and the strength of your faith," I told her. "Even if you gain mysterious powers of understanding, you will surely receive this buddha's punishment if you forget the debt you owe the Lord of Heaven.[2] And you must never say anything about this to anyone except for Shinsuke."

I later heard that Sano had gone on a trip to Nagasaki.[3] While she was away, there was no business about which Shinsuke needed to consult me. Nevertheless, to show respect for his mother's master, he continued to call on me daily without fail, taking great care not to meet anyone on the way. After Sano returned to Osaka, she became so proficient in her austerities that she surpassed me in her clairvoyant powers. I heard that she was living in Kawasaki village and had begun performing healing rituals and gathering money and goods. As an expression of gratitude to her master, she frequently had Shinsuke bring me sums of money, but I don't recall how much these came to. *(Investigators: These particulars, including Kinu's reception of money from Sano, all match those of Sano's testimony.)*

KINU'S TESTIMONY PROPER

Kinu's Encounter with Mitsugi and Initiation Into the Kirishitan Creed

I had long desired to acquire the ability to do extraordinary things, and after my husband died I decided to continue living as a widow [rather than remarry]. I became the disciple of a Shinto diviner and learned how to conduct rituals as an Inari medium, but I wasn't able to do anything particularly extraordinary. At that time Mitsugi, who was then living together with her husband, Iori, in Benten-chō in Kyoto, was conducting rituals as an Inari medium, so I took her as my master instead of the Shinto diviner. But although I followed her as best I could, at that time she didn't do anything different from an ordinary Inari medium and didn't perform any mysterious feats. It must indeed be difficult to accomplish something out of the ordinary, I decided, and I just continued doing as I had been. Then, eighteen years ago, in 1810, Iori became involved in an affair with another woman. He abandoned Mitsugi and didn't return home. Mitsugi was furious and declared she would never take a husband again. She sold her household belongings and for the moment moved in with Itoya Wasa, a woman with whom she was friendly who lived at the west end of Shinbashi street. Shortly thereafter she moved into her own quarters in Yasaka Kami-chō. Putting out a placard as Toyoda Mitsugi, she continued to make a living as an Inari medium.

Since Mitsugi was my master, I went to call on her and found things quite different from before. She was performing water austerities, and within half a year the majority of her divinations were hitting the mark, and quite a few of her clients recovered when she conducted healing rituals. Her business was flourishing much more than previously. I was envious. The Inari medium rituals that Mitsugi had taught me were just the same as fox witchery, and I wasn't able to do anything miraculous that would amaze others. I began to wonder if Mitsugi wasn't engaging in some sort of secret practice. "I have followed you faithfully," I told her repeatedly. "If you have some sort of secret practice, please license me in it, too." "This practice can't be transmitted to someone who is easily startled or who has a husband or who indulges in lust," Mitsugi responded. "If you are really committed, you should first consolidate an unwavering mind by performing water austerities at a waterfall or such, making sure that no one sees you, and by climbing Fushimi Inari mountain and other dark and lonely heights on your own. Once you have accomplished that, I'll transmit it to you."

Thereafter I performed water austerities at my house during the day. At that time Mitsugi was also avidly pursuing ascetic training, so at night I would sometimes go with her to stand under the falls at Kiyomizu or to climb one mountain or another. Fifteen years ago, in the spring of 1813, after I'd undergone ascetic training for two years or so, I felt I'd achieved an unwavering mind where nothing startled me and nothing in all the world seemed frightening. Mitsugi must also have seen this, for she told me that the time had come for her to transmit the secret practices to me. "Sometime ago," Mitsugi said, "I received the transmission of secret Kirishitan practices from a person named Mizuno Gunki at Itoya Wasa's house. On that occasion Gunki allowed me to worship a scroll he had of the Lord of Heaven. Before the practices are transmitted to you, you also should worship this scroll. But you must [vow that] you will never confess to these things, however severe a punishment you might face."

On the twenty-seventh or twenty-eighth day of the third month of that year, I went with Mitsugi to Wasa's house. Apart from Wasa, no one else appeared to be at home. Mitsugi and I went to a detached room at the rear. Gunki was already there. Evidently Mitsugi had already spoken with him about bringing me. "Please allow this woman to offer reverence to the buddha image," she said to him. Gunki took out the scroll, which he had brought with him, and hung it on the wall. "This is the Lord of Heaven," Mitsugi indicated. "If you are ready to put your faith in this deity, you should cut one of the fingers on your right hand and let your blood drip onto the deity's breast." When I looked at the buddha image, I saw that it was a paper scroll more than four feet long and one foot wide. It seemed to show a female figure with her hair hanging loose, holding a child in one hand and a sword in the other. An inexplicable feeling of reverence came over me, and I dripped blood from my finger on the image as Mitsugi had directed. As it would not do to linger there and draw people's attention, I didn't exchange any words with Gunki but simply expressed my gratitude with a silent bow and took my leave. Mitsugi remained behind.

The next day I went to Mitsugi's place and learned from her the *paraizo* mantra for praying to the Lord of Heaven, the way to make paper effigies, and the way to perform prayer rituals and divinations, just as I later transmitted them to Sano. "If you adhere firmly to the discipline in which I instructed you, knowledge of things yet to occur will well up naturally in your mind," Mitsugi told me.

> You should never forget the gratitude you owe the Lord of Heaven, even for a single day. But since this practice is something strictly proscribed by the government and people these days are quick to pick up on things, you'll be sure to attract attention unless you perform it in utmost secrecy under the pretense of being an Inari medium. For that reason, too, you must not have any relations with a man. If you faithfully pursue water austerities and preserve an unwavering mind, and also constantly chant the mantra, you'll be sure to flourish more and more.

I changed my name to Kikue, prayed single-mindedly to the Lord of Heaven, and continued to perform water austerities and walk in the mountains. The healing rituals and divinations I performed using the secret practices were more and more efficacious. I was grateful for this and wanted to find like-minded people and disseminate the practice, but I couldn't find anyone, man or woman, of sufficient caliber to enroll as a fellow devotee. Sano, though, was strong and resolute. Although she had a hard time as a widow supporting her son on her own, she seemed firm in her determination not to remarry. I thought that if I enrolled her as my fellow, she would be of help in disseminating the practice. Initially I didn't say anything about the inner secrets of the practice that Mitsugi had transmitted to me, but I told her how I had become able to make divinations. Sano seemed sincere in her wish to become a disciple, and so the two of us lived together and engaged in the same work. Sano performed water austerities and walked in the mountains at night, just as I instructed her.

Kinu and Sano Move to Osaka; Kinu's Struggle to Rent Quarters on Her Own

We pursued this ascetic training faithfully for three years, but I felt it would inconvenience Mitsugi if we continued to engage in these arts in Kyoto. I thus explained the situation to Mitsugi and talked over the matter with Sano, and twelve years ago, in the eleventh month of 1816, the two of us moved to Osaka. I turned initially to Harimaya Bunjirō (now deceased) of Nōjin-machi in Tenma, who was a relative, and while staying with him, I spread the word that I performed healing rituals. I wanted to rent a place of my own, but here in Osaka it is not possible for a woman to maintain a household under her own name.[4] As I was wondering how to overcome this problem, [I became acquainted with] Tōzō, the person who is presently my official household head. Tōzō was born in Harima and had come to Osaka about that time to work as a day laborer for several sake brewers, but he developed an ailment that made it hard to bend his arms. He tried various medicines, but he was of lowly status and couldn't [take sufficient time to] recuperate. He then came to me and asked me to perform a healing ritual. By following the secret practices transmitted to me and praying to the Lord of Heaven, I was able to cure him. Overjoyed that his ailment was gone, Tōzō brought me money as an offering of thanks. Since he was indebted to me, he would do whatever I asked, he said. I mentioned my problem with renting a place of my own and hinted that this could be solved if he acted as my household head, but at that time I didn't yet ask him outright to do so.

Just about that time, Ichimatsu, the two-year-old son of Harimaya Kahei of Tatsuta-machi in Tenma, was afflicted with an eye disease. Although Kahei consulted doctors, it was to no avail, and the boy was on the verge of going blind. Kahei came to me and asked me to perform a healing ritual, so again I used the secret practices transmitted to me and prayed to the Lord of Heaven. At first these seemed to have no effect, and Kahei and his wife were in despair. So for seven nights I went into seclusion and purified myself and prayed continuously. On the seventh night the realization that the child would be cured arose unbidden in my mind. At dawn the next morning, when Kahei came to see me, I told him that his son had now been cured. "You must be joking!" he said to me in amazement and went home to check. An hour later he came back. Thanks to the deity's grace, he declared, a waterlike substance had spurted from his son's closed eyes, rising as high as the ceiling. Shortly thereafter the boy seemed able to see again the dolls and toys that he had played with previously. Kahei and his wife were overjoyed, and he had come to express his gratitude.

Kahei was so delighted and impressed that his son had escaped blindness that he subsequently turned to me again when a maid in his employ lost a comb made of something that looked like silver that her late mother had left her. He thought that I might be able to divine what had happened to it. I prayed to the Lord of Heaven and pondered the matter throughout the night, and the realization came to me what had happened. The next day, when Kahei called on me to get the answer, I told him that the comb

Figure 2.1 Female medium with clients, who are moved to tears by what she relays to them. *Mukashigatari inazuma byōshi.* In vol. 16 of *Santō Kyōden zenshū.* Perikansha, 1994.

hadn't been stolen; another maidservant had found and kept it. "If your maid goes to the Tenma Tenjin Shrine three days from now, in the afternoon, she will meet the person who found the comb, so she can ask her about it," I told him. Kahei seemed unconvinced, but three days later he called on me again. "We did as you instructed," he said, "and, sure enough, my maid saw another maidservant with the lost comb in her hair. My maid asked the other girl about this and learned that she had found it. After some negotiation my maid was able to get the comb back. It is just amazing!" He was full of gratitude, and thereafter he seemed to have ever more faith in my powers.

"Wouldn't you like to have a place of your own even if it's rented?" he asked. "I can help to arrange it." This was just as I had hoped. "I realize you don't know Tōzō," I said, "but since he's obliged to me, I can make him my household head. With that understanding, could you find me a place to rent?" Harimaya Jirobei, my present landlord, who lives in the same block as Kahei, happened to have a vacant place for rent. Kahei said he would arrange the contract for me. "But," he said, "if Tōzō is going to be the household head, his original population register has to be transferred [to Tatsuta-machi in Tenma] so that the transaction can be recorded properly on the [Tatsuta-machi] block register." When Tōzō next came to visit, I told him that I wanted to rent a house and asked him to act as my household head. "I'm already registered in my parents' household in my native village," he said, "so I can't do something like that without asking my parents. But since I'm greatly obliged to you, I'll be happy to do whatever else you ask."

If Tōzō asked his parents, they might well not agree, I thought, so I told him that for the time being I would give up the idea that he might act as my household head. But to Kahei I made out that Tōzō had agreed. "However," I said, "since Tōzō's native village is far away, he feels it would be troublesome to have the population register forwarded and would like to ask you to come up with some alternative arrangement." Fortunately, it so happened that at the time Kahei had let a servant go but hadn't yet removed his name from the population register. "I can make it appear that Tōzō is my servant and I've set him up as a branch house," he said. "Since I'm registered with the Ikkō sect temple Rentakuji, in Tenma 1-chōme, there shouldn't be any problem if Tōzō also becomes a parishioner of that temple." In line with Kahei's proposal and with his acting as the go-between, I arranged to rent Jirobei's house with Tōzō as household head. This was eleven years ago, in the tenth month of 1817. I changed my name from Kikue back to Kinu and had myself put on the population register as Tōzō's grandmother.[5] And of course I became a parishioner of Rentakuji.

[In actuality] I continued to live alone and to pretend to be an Inari medium. Tōzō visited every once in a while, and he probably was somehow aware that I had used his name as my household head. But he behaved as if he knew nothing, perhaps, I guess, because he was obliged to me for curing his ailment. Neither of us thus said anything openly about it. *(Investigators: Reports of the interrogation of Kahei and Tōzō follow Kinu's testimony.)*

Kinu's Attempt to Recruit Koto

As I was getting on in years, I wished to set up one or two fellow devotees apart from Sano. It so happened that there was a woman called Koto; at present she lives under the name Mitsugi with her son, Edoya Jōsuke, in Sunahara Yashiki in Tenma, but at one time she used to stay in Uoyamachi in Tenma. She was also an Inari medium, and one day she came to consult me. She seemed to be unusually clever for a woman, and I thought about encouraging her to join in the practice. After Koto moved to Sunahara Yashiki, it appeared that she didn't have a husband, and as she visited me now and again to talk, we became friendly. One day I decided to invite her to become a disciple. "The Inari medium practice that you put faith in," I told her,

> is no different from fox witchery. It is like a child's game and will never bring you success and fame. The Inari practice carried out by my master, Toyoda Mitsugi, is a miraculous method unlike any other. If you attain an unwavering mind by engaging for some years in ascetic training such as walking in the mountains and water austerities, you will become clairvoyant into all things of the world and able to cure all manner of difficult illnesses easily. Most likely you will also become prosperous. Why don't you become a disciple?

But Koto said she needed to think about it. I was worried that since she hadn't given a definite answer, she might tell others what she had heard from me. I prayed as usual to the Lord of Heaven, and the realization came to me that Koto had doubts about what I had told her and had consulted someone else. She had, in fact, decided not to start ascetic training, but outwardly she was pretending that she was still interested, and therefore she was saying one thing and another [to conceal her true intentions]. When I confronted her, saying I knew what was going on, Koto was startled. "How terrifying!" she exclaimed. I realized that she wouldn't become a disciple and broke off relations with her.

Investigators' Comments on the Statements Made by Koto and Her Son

When we investigated Koto, known also as Mitsugi, and her son, Jōsuke, their testimony matched Kinu's. Koto stated as follows:

> Kinu told me that if I pursued ascetic training for some years, I could become clairvoyant into things as minute as the proverbial ant's tracks and be able to cure difficult illnesses easily. Also, I might well be able to gain a profit of one thousand *ryō* in gold. But although Kinu urged me to become a disciple, I thought Mitsugi's practices were too strange, and so I consulted my Shinto master, a person called Kawada Tosa, about what Kinu had said to me. "The methods of Inari, let alone the way of the kami, are nothing like that," he said. "What Kinu told you sounds odd, so you should take care not to be deceived." Hearing this from Tosa, I became frightened. I thought that I should refuse Kinu's proposal, but since Kinu had a fierce disposition, I put off giving her a definite answer about becoming a disciple. Then Kinu confronted me, saying that she knew I had consulted someone else and that my lack of faith was unforgivable. I was startled and found it strange that Kinu could see right into my mind. Tosa had warned me about her, and, in the end, we broke off relations. However, although I had never met Toyoda Mitsugi, I had heard that she was an extraordinary person and enjoyed a prosperous life. I didn't have faith in Mitsugi's arts, but I envied her cleverness, and thus I privately began to call myself Mitsugi, too.

Jōsuke stated as follows: "My mother told me what Kinu had said to her, but she never became Mitsugi's disciple as Kinu had urged her to do, nor did she ever receive the transmission of the Kirishitan creed or join Kinu in spreading pernicious practices. It was the height of stupidity and heedlessness for her to have envied Mitsugi's ability and to have adopted her name, and she regrets it deeply."

Kinu Initiates Sano Into the Kirishitan Creed

After breaking off relations with Koto, I decided that there was no one other than Sano on whom I could depend. Sano had settled down in Era-machi in Dōjima, but we feared that it would endanger what we were doing if we were to meet directly, so we avoided doing that. At the time Sano was still in the initial stages of her training, and I hadn't yet transmitted the secret practices to her. We thus arranged that for her healing rituals and divinations she would send her son, Shinsuke, to consult me every after-noon, under the pretense that he was going to check on a relative. Shin-suke came faithfully every day, rain or shine. Since this continued for many years and Sano consulted me about many cases, I don't remember the names of each and every client. As we had agreed, Sano gave me half the payments, however small, that she received from those who asked her to perform healing rituals or divinations. I don't know how much it came to overall. Shinsuke would bring the payments in cash, and I just used the money for daily expenses without keeping track of how much it came to.

Sano showed great commitment and continued to perform water aus-terities night and day so as to obtain an unwavering mind. When I judged that she had reached the point of firmness of mind where she would be ready to take upon herself whatever punishment she might face, I trans-mitted to her the secret practices of the Lord of Heaven. I thought that if I told Sano about how I had worshipped the drawing of the Lord of Heaven kept by Mizuno Gunki, she would want to do the same. But since I didn't have the drawing, there was no way to let her worship it. Further, if I told her about the drawing, it might lead her to think that the firmness of one's faith depended on whether or not [one had worshipped] it. In my oral transmission to her I therefore said that I'd been told that the Lord of Heaven is a buddha without shape or form.[6] There was nothing about burning a large candle in the transmission that I received from my master. [I used it merely to create an appropriate atmosphere, since] what mat-tered when transmitting the creed was that both parties remained com-posed and still in body and mind.

Shinsuke continued thereafter to come to consult me about healing rituals and divinations. I don't have any firm recollection of making a judgment about the [hairdresser's] trying to seduce Soyo, but doubtless it was one of many such judgments that I performed for Sano. After Sano returned from Nagasaki,[7] she became increasingly accomplished in her practice. Once she moved to the village of Kawasaki, she received ever greater amounts of gold, silver, and clothes from people who had become believers. She couldn't forget the debt she owed the master who had transmitted the secret practices to her, she said, and so she regularly had Shinsuke bring me gold, silver, and coppers—how much exactly I don't recall. Since I was getting on in years and finding it more and more difficult to engage in rigorous training, [I was grateful that] Sano had become proficient in her practice and shared with me the money she received. And since I felt a debt of obligation to Mitsugi as my master, I repeatedly sent her a portion of what I received from Sano, although again I don't remember how much.

I thought carefully about what to do with the gold, silver, and coppers that I kept, so as to make sure they weren't found if something should cause officials from the magistracy to become suspicious of me. Whenever I received money from Sano, I hid it in places where it wouldn't be noticed. I hid the gold and silver in the cracks of the ceiling boards, or inside the lantern stand for the kitchen god, or between the tatami and the floorboards. The coppers I hid deep in the charcoal bales.[8] Whenever I needed some money, I would just take it out and use it. *(Investigators: Calculated in silver, what is left comes to about 1,300 monme.)*

Investigators' Comments on the Sums of Money Received by Kinu

Because Shinsuke has died, as recorded previously in the addenda to Sano's testimony, it is difficult to know the total sum of the money he took to Kinu. When we questioned Kinu again on this point, she replied as follows:

Shinsuke would bring small amounts spread out over many occasions so as not to arouse suspicion. I feared that if I took the time to count the money out, someone might come by and see me, so I would immediately hide it away without checking how much it came to. You say I could have checked it at night, but I never did so because at night I concentrated totally on the secret practices. If I had allowed myself to be distracted by thoughts of money while performing the practices, I wouldn't have been able to conduct healing rituals or perform the divinations properly. I cannot remember how much I sent to Mitsugi, either.

According to Sano's calculation, Shinsuke must have taken about seven or eight thousand *monme* in silver to Kinu, so we pressed Kinu on this point again. The amount of gold, silver, and coppers that had been found hidden in her quarters came to only a little over 1,300 *monme* when converted into silver. According to Kinu, she had used the money she received over the past four years since 1824 on her daily expenses, and she had also regularly sent some to Mitsugi. The total may indeed be as Sano estimated it, but Kinu insisted that she herself didn't know the exact amount. Since it is clear where the money went and because Shinsuke is dead [and cannot supply more precise information], we have compiled the confirmed testimony in line with Kinu's statement. We have confiscated the gold, silver, and coppers that were found hidden.

Kinu's Concluding Statement

I heard that Sano and Shinsuke had been arrested, but I felt confident that Sano's mind and soul were as steadfast as a rock. I was sure that she would never reveal who her master was, or that she had received the transmission of the creed. Nevertheless, to avoid having suspicion fall on me, I went and stood next to the front gate of Tenma Tenjin Shrine until well into the night and acted as if I made a living by begging coins for reciting purification chants. Unexpectedly, however, I was nonetheless arrested. During the interrogation, I have said various false things. But since Sano has already confessed, there is nothing for me to do but confess as well, as detailed in the preceding statement.

Investigators' Summation of Their Interrogation of Kinu

We confronted Kinu additionally with the following accusation:

You [have admitted that you] received transmission of the Kirishitan secret practices from Mitsugi and did various strange things under the guise of performing healing rituals. Further, Sano, to whom you transmitted these practices, used them to cause people to take leave of their senses and contribute large amounts of gold and silver. You received a share of this in recompense for the obligation she owed you as her master, and you then sent a portion to Mitsugi. Given this behavior, undoubtedly you also were in fact plotting to do something wicked with Gunki, Mitsugi, and other members of your group whose names you may not know. Most likely you schemed from the start to raise the necessary funds [for this plot] by sending out Sano to collect whatever money she could in Osaka. And surely, apart from the transmissions described above, you also received the oral transmission of secret scriptures, spells, and practices that you have not disclosed.

We repeatedly interrogated her severely about these points.

To this Kinu responded as follows:

It is true that I became Mitsugi's follower out of a desire to acquire the ability to do things that were out of the ordinary and that I ended up receiving the transmission of the pernicious creed. But I simply sought to spread this creed in the world to help people who suffer from illness or are in difficult straits, and to enable both them and myself to live in prosperity. I never plotted anything wicked with Gunki and Mitsugi or directed Sano to gather the funds to carry out such a thing. Nor have I received the transmission of Kirishitan scriptures, spells, and secret practices apart from those I've already described. Just as Sano has said, lustful or greedy people would never be able to do the things we did even if they were initiated into this sect.

The interrogation has fully clarified the circumstances detailed in the preceding statement of how Kinu, showing not the slightest awe for the shogunal authorities, acted in a manner that was the height of audacity and committed multiple heinous crimes. She states that she has nothing to say in opposition [to what is recorded here] and is filled with remorse.

TESTIMONY OF TOSHIMAYA TŌZŌ

Toshimaya Tōzō: thirty-two years of age; household head of the aforementioned Kinu and tenant of Naosaburō, of Takama-chō, Osaka, who is being represented at the magistracy by Kameya Magobei

Under custody of the locale[9]

Summary of Tōzō's Testimony and the Checking of It Against Kinu's

Under interrogation Tōzō stated that he is the son of Sōbei, now deceased, a farmer of the village of Kyōden in Harima province. He came to Osaka eleven years ago in 1817 to work as a day laborer at sake breweries, but he became afflicted with an illness that made it difficult for him to bend his arms. He asked Kinu to perform healing rituals, and after he had been miraculously cured he offered her [money] in gratitude. These particulars all match those of Kinu's testimony.

Tōzō's Testimony Proper

When I fell ill, I consulted a doctor, but to no avail. I had heard that Kinu, who was then staying with Harimaya Bunjirō, had mysterious skills in performing healing rituals, and so I went to her regularly. Eventually I was cured, and I felt much obliged to her. Just about that time, Kinu said that she wanted to rent a room from Jirobei and asked me to become her household head. But at the time I was still registered as a member of my father's household, so I told Kinu I couldn't become her household head without consulting him, and things were left as they were.

Later I decided to go into business in Osaka. Nine years ago, in 1819, I had my population register transferred from that of my father to that of Toshimaya Izaemon of Nagahori Jirobei-chō, who is a relative. [Later] the same year I registered my name and house name [of Toshimaya] with my present landlord. I continued to make my living by working in Osaka and frequently went to see Kinu. I heard vague rumors that she had entered into a rental contract with "Harimaya Tōzō" listed as the household head. I was puzzled by this, but since I was beholden to Kinu, I acted as if I were unaware of the matter and simply let it go without looking into it. I was greatly startled to learn from the present investigation that Kinu falsely claimed that I had agreed to act as her household head, that she had arranged with Kahei to make it appear as if I were Kahei's servant whom he had set up as a branch house, and that [Kahei] had registered me [on the population register of his block] as a household head with the house name of Harimaya and with Kinu as my grandmother. I was also startled to learn for the first time that Kinu in fact practiced the secret methods of the Kirishitan sect and used them to perform healing rituals, even though she always claimed to be an Inari medium.

Investigators' Summation of Their Interrogation of Tōzō

We confronted Tōzō with the accusation that undoubtedly the preceding testimony was a lie and that in reality he had faith in the Kirishitan creed and had enrolled himself in two population registers simultaneously out of gratitude for Kinu's healing of his illness. We interrogated him severely about these points, but he insisted that such was not at all the case. He states that the circumstances of his crime having been fully clarified, he has nothing to say in opposition [to what is recorded here].

TESTIMONY OF HARIMAYA KAHEI

Harimaya Kahei: forty-three years of age; resident in Tatsuta-machi in Tenma, Osaka

Under custody of the locale

Summary of Kahei's Testimony and the Checking of It Against Kinu's

Under interrogation, Kahei stated as follows:

At the time Kinu was staying with Bunjirō, my son Ichimatsu was afflicted with an eye ailment. I asked Kinu to perform prayer rituals, whereupon something like water spurted from Ichimatsu's eyes as high as the ceiling. I was impressed by this extraordinary event and also by the fact that when I had Kinu ask Inari about my maidservant's lost comb, the girl was able to discover who had found it and get it back. When Kinu requested my help, I therefore made it appear that Tōzō was called Harimaya Tōzō and arranged with Rentakuji to take him on as a parishioner. I did this without confirming the situation with Tōzō first. I further pretended that I had set Tōzō up as a branch house and arranged for quarters to be rented from Jirobei under Tōzō's name as the household head and with Kinu as his grandmother. I even had Tōzō enrolled in the population register for this block although he was already registered elsewhere.

These particulars all match Kinu's testimony.

Kahei's Testimony Proper

Kinu's curing of my son Ichimatsu's eye disease and her ascertaining who had found my maidservant's comb seemed extraordinary events, something that no usual person could do. Saving my son from going blind, in particular, was a great deed, and although I offered payment in gratitude, I still felt obliged to Kinu and thought I could at least act as an intermediary in helping her to rent quarters of her own. That is why I agreed to negotiate the rental with Jirobei. I believed what Kinu said, so I didn't check with Tōzō. I just took advantage of the fact that a servant that I had let go hadn't yet been removed from my population register and presented Tōzō as this servant. I then [arranged for him to rent quarters from Jirobei] as if he had been set up as a branch house under the name Harimaya Tōzō and Kinu were his grandmother, and I had the two recorded on the population register as such. I was greatly startled to learn from the present investigation that Kinu is a devotee of the Kirishitan creed, that she lied in saying that Tōzō had agreed to act as her household head, and that Tōzō was already enrolled in the Takama-chō population register and thus ended up recorded in two different population registers.

Investigators' Summation of Their Interrogation of Kahei

We confronted Kahei with the accusation that undoubtedly Kinu had encouraged him to have faith in the Kirishitan creed, and that in fact he had engaged in the activities of the confraternity and secretly prayed to the Lord of Heaven. We interrogated him severely about these points, but he insisted that such was not at all the case. He states that the circumstances of his crimes having been fully clarified, he has nothing to say in opposition [to what is recorded here].

OFFICIALS' ADDITIONAL COMMENTS ON THE COURSE
OF KINU'S INTERROGATION

The particulars of Kinu's arrest are as recorded in the addendum to Sano's testimony. Just as with Sano, Kinu tried to mislead us by lying blatantly in the first stage of her interrogation. She claimed that she had learned the arts of an Inari medium from her late husband, Kihei; that she was able to use foxes and tanuki [to trick others]; and that she also had gained miraculous powers through the doings of *tengu*.[10] She continued to hold to these brazen lies, but when we had her house searched, the aforementioned effigies with nails were found, along with gold, silver, and coppers hidden in various places. Letters she had received from Toyoda Mitsugi also came to light. We interrogated Kinu severely about these matters, and at length she confessed to the particulars detailed in the preceding. Thereupon we made arrangements with the Kyoto eastern magistrate, Lord Kan'o Mototaka, to have Toyoda Mitsugi arrested and transferred to our jurisdiction.[11] The details of her interrogation are recorded as follows.

Chapter 3

Mitsugi, Mizuno Gunki, and Wasa

TESTIMONY OF TOYODA MITSUGI

Toyoda Mitsugi: fifty-four years old; yin-yang diviner under the supervision of the Tsuchimikado house; resident in Yasaka Kami-chō, Kyoto

Remanded to jail the thirteenth day of the sixth month, 1827

Investigators' Appended Comment About Mitsugi's Earlier Arrest

Mitsugi informed us that she had been found guilty of a misdeed six years ago, on the twenty-seventh day of the eighth month of 1822. The judgment pronounced then stated that although her misdeed warranted a sentence of fifty days' confinement to her house, she was exempted from further punishment because she had already been held in the jailhouse for some time [during the investigation of the incident]. We checked Mitsugi's statement with the Kyoto Eastern Magistracy, which confirmed that it is correct.[1]

Summary of Mitsugi's Testimony and the Checking of It Against Kinu's

Under interrogation the above person stated as follows:

I am the daughter of Yohei, farmer in Arama village, Niikawa county, Etchū province, and his wife, San. I have an elder brother called Kazue.

In 1775, when I was two years old, I moved with my parents and brother to Saiin village on the western outskirts of Kyoto.

I served as a maid at various places from the age of twelve and later became a prostitute. After I married Iori (later resident in Benten-chō, off Shimokawara street), I made my living as an Inari medium. Kinu had already become my disciple by the time Iori took up with another woman and absconded, leaving me behind. For a while I stayed with Itoya Wasa (now deceased). After I moved to my present house, I became much more accomplished than before in performing extraordinary feats of healing and divination, and this made Kinu envious. "If you have any secret methods," Kinu said, "please transmit them to me." Kinu appeared committed, so I instructed her to abstain from indulging in lust, to undertake water austerities, and to walk alone in the mountains at night. Kinu sometimes accompanied me to the Kiyomizu falls for water austerities. When I was convinced that Kinu's training was complete and she had attained an unwavering mind, I asked Gunki to let Kinu worship the scroll of the Lord of Heaven, which I had worshipped myself when I was still living with Wasa. At Wasa's house I directed Kinu to drip some blood from her finger onto the scroll. I also taught Kinu the mantra for praying to the Lord of Heaven and the methods of healing and divination. Kinu's training had now reached maturity, and she moved away from Kyoto to Osaka. After she had moved, Kinu continued to send me money to repay her debt to me as her master. *(Investigators: These particulars all match those of Kinu's testimony.)*

MITSUGI'S TESTIMONY PROPER

Mitsugi's Youth and Marriage

I worked as a maid in various places from the time I was twelve or thirteen, while my brother, Kazue, set himself up as an *Yijing* diviner in Uchino Niban-chō under the name of Watanabe Kazue. Both my parents moved in with Kazue. My father soon fell ill and died, and my mother took the tonsure and adopted the [Buddhist] name of Eshū, while continuing to stay with Kazue. When I was twenty-four or -five, I came to depend on a woman called Akashiya Iwa, who ran a teahouse in Nijō Shinchi, and I worked for Iwa as a prostitute under the name of Onoe.[2]

According to what I have heard, Iori was the son of a man called Saitō Dewa, a priest at a Hachiman shrine somewhere in Ōmi province—I don't know the name. Iori led a dissipated life. He came to Kyoto for amusement and had an affair with me. We became husband and wife and temporarily moved in with Kazue. Since Iori had been born in a priestly household, he had learned how to call down Inari by shaking a wand, and he was also quite proficient in *Yijing* divination. Iori had some capital, so with the sponsorship of Takeuchi Chikugo (now deceased), the father of Takeuchi Ōmi and a Tsuchimikado retainer, he became a yin-yang diviner under the supervision of the Tsuchimikado house. We rented a house in Benten-chō and moved there. Iori earned his living as an Inari medium and an *Yijing* diviner, healing people's illnesses and determining what good or bad fortune awaited them.

I had no interest or training in ordinary women's work [such as weaving and spinning], and from the time I worked as a prostitute I wanted to try my hand at performing mysterious feats. Fortunately Iori knew the arts of an Inari medium, so I studied them with him and learned both the universal purification prayer and *Yijing* divination.[3] I made a living in this way for some four years, and gradually I won more clients. [Yet I had doubts about this profession.] Inari mediums, I reckoned, are no more than practitioners of fox witchery; their profession is just a game, getting people excited by shaking a wand and tricking ignorant men and women. Some people may escape hunger and cold with the help of such crude trickery, but no amount of prayer rituals of that sort will actually heal, and the true future remains out of sight. In the end it would be impossible, I realized, to astound people and make a name for myself in the city and beyond by sticking to such methods. In my heart, I mocked [the entire profession].

In the meantime, Iori fell in love with a woman called Katsura, who lived in Miyagawa-chō in Kyoto (she came originally from Hiroshima, in Aki province), and started an affair with her.[4] Eighteen years ago, in the ninth month of 1810, Iori absconded. He left behind all his household possessions and savings, and also a letter of divorce addressed to me. I didn't know where he had gone but suspected that he was probably hiding in Katsura's place. I asked around and found that my suspicions were correct. I sent letters to Iori, but he had lost all interest in me. He told me, though, that I could keep everything that he had left in the house. Soon

I heard that he had set off from Kyoto together with Katsura and gone to Aki. "How heartless!" I thought, and more than once I became so distraught that I was determined to knife Katsura to death.

Itoya Wasa was a widow who ran a teahouse. At heart she was a solid character, and we had been on friendly terms since the time I married Iori. Wasa, too, was exasperated at Iori's infidelity, but she restrained me from seeking revenge. "You should give up that faithless man!" she told me. "Let the house go, sell off the furnishings, and move to my place for the time being. The rest we can decide later." Following her advice, I sold off all the household effects. Together with the savings that Iori had left behind, this amounted to about thirty *ryō* in gold. I took this sum with me and moved in with Wasa in the tenth month of 1810 for about sixty days.

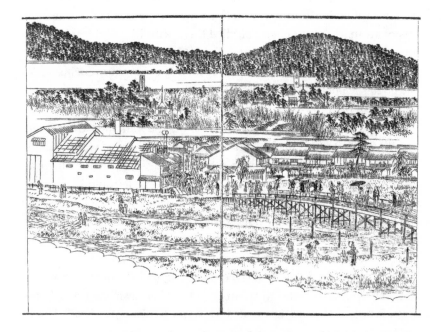

Figure 3.1 The area along the east bank of the Kamo River. In the left middle ground is the pagoda at Yasaka, near where Mitsugi eventually lived. The pagoda at the rear right is at Kiyomizu, one of the places where she performed austerities. At the back lie the Higashiyama hills. Wasa's house was located north of the area depicted. *Karaku meishō zue*, "Matsubara tokō, sono ni (Matsubara gawara)." International Research Center for Japanese Studies.

Mitsugi's Encounter with Mizuno Gunki and Her Initiation Into the Kirishitan Creed

I noticed that Mizuno Gunki visited [Wasa] often, and I asked Wasa who this gentleman was. Wasa told me that he was a retainer of the Kan'in princely house and that he lived in rented quarters in Samegai, south of Gojō street, owned by Tomitaya Riemon. I soon came to know Gunki. "There is something out of the ordinary about your facial features," he said to me. "What have you been doing up to now?" I told him all about my earlier profession. Then I said, "My husband deceived me. He had an affair with Katsura, left me behind, and eloped with her. I became so jealous that I wanted to kill both Katsura and myself, but Wasa stopped me. All I could do was to depend on her. It is so infuriating!" "If you hate Katsura so much, why don't you describe her to me in detail," Gunki said. "I can then show her to you, and you'll be able to free yourself of your despair and hatred." Surely he can't be serious and is just making fun of me, I thought. But Wasa said, "Gunki is no common man. He has mastered many mysterious arts. Let Gunki show Katsura to you!" I was still skeptical, but I described Katsura's looks and age to Gunki. He impressed on me that what he was about to show me should not be revealed to others and that I should never tell anyone about it.

The three of us went to a detached room [in the garden] of Wasa's house. Wasa had two adoptive daughters, Ito and Toki. She had sent Ito off in service elsewhere as a maid. Toki usually served sake at parties [held at the teahouse], but on this evening Wasa didn't have her attend the gathering. Without getting up from his seat, Gunki extinguished the candle that stood twenty-five or thirty feet away. When he did this a dim light filled the room, and he went out onto the veranda. Suddenly Katsura appeared, walking into the garden from the alley beyond, accompanied by a girl who looked like a maid. When I saw them, clearly distinguishable, about to step onto the veranda, my feelings of despair and hatred exploded. I gnashed my teeth and flew at Katsura, trying to grab her. Wasa silently held me back, and when I calmed down, Katsura's figure disappeared. Wasa lit the candle and thanked Gunki. "You certainly showed us something mysterious!" I said to Gunki. The apparition had left me both enraged and exhilarated. "How is it that you can do such extraordinary things?" I asked. "That was nothing special," Gunki said. "Let me show you a remarkable art!" He asked Wasa to fill a pot with water. Gunki

Figure 3.2 A Kyoto teahouse. Separate parties are being entertained in rooms on the first and second floors. In the left foreground is a detached room of the sort where Mitsugi and Wasa met with Gunki. *Karaku meishō zue*, "Dō minamigawa Ichiriki zashiki (Ichiriki chaya)." International Research Center for Japanese Studies.

performed some spell over it, and the water rose two feet up in the air. By now, I was thoroughly impressed.

As I said, I already regarded what Inari mediums do as nothing more than a game, and I had the ambition to do something extraordinary. If Gunki would be willing to teach me the kind of things he had just done, I thought, people would surely be astounded. When I asked Gunki about this, he said,

> That was sorcery, and not something you should trouble yourself with. But if you master the other arts that I can transmit to you, you'll be able to foresee things before they occur and predict fortune and misfortune correctly when people come to consult you. You'll be able to heal people by performing prayer rituals, and you'll never be short of money. However, I can't transmit these things lightly. You might be able to perform these arts for a while, but unless you commit yourself totally to your

training, without taking a husband for the rest of your life, you will die before your time. I will teach you, but only if you keep these things well in mind.

I had been a prostitute, so I knew how fickle men's affections are. After Iori's betrayal, I was all the more fed up with men, so I made up my mind not to take another husband for the rest of my life. Following Gunki's instructions I went by myself to such places as Nyakuōji in Higashiyama and stood under one of the falls there every night for thirty days. After I had done this, Wasa told me [about the further steps of initiation]. "The creed of the Lord of Heaven is strictly proscribed," she said, "and is not to be transmitted lightly. You will have to pay Gunki one thousand *monme* in silver in gratitude for transmitting the secret arts to you and for allowing you to worship the scroll of the Lord of Heaven." I took that sum out of the money that I had gained by selling the furnishings of my previous house and sent it to Gunki.[5]

Sometime later, Gunki allowed me to worship the buddha scroll at night in the detached room at Wasa's house. The buddha figure was a standing woman with her hair hanging loose, holding a child in her left hand and a sword in her right. *(Investigators: This matches Kinu's description.)* It was an old drawing, however, and hard to make out clearly. This image is called the Lord of Heaven, I was told. Following Gunki's instructions, I cut the middle finger of my right hand and dripped blood onto what appeared to be the buddha's breast. "If you remain unmarried," Gunki told me, "are single-minded in your faith, and practice water austerities diligently, all the while secretly giving thanks to this buddha and reciting the *paraizo* mantra, you will find success and prosperity once your repeated performance of water austerities has reached fruition." *(Investigators: The method to heal people and collect money was the same as that later transmitted from Kinu to Sano and described by Sano in her testimony.)*

"You must make sure," Gunki continued,

to maintain a firm faith in your heart. The ascetic training is hard, but if I were to teach you straightaway the sorcery that I perform, and you began to want to show it to others, just like entertaining guests at a party with conjuring tricks, you would attract suspicion and get arrested. Therefore I won't teach you sorcery. In the end, sorcery is no more than a lead to pull people into the pernicious creed, and you'll be able to focus on your training more effectively if I don't transmit it to you. However, if you find someone who you think would be suitable as a disciple, you won't be able to make him a true follower unless you can astound him to the depths of his soul with some remarkable art. When you take him to a waterfall somewhere to perform water austerities, you should lock up his eyes and mouth by drawing a secret sign on his back and eyes with your finger.

Investigators' Comments on the Secret Sign

[We asked Mitsugi] what kind of sign this might be, and whether she had some samples of calligraphy or pieces of writing by Gunki; she said she did not. The sign was like this: ⓐ.

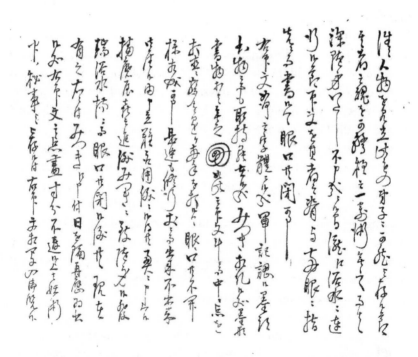

Figure 3.3 Page from the Kōda-bon MS depicting the secret sign. The indented passage that starts six lines from the right shows the format used for the addenda written in red ink. "Jashūmon ikken kakitome," traced facsimile copy. Historiographical Institute, University of Tokyo.

"When you put the dot in the center, you shout at the same time and clap your hands," she said. "The person will be unable to open his eyes and mouth. Whether you can make this work depends on the extent of your training."

This appears hard to believe, but as noted below, it was in fact after Mitsugi had closed his eyes and mouth at a waterfall that Harimaya Kinoshin became her follower. We raised this issue with Mitsugi some days later and had her draw the sign once again. Every stroke and dot were exactly the same as what she had drawn before, so this must be one of the ultimate secrets of their sorcery. That is why we have copied it and include it in this report. Mitsugi maintains she has not transmitted this sign to Kinu.

Gunki Provides Mitsugi with a Substitute Scroll and Emblem

"Originally the Lord of Heaven had no sacred icon," Gunki continued.

But people felt as if they were praying to emptiness, and their faith remained shallow. So, even though the Lord of Heaven by nature has no shape or form, people in the lands of the southern barbarians began to make drawings of the Lord of Heaven like the one I have—so I've heard. This creed is strictly proscribed at present, though, and we would soon be discovered unless we found a way to disguise our object of worship. Therefore I have devised an image consisting of three figures: Otafuku, wearing a red *hakama*, Shōki, and Kikudōji. I call this Otafuku "the divine Uzume," but in fact it is a stand-in image for the Lord of Heaven.[6] You should have drawings made of these three figures. But if you have the three drawings fashioned into scrolls of the same style, people may suspect that they form a set, so have them mounted and arranged in different ways. Keep firmly in mind that these represent the Lord of Heaven, but you should continue to act outwardly as an Inari medium.

[To that end you need an appropriate emblem.] Hōkoku Daimyōjin is the posthumous deity title of Lord Toyotomi Hideyoshi, but people tend to be ignorant of this [and simply associate this deity with prosperity].[7] Even if you use this title as the name of your Inari,[8] people will not realize that it is the deity title of Lord Hideyoshi. Since he used the "thousand gourds" as his battlefield emblem, from now on use a single gourd as your crest. Whatever one does today, one can never become as prosperous as Lord Hideyoshi. Yet, if you worship the Lord of Heaven and act with determination—even as a woman—you are sure to attain the greatest success possible. I congratulate you in advance!

I was pleased with the deity name and crest that Gunki had given me. I devoted myself to practicing water austerities and walking in the mountains, and I prayed to the Lord of Heaven through the night without sleeping.

Mitsugi's Success as a Diviner

In the twelfth month of 1810 I requested Wasa's temple of affiliation, the Nichiren temple Daijōin in Nijō Shinchi, to accept me as a parishioner. I also decided to place myself under the supervision of the Tsuchimikado house as a yin-yang diviner. Chikugo (now deceased), the father of Take-uchi Ōmi, was a retainer of that house and supervised yin-yang diviners on their behalf. As mentioned previously, this Chikugo had earlier arranged for Iori to become a yin-yang diviner under Tsuchimikado supervision. Therefore I asked Chikugo's assistance once again, and I joined the ranks of licensed yin-yang diviners. With the money I had left I bought a dilapidated house in the location where I am presently living and had it repaired. When the repairs were finished, I moved from Wasa's place to this house. I hung out a sign reading, "*Yijing* divination, Inari medium," and began earning my own living.

I set up an Inari shrine at my house, using a piece of wood wrapped in silk as the deity body. Following Gunki's instructions, I advertised [my deity] as Hōkoku Daimyōjin, and I displayed this name in large lettering on the shrine lanterns. I had shrine furnishings made, dyed with the crest of the single gourd. Since it was a special emblem, I didn't use it for everyday purposes. I also had an ukiyoe artist draw Otafuku, Shōki, and Kikudōji; I had the drawings mounted and rimmed in different styles and placed them [in the shrine].

Investigators' Comments on the Substitute Scroll

Concerning these images of Otafuku, Shōki, and Kikudōji, we conferred with [the Kyoto eastern magistrate,] Lord Kan'o Mototaka. He had Mitsu-gi's house searched and confiscated these three drawings, which have

Figure 3.4 Mitsugi's three scrolls that served as a substitute for an icon of the Lord of Heaven perhaps looked something like this: (*left*) Shōki with sword; (*center*) Otafuku/ Uzume; (*right*) the child Kikudōji. *Hokusai manga*, vol. 3. Katano Tōshirō, 1878. National Diet Library Digital Collection; *Hokusai manga*, vol. 5. Katano Tōshirō, 1878. National Diet Library Digital Collection; *Japanese pottery: with notes describing the thoughts and subjects employed in its decoration and illustrations from examples in the Bowes collection*, "Kiku-jido. From Senriodo gwafu, by Takizawa Kiyoshi." International Research Center for Japanese Studies.

been transferred to Osaka. If Mitsugi's account is correct, a drawing of Otafuku alone should have been sufficient to represent the Lord of Heaven, and Shōki and Kikudōji would be superfluous. We therefore questioned Mitsugi further about this point, and she responded as follows:

> The figure on the scroll owned by Gunki, as I said, held a child in her left hand and a sword in her right. Shōki's sword corresponded to the sword of the Lord of Heaven, and Kikudōji to the child. It was only later that I realized how ingenious Gunki had been in devising this arrangement, so that an ordinary person who saw these drawings wouldn't understand [what they were]. This is my own conjecture; Gunki never gave me a specific oral transmission stating as much. I gradually came to understand [that the acquisition of mysterious powers] depends solely on the extent of your training, not the possession of drawings of this

sort. Therefore I didn't tell Kinu anything about the drawings of Ota-fuku and the others when I transmitted the secret method to her; I merely had her worship Gunki's scroll.[9]

Mitsugi Arranges for Kinu's Initiation

Kinu had been living for some time in Nushiya-chō. She had already become my disciple when I was still married to Iori, and after I moved to Yasaka Kami-chō she continued to visit me there. Kinu saw me engage in water austerities, and she grew envious when she noticed that I was successful whenever clients asked me to perform healing rituals or to predict good or bad fortune. She asked me to transmit the secret methods to her, and as she promised never to take a husband, I taught her to practice austerities by walking in the mountains during the night and standing under waterfalls so as to attain an unwavering mind. After Kinu had followed this ascetic training for two years, I saw that she had indeed gained an unwavering mind. I believed that her faith wouldn't be strong unless she was allowed to worship the image of the Lord of Heaven, so I discussed her situation with Gunki in private. Fifteen years ago, in the evening of the twenty-seventh or the twenty-eighth day of the third month of 1813, I took Kinu to Wasa's house and had her drip blood onto the drawing owned by Gunki. I taught her how to recite the *paraizo* mantra, when to hammer nails into an effigy and when not to, and how to perform prayer rituals and divine good or bad fortune.

Mitsugi's Failure to Recruit Toki

Wasa was committed, but she was an old woman and couldn't perform such austerities as standing under a waterfall. She said that she wanted Ito and Toki, or at least Toki, to begin training and asked me to teach Toki. I took Toki along to a waterfall and told her to stay away from men. However, she appeared to dislike such training, and I thought that probably she was unable to practice the austerities because she was secretly seeing a man. After I had discussed this in private with Wasa, I tried all sorts of measures to bring Toki around. I drew a dagger and threatened her. I tied her hands behind her back and beat her. When I fed her, I mixed rice and soup in a tub as one would when feeding a dog. In the face of such treatment, Toki insisted that she wouldn't bend to my will even if it meant her death. I continued this treatment for about sixty days, but Toki wouldn't come around.

This annoyed me, and I talked the matter over with Wasa. "That hateful daughter of mine is too stubborn," Wasa said. "We should put her under Gunki's charge and have him bring her to her senses." We sent Toki to Gunki, but Gunki was a clever man who could instinctively tell who had potential and talent and who did not. He never revealed his real intentions to people whom he found lacking in potential, even if they were family members or close relatives. Perhaps Gunki saw that Toki had a weak character and would never be able to train successfully. It appears that he didn't pressure her to perform water austerities and just had her stay with him for a while. I heard that this angered Wasa, who then made Toki into a prostitute.

Investigators' Comments Regarding Their Questioning of Wasa's Adoptive Daughters, Ito and Toki

We contacted Lord Kan'o Mototaka, the Kyoto eastern magistrate, about Ito and Toki and arranged to have them sent to Osaka, where we questioned them. The particulars of their statements matched [those of Mitsugi's].

Ito stated as follows:

I am the daughter of Wataya Zenbei (now deceased), who resided in Teramachi, north of Gojō street, in Kyoto. When I was eight years old, Wasa, who was running a teahouse at the intersection of Shinbashi and Nawate streets, took me in as an indentured adoptive daughter.[10]At the age of sixteen I went into service as a maid in the house of Karakiya Mansuke (present domicile unknown), who at that time resided in Daikoku-machi, south of Matsubara street. Later I became this man's wife. When my son Ichimatsu was born, I called on Wasa to pay my respects, but I didn't know much about the situation of her household. At present, I am living on Higashi-no-tōin street, north of Nijō street, with Ichimatsu registered as the household head.

Toki stated as follows:

I was adopted by Wasa at birth. I don't know who my true parents are. I was raised by Wasa and have lived with her the whole time. Mizuno

Gunki visited often, and Wasa was on particularly close terms with him. She was already on very close terms with Mitsugi, too, when Mitsugi was still married to Iori. When Iori absconded, Mitsugi moved in with Wasa. At times, Gunki, Mitsugi, and Wasa would withdraw to the inner room at Wasa's house to have private discussions. Nobody was supposed to enter that room unless teahouse guests were being entertained, so I found this strange. After Mitsugi had moved to the house in Yasaka Kami-chō, Wasa started to pay less attention to her business and visited Mitsugi often.

Strange rumors began to circulate in the neighborhood about Wasa, and I saw that she was getting up in the middle of the night to pray and that she made effigies out of paper. When I asked her what she was doing, she scolded me angrily, saying, "That is none of your business!" I found this all the more suspicious and made so bold as to tell her she shouldn't be doing such things, but she paid no attention. Wasa was growing old and was unable to practice austerities, so she ordered me to go and train with Mitsugi in her stead. I had no choice but to move in with Mitsugi and follow her commands to accompany her to the falls where she performed austerities. In my heart I was already suspicious, but now I saw how Mitsugi became as powerful as a demon when she practiced water austerities. It was so frightening that my hair stood on end.

It soon became clear that I wasn't suited to such training, and I was treated harshly. *(Investigators: This is as Mitsugi stated in her testimony.)* In particular, Mitsugi accused me of having secret relations with a man, which was not true. I protested again and again that this accusation was wrong and that I didn't want to do the training, and in the end I escaped from Mitsugi and returned to Wasa's house. But when I complained to Wasa about what had happened, she only became even angrier with me. I was in a hopeless situation. I became so desperate that I decided to kill myself, but Ito would visit every once in a while, and she held me back.

After this, Wasa arranged to send me to Gunki, who at that time was living in rented quarters owned by Tomitaya Riemon. Gunki didn't force his views on me, and in the end Wasa took me back and instead made me into a prostitute. After Wasa's death I became the wife of Suehiroya Kahei, who presently resides in Kyōgoku-chō, south of Gojō Bridge.[11]

Ito and Toki maintain that they never became believers in the Kirishitan sect, but both are held in the Osaka jailhouse for the time being.

Gunki's Decline

Thirteen years ago, in 1815, I decided to host a party for Gunki, since I had not yet acknowledged my debt to him as my master or thanked him for allowing Kinu to worship the drawing of the Lord of Heaven. By way of Wasa, Gunki replied that a man called Fujii Umon, who was even more versed in remarkable arts than himself, happened to be staying with him and that he wanted to bring Umon along to this party. My house wasn't a suitable place to hold such a gathering, so toward the end of the third month I had Wasa reserve a room at the Twin Teahouses in the precincts of Gionsha,[12] and we feasted Gunki and Umon there. At this party, too, Gunki praised Umon as an extraordinarily talented man, and so I treated him with great respect. The party cost two or three *ryō* in gold, and of course I paid for it. *(Investigators: This Fujii Umon is Irakoya Keizō from Sonezaki village in Settsu province. We report in a later section on how we immediately sought him out and arrested and interrogated him.)*

Twelve years ago, in the ninth month of 1816, Gunki visited me and said that he was on the spot for some money he had to come up with. "Since you're doing so well," he said, "won't you lend me a small amount?" I gave him the eight *ryō* that I had at hand.

In the same year, Sano once came along when Kinu visited me, but I made a point of not talking to her. Kinu was making progress in her practice, and she told me that she wanted to move to Osaka and spread the creed there. I subsequently heard that she had given up the house where she and Sano had lived together and that the two had moved to Osaka. Kinu continued to keep in frequent contact with me, either by sending me letters or by coming up to Kyoto to see me.

Around the same time, my former husband, Iori, returned to Kyoto because Katsura had abandoned him. He was surprised that I was doing so well. "Let's get together again as husband and wife," he said. "Please let me stay with you." Because of the business I was pursuing, I disdained having a man and practiced austerities single-mindedly. Carnal feelings were defiling, I thought, and I refused to take him in. Iori had no choice but to leave. Later, I heard that he had gone to Edo, where he fell ill and died.

Eleven years ago, in the twelfth month of 1817, I heard that Gunki had absconded in connection with irregular financial dealings at the Kan'in princely house.[13] I was shocked, but my relationship with Gunki went beyond the ordinary since I had received dangerous transmissions of the creed from him. I pretended not to know what had happened and made sure not to visit his house. Ten years ago, in the fourth month of 1818, Gunki was dismissed by the Kan'in princely house. He gave up his old quarters and moved into rental quarters owned by his friend Nakamuraya Shintarō, who resided north of Matsubara street in Kyoto.[14] I heard that Gunki had no regular employment and was in dire financial straits. One day early in the fifth month, he came once again to my place to ask for money; this time I lent him six *ryō*.

In the seventh month of that same year Wasa fell ill, and she died on the tenth day of the eighth month. I went to her place immediately and found that a Nichiren-sect rosary was draped on her body. This weak-kneed display was not at all in keeping with Wasa's feelings when she was still alive, so I took the rosary and threw it away. Toki and the others there were shocked and protested, and since I was outnumbered, I left immediately. I felt like I had lost my right arm and was utterly deflated.

Since I knew that Gunki had lost his position and fallen on hard times, I thought that he might well be willing to sell me the scroll of the Lord of Heaven that I had previously worshipped, maybe for ten *ryō* or so. If I had that scroll, and I happened to find people who wanted to become fellow devotees, I could deepen their faith by having them drip blood onto it rather than [just] swear an [ordinary] oath. Nine years ago, on some day (I don't remember exactly which) in the fourth month of 1819, I secretly visited Gunki and asked him about this. "I have made progress in my practice thanks to you," I told him. "The only thing that I could wish for now is that you sell me the scroll that I worshipped at the time [of my initiation]." "If you had come a little earlier," Gunki answered, "I could have arranged something. When I lost my position, I fell ever deeper into poverty. I had no other choice but to ask a wealthy friend of mine to take that scroll in pawn for a great sum of money, so I no longer have the real image. It is a great pity, but I could borrow it back and make a copy. But, still, it is a proscribed buddha image, so even copying it wouldn't be possible for less than forty or fifty *ryō*." "I have no use for a copy," I told him, "and that price is extremely high, so let me think about it." Then I left.

Eight years ago, in the third month of 1820 (I fail to remember what day), Gunki came to take his leave, saying he was planning to set off on a trip to the western provinces. As a travel present, I gave him a further three *ryō*. I heard that Gunki's wife and son were taken in by one of his calligraphy students after he had left, but Gunki and I had agreed that I wouldn't visit them.

Mitsugi's Encounter with Kinoshin and Pilgrimage to Konpira

I was fond of *renga* and *haikai* poetry, and by way of those arts I had earlier gained permission to enter the mansion of the Yamanoi noble house. I was now asked to make a proxy pilgrimage to Konpira in Sanuki province on behalf of this house.[15] I found it difficult to say no, but I needed to find some trustworthy person to take along as a travel companion. Harimaya Kinoshin, who at that time was called Kinuya Mitsuemon and was living in Tatsuta-machi in Tenma [in Osaka], had called on me sometime earlier, I cannot remember exactly when, to seek assistance about some money that he wanted to collect. *(Investigators: This Kinoshin has been mentioned previously in the addendum [about the secret sign]; he resides presently in Osaka in Tenma 7-chōme.)* He had asked me to consult Inari and ask the deity whether he would be able to collect this money or not. I had made a paper effigy in the usual manner, sprinkled it with pure water during the night, and prayed to the Lord of Heaven. In the end, Kinoshin did get hold of his money. He was greatly impressed and became my disciple. When I took him along to the falls at Kiyomizu, I drew the sign that I mentioned earlier on his eyes and back, and for a while he was unable to open his eyes and mouth. This amazed him even more.

I intended to let Kinoshin stay with me for a while, but he wasn't strong or bold of character and wasn't the kind of person who could be told about the Lord of Heaven, let alone be trusted with transmission of the creed. Then he did something that annoyed me, and so I expelled him as my disciple. He went to Osaka and registered under the new name [of Kinoshin] with the help of Kinu, and I heard that he was working as an Inari medium there. I thought I could lift his expulsion and take him along as my travel companion [on the pilgrimage to Sanuki], so I sent someone to ask him to visit me. He came immediately, accompanied by Kinu. I had Kinoshin change his name to Tamaki Kurando,[16] and we set out from Kyoto seven years ago, in 1821, on the second day of the tenth month.

On the road to Sanuki I was angered by the post-station officials at Minami Takinomiya, who didn't treat us in a proper manner,[17] and I ended up hitting a village alderman. When we returned to Kyoto, we were arrested and questioned about this at the Kyoto Magistracy. *(Investigators: The verdict was as described in the note appended at the beginning of Mitsugi's testimony.)*

Investigators' Comments on Their Questioning of Kinoshin

The rumors we heard about this Kinoshin invited suspicion. We therefore arrested and interrogated him. The particulars of his statement all matched those of Mitsugi's testimony.

Kinoshin stated as follows:

I am the son of Ryūzō (now deceased), a farmer from Tōrinji in Awa province [in Shikoku]. I left my native village at a young age, and ten years ago, in 1818, I entered into service as a retainer at a Kyoto temple. I have long been attracted to Shinto, and since Mitsugi was well known, I wanted to meet her. I had an acquaintance in the Nijō area called Hisa (now deceased), the elder sister of the sumo wrestler Inagawa. Hisa was running a mutual credit group. One member of this group, Kakiya Jirobei (now deceased) of Ogawa-chō, had gained the right to use the funds accumulated by the group up to that point, but then failed to pay the ongoing installments. (The arrears came to a total of 3.25 *ryō* in gold.) Hisa complained to him about this, but Jirobei knew that even if she filed a suit, the authorities wouldn't take the matter up because it involved a mutual credit group rather than an ordinary money suit.[18] Thus he didn't pay any heed to her complaint.

Hisa wondered whether something couldn't be done, and she asked me about it. I told her that I had no way to collect this money either, but I would ask Mitsugi to consult Inari, since Mitsugi had a mysterious clairvoyance into all kinds of matters. Around the twentieth day of the eleventh month I visited Mitsugi and talked to her about this. She told me to come back seven days later, and I called on her again on the specified day. Mitsugi told me that she would send one of Inari's messenger spirits to Jirobei on the evening of the last day of that month to urge him to pay up the money.[19] At first, I didn't believe her, but on the appointed

day and time I went to Jirobei's house. He was not at home, so I waited
for him to return, and late that evening he appeared. When I pressed
him for the money that he owed to the credit group, Jirobei gave me two
ryō and begged forgiveness for failing to pay the rest.

This was so remarkable that I wondered whether Mitsugi might have
secretly visited Jirobei and given him this money, just to spread word of
her skills and sell her name by astounding me. Even if that was so, I
now had in hand more than half the installment money that had proved
so hard to collect. I took the money and gave it to Hisa, who was very
happy with the outcome. She gave me a quarter *ryō* as an expression of
thanks and entrusted me with another quarter *ryō* to pass on to Mitsugi
as an offering of gratitude to Inari. I took this offering to Mitsugi, but I
still couldn't let go of my suspicions. I asked here and there and heard
various rumors passed around by Mitsugi's clients. I learned that she
was said to be able to do many mysterious things. I also looked more
closely into Jirobei's affairs, and it became clear that this man didn't have
any connection with Mitsugi. Now that my suspicions were cleared up,
I finally became convinced of Mitsugi's miraculous powers. I thought
that if I became her disciple, I could learn how to perform the same kind
of extraordinary feats.

I asked Mitsugi to take me on as a disciple and told her that I was
willing to work for her as her manservant. Mitsugi told me that her practice was different from that of ordinary Inari mediums. Since ascetic
training is crucial, she said, she couldn't transmit anything to me until
I reached a certain level. I told her that I was determined to follow this
through and moved in with her as her manservant. One night, when
Mitsugi went to the falls at Kiyomizu, she told me to stand under them
as well, and I took off my clothes. Mitsugi drew something on my back
and my eyes with her fingers and shouted at the same time. I was unable
to open my eyes and felt as though my body had been tied up. I stood
under the waterfall in that state, and after a while I was finally able to
open my eyes and move freely again. When we had finished the water
austerities we went home. Shocked by these mysterious events, I began
to fear Mitsugi as a person of extraordinary powers. But Mitsugi said
that she wouldn't teach me anything unless I attained an unwavering
mind by practicing austerities.

I also knew how to do stomach massage. To my shame, one evening
I became aroused when I was massaging Mitsugi's stomach. With her

clairvoyance, Mitsugi saw into my mind and became angry. "Even a single such thought is defiling!" she said. "I will never grant you the true transmission!" She told me that a man like me was fit only to work as an ordinary Inari medium, and she declared that she was expelling me as a disciple. I had no choice but to leave. Since Kinu visited Mitsugi regularly, I decided to rely on Kinu and went down to Osaka, where I rented quarters in Tatsuta-machi with her help.

In 1821 Mitsugi sent me a message, saying that my expulsion was suspended and that I should return to Kyoto. Since Kinu lived nearby, we went up to Kyoto together. Mitsugi had recovered her good temper. She said that she would be making a pilgrimage to Konpira in Sanuki province on behalf of the Yamanoi house, and since she needed a reliable companion, she wanted me to join her as her attendant. I had no objections and agreed. Calling myself Tamaki Kurando, I joined Mitsugi on this journey. Her behavior on the road was haughty and bold. She wouldn't listen when I told her that this was not the way a woman should behave, and in the end she caused a tremendous ruckus in Minami Takinomiya. We were arrested after returning to Kyoto and interrogated at the Kyoto Magistracy. When Mitsugi was sentenced, I was also sentenced to thirty days' handcuffing as her accomplice.

After this I became more and more afraid of Mitsugi and fearful of the consequences [of consorting with her], so I kept my distance. Now I have been arrested and investigated once again. I repent deeply [my involvement with her].

We confronted Kinoshin with the following accusation: "Since you became Mitsugi's follower, surely you also received transmission of the Kirishitan creed from her and plotted other wicked deeds with her." We interrogated Kinoshin severely multiple times, but he denied these accusations. For the moment, he is held in the jailhouse.

Mitsugi's Account of Gunki's Last Years and Death

After I was sentenced [for the incident at Minami Takinomiya], my unwavering mind became all the more firm, and I grew supremely confident in my powers. I had received the transmission from Gunki, but even though Gunki had once been an extraordinary person, he had stopped practicing water and mountain austerities when he became an official [in the Kan'in princely house]. He didn't stay away from women and he was as unable to undertake purification austerities as any layperson. In contrast, I continued to engage in hard training and was so determined that I not only had nothing to do with lust but even refused to take back my former husband. Year after year, I had prayed to the Lord of Heaven, and I had gained miraculous powers to foresee fortune and misfortune. Gunki, on the other hand, was quite unable to do any of this. I thought that [Gunki's backsliding] was why he had gradually fallen into poverty after flourishing for a while, and I felt that I should encourage him [to return to his practice].

One day in the tenth month of 1821, Gunki visited me with his son, Makijirō. He had just returned from Nagasaki, and we met for the first time in three years.[20] Gunki said that his wife and son had been in dire straits while he was away and that he had to pay back money borrowed from various people. He asked me to lend him some further funds. "I acted in a haughty and bold way when I made a pilgrimage to Sanuki on behalf of the Yamanoi house," I told him. "As a result, I was remanded to jail for a while, but the matter ended well. If I am successful in my business now, that is the result of my determined resolve. I don't lack for money, but you have yet to repay what I lent you earlier. I happen to have a hair ornament that should be worth one and a half ryō in gold. Though its value may be small, let me give this ornament to you; it would please me greatly if it could pay at least for some of Makijirō's clothing." In this way I sought to encourage him [to practice] without saying so. Gunki was a magnanimous man, and he kept his calm. He praised me for my bold action on the Sanuki road and left after saying that he would accept the hair ornament as a token of my sentiments for him. He seemed oblivious to my encouragement, and I couldn't guess what he was really thinking.

After this Gunki visited me from time to time. Four years ago, in 1824, toward the end of the twelfth month, I heard that he had fallen ill and died, and I couldn't help shedding tears for him. I remained unmarried and continued to pray to the Lord of Heaven night and day. Owing to my vow, I was able to see the answers to the questions of the clients who sought me out. Just as I had hoped, I became famous not only in the capital but even in neighboring villages. I was called the clairvoyant of

Yasaka, and I flourished more and more. I bought plenty of clothes and other paraphernalia, and I was able to enlarge my house so it became quite spacious. For all this I never forgot my debt to the Lord of Heaven. *(Investigators: So many clients visited Mitsugi for healing rituals or divinations over the years that their names and addresses cannot be recovered.)*

MITSUGI'S RELATIVES AND ADOPTIVE SON

My elder brother, Kazue, was living in poverty, and he appealed to me on behalf of our mother, Eshū. Although he came begging for my help again and again, I firmly refused.

Investigators' Comments on Mitsugi's Relatives

We contacted [the Kyoto eastern magistrate] Lord Kan'o Mototaka about Eshū and Kazue and asked him to summon them and send them here. It transpired that Kazue fell ill and has died, while Eshū is now eighty-five years old, senile, and incontinent. She lacks all understanding of what is going on around her and has not been interrogated. She has been placed in the custody of those responsible for the matters of her locale. Mitsugi insists that she has not transmitted the pernicious creed to Eshū and Kazue, nor talked to them about it. This would appear to be correct.

Mitsugi's Adoption of Kamon

I wanted to make sure that I prepared someone to carry on my efforts, but few appeared suitable to me. It so happened that Iku, the wife of Mokuzaemon of Katagihara village [west of Kyoto], suffered from a difficult illness, and she asked me to perform a healing ritual. I prayed for Iku using the secret arts, and she evidently felt that she was recovering, and so she visited me often. I could perceive that Mokuzaemon's eldest son, Kamon, was also very pleased, and I asked [Mokuzaemon] to allow me to adopt Kamon. Since [Mokuzaemon and Iku] were indebted to me, they agreed in the end, and I adopted Kamon four years ago in the eighth month of 1824. I thought it best to allow some time to appraise his disposition before taking him along to perform austerities at a waterfall and to let him embark on practice at a leisurely pace. First I sent him into service with various noble houses, including the Washinoo house.[21] But Kamon became ill and was sent back to my house to recover. Since it would interfere with my performance of the secret practices to have him in the house, I sent him on to Mokuzaemon until he got better. I did not transmit any pernicious practices to Kamon.

Investigators' Comments on Their Questioning of Kamon

We contacted Lord Kan'o about Kamon and asked to have him summoned and sent here. When we questioned him, the particulars of his statement matched those of Mitsugi's testimony. He stated as follows:

> My parents were grateful that the healing ritual had been effective, so they sent me to Mitsugi as her adoptive son. Since this was her wish, they did this even though I am their firstborn son. After my adoption I went into service with noble houses, including the Washinoo house, and I never stayed with Mitsugi. I firmly believed that Mitsugi owed her clairvoyant powers to Inari. This interrogation is the first time for me to hear what she has testified. I repent deeply [my involvement with her].

We confronted Kamon with the following accusation: "Since you were adopted by Mitsugi, surely you must have lived in her house the whole time, received transmission of the Kirishitan creed from her, and plotted other wicked deeds with her." We interrogated him severely on these points, but he insisted that this was not the case. This appears to be correct, but since he is Mitsugi's adoptive son, of whom she had high expectations, we have ordered him remanded to jail for the time being.

MITSUGI'S ARREST AND INTERROGATION

Kinu has regularly sent me money for the past three or four years to repay her debt to me as her master; how much, I don't know. I accepted this money but worried that it would lead to trouble later. "I've secretly been practicing arts that are proscribed as pernicious," I thought, "and although Kinu has promised [that she will keep our practice secret], it might happen that it somehow comes to light. If I put the money in a chest of drawers and happen to be arrested and my house is searched, it will surely raise suspicions." Therefore, I filled the bottom of a large brazier with dirt and buried thirty-five *ryō* in gold deep in it. When Sano's interrogation revealed that the practices transmitted to her originated from me, I was arrested and interrogated. "Sano received the transmission from Kinu, used Yae and others as her agents, and caused people in Osaka to take leave of their senses," I was told. "She has appropriated money and clothing and shared the proceeds with Kinu. Kinu must have passed on part of her share to you as her master." Although I told various lies in the hope of getting out of the jailhouse, I realize I will not be able to escape your investigation, so I have confessed as recorded here and repent most deeply. Since Gunki has already died, I accept the responsibility for having started all this, especially since everything originated from my transmission of the practices to Kinu. Therefore I ask you to let me take upon myself all the blame and punish me alone for these crimes.

Investigators' Summation of Mitsugi's Interrogation

We confronted Mitsugi with the following accusations:

> You received transmissions of the Kirishitan creed from Gunki. Follow-ing Gunki's directions, you built an Inari shrine that did not in fact enshrine Inari, to which you gave the name of Hōkoku Daimyōjin, the deity title of Lord Toyotomi Hideyoshi. You even knowingly adopted a variation of Lord Hideyoshi's gourd emblem as your crest. You pretended to act as an Inari medium while in reality you were using Kirishitan arts to heal illness and carry out divinations, and in that way you drew peo-ple to you. Kinu, who had received your transmission, took Sano as a disciple, and here in Osaka Sano did strange things that caused people to take leave of their senses. She appropriated large amounts of money and goods from them, and you received part of the proceeds by way of Kinu. Surely you did all this because you secretly plotted wicked deeds together with Gunki and others whose names you may not know. And since you needed money for those purposes, from the outset you must have schemed to collect funds not only through your own practice but also by dispatching Kinu and Sano to gather even more money. With-out doubt, you must still be hiding orally transmitted secret scriptures,

spells, and practices apart from the transmissions [that you have confessed to already].

We submitted Mitsugi repeatedly to severe interrogation. [To our accusations, she responded as follows:]

From the start, I had the ambition to make a name for myself by performing extraordinary feats. I was impressed by Gunki's sorcery and ultimately learned the pernicious creed from him. Since Lord Toyotomi Hideyoshi was a hero who rose high from humble beginnings and achieved great fame, I followed Gunki's advice in the hope of becoming successful and wealthy, and without thinking deeply about it, I took Lord Hideyoshi's deity title of Hōkoku Daimyōjin for my shrine and even adopted his gourd crest. However, I never conspired with Gunki to use this as a cover to plot further wicked deeds, nor did I scheme to collect money for such a purpose. Also, I have not received oral transmissions of any Kirishitan scriptures, spells, or practices in addition to the transmissions that I have described above. Just as Sano and Kinu have said, lustful or greedy people would never be able to do the things we did even if they were initiated into this sect.

Mitsugi's testimony is the same in this regard as Kinu's.

The interrogation has fully clarified the circumstances of how Mitsugi, as detailed here, showing not the slightest awe for the shogunal authorities, acted in a manner that was the height of audacity and committed multiple heinous crimes. She states that she has nothing to say in opposition [to what is recorded here] and is filled with remorse.

Investigators' Comments on the Investigation of Mitsugi

Mitsugi seems to have persevered in her hard practice without taking a husband. But before she received the transmission, she trained at the Nyakuōji falls for a mere thirty days. By contrast, Kinu performed water and mountain austerities for two years, and in Sano's case, it took seven years before she finally received the transmission. Sano joined Kinu while she was still living in Kyoto, and she continued to perform water austerities after she had moved to Osaka. We questioned Mitsugi about the reason for this extreme difference in the length of training prior to receiving the transmission. "People are born with different dispositions," she responded, "some stalwart and others soft. Some are quick to attain an unwavering mind, others slow. That is the reason why the time required to receive the transmission varies."

Lord Kan'o Mototaka has had Mitsugi's possessions examined and inventoried. He has sent us this inventory together with the scrolls of Ota-fuku and the other figures described previously; all have been duly received. They confirm that Mitsugi owned numerous items of clothing and other goods beyond her status. Money was found hidden at the bottom of her brazier, as noted earlier.

When first interrogated, Mitsugi proffered many lies. She claimed glibly that she had far-reaching insight because of her proficiency in *Yijing* divination and as an Inari medium and thus people had faith in her. Telling different stories, she also asserted that her master was an extraordinary person whom she met at Wasa's place and whose name she did not know. However, since we already had the testimonies of Kinu and Sano, in the end Mitsugi, too, confessed that she belonged to the pernicious sect. Even so, she prevaricated about the line of transmission. She initially claimed that she had received the transmission from Wasa, and that it was Wasa who owned the drawing of the Lord of Heaven; she claimed that the drawing had disappeared when Wasa died ten years ago, in 1818. Mitsugi said that Wasa had no sons or daughters, neither her own nor adoptive, and lived alone as a widow. Mitsugi had thus gone to collect the scroll when Wasa died, only to find that Wasa had already given it away, to whom she did not know. In any case, she claimed, Wasa was not able to attain the level of clairvoyant powers Mitsugi had and thus had not been successful in collecting money. Even if Wasa were still alive today, [she would not deserve severe punishment because, unlike Mitsugi,] her proficiency in the practices was not great enough to make her a master in anything but form. Mitsugi repeatedly begged us to let her take all punishment upon herself and to desist from investigating what happened after Wasa's death and the whereabouts of the scroll, and she asked us to spare the lives of Kinu and Sano.

What Mitsugi said invited even greater suspicion. We thus contacted Lord Kan'o again, with the request to investigate whether Wasa had any descendants, and whether the buddha image of the Lord of Heaven might be kept hidden away by those who took over her possessions after her death. After some investigation in Kyoto, it became clear that although Wasa had no children of her own, she had two adoptive daughters: the abovementioned Ito and Toki, who were already married into other households. Ito and Toki testified that the caretaker of Wasa's possessions was a man called Minoya Sahei, who resides along Higashi-no-tōin street north of Nijō street. Lord Kan'o immediately had Sahei's house searched; Sahei asserted that he had found no suspect buddha images among Wasa's belongings, let alone a scroll of the kind mentioned. Nevertheless, since Sahei had taken charge of Wasa's possessions, Lord Kan'o sent him to Osaka, together with Ito and Toki.

When we questioned Sahei, nothing in what he said was suspicious. The results of our interrogation of Ito and Toki are reported in an earlier addendum. Toki's statement made it clear that Mizuno Gunki visited Wasa often and conferred with her in private in a detached room. We thereupon cross-examined Toki and Mitsugi together and subjected Mitsugi to severe interrogation about her relations with Gunki. She said that she had firmly promised Gunki that she would never confess, however severe a punishment she might face. Now that Toki had appeared as a witness, however, there was nothing to be done but confess the truth. Mitsugi declared that she was ignorant about the whereabouts of Gunki's scroll, but when we probed further she stated as follows: "I have heard that when Gunki died four years ago, in 1824, in temporary lodgings on Kiyamachi street, south of Matsubara street, those who looked after his possessions were from the circle of his calligraphy students.[22] You may find the scroll among the papers that these people took charge of, or with the person who took in Makijirō, Gunki's son."

Again, we contacted Lord Kan'o, who ordered an investigation to find out who had taken over Gunki's possessions after his death. It was learned that the following persons had arranged for Gunki's funeral:

Hōki Masasuke, Gunki's calligraphy student, resident in Butsuguya-chō, north of Kitakōji street, Kyoto
Also, the following friends and acquaintances:
Tsuchiya Shōni, also known as Mimura Jōnosuke, resident in Furu-monzen Moto-chō, Kyoto
Matsusakaya Nihei, resident along Nishi Ishigaki street, south of [Shijō] street, Kyoto

Teradaya Kumazō, resident near the intersection of Yanagi-no-banba and Maruta-machi streets

Minoya Kohachi, also known as Yōzō, resident in the area on the west side of the Takase River, south of Matsubara street

The one who took possession of Gunki's papers and scraps of writing was Shōni. Makijirō was taken in by a relative, Momijiya Jinbei of Kita-machi, Minakuchi post station, in Ōmi province, and was still living with this person. Lord Kan'o thereupon sent all the persons listed here to Osaka. Details about their interrogation and the whereabouts of the scroll of the Lord of Heaven are given in the following sections, both as written testimony and in addenda.

Chapter 4

⁓

Gunki's Male Disciples Umon and Heizō

TESTIMONY OF FUJII UMON

Fujii Umon, also known as Irakoya Keizō: sixty-one years old; resident in quarters rented from Edoya Kichibei, village of Sonezaki, Nishinari county, Settsu province, in the district under the jurisdiction of the intendant Kishimoto Budayū

Remanded to jail on the eighteenth day of the intercalary sixth month, 1827

Under interrogation Umon stated as follows:

I was separated from my parents at the age of eight or nine. I am not certain about the province where I was born or where my forebears came from, but I understand that my father served a princely house as a retainer. I was looked after by various acquaintances here and there, and from the age of twelve or thirteen I went into service at temples and shrines, where I picked up some knowledge of Buddhism and Shinto. I hoped someday to become famous and successful, but for the moment I started as an *Yijing* diviner at Kami Goryō-mae in Kyoto under the name of Fujii Umon. This was around 1791. I also got some training as a physician, but there was no chance of achieving glory and prosperity by making a living in these ways. They didn't match my ambitions, and therefore I moved to Osaka.

In Osaka I met a man called Gengenshi (now deceased), residing in Minami Horie, a lapsed monk who had once practiced Kangiten rituals [at Kannonji] in Yamazaki.[1] Gengenshi was familiar with Shingon mantras and spells. Through friends I was able to develop a connection with him, and he transmitted Kangiten rituals to me. I practiced them for a while, but I obtained no real results, and they didn't seem to be leading me where I wanted to go, so I temporarily returned to Kyoto. Since I had given up my former residence there, I drifted from place to place.

I met Mizuno Gunki in 1801 at a restaurant in Sanbongi.[2] I had heard about him before then but didn't know about his involvement with the pernicious creed. I was leading a fast life at the time, consorting with kabuki actors and traveling here and there. But I thought that this lifestyle was contrary to my earlier ambitions and that I would never excel at anything if I let myself fall in with such people, so I pulled myself together. When I met Gunki, he seemed knowledgeable and bold, and I felt that if I could talk to him, I would know what to do.

In 1805, when Gunki was living in rental quarters owned by Tomitaya Riemon (whose name I didn't know at the time), I went to call on him and met him for the first time in a long while. I told him about the difficulties I faced, and he allowed me to stay with him for a time. "Isn't there some superior way that is sure to bring fame and success?" I asked Gunki. "You could do well practicing Kangiten rituals," he said. I told him that I had received Kangiten transmissions earlier from Gengenshi, but that they hadn't done much for me. I had doubts about Kangiten rituals and had stopped practicing them. Gunki laughed at this. "What you learned from Gengenshi are the kind of Kangiten rituals that a mediocre priest or even an ordinary person can manage," he told me.

It goes without saying that there is nothing to gain from those. My own Kangiten practice is extremely demanding, but all [who have attempted it] in the past have achieved unsurpassed feats, depending on their training and prayers. But even those who are firmly committed cannot begin this practice without money, so the first thing to master is a method to collect money. I concentrate fully on practicing Kangiten rites, but I am hindered by everyday circumstances and cannot pursue this practice in the way I would like. Since you appear to be a stalwart person, I will allow you to worship my drawing of Kangiten if you agree to be my follower. However, I have spent a large sum to acquire this drawing. At present you may be just drifting from place to place, but if you have faith, your sincerity should enable you to come up with four or five *ryō* in gold. And if you write out a sacred oath and seal it in blood, I will grant you the transmission.

Since I had become acquainted with Shinto and Buddhism when I was a youngster, I realized that the Kangiten worshipped by Gunki must be in fact a demonic buddha outside the Dharma. I couldn't ask outright about the nature of this deity so long as Gunki did not reveal it, but I became more and more interested in receiving the transmission. It seemed reasonable for Gunki to expect some payment from me to demonstrate my sincerity, so I asked acquaintances for a quarter or half a *ryō* each, and I went out into the streets to work as a diviner. In thirty days I had collected three *ryō*. I took this money to Gunki, who was impressed. He had me write out a sacred oath and seal it with blood: "However severe a punishment I might face, I shall never confess," I wrote. "May I receive punishment as severe as decapitation should I reveal this to others."[3]

At a time no one else was at home, Gunki took me to a room he never permitted anyone else to enter and allowed me to worship a buddha image that he kept there. It was a little more than four feet long and one foot wide, an old image showing a standing woman with her hair hanging loose, holding a child in her left hand and a sword in her right. "Is this really Kangiten?" I asked. "To avoid trouble with the law I call it Kangiten," Gunki replied,

> but in fact, it is the Lord of Heaven. It is because this [buddha] is proscribed that I made you write out a sacred oath. You must not say anything about this image to anybody, not even to your parents, your siblings, or your wife, unless you are sure about their character. You must perform water austerities day and night, making sure that no one sees you, silently chant the mantra *Zensu Maru paraizo*, and pray to the Lord of Heaven. If you do this, gold and silver will come to you, you will become more and more skillful, and your wishes will come true. But the power of this method depends completely on the devoted performance of water austerities, and you will not be able to do anything extraordinary unless you dedicate yourself to that practice over a long period. Whenever you have some free time, day or night, you must concentrate on the water austerities.

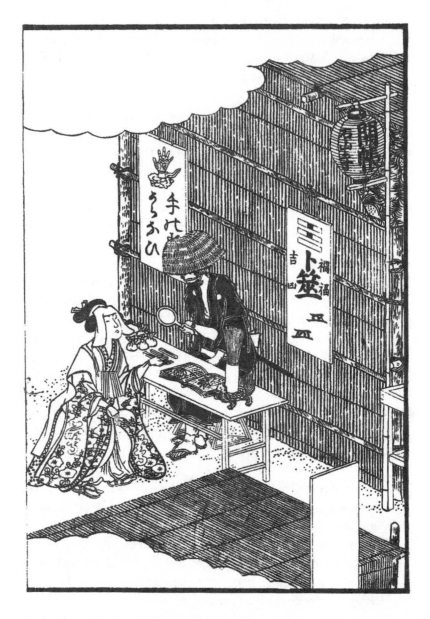

Figure 4.1 A male *Yijing* diviner who has set up a street-side stand. *Mukashigatari ina-zuma byōshi*. In vol. 16 of *Santō Kyōden zenshū*. Perikansha, 1994.

At this point I realized that this was a pernicious creed, but being reckless by nature, I agreed. Gunki explained to me what is written in such works as *The True Principles of the Lord of Heaven* and *Ten Pieces Transcending Common Sense* by the southern barbarian Matteo Ricci,[4] and from this I came to understand the fundamental nature of the Lord of Heaven. Even though these works are proscribed, what they have to say sounded convincing to me. This sect, I believed, enters into the true by way of the pernicious. From that time onward, I performed water austerities at different waterfalls, but I suffered from chronic diarrhea, and the austerities made this worse, so in the end I was unable to keep up my training.

I decided that I would first establish myself as a physician or such while continuing [to worship the Lord of Heaven]. In 1806 I stayed for a time with Mizuhaya Hida (now deceased), priest of Hiraoka Myōjin Shrine in Kawachi province, an acquaintance who was quite skilled in medicine.[5] While I was there, I happened to meet a person named Fujita Kenzō, who also made a living as a physician. *(Investigators: This Kenzō is currently staying with Zenbei, resident in Funadaiku-machi in Dōjima, Osaka, who is represented before the magistrate by Okamotoya Tamizō. At the time he resided in Shinchi 1-chōme in Dōjima.)* Kenzō was friendly with Hida. Once I went to Kenzō's place on an errand for Hida to borrow the medical work *Comprehensive Compendium of Healing*.[6] I met Kenzō on the way and put Hida's request to him, but Kenzō said that he had already lent the book to someone else. When I passed this reply on to Hida, he told me that Kenzō had a large collection of rare books. "Kenzō even has books of the Jesus creed," Hida told me. I asked about the titles of these books, and to my surprise they seemed similar to the books by Matteo Ricci that Gunki had expounded to me earlier. I had heard that Kenzō, too, was a bold man, so I wondered whether he was in secret contact with Gunki, and whether his dealings with such books had anything to do with that. But I couldn't mention Gunki to Hida, and neither could I carelessly ask Kenzō whether he knew him, so I didn't follow up on my suspicions.

Hida told me that he could arrange for me to become the adopted second husband of Fusa,[7] widow of the farmer Yohei of Kadoma Niban village in Kawachi province. I worked as a physician in that village under the name of Iwai Onjaku for three years. However, I ran into economic difficulties [and so had to abandon our holdings in the village]. I moved with my wife into rented quarters in Kyōmachibori 4-chōme [in Osaka] owned by Izumiya Denbei, and we became parishioners of the Ikkō

Figure 4.2 A physician. *Inchū hachinin mae.* From *E de yomu Edo no kurashi fūzoku daijiten.* Kashiwa Shobō, 2004.

temple Jōkōji in Shirokoura-machi. I continued to work as a physician in Osaka while making occasional trips to Kyoto to see Gunki. Gunki told me never to reveal these visits to my wife, and I pretended to visit Kyoto on medical business. Fifteen years ago, in 1813, we moved to the village [of Sonezaki], where we live currently.

Thirteen years ago, in the third month of 1815, I traveled up to Kyoto to see Gunki—telling my wife that I was going on a trip to Izumi province. "Sometime ago, I transmitted the creed of the Lord of Heaven to Toyoda Mitsugi," Gunki told me.

> Although she is a woman, she is stalwart and resilient, and she has made such great progress in her practice that even valiant men would not be able to match her. She has recently invited me to a feast at the Twin Teahouses in the precincts of Gionsha, and since by lucky coincidence you happen to be in Kyoto, you should come along. But don't act as my disciple; pretend to be my master. Mitsugi has kept asking me about my master. I know this is awkward, but I hope you'll be willing to play this role.

I found it hard to refuse and accompanied Gunki to the Twin Teahouses. Here I met Mitsugi and Wasa for the first time and in the guise of Gunki's master enjoyed lavish hospitality far beyond what I could otherwise have expected. Mitsugi was deferential toward me, and when the party was finished and Gunki and I returned to his house for the night, he praised her while encouraging me to work harder at my deficient training. "I have faith," I told him, "but my chronic ailment makes it hard for me to undertake water austerities. Regrettably, I fear that I will end my days as a mediocre doctor." I left and returned to Osaka.

Gunki was later dismissed by the Kan'in princely house and moved to the area near the intersection of Akezu and Matsubara streets. When I heard from Gunki that he would be traveling to Nagasaki, he said he would be staying somewhere in the Ue-machi area in Osaka [on his way to Nagasaki], but I was ill at the time and didn't visit him there.[8] *(Investigators: It appears that the households where Gunki stayed in the Ue-machi area were those of Takamiya Heizō and Matsuya Jihei in Matsuyama-machi. Jihei died sometime ago. We have arrested and interrogated Heizō. He put Gunki up and looked after him. Their relation was thus that of master and disciple, making Heizō culpable of crimes. The results of his interrogation are reported following Umon's testimony.)*

Four years ago, in 1824, I was shocked to hear that Gunki had died. Without telling my wife, I continued as before to pray secretly to the Lord of Heaven, all the while pretending that I was praying to Kangiten. Yet, contrary to my hopes, I grew ever poorer.

Investigators' Summation of Umon's Testimony

Initially Umon stated that in his old age he finally realized that he had been deceived by Gunki and regretted what he had done. He declared that now that he had been arrested, he deeply repented his behavior. However, he [originally] claimed falsely that he knew neither Mitsugi nor Gunki. Why did he not tell the truth?

Moreover, Mitsugi and others dripped blood from a finger onto the drawing of the Lord of Heaven that Gunki owned. Surely, Umon must have done the same, but he stated that he wrote out a sacred oath on a separate piece of paper and sealed it in blood. We cross-examined Mitsugi and Umon together and questioned him further about these points. [In Mitsugi's presence,] he had no choice but to confess as follows: "Gunki and Mitsugi engaged in practice of the banned Kirishitan creed, and although I was unable to carry that practice through, I was once Gunki's follower. I worshipped the drawing of the Lord of Heaven, and I even wrote out a sacred oath. I accepted Mitsugi's hospitality as Gunki's companion. However, I concealed this because I feared [punishment] for having once prayed [to the Lord of Heaven], even though I now regret this."

He continues to insist, however, that he never heard from Gunki that Mitsugi dripped blood onto the drawing of the Lord of Heaven. All he personally did was to write out a sacred oath on a sheet of paper and seal it with blood, and he recalls that the oath said, "Having received transmission of this creed, I will never say anything about this to others, including my parents, children, and siblings. May I receive punishment as severe as decapitation should I reveal this to others." He says he does not know why the form of his pledge differed from Mitsugi's, or what Gunki's reasons for this may have been.

We confronted Umon with the following accusation: "Surely apart from transmission of the creed, you must have received transmissions of other scriptures, spells, and secret practices. You must have conspired with Gunki to engage in wicked deeds, and there must be other members of the same group. Tell us the truth about this." Again and again, we interrogated him severely. He insists that this is not the case. However, the interrogation has fully clarified the circumstances of how he, as detailed above, showing not the slightest awe for the shogunal authorities, committed multiple heinous crimes. He states that he has nothing to say in opposition [to what is recorded here] and is filled with remorse.

Investigators' Comments on Their Questioning of Umon's Wife

We questioned Umon's wife, Fusa. According to her statement, she is the widow of the abovementioned Yohei and took Umon as her second husband, with Mizuhaya Hida acting as a go-between. Subsequently, Umon met with financial difficulties and had to abandon the village holdings [left by Fusa's late husband]. They then moved to Osaka, where Umon practiced medicine. Her statement on these particulars matches that of Umon. She further stated as follows:

I have never heard even the name Gunki. Whenever Umon went to Kyoto, he told me that it was for reasons connected to his medical practice, and I believed him. I never knew that he received transmission of the pernicious creed from Gunki, or that he wrote out a sacred oath, let alone that he was entertained by Mitsugi together with Gunki. For a long time Umon didn't set up a Buddhist house altar to the ancestors. I told him that this gave a bad impression to the neighbors, but he said that he didn't care because his prayers were focused solely on Kangiten. I thought this strange and couldn't understand why he took this attitude. Now that I am told what Umon has testified as a result of this investigation, I am shocked. I repent deeply that I failed to realize that Umon was praying to the Lord of Heaven under the pretext of praying to Kangiten.

We confronted Fusa with the following accusation: "Undoubtedly you not only knew that Umon was Gunki's follower and that he was praying to the Lord of Heaven, but you also practiced the pernicious creed and collected money under the guise of joining him in his prayers and rites." We interrogated her severely, but she insisted that this is not the case. For the time being, she is detained in the jailhouse.

TESTIMONY OF TAKAMIYA HEIZŌ

Takamiya Heizō: forty-six years old; resident in quarters rented from Kawachiya Iemon, Matsuyama-machi, Osaka

Remanded to jail on the twenty-first day of the intercalary sixth month, 1827

Heizō's Early Life and Encounter with Mizuno Gunki

Under interrogation Heizō stated as follows:

I was born of the physician Takami Genryū (now deceased) of Kusukuri village in Harima province and his wife, Sano. Both my parents are dead. My childhood name was Eijirō. I took the tonsure at the age of twelve and became a novice under Zenpō, abbot of Chōkeiji of the Sōtō Zen sect in the same village. Zenpō gave me the name Hōzui. From the age of seventeen or eighteen, I traveled from province to province as an itinerant monk,[9] and in the eighth month of 1803 I received the transmission of the Buddha and the patriarchs, the lineage chart, and the Dharma precepts from Zenpō. I advanced to the grade of senior monk and continued my studies of Zen, but I found it difficult to keep the precepts and worried that I might slide into corruption. Eighteen years ago, in 1811, when I was twenty-nine years old, I returned to lay life and adopted the name of Takamiya Heizō.

After this I lived in rented quarters in the port town of Hyōgo in Harima province,[10] where I made my living as an *Yijing* diviner. I found it hard to live on my own, so I married Mutsu, daughter of Kohei (now deceased), farmer of Satani village in Harima. Fifteen years ago, in 1813, I asked the temple of Kanzanji in Nishi Tera-machi in Tenma to register me as a parishioner and rented quarters from Yahataya Ihei of Sakata-chō [in Osaka]. I worked on the streets in various spots around the city as a diviner. Later I read Japanese and Chinese military tales in my free time, with the intention of becoming a storyteller specializing in such works.[11]

Ten years ago, in 1818, I moved to quarters that I rented from Kashikiya Otomatsu of Owarizaka-chō. I was then working as an *Yijing* diviner and a teacher of calligraphy. Yuki, the daughter of Matsuya Jihei *(Investigators: mentioned earlier in an addendum to Umon's testimony)* of the

Figure 4.3 A storyteller specializing in military tales. *Chūshingura jūnidanme.* From *E de yomu Edo no kurashi fūzoku daijiten.* Kashiwa Shobō, 2004.

same place, was one of my calligraphy students, and I was on good terms with Jihei, too. Jihei told me that he was almost like Mizuno Gunki's subordinate. "Gunki is knowledgeable about many things and is a good speaker," he said. "I will introduce you to him the next time he comes down to Osaka, so you can meet him." Around the seventh month of that same year, I heard that Gunki was visiting Osaka and invited him to my place. I was impressed with Gunki's knowledge about military tales of both Japan and China and with his detailed grasp of Buddhism and *Yijing* divination; also, I was struck by his account of how his unwavering mind had allowed him to cope with being incarcerated at the Kan'in princely mansion. Although I had returned to lay life, I was nonetheless a man who had reached the status of senior monk in the Zen school, and I had met many monastics and scholars. Most of these, I felt, knew only the Way that they themselves professed, and very few were well versed in other matters. Gunki was truly exceptional in this regard, as Jihei had already told me, and judging from his appearance, I thought he might well be familiar with other unusual things, too. I came to respect Gunki, and whenever he stayed with Jihei or myself we discussed military tales, Buddhist treatises, and a variety of other matters.

Then, one day, Gunki spoke to us about the books of the southern barbarian Matteo Ricci of Europe, who had traveled to China to spread the teaching of the Lord of Heaven. Although Gunki hadn't brought such books along on that occasion, I listened to his account of them and suddenly realized that the essential points of the teaching of the Lord of Heaven made good sense. I felt that even though this teaching is condemned as the Jesus creed, neither Confucianism nor Buddhism is equal to it. Since Gunki knows about this European Ricci, he must also practice the sorcery that pulls people into that sect, I thought. But I knew that it wouldn't do to ask him about this haphazardly; he would never perform such things lightly.

One evening, Gunki happened to visit when my wife was out. "Since the time I was a monk," I told him, "I have mingled with many kinds of people, but none of them had any knowledge of the teaching of the Lord of Heaven. You are so extraordinarily knowledgeable, I am sure you must have learned to perform sorcery. Could you show me some of it?" However, Gunki denied knowing anything about such things and repeatedly put me off. When I insisted, he scolded me. "Why would you fancy sorcery, you who have studied Zen?" he said. "Not only Zen but all the other [Buddhist] sects, too, are no more than stories made up to scare old fools," I replied.

> They are quite without interest. Here [in Japan] we ban the European teaching of the Lord of Heaven as the Kirishitan [heresy], but it makes perfect sense and enables people to do extraordinary deeds. I have studied military tales, and although accounts of the Amakusa rebellion may not all be true, they record various instances of Kirishitan performing extraordinary feats and being able to know everything before it occurred.[12] I have long been fascinated by this and envied them their knowledge. I believed that there couldn't be anyone left today who knows the Jesus creed, because it is subject to such a strict ban—and certainly I didn't believe that there could be someone who is familiar with the books of Ricci. But now you have given a detailed explanation of his works on the teaching of the Lord of Heaven. Seeing the glint in your eyes and your sturdy build, I am convinced that you must possess the knowledge and capabilities of a true general. In my opinion, there can be no doubt that you must have mastered sorcery. I am willing to write an oath sealed with blood and pledge that I will never tell my wife or anybody else. Please show me a secret display of your remarkable arts!

"If that is your wish," Gunki answered,

> it cannot be granted with a mere blood seal. I have a buddha scroll that I carry along with me even on my travels. If I let a man worship this scroll, and he draws blood from the tips of the five fingers of his left hand and drips it onto this image, and he swears that he will enter into a relationship of master and disciple with me, and that he won't reveal anything to others whatever may happen—then I can show him sorcery. If he does tell anybody about this after he has made this oath, he will suffer punishment as severe as decapitation. Even if they have made an oath, weak persons are likely to ignore it and confess immediately when their life is threatened. Therefore I will never talk about Ricci's books— let alone demonstrate sorcery or show the buddha image—to a man or a woman who lacks boldness, courage, and an unwavering mind. Up to this day, I have never revealed anything to weak persons, even if they were my friends or relatives, no matter how long I have known them. To them, I always pretend that I worship Kangiten. You may be a lapsed

monk, but you engaged in training in the Zen school to obtain an unwavering mind, and you appear to me to be a bold man by nature. Your features and your build tell me that you are a man who will not keep company with the weak of this age. If you agree to keep this oath firmly and never betray our relation of master and disciple, I will allow you to worship the buddha image and start praying to the Lord of Heaven.

"I am grateful to you for looking into my heart and recognizing that while unfit for this world, I am a man of some caliber," I replied. "It is my wish to become your follower, so please allow me to worship the buddha image!"

Heizō's Initiation

That night Gunki left my place after this exchange. The next evening, I sent my wife away on an errand and invited Gunki to my house again. We shuttered the door and went upstairs. Gunki unfolded a wrapping cloth and revealed a paper scroll about four feet long and a bit more than one foot wide. It was an old drawing and not easy to make out, but it showed a standing woman with her hair hanging loose, holding a child in her left hand and a sword in her right. Gunki explained that this was the Lord of Heaven. "If you worship this image once," Gunki said, "and year after year perform water austerities day and night at a place where people cannot see you, all the while reciting the mantra *Zensu Maru paraizo* in your heart and praying to the Lord of Heaven, you are sure to grow prosperous as your merit accumulates." I drew blood from the tips of the five fingers of my left hand, let it drip onto the breast of the buddha image, and worshipped it.

Gunki wrapped up the image. "Now," he said, "I will show you some sorcery. First, bring a big lighted candle on a stand." The second floor of my house had two rooms separated by sliding doors. When the doors were opened, the space came to about twenty mats. I put the candle in one of the rooms, about twenty-five feet away from where Gunki was sitting in the other room. Without getting up from his seat, Gunki extinguished the candle. One would have expected the entire upstairs area to become dark, but somehow there was still a dim light. From some unidentifiable place, a woman appeared. This was spooky, and I became agitated. "I am very impressed with your skill," I exclaimed, "but please stop it now!" Immediately the woman disappeared and the room became dark.

Gunki told me to bring a light, and I did so immediately. I praised Gunki's frightening sorcery. "What you do is very different from the usual conjuring tricks. Could you transmit these arts to me?" "You may have undergone Zen training to obtain an unwavering mind and practiced zazen," Gunki replied,

> but you have not yet gathered merit by performing the water austerities of this [Kirishitan] sect, and you haven't learned how to pray to the Lord of Heaven. Right now I could see that you were already becoming agitated, and if I were to transmit this sorcery to you and you carelessly performed it at some party in the way of a conjuring trick, people would be astounded and start spreading rumors. This would never do. It's not you alone. Although I can't mention names, there are three or four people whom I have found worthy of worshipping the Lord of Heaven, after looking deep into their hearts. But I have refused to transmit this sorcery to them until they attained an unwavering mind by practicing water and mountain austerities.

I agreed that this was reasonable. I swore never to reveal anything, however severe a punishment I might face, as stated in the oath. It was late in the evening when my wife came home. "Gunki is an *Yijing* expert," I told her, as though it were nothing special, "so I have received a transmission from him and entered his lineage. Since I have become his disciple and sealed my word in blood, we must assist him with everything and make sure never to treat him with disrespect." My wife believed me and was very accommodating toward Gunki. In the ninth month of the same year Gunki returned to Kyoto, and we stayed in contact through letters. I secretly doused myself with water at night, but I found it hard to make a living while dedicating myself to such austerities. I am by nature a lover of carnal pleasures, and I found it hard to keep my mind from wandering while praying to the Lord of Heaven. I realized that I wouldn't be able to hold to this practice.

Heizō Looks After Gunki's Wife and Son; the Alternative Drawing of the Lord of Heaven

Eight years ago, in 1820, I moved to my present rental quarters. Gunki visited me in the middle of the fourth month of that year. "I would like to travel to Nagasaki by way of the western provinces," he said. "My travels may take some years, so I will move out of my house. Because of various complications, I would like to leave my wife and son here in Osaka. Could you look after them while I'm away? If there are any issues, you can consult my calligraphy disciple Hōki Masasuke." Although I had failed to perform the water austerities, Gunki was still my master and I his disciple, so I could hardly refuse. I talked it over with my wife, and since I had earlier told her that we must treat Gunki with respect, she agreed. Gunki left his wife, Soe, and his son, Makijirō, in my care and set sail from Osaka on the twenty-seventh day of the sixth month of the same year. I thought Soe and Makijirō would feel constrained if they moved in with us, so I rented additional quarters at the back, pretending it was for storage.[13] I installed Soe and Makijirō there and looked after their needs.

By the spring of the following year, 1821, there was still no news from Gunki, and Soe appeared worried and ill at ease. I thought she probably felt bad about having to depend on others for such a long time. She said that she wanted to go to Kyoto and see Hōki Masasuke. I objected that I had an agreement with Gunki, who certainly would be angry if he returned and found that I had allowed her and Makijirō to return to Kyoto. I tried to get them to stay, but Soe said she wanted to make her own living by doing piecework and wouldn't be stopped, so I asked Jihei to accompany her to Masasuke's place. I was struggling to make ends meet. I had stopped doing divination and teaching calligraphy. Instead I was performing in various places as a storyteller of military tales.

Six years ago, in the summer of 1822, Gunki returned from Nagasaki and visited me. I told him how I had taken care of his wife and son, and how Soe had wanted to support herself by doing piecework and had moved to Masasuke's place. Gunki was pleased that I didn't try to conceal what had happened. While Gunki was staying with me, he drew a scroll for me showing Otafuku, wearing a scarlet *hakama* and driving away demons by throwing beans. "Under today's strict regime," he said,

> it would immediately raise suspicions if I were to give you a copy of the true drawing of the Lord of Heaven. Some years ago I therefore devised this drawing expressly to avoid notice. Because Otafuku is a divergent form of the divine Uzume, I call the image Uzume, and I think of it and pray to it as the mother of the Lord of Heaven. Since the characters

of Uzume are not unrelated to the name of the Lord of Heaven, it is the same as worshipping the true drawing. I have sold the drawing that I allowed you to worship earlier to a rich household of our faith, in great secrecy, and it is no longer in my possession. Since then, I have told everyone to pray to this Uzume. I myself have taken the name Recluse of Mount Usu, so as to preserve a connection to the name of the Lord of Heaven. I am using this name in private and never mention it to ordinary acquaintances.[14]

Gunki went on to encourage me. "You must pray to Uzume. You say you can't practice austerities because you are too busy making a living, but that is just because your commitment is weak. You must keep doing water austerities." I was vaguely aware that Gunki secretly organized a faith confraternity at Jihei's place while he was staying there and that he [had the members worship] Uzume as the Lord of Heaven. But since I found myself unable to keep up the practice, I never went there to take part.

Investigators' Comments About Earlier Rumors of a Confraternity That Worshipped the Lord of Heaven

Four or five years ago, in 1823 or 1824, it was rumored that a group of people was gathering at night somewhere along Honeya-machi street in the Ue-machi [area of Osaka] to worship the Lord of Heaven. A rigorous search was made, but Honeya-machi street runs for some two or three miles from north to south, and we were unable to identify the place. We continued sending people to make inquiries, and on the occasion of this investigation we interrogated Heizō about this rumor. Since both Heizō and Matsuya Jihei lived on Honeya-machi street, one of their houses may well have been the place in question. Heizō testified as recorded previously, but it is possible that the group actually gathered at his house and engaged in worship there. We suspected that he might be falsely claiming ignorance and shifting the blame to Jihei, who (as noted earlier) is dead. Therefore we questioned him about this multiple times, but he has not changed his testimony. Now that Jihei is dead, it cannot be ascertained who the members of this confraternity were, but it appears that when our investigation into these rumors became known, the worship ceased immediately.

Heizō's Subsequent Relationship with Gunki

After Gunki's return to Kyoto, I fashioned Gunki's drawing of Uzume into a hanging scroll and kept it with me.

I have no children of my own, and on Gunki's recommendation I took into my care Hisae, daughter of Kimoto Kazuma in Kyoto. I planned to adopt Hisae and took her in with the intention to formalize the adoption later. Since Gunki was close to her family, we all kept in touch regularly as if we were relatives.[15]

Four years ago, late in the twelfth month of 1824, Gunki fell ill and died. I heard that his acquaintances gathered, held a funeral for him, and disposed of his possessions, and also that Makijirō was taken in by relatives in Ōmi province. The news shocked me, but in my heart I was also relieved that Gunki was dead, because I had been unable to hold to the practice and was beginning to fear Gunki's exhortations to follow the pernicious creed. Then, recently I heard that people in Kyoto and here in Osaka were being arrested for engaging in suspicious practices, and I guessed that the investigators were seeking out Gunki's followers. If that was the case, I thought, doubts might fall on me, too, and lead to my arrest. If I still had Gunki's scroll of Uzume, and it attracted the investigators' attention, how could I allay their suspicions? I thought up a reason to send the others in my household out of the house and burned the Uzume scroll. Nevertheless, I was arrested and questioned. I confess to the circumstances described above, but in fact in the end I wasn't able to carry through the practices of the pernicious creed. From before I already regretted my involvement with it, and I continue to repent this deeply.

Investigators' Summation of Heizō's Interrogation

Heizō testified as above. However, whereas Mitsugi and Umon had paid money to Gunki when they worshipped his drawing of the Lord of Heaven, Heizō claimed that he had not made such a payment. When we pressed him on this matter, he stated as follows:

> Gunki was a man of forethought. Maybe he did not ask me for any payment when I worshipped the drawing because he had already made up

his mind to travel to Nagasaki and planned to have me take care of his wife and son while he was away. And then, he also expected me to cover all the expenses for his stays at my house. I spent four or five hundred *monme* in silver to look after his wife and son and to cover Gunki's expenses. My wife, Mutsu, being a woman, was always complaining to me about the costs, and it required some effort to reason with her.

We confronted Heizō with the same accusation of further crimes as we did with Umon and repeatedly interrogated him severely, but he held to his previous testimony. However, the interrogation has fully clarified the circumstances of how he, as detailed above, showing not the slightest awe for the shogunal authorities, committed multiple heinous crimes. He states that he has nothing to say in opposition [to what is recorded here] and is filled with remorse.

Investigators' Interrogation of Mutsu

We also questioned Heizō's wife, Mutsu. According to her statement, she is the daughter of Kohei (now deceased), farmer of Satani village in Harima province. She moved to Hyōgo when she married Heizō and then later moved with him to Osaka. When Gunki went to Nagasaki, Heizō took in his wife and son and looked after them. Her statement on these particulars matches that of Heizō. She further stated as follows:

According to Heizō, Gunki began to visit him some years ago as a result of Jihei's introduction. He told me also that he received transmissions in *Yijing* divination from Gunki and that we should never treat Gunki with disrespect. I believed him and thus obeyed his instructions when Gunki left for Nagasaki. Heizō rented additional quarters at the back for Gunki's wife and son and looked after them. Expenses piled up as time passed, and it was hard to make ends meet. I wasn't happy about the situation, but there was nothing I could do about it. I never realized that Gunki encouraged Heizō to practice the pernicious creed, or that Heizō worshipped a drawing of the Lord of Heaven and prayed to the Lord of Heaven. It is only as a result of your investigation and hearing what Heizō has testified that I have come to know of this, and I am deeply shocked.

We confronted Mutsu with accusations in the same manner as with Umon's wife, Fusa, and interrogated her severely, but she insisted that none of these were true. For the time being, she is detained in the jailhouse.

Chapter 5

~~

Gunki's Associates and Son

TESTIMONY OF SHŌNI

Tsuchiya Shōni, also known as Mimura Jōnosuke: sixty-five years of age; resident in Chion'in Furumonzen Moto-chō, Kyoto

Remanded to jail the twenty-first day of the sixth month, 1827[1]

Shōni's Background and Encounter with Gunki

Under interrogation, Shōni stated as follows:

I was born in Takada Shibazaki village in Bungo province, the son of the farmer Zenzō and his wife, In. As a child I was known as Kichisaburō. My parents both died some years ago, and in 1791, when I was twenty-nine, I left my native province. Relying on an acquaintance in Kyoto, I found a live-in position at a princely house, where I was known as Abe Kageyu. It was while I was working there, in 1795, that I first met Mizuno Gunki at the rental horse grounds north of Gionsha.[2] Gunki told me that he had been born in Nagasu in Buzen province *(Investigators: This is in a district under the jurisdiction of Shimabara domain in Hizen province)*, and since this province was next to the one I came from, I immediately felt a certain bond with him.[3] After that, Gunki came to visit me every once in a while. He told me that he had traveled from his native province to Edo and Osaka, where he had studied calligraphy, and that he had various other skills as well. At that time it didn't seem as if he had any evil intentions. He asked me to recommend him to the princely house as a scribe. I felt I couldn't refuse and went through the motions of making inquiries, but then I left that princely house and instead was taken on as a retainer by Lord Nijō.[4]

By happenstance the Nijō house needed a chief scribe. At the time Gunki was staying with someone in the Ōmi countryside, but since he had asked me earlier to recommend him for a position, I arranged for him to be taken on by the Nijō house as a live-in chief scribe. However, Gunki behaved extravagantly and willfully while on duty. I cautioned him repeatedly, but his attitude had changed since the time when he had asked me to recommend him. He was boastful of his own intelligence and paid no heed to my words, and in the end he was dismissed by the Nijō house. I didn't know where he had gone thereafter and had no word from him for some time. Then, around 1799 or 1800, he came by to announce that he had obtained a live-in position with the Kan'in princely house. He told me that he was staying in rental quarters owned by Tomitaya Riemon and that I should come and visit him there sometime.[5] But at the time I was frequently traveling to the provinces on business for my master and was extremely busy, so I again lost contact with Gunki.

Sometime thereafter I left the Nijō house. I changed my name to Mimura Jōnosuke and moved around from one temporary lodging to another.[6] [I made a living] by giving lessons in playing the small drum. One day Gunki reappeared unexpectedly. He apologized for not having been in contact and urged me to stay in touch. But I was preoccupied with various things and didn't see him often. Meanwhile Gunki became involved in irregular financial dealings at the Kan'in princely house. He was arrested, and ten years ago, in the fourth month of 1818, that house dismissed him and put a ban on his taking up service with any other princely or noble house. His household possessions and other belongings were all confiscated on behalf of the Kan'in house, leaving him in severe straits.[7] Three people, however, were said to be somehow deeply connected to Gunki—his landlord Riemon; Kamaya Kyūbei, who lived on the northern side of the intersection of Akezu and Gojō streets; and Nakamuraya Shintarō—and I heard rumors that Gunki had removed some important items [before his belongings were confiscated] and entrusted them to Riemon and Kyūbei.

In the middle of the fourth month of 1818, after Gunki had moved to rental quarters owned by Shintarō, I went to visit him there. As far as I could see, Gunki wasn't engaged in any kind of occupation and was leading a life of leisure. When I asked him about this, Gunki replied that he was greatly beholden to Riemon, Kyūbei, and Shintarō. Shintarō, in particular, had come to Gunki's assistance when he was in difficulty. Shintarō had allowed Gunki to move into rental quarters that he owned and to stay there free of charge. Gunki's previous landlord, Riemon, had done the same, Gunki said, but perhaps Shintarō felt a special obligation to him because he had taught Shintarō's son, Yatarō, calligraphy. In addition Shintarō even lent Gunki money, enabling him to live in leisure. Gunki repeated the same thing to me on several occasions, and I thought it strange that these well-to-do townspeople held him in such respect. I knew that Gunki regularly practiced rites to Kangiten and decided that perhaps it was owing to their miraculous efficacy.

Eight years ago, in 1820, Gunki came to call, saying he was about to set out on a trip to the western provinces. I heard that Gunki first took his wife, Soe, and son, Makijirō, to Osaka [and left them there, and that they then returned to Kyoto, where] Hōki Masasuke looked after them. Gunki returned to Kyoto six years ago, in the summer of 1822, and moved into temporary lodgings on Kiyamachi street north of Matsubara street. Soe fell ill and died five years ago, in 1823, and on the twenty-second day of the twelfth month of 1824, Gunki died as well. Since there were no immediate relatives, Masasuke conferred with Teradaya Kumazō, Matsusakaya Nihei, Minoya Kohachi, [and myself] about what to do. Gunki had been a parishioner of the Ikkō temple Unseiji, located at the intersection of Samegai and Uonotana streets, south of Gojō street, so we arranged with this temple to have Gunki cremated. I took charge of selling his few possessions, and Nihei used the proceeds to cover the funeral costs. Almost all of Gunki's household effects had been confiscated at the time the Kan'in princely house dismissed him, and there was nothing notable in the way of objects. The group decided that I should look after Gunki's papers, diaries, and miscellaneous scraps of writing. Makijirō was the son of Gunki's concubine, who was the younger sister of Momijiya Jinbei, resident in Kita-machi, Minakuchi post station, in Ōmi. She had gone back to stay with Jinbei and had died there some time previously. Because of this connection, we arranged with Jinbei to take Makijirō in.

I subsequently rented the quarters where I live at present, registered my house name and name [with those responsible for the locale], and made a living by teaching noh songs.[8] I intended to keep Gunki's papers as mementos for Makijirō once he grew up, but it so happened that I needed a large paper mat [to cover] the floor of my room. To make such a mat, I ended up using most of the scraps of paper Gunki had kept for calligraphy practice as well as his correspondence, although I set aside his diaries.[9] There were also a few incomplete copies of books (these were not written entirely in block characters),[10] so I used those as well for the mat. I spread the mat on the floor to keep the tatami from getting soiled, but since my quarters were small, the mat soon became torn, and I sold it to an itinerant scrap-paper dealer.

When Mitsugi was interrogated about Gunki's transmission to her of the pernicious creed, the investigators looked into the whereabouts of the scroll with the buddha image that Gunki had possessed. Since I had taken charge of Gunki's written materials when he died, I came under suspicion and was arrested. Initially I tried to hide the fact that I had taken charge of the writings and that I had used the scraps to make a paper mat, but after repeated interrogation, I have testified to the circumstances of what actually happened, as recorded here.

Investigators' Comments on the Papers Kept by Shōni

Shōni initially tried to hide that he had taken Gunki's papers home with him and had used scraps from them to make a paper mat. But when we interrogated him again, confronting him with the testimony of Masasuke and the others, he admitted what had actually happened. We then had the remaining papers sent to us [from Kyoto] and investigated them. They consisted of fragments of diaries in Gunki's own hand, a notebook with an account of his dismissal from the Kan'in princely house, letters, and other scraps. There was nothing of any significance, but among the scraps were some that were written entirely in block characters. These appeared to be from *Refutations of the Pernicious Sect*, which in the past was burned in Nagasaki and is included among the list of proscribed books of the Jesus creed that was distributed to the booksellers of this city [in 1698].[11] Since illicit transcriptions of this sort were found among the scraps of paper possessed by Gunki, it seemed quite likely that Shōni might have found other writings of the Jesus creed among Gunki's papers and knowingly used them as well for the paper mat. We thus interrogated him further, confronting him with the accusations described in the next passage.

Investigators' Summation of Shōni's Testimony

We confronted Shōni with the following accusations, repeatedly interrogating him severely:

> You concealed the fact that you took charge of Gunki's papers. Among those, just as with the scraps of writing, there must have been copies of proscribed works of the Jesus creed. Since you were close enough to Gunki to recommend him for a position, undoubtedly you conspired with him to do wicked deeds and were one of the first to receive from him the transmission of the pernicious Kirishitan creed. Surely you must have become a believer, worshipping the drawing of the Lord of Heaven and listening to Gunki's expositions of the Jesus creed. When Gunki died you undoubtedly decided to conceal the drawing of the Lord of Heaven and the writings on the Jesus creed [from the others present] by mixing them among the other papers, such as Gunki's diaries. Then [later at home] you must have separated them out and hidden them. Now you must be making up false stories [to conceal that you still have the drawing and the writings on the Jesus creed].

To this Shōni responded as follows:

> Gunki was able to discern people's mental capacity, regardless of whether they were of high birth or low. When he met people who shared his own inclinations and whom he thought he could trust, he would treat them as if they were blood relations, even if they were only recent acquaintances. But Gunki would never readily disclose his thoughts to someone he looked down on as timid or untalented, even if the person was a blood relation or a friend of long standing. I myself and others such as Masasuke probably didn't measure up to Gunki's standards, and as a result our contact with him was quite superficial. I definitely never received the transmission of the Kirishitan creed from him, let alone worshipped the drawing of the Lord of Heaven. Nor did I listen to expositions of the Jesus creed or set aside writings about the Jesus creed that Gunki had owned.
>
>   As for the whereabouts of the drawing, it was no longer among Gunki's possessions when I went through them together with Masasuke and the others at the time of his death. The only things I brought home

were papers such as the diaries. I don't know what happened to the drawing, but after Gunki was dismissed from the Kan'in princely house and went to live in the rental quarters owned by Shintarō, he set off on a trip of more than three years to Nagasaki. It surely would have been difficult for him to do this without funds for travel expenses. Further, Gunki's landlord Shintarō was extremely friendly toward him, letting him stay without paying any rent and lending him money. It is possible that Shintarō took the drawing in pawn or that Gunki sold it to him. According to rumor, Riemon's and Kyūbei's financial circumstances had deteriorated, and I didn't hear anything of Gunki associating with any well-to-do townspeople apart from Shintarō after he had been dismissed by the Kan'in princely house. Shintarō is thus the most likely suspect.

Shōni insisted throughout that he knew nothing whatsoever about the drawing, but he acknowledged that he was culpable of the offense of having heedlessly used various scraps and transcriptions to make the paper mat, while setting aside Gunki's diaries and other papers. He acknowledged also that he had concealed the fact that he had taken charge of Gunki's papers. Since the remaining scraps left by Gunki included some transcriptions of works about the Jesus creed, it also was possible, he admitted, that he had carelessly used other pernicious writings of this sort to make the paper mat, without realizing it. He stated that he regretted his mistaken conduct and repented deeply. The interrogation having fully clarified the circumstances of his crimes, he states that he has nothing to say in opposition [to what is recorded here] and is filled with remorse.

INVESTIGATORS' ADDENDUM REGARDING HŌKI MASASUKE

When we interrogated Masasuke, the particulars of his testimony about the arrangements made when Gunki died matched Shōni's. He stated as follows:

I became Gunki's calligraphy disciple at the time he was living in rental quarters owned by Riemon, and eventually I [became skilled enough] to take disciples of my own. If I failed to visit Gunki regularly, he would require me to write out a letter of apology. I found this troublesome, but since I was obliged to him, I continued to call on him whenever I was free. As Shōni has testified, Gunki was a good judge of people, and he often berated me and others for being stupid and of no use. When Shintarō, Kyūbei, and Riemon came to call, they would often go into a secluded room that Gunki didn't allow outsiders to enter. It was difficult for me to ask what they were doing. Although I periodically encountered the three of them at Gunki's place over the years, for some reason I was never introduced to them or to [Shintarō's son,] Yatarō. While I knew their faces and names, I never spoke with them.

When Gunki was dismissed as a result of his misdeed at the Kan'in princely house, Riemon, Kyūbei, and Shintarō arranged for him to move into rental quarters owned by Shintarō. Shintarō's son, Yatarō, Riemon, and Kyūbei continued to call on him there regularly. I often heard Gunki say that Shintarō wasn't only taking care of his financial needs but also allowing him to stay free of rent, just as Gunki's former landlord, Riemon, had done earlier. Gunki was thus able to lead an easy life. I then heard that Gunki had set off on a trip to distant parts, but he didn't say anything to me about this, and for a while I didn't know anything either about the whereabouts of Gunki's wife, Soe, or his son, Makijirō. After about a year, Soe and Makijirō came to call. Soe told me that Gunki had gone to Nagasaki and that Takamiya Heizō in Osaka was looking after them in the meantime. She felt sorry for imposing on Heizō, she said, and wanted to return to Kyoto, and she begged me to take care of the arrangements. I was afraid that if I refused, Gunki might use his status as my master to make trouble for me when he returned to Kyoto. I didn't want to get involved, but I felt I had no choice but to do as Soe asked. So I rented quarters in a back tenement and set Soe and Makijirō up there. Soe eked out a living by doing tie-dye preparation piecework.[12]

In the summer of 1822, six years ago, Gunki returned to Kyoto and moved Soe and Makijirō to the room he rented on Kiyamachi street south of Matsubara street. But Soe fell ill and died in 1823, and on the twenty-second day of the twelfth month of the following year, Gunki died as well. Shōni and the others saw to the necessary arrangements. Shōni took the papers and such home with him, and Makijirō was sent to live with Jinbei. Afterward I thought I would like to have a scrap of Gunki's writing as a memento. I spoke to Shōni about this, but Shōni said that he had used the writing scraps to make a paper mat. I thought it was wrong of Shōni to dispose heedlessly of things he had been entrusted with, even if they were just paper scraps. But nothing was to be gained by complaining about a done matter, so I let it go.

When we interrogated Masasuke about the whereabouts of the drawing of the Lord of Heaven owned by Gunki, he said the same thing as Shōni. He repented deeply that he could not be of assistance, but when he joined Shōni and the others to go through Gunki's belongings after his death, there was nothing of that sort among them. Among those who were closest to Gunki, Shintarō had been especially solicitous. Shintarō had lent Gunki money and had let him stay in housing he owned without paying any rent. Before Gunki set off for Nagasaki, perhaps he raised funds [for the trip] by seeking Shintarō's aid and secretly leaving the scroll with him as a pledge.

We confronted Masasuke with the following accusation: "Undoubtedly you received transmission of the Kirishitan creed from Gunki, and since you were his calligraphy disciple, you must have conspired together with him." But Masasuke continued to insist that such was not the case. His statement appears to be truthful.

ADDENDA REGARDING THE INVESTIGATION OF OTHER FRIENDS OF GUNKI'S

Investigation of Teradaya Kumazō

When we questioned Teradaya Kumazō, he stated as follows:

I was not a disciple of Gunki's. I am a scabbard maker and came to know him through this business. Although I became friendly with him, there was something frightening about Gunki. He urged me to become a follower of Kangiten, but I refused. I told him that I didn't like monkish things very much and saw no point in getting involved in them. Matters stayed that way, but the night before Gunki absconded after committing a misdeed at the Kan'in princely house, he came to my place. I kept him hidden that night and the next morning sent him in a palanquin to the Fushimi river port.[13] As a result, I came under suspicion from the Kyoto officials. I had no choice but to tell them where Gunki had gone, and in the end Gunki was arrested and dismissed by the

Kan'in princely house and his possessions were confiscated. As this happened because I had divulged Gunki's whereabouts, it would have been quite natural for him to be angry and break off relations. However, after he moved to the rental quarters owned by Shintarō, he sent a message saying that we should stay on good terms with each other. I guessed that he did this because I knew that he had entrusted the valuable items among his possessions to Riemon and Kyūbei [before he absconded and the order for confiscation of his belongings was carried out]. Gunki probably feared that if he fell out with me, I might report things about him to others. I thought it wouldn't do to refuse and thus continued to be friendly with him, but after this Gunki never told me anything notable.

Kumazō's statement regarding Gunki's return from Nagasaki and death in the temporary lodgings south of Matsubara street was the same as that of Shōni and Masasuke. We pressed him on the whereabouts of the scroll with the drawing of the Lord of Heaven, but he insisted that he knows nothing about this. He stated as follows:

Gunki's previous landlords Riemon and Shintarō long let him stay in their rental housing without paying anything. Since Kyūbei looked after Gunki's belongings when he absconded [from the Kan'in princely house], he might [have once kept the drawing for Gunki]. But [Gunki's friends] returned all of Gunki's belongings to him when he moved into the rental quarters owned by Shintarō, both the things that Kyūbei had taken charge of and the few that Riemon had kept for him. It thus does not seem likely that Kyūbei or Riemon still have any of Gunki's belongings in their possession. When Gunki set off for Nagasaki, he would have needed money for the trip. Since Shintarō was especially close to him, perhaps Gunki secretly went to Shintarō to raise funds by pawning or selling the scroll. Otherwise the scroll should have been among Gunki's belongings when he died, but as Shōni and the others have testified, nothing of that sort was found among his possessions. Most likely he had earlier entrusted it to Shintarō to raise funds.

We confronted Kumazō with the following accusation: "Since you were friendly with Gunki, undoubtedly you received transmission of the Kirishitan creed from him." We pressed him severely, but he insisted that such was not the case. His statement appears to be truthful.

Investigation of Minoya Kohachi

When we questioned Minoya Kohachi, he stated as follows:

> I am a palanquin bearer and long had dealings with Gunki. I ran all
> sorts of errands for him and frequently carried messages from him to
> Itoya Wasa, Kyūbei, and Shintarō. I don't know when Gunki's landlord
> Riemon and the other three came to be on familiar terms with Gunki,
> but they were always in close contact with one another and would often
> confer in a secluded room. I never heard anything of what they said.
> When Gunki absconded, he employed me to carry his household
> belongings to Kyūbei's house. Then, when Gunki moved into the rental
> quarters owned by Shintarō, I retrieved the items that Kyūbei had kept
> hidden for him. But I don't know anything about the nature of those
> items. After that, Gunki's landlord Shintarō came frequently with his
> son, Yatarō, and with Kyūbei and Riemon to confer privately with Gunki,
> just as before. I was sick during much of the time that Gunki was in
> Nagasaki, but after he returned to Kyoto, he employed me once again.
> The situation at the time of Gunki's death was as Shōni and the others
> have testified. I have never seen the scroll with the drawing of the Lord
> of Heaven and know nothing about it, but during the time Gunki lived
> in the rental quarters owned by Riemon, Wasa's daughter Toki and
> Kyūbei's daughter Moto stayed with him for long periods. You probably
> would be able to find out most of the secret matters of Gunki's house-
> hold if you asked them. I never went into the back rooms of Gunki's
> house.

Kohachi's statement appears to be truthful.

Investigation of Matsusakaya Nihei

When we questioned Matsusakaya Nihei, he stated as follows:

> I run a restaurant, and I became friendly with Gunki ten years ago, when
> he came to my restaurant with a retainer from another princely house.
> When Gunki returned from Nagasaki, he said he wanted to live some-
> where around the intersection of Kiyamachi and Matsubara streets, and
> he asked me to arrange for him to rent temporary lodgings there. I acted

as the intermediary in the transaction and stood as the guarantor. But since I was occupied with my business, I never went to visit, and I knew nothing of the circumstances of Gunki's household. As for what happened when Gunki's wife died and then Gunki himself fell ill and died, it was just as Shōni and Masasuke have testified. We and the others gathered together, held the funeral, and sold Gunki's possessions. I took charge of the money resulting from the sale and used it to pay for the funeral expenses.

Nihei stated that when he disposed of Gunki's possessions, he definitely had not seen any sort of strange scroll. In the course of the present investigation, he had been asked about the whereabouts of the drawing of the Lord of Heaven, but there had not been anything of that sort among Gunki's possessions when he died, and so Nihei knew nothing of it. His statement appears to be truthful.

Reinvestigation of Wasa's Adoptive Daughter Toki and Investigation of Kyūbei's Daughter Moto

To follow up on Kohachi's statement, we questioned Wasa's daughter Toki once more. She again stated, as in the previous addendum [to Mitsugi's testimony], that she was sent to stay with Gunki because she would not agree to Mitsugi's demands. During that time, she said, Moto was also put in Gunki's charge. Gunki always worshipped a deity that he said was Kangiten, and there was one room in the house that outsiders were not allowed to enter. When Riemon, Kyūbei, and Shintarō visited, they would confer together in that room, but on those occasions Toki and Moto were never allowed to enter, so Toki does not know what they discussed.

We consulted with [the Kyoto eastern magistrate] Lord Kan'o about Moto and had her summoned to Osaka for interrogation. She stated that she had become involved in an affair with a man, and after this relationship had been terminated, her father, Kyūbei, asked Gunki to take her under his charge. At the time Toki was also staying at Gunki's house. Moto's statement that there was one room that outsiders were not allowed to enter matches Toki's statement. Moto also stated as follows:

When Gunki absconded, my father took him in and also took charge of his possessions. After Gunki had been dismissed by the princely house, he stayed for a while at my father's house. Upon conferring with Riemon and Shintarō, he moved to rental quarters owned by Shintarō, but my father continued to visit him there, and I did so as well.[14] One day, I don't remember when, I overheard Gunki tell Soe that the confiscation of his belongings on behalf of the princely house at the time of his dismissal had left him in terrible straits, and at this point his only choice was to pawn or sell the important things still in his possession. He and Soe indeed looked to be penniless, and I felt sorry for them, but since I couldn't do anything about the situation, I just let the matter go.

Nine years ago, on the twenty-fifth day of the ninth month of 1819, my mother, Fuji, died, and shortly thereafter my father died as well. At the time my parents died, Gunki and his wife both came to help. My elder brother, the present Kyūbei, succeeded as head of the household, but as he had been deaf for some time, he never talked with Gunki. I myself never received the transmission of the Kirishitan creed from Gunki and knew nothing about the drawing.

Moto's statement appears to be truthful.

Investigation of Riemon's Widow, Kiyo, and the Present Kyūbei

In principle we should have followed up the leads gained from the statements of the abovementioned figures by interrogating Riemon and Kyūbei. As both were deceased, however, we arranged with [the Kyoto eastern magistrate] Lord Kan'o to summon and question Riemon's widow, Kiyo, and the present Kyūbei. The results are as recorded here.

When we interrogated Riemon's widow, Kiyo, she stated as follows:

I am the daughter of Tsuchiya Chōbei, who resided along Nishi-no-tōin street south of Shijō street in Kyoto, and I married Riemon thirteen years ago in the eighth month of 1815. At the time Mizuno Gunki was living with his wife in rental quarters that Riemon owned. They had been living in these rental quarters from before the time I married Riemon. Riemon was very close to Gunki, and for some reason that I did not understand, no one ever seemed to come from Gunki's place to bring the rent. I thought this strange and asked Riemon about it, but he only scolded me, saying that Gunki hadn't paid rent from the start and it would be difficult to urge him to do so now. It wasn't something that I should concern myself with, being a new wife who had only recently entered the household. So I said nothing further about Gunki's situation. I didn't know anything about his having absconded eleven years ago in the twelfth month of 1817, or of his dismissal by the princely house in the fourth month of 1818. It is only now that I have heard of these things.

Gunki and his wife and child were later taken in by Kyūbei for a while, and they then moved to rental quarters owned by Shintarō. Riemon seemed to continue to visit him there. Riemon had originally been quite well-to-do, but perhaps because of his involvement with Gunki, he appeared to have various irregular expenses, and his finances became ever more straitened. I worried about this, and then, four years ago, in 1824, Riemon fell ill and died on the twenty-fourth day of the eleventh month. He had no son and all his blood relatives were deceased, so there was no one to inherit the household headship. Matsuya Kihei, who was related to my natal house and resided on Aburanokōji street, south of Gojō street, was thus asked to serve as my guardian. I continued the household under the status of "widow" and began a business selling secondhand clothes and other goods. I have made my living in this way up to the present.

In the course of the present investigation I have been asked whether Riemon prayed to the Lord of Heaven, what he talked about secretly with Gunki, and what items he took charge of when Gunki absconded. But, as I stated, I never heard anything about Gunki's dismissal by the princely house, let alone his absconding. I thus know nothing about such matters. It was only when I was told about the testimony of the other parties that I learned [of Riemon's involvement]. I deeply repent [his involvement], but I have no knowledge whatsoever whether or not he received transmission of the Kirishitan creed from Gunki.

When we interrogated the present Kyūbei, he stated as follows:

At present four people live in my household, including my wife and child and my younger sister, Moto. My late father, the former Kyūbei, was very friendly with Gunki, and I heard that he put Moto under Gunki's charge. However, until ten years ago I lived in a different house, and apart from that, I became almost totally deaf and wasn't able to communicate about anything. As both my parents died and there was no one else to succeed [to the position of household head], I became the successor despite being impaired. Although I knew Gunki by sight, I never conversed with him. My sister, Moto, in fact knows much more about Gunki's situation. I first learned about the testimony of those involved in the incident from the present interrogation. Although I have no knowledge whether or not my late father received transmission of the Kirishitan creed from Gunki, I repent deeply [his involvement with Gunki].

As it was possible that the former Kyūbei and Riemon might have secretly received writings of a suspicious nature from Gunki, we asked Lord Kan'o to have their households searched. He sent us a list of the items found, but those items did not include any suspect writings.

Investigators' Conclusions Regarding the Whereabouts of Gunki's Scroll of the Lord of Heaven

According to the statements of Kiyo and the present Kyūbei, neither of them knew much about Gunki, and thus they had no way of knowing anything about the drawing of the Lord of Heaven. Nor could the whereabouts of the scroll with the drawing of the Lord of Heaven be readily deduced from the testimony and statements of Shōni, Masasuke, Kumazō, Kohachi, Toki, and Moto. However, as recorded in the preceding addenda [about these people], Shōni took charge of a number of writings in Gunki's own hand. In one of these Gunki recorded that his belongings had been confiscated when the Kan'in princely house dismissed him ten years ago, in the fourth month of 1818. Nevertheless, he wrote, the scroll of the divine image and the sacred objects that he always kept with him, even when traveling, [had escaped confiscation and] had been safely returned to him by his landlord Riemon. Kyūbei had subsequently kept them for Gunki for a while, and Gunki had then taken them with him when he moved to the rental quarters owned by Shintarō. What Gunki referred to as the "scroll of the divine image" surely was the drawing of the Lord of Heaven. It seems that although Gunki put great store by it, he thought it was not something for an absconder to carry with him, and so he secretly entrusted it for the time being to his confidant, Riemon. Once the incident was over and he had moved to the rental quarters owned by Shintarō, he must have retrieved the scroll.

Soon Gunki and his wife found themselves in straitened circumstances, and Moto, as noted, heard them talking about pawning an "important object." Most likely this "important object" was the drawing of the Lord of Heaven, and for that reason they did not name it as such but simply referred to it as "important." Subsequently Gunki came to Osaka from the seventh to the ninth month of 1818 and had Heizō worship the drawing of the Lord of Heaven. Thus, although Moto overheard Gunki and his wife talking about pawning an important object, at that point this must have been just something they were considering, and Gunki had not yet actually pawned the scroll. However, the following year, when Mitsugi sought to obtain the scroll from Gunki in the fourth month of 1819, he told her that he had turned it over to a wealthy person in return for a large sum of money. Gunki then proposed to borrow it back and let Mitsugi copy it for a sum of forty or fifty ryō. Judging from these facts, in the span of the half year between the time Gunki brought the scroll back after showing it to Heizō and the time when Mitsugi tried to obtain it from him, he must have pawned or otherwise relinquished it.

It is difficult to know with certainty who received the scroll from Gunki. But the abovementioned Shintarō had long had close relations with Gunki, and after Gunki had been dismissed by the princely house and no longer had the possibility of serving elsewhere, Shintarō allowed him to stay in one of his rental properties without paying any rent. He even lent Gunki money. Further, Shintarō and his son, Yatarō, visited Gunki often. All this invites suspicion. Since Shintarō had a pawnshop, if we put together the statements of Shōni, Masasuke, and Kumazō, most likely Shintarō either took the scroll in pawn or otherwise obtained it from Gunki. It would have been best to investigate Shintarō directly, but he had died sometime previously. As his son, Yatarō, had taken over the name Shintarō and continued the household, we consulted Lord Kan'o and arranged to have him arrested. Staff from our office were dispatched to Kyoto to take charge of him [and bring him to Osaka]. The record of our interrogation of Yatarō follows.

TESTIMONY OF NAKAMURAYA YATARŌ

Nakamuraya Yatarō, also known as Shintarō: forty-one years old, residing on Akezu street south of Matsubara street

Remanded to jail the eighteenth day of the seventh month, 1827

Yatarō's Relationship to Gunki

Under interrogation, Yatarō stated as follows:

My childhood name was Yatarō. I live together with my mother, Wasa; my wife, Nobu; my son, Sutejirō; and my daughter, Kyō, a household of five. I make my living as a pawnbroker. I have a concubine, Tsugi, whom I have accommodated in rental quarters, with my younger sister, Mume, listed as the tenant; Mume is married to my father's adoptive son, the present Nakamuraya Shinbei. Tsugi has borne me a daughter, called Ai.

My deceased father, Shintarō, was the son of the deceased [previous] Nakamuraya Shinbei, who resided on Higashi-no-tōin street north of Gojō street. In the Meiwa years he was sent as a child to Edo to work as an apprentice, and he returned to Kyoto in 1786 at the age of twenty-one.[15] Straightaway he was adopted by Nakamuraya Jirobei, the head of the main house, who resided in the same area, and married Jirobei's daughter Wasa.[16] Wasa is my mother. In the same year, my father established a branch house at the place where our house is located today and registered himself under the name of Nakamuraya Shintarō. I was born in the following year, 1787.

It appears that my deceased father, Shintarō, was already on friendly terms with Mizuno Gunki and used to call on him in secret. I don't know when they became friends, or who introduced them to each other. At my father's instructions, I became Gunki's calligraphy disciple when he was serving as a retainer of the Kan'in princely house and living in rental quarters owned by Riemon. Gunki provided calligraphy models for me to copy, but I preferred to frequent places of amusement and had little interest in calligraphy, so I often skipped my sessions with him. My father kept his closeness to Gunki hidden even from me, my mother, and our relatives. I have heard that Gunki spent time in Edo, so I would guess that my father became friends with him while he was an apprentice there. If that isn't correct, I don't know how they may have met.

Ten years ago, in the fourth month of 1818, Gunki was dismissed by the Kan'in princely house and banned from entering the service of other princely and noble houses. He vacated the rental quarters owned by Riemon, and my father arranged for him to move instead into rental quarters that my father owned and where he saw to Gunki's needs. My concubine, Tsugi, lives opposite the house where Gunki stayed. My father continued making secret visits to Gunki, and I, too, called on him whenever I went to Tsugi's house.

I don't know why, but Gunki didn't introduce me to [his calligraphy disciple] Masasuke, and so I didn't even know Masasuke's name at the time. Gunki lived in this house from the fourth month of 1818 until the fourth month of 1820, eight years ago. Then he left for Nagasaki, and I heard that subsequently this Masasuke looked after his wife and son. I understand that Gunki came back to Kyoto six years ago, in 1822, and moved to Kiyamachi. The members of my family don't know whether my father visited him there, since he kept his friendship with Gunki secret, but I didn't call on Gunki in Kiyamachi.

Four years ago, in the twelfth month of 1824, I heard that Gunki had died. In the eighth month of the following year, my father began to suffer from a lump in his throat, and he died last year, on the twenty-sixth day of the third month of 1826. I inherited the household and took over the name Shintarō.[17]

Before my father died, he chose a moment when none of the people who were taking care of him were present and spoke to me as follows:

> I won't be able to recover from this illness, and I have only one remaining concern to pass on to you. You must make sure not to associate with someone like Gunki; just put all your efforts into our household and our business. I was close to Gunki and helped him financially, and then he asked me to secretly keep as a kind of pawn a certain scroll with a buddha image. I lent him a large amount of money in return, and soon after, he set off for Nagasaki. After he returned, he never came to retrieve [the drawing], perhaps because he couldn't come up with the money to repay me. As one thing followed the other, he fell ill and died, and much to my chagrin I am now left with this drawing. As I was worrying about what to do with it, I caught this fatal illness. If this drawing remains in our household, it is hard to know what might happen. Since Gunki had unusual powers, who knows what untoward events might occur after his death. That would inevitably cause suspicion to fall on us and bring disaster to our house. After my death, tear that drawing to pieces and throw them into the river, or burn it and throw away the ashes. Make sure that your mother, your wife and children, our relatives, and our servants know nothing about it.

Two or three days later, my father's condition suddenly deteriorated, and he died. After the funeral, I was overwhelmed with grief for my father's death. I didn't take the matter of the scroll very seriously and forgot about it until the summer of this year, when I heard rumors that Gunki was said to have transmitted the banned pernicious creed to his disciples, and that even Gunki's acquaintances were being arrested on orders from Osaka by way of the Kyoto magistrate. I didn't think that my father had entered Gunki's banned sect, but I suddenly recalled his deathbed instructions to burn the buddha image. I worried what might happen if I were summoned and questioned and if this led to our house being searched. Just as I was planning to carry out my father's instructions, most strangely our well for drinking water became infested with insects on the eleventh day of the intercalary sixth month. My father had had this well dug thirty years ago to last forever, and it was lined with stone walls from the bottom to the top, rather than just tiles. Nevertheless, the water became so unclear and smelly that we couldn't drink a single sip. I felt that this might be an omen of impending disaster.

I searched the storehouse, and there it was, in a chest of drawers left by my father that we ordinarily never opened. I unrolled the scroll in secret; it was a bit more than four feet long but I can't recall how wide it was. It seemed to show a woman of unusual appearance holding something in her hands, but it was an old drawing, and it was difficult to make out just exactly what it was. I became afraid and rolled the scroll up again. I took it out from the storehouse, making sure nobody in the household saw me. There is an old stove between the storehouses that we use to heat water for bathing. I threw the scroll into this stove and burned it to ashes. If any cinders remained, I intended to say that I had found some old shrine amulets and burned them. To my relief, luckily no servants turned up and no one asked me any questions. But then I came under suspicion and was arrested. I repent deeply what has happened.

The Investigators' Suspicions About Yatarō

When we first began to investigate Yatarō, [currently known as Shintarō,] he asked his cousin Nakamuraya Yazobei not to tell the magistracy that as a child he had gone by the name Yatarō. He also told us various lies, such as that neither he nor his father had known Gunki for any length of time. Gunki was really just a recent acquaintance, he said, whom he and his father had visited occasionally after Gunki moved into the rental quarters they owned.

Investigators' Comments on Yatarō's Relationship with Yazobei

Yazobei is the younger brother of Nakamuraya Jirobei, the [current head of the] main house of Yatarō's family. [Yatarō's mother,] Wasa, is Yazobei's aunt.[18] Since Shintarō was the adopted husband of Yazobei's aunt [Wasa], Yazobei went to help Shintarō out in his shop from the time he was a child, at which time he was known as Mannosuke. Ten years ago, in 1818, he established his own household, separate from Jirobei's. Since Shintarō had rental quarters that were vacant, Yazobei started a dry goods business there. Our investigation revealed that Shintarō told Yazobei to have Gunki inscribe the street sign for his shop.

At first, Shōni and the others made statements that gave the impression that Shintarō was still alive, and that Yatarō was the one who had opened the dry goods shop. Further, in the papers that Gunki left, Yatarō's name appears in a more prominent position than Shintarō's. It seemed that Yatarō might not be Shintarō's son but someone with a household of his own. We were unsure about the truth of the matter. Moreover, we didn't yet know that Gunki's buddha image had been burned, and we were determined to confiscate it safely. We dispatched staff officials to Kyoto to confer with their counterparts in the Kyoto Magistracy, and they carried out a wide-ranging investigation. From this we learned that Shintarō had died, but we confused Yatarō with Yazobei. As a result, we arranged through the Kyoto eastern magistrate, Lord Kan'o, to have the two of them arrested and handed over to us. Yazobei's childhood name in fact was Mannosuke, whereas [the present] Shintarō's was Yatarō, but when they were arrested, Yatarō asked Yazobei to gloss over the situation and not tell the magistracy that Yatarō had been called by that name [before he assumed the name of Shintarō]. However, when Yazobei realized that the magistracy had arrested him because they believed he was Yatarō, Yazobei told Yatarō that he could not do what Yatarō had asked. And indeed, when interrogated, Yazobei stated that he would tell the truth and that it was the current Shintarō who was formerly called Yatarō.

Gunki and [Yatarō's father,] the former Shintarō, appear to have been skilled in trickery. Perhaps they feared that the evil in which they engaged would come to light after their death if not during their lifetimes and lead to an investigation. They may even have thought to make it difficult to figure out who was who by having Gunki inscribe the sign for Yazobei's dry goods shop, [suggesting that it was Yazobei who had a connection to Gunki]. This made it difficult for us to untangle the confusion over the names of Yatarō and Yazobei. According to the statements of Masasuke and the others, Gunki never introduced Yatarō by name to outsiders [such as Masasuke]. Considering all these things together, it would appear that there must have been a reason for this, but now that both Gunki and Shintarō are dead, it is no longer possible to find out the true facts of the matter.

As we continued our questioning of Yazobei, it became clear that he did not associate with Gunki, let alone receive transmissions from him. As recorded in the following section, we thereupon confronted Yatarō with accusations as to why he asked Yazobei not to mention his name.

Investigators' Summation of the Interrogation of Yatarō

We confronted Yatarō with the following accusations:

> Undoubtedly you must have received transmissions from Gunki about the practices of the Kirishitan sect and conspired with him to commit wicked deeds. The people of your household must all have known that your late father, Shintarō, received the aforementioned drawing of the Lord of Heaven and worshipped it together with him. Surely you have hidden the drawing with fellow members of your group [whom we have not yet identified], and you must be lying when you claim that you burned the image in accordance with Shintarō's deathbed instructions.

We repeatedly subjected him to severe interrogation about these points, but he denied our accusations, stating as follows:

> I was Gunki's calligraphy disciple and I carelessly burned a dangerous scroll on account of Shintarō's deathbed instructions. I was afraid that if

it came to light that my former name was Yatarō, my relationship to Gunki as my calligraphy master would be undeniable. If that happened, I feared, not only my late father but also I myself might be held to be Kirishitan, and I might be punished severely. Although I realized that these matters would come out eventually, I asked Yazobei to keep them concealed for a while at least. But I have not done what you are accusing me of.

The interrogation has nevertheless fully clarified, as detailed above, the particulars of Yatarō's crimes. He states that he has nothing to say in opposition [to what is recorded here] and is filled with remorse.

Investigators' Interrogation of Yatarō's Mother, Wife, Concubine, and Shop Manager

We contacted the Kyoto eastern magistrate, Lord Kan'o, and arranged to summon Yatarō's mother, Wasa; his wife; his concubine; and his main clerk. Upon being questioned, Wasa stated as follows:

I do not know how my husband, the late Shintarō, became acquainted with Gunki, but I believe that they became close while Shintarō was in Edo. I didn't like it when Shintarō invited guests, let alone a retainer of a princely house [like Gunki], and I found Gunki's frequent visits unpleasant. I complained about it to Shintarō, but he wouldn't listen to me. Shintarō told me that he had arranged for our son, Yatarō, to become Gunki's calligraphy disciple. I objected that Yatarō was too old for this and said that there was no point in having him study calligraphy at this stage. But Shintarō was a stubborn man who had no use for my opinion. When Shintarō offered to let Gunki stay in one of the rental quarters he owned, he initially didn't tell me about this, so I knew nothing about it. After Gunki had moved in, Shintarō started to go out very often, and I asked him where he went. He then told me that he had allowed Gunki to move into one of his rental quarters and was visiting him there. When Shintarō fell ill and died, he didn't leave any testament—not even a word—either with me or his relatives, which I found strange. This investigation is the first time for me to hear what my son has testified, and I am deeply shocked.

We pressed Wasa with the following accusation: "This statement is undoubtedly false. In fact, you must have been Gunki's follower together with Shintarō and are a believer in the Kirishitan sect. You must have received the drawing of the Lord of Heaven together with Shintarō and prayed to it all along." We interrogated her about these points, but she denied them: "That is not at all the case. Until this investigation, I had no idea that Shintarō had received this scroll from Gunki in pawn, that he gave instructions on his deathbed to Yatarō to burn it, or that my son did indeed burn it."

Yatarō's wife, Nobu, is the daughter of Ōmiya Ihei, who resides along Nishi-no-tōin street east of Shijō street. She married Yatarō fourteen years ago, in 1814, and has borne him two children: their son, Sutejirō, who is seven years old this year, and their daughter, Kyō, who is four years old. According to her, the household has been managed by her parents-in-law, and when her father-in-law, Shintarō, died, Yatarō took over. Nobu has not been involved in any external business of the house, occupying herself exclusively with sewing the household's clothes and looking after the children. She stated that she knew nothing about Gunki living in rental quarters opposite Yatarō's concubine, Tsugi, or that Yatarō often called on Gunki when he visited Tsugi because Gunki had once been his calligraphy master. It was only as a result of the present investigation that she learned what her husband had testified, and she was deeply shocked.

Yatarō's concubine, Tsugi, is the adoptive daughter of Izutsuya Jiro-saburō of Gion-machi.[19] Yatarō took her as his concubine fifteen years ago, in 1813, and set her up in her own household in the abovementioned rental quarters. Her daughter, Ai, is fourteen years old this year. Tsugi stated as follows:

I saw that both Shintarō and Yatarō visited Gunki regularly after Gunki had moved into the rental quarters opposite my own. Because both my own house and Gunki's were rear houses, [built in the space behind the houses that face the street,] I became acquainted with Gunki's wife and son and was friendly with them. However, Yatarō told me not to call on Gunki, because Shintarō often visited him, and it would be awkward were Shintarō to encounter me there. So I never went there and don't know anything about the circumstances of Gunki's household. It is only

as a result of the present investigation that I have learned what Yatarō
has testified, and I am deeply shocked.

Among the clerks employed by Yatarō, Tsunehachi has worked for the
house for more than twenty years. He is the son of Kamiya Yasubei of
Kizu village in Yamashiro province. He stated as follows:

> I became an apprentice at the Nakamuraya house in 1808 at the age of
> fourteen, and I am currently the manager of the shop. From the time
> Gunki lived in the rental quarters owned by Riemon, he often visited my
> master's house. Shintarō seemed to be particularly taken with him, but I
> don't know how they came to be friends. After Shintarō allowed Gunki to
> move into the rental quarters that he owned, he treated Gunki with par-
> ticular consideration, and although I don't believe Gunki ever paid any
> rent, Shintarō never seemed to press him. I found it strange that Shintarō
> lent Gunki excessive amounts of money in exchange for goods that
> seemed worthless, but as to Gunki's leaving the scroll with Shintarō, they
> must have kept this a complete secret between themselves, and I had no
> way of knowing about it. It is only as a result of the present investigation
> that I have learned what Yatarō has testified, and I am deeply shocked.

All these statements appear to be truthful. Except for Tsunehachi, all the
servants [of the Nakamuraya house] have been taken on recently and have
not been called in for questioning.

Investigators' Comments on Shintarō's Daughter's Household and the Search of Yatarō's House

The late Shintarō had a son and a daughter; the son is Yatarō, and the
daughter the aforementioned Mume. Some time ago Shintarō adopted
Shinbei, son of Tashiroya Shinroku of Kami Saga in Yamashiro province,
as Mume's husband. He had a house built for them on the plot of land he
owned next to his own house and set up the married couple, Shinbei and
Mume, as a branch house. Shinbei registered himself as Nakamuraya
Shinbei and started his own business. We arranged through Lord Kan'o
to summon and question Shinbei and Mume. Their statements were identical to Wasa's, and they said that they had not known anything [about

the circumstances described in Yatarō's testimony] prior to the present investigation. This appears to be truthful.

We arranged through Lord Kan'o to have Yatarō's house searched, and he sent us Yatarō's account books. No pieces of writing transmitted from Gunki were found. The scroll that belonged to Gunki and that Yatarō burned appears to have been of the same size and to have had the same drawing and faded colors as the one on which Mitsugi and the others dripped blood. It must have been that scroll.

TESTIMONY OF MAKIJIRŌ

Makijirō: fourteen years old; son of the aforementioned Mizuno Gunki (now deceased); living together with Momijiya Jinbei in Kitamachi in the post station of Minakuchi, Kōga county, Ōmi province, in the domain of Lord Katō Akikuni[20]

Remanded to jail on the eighteenth day of the seventh month, 1827

Summary of Makijirō's Testimony

Under interrogation Makijirō stated that when his father, Gunki, traveled to Nagasaki, his stepmother, Soe, and Makijirō himself were left behind in the care of the aforementioned Heizō and Masasuke. When Gunki returned to Kyoto he moved to temporary lodgings on Kiyamachi street, south of Matsubara street. Soe and Gunki subsequently both fell ill and died, and Makijirō was taken in by Jinbei. These particulars match the testimony of Shōni and the others.

Makijirō's Testimony Proper

My actual mother was Tomo, who was Jinbei's younger sister. When Gunki was living in rental quarters owned by Riemon, Tomo entered his service as a maid. After a while she became his concubine, and I was born fourteen years ago, on the fifteenth day of the fifth month of 1814. Not long afterward, Tomo left Gunki's service and returned to Jinbei's household, where she fell ill and died. I was raised by Soe, whom I thought of as my real mother.

After Soe's death I began to roam about town, and even Gunki could not control me. Four years ago, in the eleventh month of 1824,[21] after he had already fallen ill, Gunki decided to discipline me. He suspended a wastepaper basket with the paper still in it [from the ceiling] of the second floor, using the hair of a woman. He threatened me, saying that if I didn't change my attitude, he would hang me from my hair in the same way as that basket; that, he said, was the Kirishitan method. As I was only a child, this scared me for the moment. Then, in a small room that was just six mats in size, he took a spear twelve feet long, pinned me to the wall with it, and drew his sword.[22] He also made the first and the second floor shake. I promised to mend my ways there and then, but it was hard to break long-established habits, and soon I went back to my bad behavior. Gunki became angry, and it seemed he intended to poison me. I became afraid, and I made sure not to eat anything in the house. I ate only things that I got elsewhere from people I knew. While this was going on, Gunki's illness grew worse and he died. I was then taken in by my uncle Jinbei. It was only after I was arrested and as a result of the present investigation that I have heard that my late father, Gunki, transmitted the practices of the proscribed Kirishitan sect to others. I am deeply shocked.

Investigators' Summation of Makijirō's Interrogation

We confronted Makijirō with the accusation that he, too, must have received transmissions of Kirishitan practices and of sorcery from Gunki, even though he was still young, and that he must have witnessed other strange things as well. We interrogated him severely, but he insisted that this was not the case. However, when we declared to him that his father had committed heinous crimes, he stated that as Gunki's son, he has nothing to say in opposition [to what is recorded here] and repents most deeply [what Gunki did].

Investigators' Comments on Their Interrogation of Makijirō's Uncle

When we interrogated [Makijirō's maternal uncle] Jinbei, he stated that his younger sister Tomo had been sent into Gunki's service as a maid, later became his concubine, and left Gunki's service soon after Makijirō was born. Jinbei took her in, but she fell ill and died. In these particulars

Jinbei's statement matches the testimony [of Makijirō and the others]. So does his declaration that he took charge of Makijirō after Gunki's death because of his relationship [to Makijirō as his uncle] and let him stay in his house. Jinbei further stated as follows:

> When I, too, was summoned in connection with the present investigation, I assumed that Gunki must have done something bad and that this had come to light. I asked Makijirō whether Gunki had done anything wrong while he was still alive. Makijirō told me that Gunki had threatened him with sorcery and had been about to poison him *(Investigators: This is as Makijirō stated)*. This was strange, I thought, and narrow-minded countryman that I am, I feared that if Makijirō spoke frankly about these things, suspicion might fall on me as well, even though I know nothing about what happened, and I might be punished severely. Therefore I warned him not to speak carelessly about them. Beyond that, I know nothing about Gunki.

This appears to be the truth.

Investigators' Conclusions About the Origins of Gunki and His Wife

When we looked into the origins of Gunki and his wife, Soe, the aforementioned Shōni said that Gunki was from Nagasu in Buzen province (Nagasu is under the jurisdiction of Shimabara domain based in Hizen province), but he did not know the name of the specific place where Gunki was born or the names of his parents. Masasuke said that he had once heard that Gunki was born in Edo, but he did not know whether he was born as a samurai or a townsman. Kumazō said that Gunki had told him that he was born in Utsunomiya in Shimotsuke province but had grown up in Edo and Osaka; Mitsugi, too, was told that Gunki hailed from Utsunomiya. The others summoned in connection with the investigation had merely heard that he was "from Edo" or "from somewhere in the western provinces." Nobody knows the name of the place where Gunki was born, or the names of his parents. Of course, we also questioned Makijirō about this; he said that he had been too young to think of asking Gunki about the province where he was born, so he did not know. We are left without a clue. Gunki was hiding evil deeds, so he likely kept the place of his birth secret, spreading falsehoods to make sure that it could not be traced. It would seem that this was a ruse to ensure that if his evil deeds were discovered in the future, his relatives would not be implicated.

We assume that Gunki would not have traveled all the way to Nagasaki if he had not had any connections there, so Nagasu in Buzen may well have been his real place of birth, as Shōni testified. However, it is impossible to know for sure.

Soe was [earlier] registered under the name of Ōmiya Suma, resident in rental quarters owned by the aforementioned Riemon (now deceased). It is unclear when she married Gunki. She lived in Riemon's rental quarters for many years. When Gunki was dismissed by the Kan'in princely house, Riemon arranged for the registered name "Suma" to be transferred to the household of Minoya Bunsuke, who resides in Shichiken-chō on Nishikikōji street east of Ōmiya street. In the meantime, Gunki and Soe herself were first taken in by the aforementioned Kyūbei (now deceased) for a little while, and after that, they moved to the rental quarters owned by Shintarō (now deceased).

We arranged through Lord Kan'o to summon and question Bunsuke, and he stated as follows: "I was on friendly terms with Riemon. Riemon told me that Suma had absconded, and since there was nobody to transfer her name to, they couldn't finalize matters with those responsible for town block matters. He asked me to have just her name transferred to my household. Without thinking more about it I agreed. I had no idea that Suma was also called Soe or that she was Gunki's wife; in fact, I did not know this Gunki at all."

It appears that Bunsuke was deceived by Riemon, and since Riemon is now deceased, we do not know where Soe was born.

According to some parties to the incident, three other people were friendly with Gunki and might well know where he was born. These were Shimada Kinzaemon (also known as Sairin), who resides together with Shimadaya Uta in the first block of the highway running east of Shichiku village; Chūjirō Isshin, who resides together with Wakasaya Yūjirō in Gion-machi; and Uneme, an unregistered person. We arranged through Lord Kan'o to summon and question Sairin and Isshin. Uneme was formerly called Sugihara Umon and was a retainer of the Kan'in princely house. Twelve years ago, in the third month of 1816, he committed a crime in Osaka and was condemned to distant exile;[23] not long ago, he entered a place that was off-limits to him and was arrested for this. We questioned these three persons about Gunki's place of birth, but, just as with the people mentioned above, they all gave divergent answers, and it remains unclear.

In this manner, we extended our investigation to try to uncover the line of transmission to Gunki of Kirishitan practices and the origin of the drawing of the Lord of Heaven, but we found no answers. The circumstances of the case of Uneme's breach of exile have been clarified [and the testimony confirmed]. We have consulted with you separately [regarding the appropriate punishment].

Chapter 6

~

Kenzō and Others Implicated in the Investigation

TESTIMONY OF KENZŌ

Kenzō: fifty-seven years old; residing together with Zenbei in rented quarters in Funadaiku-machi in Dōjima in Osaka, managed by Matsumotoya Yuzō, who is represented before the magistrate by Okamotoya Tamizō

Remanded to jail on the twenty-first day of the intercalary sixth month, 1827

Under interrogation Kenzō stated that he had been on friendly terms with the abovementioned Mizuhaya Hida (now deceased); this matches the testimony of Umon.

Kenzō's Testimony Proper

I am the son of Genzō, farmer in Yamasaki village, Awa province [in Shikoku]. In 1798 I was adopted by the physician Fujita Kyōan of Shinchi 1-chōme in Dōjima in Osaka as the husband of his daughter Shū.[1] My adoptive father died on the eighth day of the sixth month of 1803. I have read most of the medical works and Confucian literature available. I have been particularly interested in Western medicine, and I have regularly purchased rare books. Although works of the Jesus creed are proscribed, I used to buy them whenever I came across any, without giving any thought [to the proscription]. *(Investigators: Kenzō declared that he did*

not remember where or from whom he had bought such books, because it was
a long time ago. Because these dangerous books are strictly proscribed, we
interrogated him severely about his suppliers. He insisted that he did not
remember the sellers because so many years had passed, and he said he
repented this deeply.)

Hida was a fellow physician and a friend, and we used to lend each
other medical books. Some years ago, I met a messenger from Hida on
the road, who asked me to lend [Hida] the work *Comprehensive Compen-*
dium of Healing; but if I remember correctly, I had already lent this book
to someone else, so I declined. Perhaps it was Umon who brought Hida's
request, but this person did not give his name and I do not remember
his face.[2]

My business was not doing well, and I fell into poverty. I speculated
on the Dōjima rice exchange and suffered losses.[3] I borrowed money elsewhere to make up for those losses, but it was not enough. I pawned
everything I could, including the house owned by my late adoptive father
and out-of-town rental properties, but my creditors constantly harassed
me to repay my debts, and in the end it became impossible to sustain my
household.[4] I sold the more expensive among my medical works and Confucian books, but I kept the books on Western medicine, astronomy, and
geography, and also the works of the Jesus creed.

Six years ago, on the sixth day of the eleventh month of 1822, I fled
Osaka, leaving behind my adoptive mother, Tame, and my wife, Shū. I
went into hiding here and there before returning to the city in the fifth
month of the following year, 1823. I contacted some acquaintances and
asked them what the situation was. They told me that when I failed to
return the previous year, my creditors had petitioned the magistracy to
allow them to redeem what they were owed. The remaining household
goods were transferred to Tame, but the houses and land were all handed
over to those who had received them in pawn. Tame and Shū had been
taken in by Hirotaniya Sōyū of Shinchi 1-chōme in Dōjima, and all the
debts were cleared.

My immediate worries having been alleviated, I went to Sōyū's place
on the eighth day of the sixth month of the same year. I reported my
return to the magistracy and petitioned to have my name removed from
the list of absconded persons.[5] Then Matsumotoya Rihei of Funadaiku-
machi in Dōjima agreed to take in myself, Tame, and Shū. Since I had
forfeited the household of my adoptive father, I could not show my face to

the world and stayed inside as though I were under house arrest.[6] Yet I still had the ambition to improve my skills in Western medicine. I was convinced that unless I thoroughly studied various aspects of the countries of the West, I would not be able to grasp the deeper meaning of their medical learning. Therefore I held on to my books about [Western] astronomy and geography as well as those of the Jesus creed. I also noted down what I had learned in a small booklet that I titled "The Torch of Rhinoceros Horn, Draft."[7] Then Umon's testimony cast suspicion on me, and I was arrested and placed under investigation. I repent deeply that this has happened.

Mizuno Gunki was not an acquaintance of mine. Although I own books of the Jesus creed, I have never worshipped the Lord of Heaven nor engaged in the practices [of the Kirishitan sect].

Investigators' Comments on the Books Confiscated from Kenzō

We confiscated the Western works of medicine, astronomy, and geography, as well as the books of the banned Jesus creed in Kenzō's possession, and we have submitted them [to the Osaka governor] together with a list of their titles.[8] When we questioned Kenzō about his possession of four copies of *fumie*, he stated that he had gotten them when he visited Kyoto some years ago. The person from whom he received them looked like an itinerant Zen monk and was staying in the same inn. Kenzō said that he didn't know the monk's name or where he was from.

Investigators' Summation of Kenzō's Interrogation

We confronted Kenzō with the following accusation:

> After you ruined the household of your adoptive father, you were no longer in a position to practice your profession openly even if you kept studying, however proficient you might become in astronomy, geography, or medicine. Yet, using the study of Western medicine as a pretext, you delved into astronomy and geography, and on top of that you were in possession of proscribed books of the Jesus creed. Certainly you must have been an acquaintance of Gunki's, and you must have received these

books of the Jesus creed from him. You must have conspired with Gunki for a long time, plotting wicked deeds and praying to the Lord of Heaven.

We repeatedly subjected Kenzō to severe interrogation on these points. To this he responded as follows: "That is not at all the case. To be sure, having read widely in all kinds of miscellaneous works of deviant schools, I searched out these proscribed books and I rashly engaged in writing [about what I learned from them]. I regret this and repent deeply my behavior." When we declared to him that the interrogation had clarified that these actions, as detailed above, constitute crimes, he stated that he had nothing to say in opposition [to what is recorded here] and is filled with remorse.

Investigators' Comments About Whether Kenzō Should Be Included in This Case

Umon's testimony gave the impression that Kenzō was a member of Gunki's group, and we had an investigation conducted to see if there were any rumors about this. Although nothing specific could be discovered, there is no doubt that Kenzō did own suspect books, as Umon has testified. When Kenzō was arrested, we had his house searched and found that he owned the books described in the preceding addendum. Under interrogation he maintained that he had no relations with Gunki, but since he is the owner of such criminal books, we inquire whether we should include him as one of the parties to this case.

TESTIMONY OF THE PRIEST OF THE TEMPLE WITH WHICH MIZUNO GUNKI WAS AFFILIATED

Daizui: thirty-one years old in 1827; priest of the [Nishi] Honganji branch temple Unseiji,[9] Kyoto, located at the intersection of Samegai and Uonotana streets, south of Gojō street, the temple where the deceased Mizuno Gunki was registered; provisionally confined to his temple

Also summoned: the priests of Unseiji's temple group

Under interrogation Daizui stated that Shōni and his fellows asked Unseiji to take care of Gunki's remains following his death and to arrange for his cremation. In these particulars, Daizui's testimony matches that of Shōni and his fellows. His testimony is as follows:

At the time of his death, Gunki was living in temporary lodgings and had no settled rental residence, but he had been a parishioner of Unseiji since the time he lived in the rental quarters owned by Riemon, [and thus I agreed to handle this matter]. As I was ill, I sent a deputy priest, who checked the corpse and determined that Gunki had died of natural causes. The temple thus saw to the cremation. As the Kirishitan sect has long been proscribed, I have always scrupulously checked [to make sure my parishioners are not Kirishitan]. It is only as a result of the present investigation that I have learned that Gunki had his fellow devotees worship a drawing of the Lord of Heaven, write out sacred oaths, and drip blood on the drawing. Not only that, he also transmitted the practices of the pernicious creed to them, explained things written in books of the Jesus creed, and even engaged in sorcery. This indeed shows that Gunki was without question secretly a believer of the Kirishitan sect, and I repent deeply [not having realized this].

Investigators' Summation of Their Interrogation of Daizui

We declared to Daizui that the investigation has fully clarified that his dereliction in his duty to look properly [into Gunki's behavior prior to] certifying his temple affiliation constitutes a misdeed. He states that he has nothing to say in opposition to this.

Investigators' Addendum Regarding Whether or Not Gunki Had a Grave

We questioned Daizui about whether or not Gunki had a grave. He replied that the bones and ashes had been abandoned after the cremation and that there was no grave or gravestone for Gunki, either within the temple grounds or elsewhere. We again questioned Shōni and Masasuke, who had seen to Gunki's funeral at the time of his death, as to why they had not erected a gravestone. They responded as follows:

Gunki had greatly changed from before and at the time of his death was in a miserable condition. On his deathbed he said repeatedly that he bitterly regretted that he had deviated from the purpose he had set himself when he was in his prime. When he died, he told us, we should just have his body cremated and abandon the bones and ashes. If we were to erect a gravestone it would simply call attention to his disgrace. But although we did not erect a gravestone, we recovered the throat bone from the ashes and had it deposited in the opening in the side of the [Nishi Honganji] ossuary at Ōtani.[10]

We also interrogated Makijirō on these points. He testified that as he was still a child at the time, he was not aware of any of the decisions made. He had assumed that Shōni and the others had kindly arranged for a gravestone and had not pursued the matter any further. It was only as a result of the present investigation that he learned that Gunki on his deathbed had told Shōni and the others simply to have his body cremated and to abandon the ashes.

Regarding [the lack of a gravestone], Daizui additionally stated as follows: "I didn't know anything about Gunki's having left a statement at the time of his death. I assumed that as he had fallen into penury, it wasn't possible to put up a gravestone. Following the directions from Shōni and the others, I had him cremated in the same manner as other paupers and didn't encourage them to put up a gravestone. That is how things remained up to the present investigation." The place called Ōtani is in the Higashiyama area on the outskirts of Kyoto. When parishioners of the Ikkō sect die, they are cremated and their throat bones are put in one of the ossuaries there.

TESTIMONY OF THE PRIESTS OF THE TEMPLES WITH WHICH THE OTHER MAIN PARTIES TO THE INCIDENT WERE AFFILIATED

Shōryū: forty-four years old in 1827; priest of the Ikkō temple Enkōji, a branch temple of Bukkōji, located in the village of Kita Miyahara, Nishinari county, Settsu province, in the holdings of Amenomiya Gonzaemon, the temple where Kyōya Shinsuke's mother, Sano, is registered; provisionally confined to his temple
Also summoned: the priests of Enkōji's temple group

Zenshō: fifteen years old in 1827; priest of the Higashi Honganji branch temple Rentakuji, located in Tenma 1-chōme, Osaka, the temple where

Kinu, resident together with Harimaya Tōzō, is registered; provisionally confined to his temple
   Also summoned: the priests of Rentakuji's temple group

Zekan: twenty-nine years old in 1827; priest of Daijōin, a subtemple of the Nichiren temple Chōmyōji, located on Nijō street, on the east side of the Kamo River, Kyoto, the temple where Toyoda Mitsugi is registered; provisionally confined to his temple
   Also summoned: the priests of Daijōin's temple group

Kanryō: thirty-nine years old in 1827; priest of the [Nishi] Honganji branch temple Jōkōji, located in Shirokoura-machi, Osaka, the temple where Fujii Umon is registered; provisionally confined to his temple
   Also summoned: the priests of Jōkōji's temple group

Kōhō: thirty-six years old in 1827; priest of the Rinzai Zen Myōshinji branch temple Kanzanji, located in Nishi Tera-machi in Tenma, Osaka, the temple where Takamiya Heizō is registered; provisionally confined to his temple
   Also summoned: the priests of Kanzanji's temple group

Under interrogation, these priests all testified as follows:

Sano, Kinu, Mitsugi, Umon, and Heizō are without doubt our respective parishioners. As the Kirishitan sect has long been proscribed, we have always scrupulously made sure [that our parishioners are not Kirishitan]. It is only as a result of the present investigation that we have learned that these parishioners worshipped a drawing of the Lord of Heaven possessed by Mizuno Gunki, submitted sacred oaths to him, dripped their blood on the drawing, prayed regularly to the Lord of Heaven, and engaged in the practices of the pernicious creed. We repent deeply [not having realized this].

Investigators' Summation of Their Interrogation of the Other Temples

We declared to these priests that the investigation has fully clarified that their dereliction in their duty to look properly into their parishioners' behavior before issuing certificates of sectarian affiliation constitutes a misdeed. They state that they have nothing to say in opposition to this.

Investigators' Addendum Concerning the Temple Affiliation of Itoya Wasa

As recorded in the report on Mitsugi's interrogation, Itoya Wasa had been registered as affiliated with Daijōin. This was confirmed through the questioning of Zekan and also of Wasa's daughters, Ito and Toki. When Wasa died ten years ago in the fourth month of 1818, the priest at the time, Ijō, handled [the funerary arrangements]. Ijō himself died subsequently, and Zekan became the temple priest only five years ago, in 1823. He has testified as follows: "Although I did not personally know Wasa, I understand that Daijōin arranged her cremation, and her grave is indeed within the temple precincts. It was only as a result of the present investigation that I learned that Wasa, too, was a follower of Gunki's pernicious creed, and I am deeply shocked."

TESTIMONY OF TAKEUCHI ŌMI

Takeuchi Ōmi: forty years old in 1827; retainer of the Tsuchimikado house

Under interrogation, Takeuchi Ōmi stated that some years ago Mitsugi became a yin-yang diviner under the supervision of the Tsuchimikado house through the sponsorship of his father, Chikugo. His testimony in this regard matches that of Mitsugi. His testimony is as follows:

> Five retainers of the Tsuchimikado house supervise the yin-yang diviners of Kyoto. Mitsugi was under the supervision of Chikugo, but he had grown old and feeble, so I performed his duties as supervisor in his stead. We have always stressed to all the diviners, including Mitsugi, that no diviner is to engage in activities unbefitting of the profession. We heard that Mitsugi's business was flourishing, but both Chikugo and I had the impression that she had so many clients because of her skill at *Yijing* divination. Subsequent to Mitsugi's arrest, Chikugo fell ill and died on the seventeenth day of the eighth month of 1827, and the Tsuchimikado house directed me to take over his position. It is only as a result of this investigation that I have learned that Mitsugi was merely

acting nominally as a yin-yang diviner. In fact while performing in the guise of an Inari medium, she had received secret transmissions of the Kirishitan creed from Mizuno Gunki and was practicing its pernicious arts. It is also only now that I have learned that Mitsugi was involved in the evil deed of transmitting these arts to Kinu and others. I am deeply shocked.

Investigators' Summation of Their Interrogation of Takeuchi Ōmi

We confronted Ōmi with the following accusation and interrogated him severely: "In fact you undoubtedly long realized that Mitsugi was practicing pernicious arts but simply took bribes from her and pretended not to know." He insisted that this was not the case, whereupon we declared that the present investigation has fully clarified that he had been extremely inattentive and that his laxity in giving instructions to the yin-yang diviners constitutes a misdeed. He states that he has nothing to say in opposition to this.

Investigators' Addendum Regarding the Investigation of Takeuchi Ōmi

Since Mitsugi had been practicing pernicious arts, it appeared that the Tsuchimikado retainer responsible for supervising yin-yang diviners had been negligent in his duties. We sent a memorandum to [the Osaka governor], asking whether it would be appropriate to consult the supervisors of court personnel about directing the court liaison officers to have the Tsuchimikado house dispatch this retainer to us together with an accompanying responsible figure.[11] We received instructions from the governor to do so, and when we consulted the supervisors of court personnel, they arranged for the Tsuchimikado house to send Takeuchi Ōmi to us, accompanied by another Tsuchimikado retainer. Upon our questioning of Ōmi and the other retainer, they confirmed the points stated in Ōmi's testimony. That is, yin-yang diviners are divided into groups, each of which is under the supervision of a retainer of the Tsuchimikado house, and Mitsugi did indeed belong to the group under Ōmi's supervision. They further stated as follows:

The yin-yang divination conducted by the Tsuchimikado house is based solely on the *Yijing*. The things Mitsugi did—making effigies, piercing them with nails, issuing strange judgments, collecting money at will, engaging in ascetic training to secure an unwavering mind by standing under waterfalls or going into the mountains at night, closing people's eyes with deviant secret spells—are all without question pernicious arts. We repent deeply [that we did not realize she was doing such things].[12]

We attach a separate report on their statement.[13]

TESTIMONY OF THOSE RESPONSIBLE FOR THE LOCALE

The landlords, village headmen, and village aldermen of the rural districts where Sano and Fujii Umon resided

The landlords, block aldermen, and five-household groups of the urban districts where Kinu and Takamiya Heizō resided

The block alderman and five-household group of the town block where Toyoda Mitsugi resided

Under interrogation, these persons testified as follows:

As the Kirishitan sect has long been proscribed, we have always scrupulously checked [to be sure that those for whom we are responsible are not Kirishitan]. Nevertheless we remained unaware that Sano, Kinu, Mitsugi, Umon, and Heizō received transmissions of the pernicious Kirishitan creed, prayed to the Lord of Heaven, and, in addition, engaged in pernicious arts and appropriated people's money and goods. Moreover, Kinu's landlord and those responsible for the matters of her locale did not realize that she had asked Kahei to register Tōzō as her household head without Tōzō's consent, that Kahei presented Tōzō's name and house name as being that of one of his servants, and that Tōzō consequently ended up listed in two different population registers. It is only as the result of the present investigation that we have learned these things, and we deeply repent [our lack of attention].

Investigators' Summation of Their Interrogation of Those Responsible for the Locale

We declared to these people that the investigation has fully clarified that their laxity [in failing to look properly into the behavior of those for whom they are responsible] constitutes a misdeed. They state that they have nothing to say in opposition to this.

Investigators' Addendum Regarding the Investigation of Those Responsible for the Locale Where Itoya Wasa Resided

Wasa, who is mentioned in an addendum to Mitsugi's testimony, arranged for Mitsugi to become Gunki's disciple, and Gunki engaged in sorcery at her house. Moreover, Wasa's adoptive daughter Toki saw Wasa herself make paper effigies and pray. Wasa even tried to force Toki to undergo ascetic training in her stead, sent Toki to Mitsugi, and punished her mercilessly when she resisted. All this leaves no doubt that Wasa was one of the followers of Gunki's pernicious creed. As Wasa would have faced severe punishment if she were still alive, we thought we should investigate her landlord, the people who had served at the time as block aldermen, and the members of her landlord's five-household group. We thus arranged through the Kyoto eastern magistrate, Lord Kan'o, to have these people summoned and questioned. However, it turned out that her landlord, Iseya Rihei; her block alderman, Izumiya Mataemon; and the members of Rihei's five-household group at the time had all died more than eight years ago. Responsibility for the locale has thus passed into new hands, and the successors have no knowledge whatsoever of events in Wasa's time. We therefore did not carry this line of investigation to a conclusion.

Investigators' Addendum Regarding Having the Parties to the Incident Tread on *Fumie*

Sano, Kinu, Mitsugi, Umon, and Heizō have all confessed their involvement with the pernicious creed and face severe punishment; therefore, we have not ordered them to tread on *fumie*. Among their associates and relatives, Iseya Kanzō's wife, Toki; Mitsugi's adoptive son, Kamon; Umon's wife, Fusa; Heizō's wife, Mutsu; Tsuchiya Shōni; Gunki's son, Makijirō;

and Itoya Wasa's adoptive daughters, Ito and Toki, will likely face exile to a remote island or another form of exile. We therefore had all of them tread on *fumie* at the magistracy.[14] They all trod upon the image without resisting, and none among them behaved in a suspicious manner.

Part II

THE JUDICIAL REVIEW PROCESS

The first stage of the investigation of the Keihan Kirishitan incident concluded with the compilation of the confirmed testimonies. As mentioned in the introduction, the Osaka Magistracy had broad investigative authority, but its prerogatives regarding sentences were constrained. The Osaka magistrates had to consult the Osaka governor about all sentences before handing them down, and the governor in turn frequently forwarded the inquiries he received to the senior councillors in Edo, particularly if a case presented complications. In the ninth month of 1827, Takai Sanenori, the Osaka eastern magistrate, set this process of judicial review in motion by submitting the materials on the investigation of the Keihan Kirishitan incident to the Osaka governor. The governor directed Takai to make some adjustments and then sent the amended dossier on to Edo. There the dossier underwent further examination. The review process produced the documents translated in chapters 7, 8, and 9. For convenience, we have numbered these documents in chronological order and given them headings, and we refer to them here by those numbers.

PRECEDENT AND THE ROLE OF THE DELIBERATIVE COUNCIL

A key feature of deciding upon a sentence was evaluation of the case in light of the precedents provided by earlier decisions. When an Osaka magistrate submitted a case for review by the governor, he prepared a dossier of the confirmed testimonies. To this he added summations of the charges against the various parties to the case, each of which usually concluded with the punishment that the magistrate regarded as appropriate. The summations (known as *kigami*, "yellow papers," perhaps because originally they were written on yellow paper) were in effect a draft of the verdict to be pronounced at the ultimate sentencing. The proposed punishment was phrased in a tentative manner, as being subject to the governor's approval. On occasion the magistrate did not include the proposed punishment in the summation and instead appended a separate "proposal for punishments" (known as *oshiokizuke-gaki* for serious crimes and *otogamezuke-gaki* for lesser misdeeds). In these proposals he weighed the relative degrees of culpability of the different parties in comparison with one another, as well as with similar cases decided previously and kept on file in the magistracy. If the governor held the case to fall fully under his competence, he would append his response and directions to the dossier and return it to the magistrate. If the governor felt that the case required further consideration at a higher level, he would forward it to Edo, where the dossier would receive additional scrutiny.[1] For this further review, the senior councillors often sought the opinion of the Deliberative Council.

The Deliberative Council was a kind of judicial cabinet made up of the officials serving in the three main Edo-based administrative magistracies: the two town magistrates (or Edo magistrates, *machi bugyō*), the two financial and judicial affairs magistrates (*kanjō bugyō*) responsible for managing judicial matters, and the four temples and shrines magistrates (*jisha bugyō*). These members of the council were supported by a permanent staff of judicial clerks (*tomeyaku*) who did the groundwork for the deliberations. The Deliberative Council did not function as a court of appeal, and it did not reconsider the facts of the case or try to gather additional evidence. Rather, it focused on the appropriateness of the proposed sentences. It might affirm the punishments proposed by the investigating official, or it might recommend that they be adjusted in one way or another. In either instance it submitted its recommendations to the senior councillors, who by and large adopted them and directed the official who had referred the case to proceed accordingly in pronouncing and implementing the sentences.[2]

By the first decades of the nineteenth century the senior councillors and Deliberative Council standardly made use of two resources in their evaluations of proposed sentences. The first was Rules for Deciding Judicial Matters (*Kujikata osadamegaki*), a set of standardized criteria for punishments compiled in the 1730s and 1740s under the eighth shogun, Yoshimune (1684–1751; r. 1716–1745). This collection listed a wide range of crimes; for each it drew from earlier edicts and decisions to specify the punishments appropriate to particular circumstances, such as whether the person being sentenced had been the main perpetrator or had played an abetting role, and so forth.[3]

The Rules for Deciding Judicial Matters were compiled for use by the central administrative offices, and in principle the work was open only to them and to the two major regional representatives of shogunal authority, the Kyoto and Osaka governors. In actuality, copies of it circulated widely, and local magistrates such as the Osaka magistrate put together dossiers on criminal cases with its provisions in mind, even if they did not refer specifically to the Rules in their summations and proposals for punishments. Because the Rules were intended to serve as a general standard, however, they alone were often not a sufficient basis for arriving at a judgment in a given case. The body of specific decisions in individual cases that had accumulated over the years of Tokugawa rule was thus the second resource that officials looked to as a guide for reaching and evaluating judgments. Local officials (in this case the Osaka magistrate and governor) would already have turned to precedents of similar cases on file in their own jurisdiction; the Deliberative Council in Edo had at its disposal a much larger archive of cases submitted for review from the entire range of shogunal administrative offices. The adjustments in sentences that it recommended frequently set aside precedents adduced by the referring official in favor of others that the council saw as more pertinent to the case under consideration.

To facilitate the identification of appropriate precedents from within its ever-expanding archive, the Deliberative Council began at the end of the eighteenth century to compile indexes of representative cases. The initial volumes of the most notable of these indexes, the Precedents of

Criminal Judgments Organized by Category (*Oshioki reiruishū*), were compiled in 1804 and comprised cases dating from 1771 to 1802. By 1827 there were three such compilations. Eventually there would be five, covering up to 1852. The fifth was lost in the 1923 Kantō earthquake and is no longer extant, but the four existing compilations come to sixteen volumes in a modern printed edition. Copies were provided to the Kyoto and Osaka governors, and they were permitted to allow the Kyoto and Osaka magistrates under their supervision to view precedents from the compilation in their presence.[4]

Given the weight placed on precedent in Tokugawa jurisprudence, one of the major challenges of the Keihan Kirishitan incident was the lack of similar cases in the recent or even more distant past. Takai Sanenori, the Osaka eastern magistrate, noted this lack in a statement that he appended to the end of the confirmed testimonies when he consulted the Osaka governor about how to proceed (document 1): "Never before has there been an investigation in this city [of Osaka] of perpetrators of these kinds of evil acts. . . . Thus there appear to be no appropriate precedents to cite [in recommending punishments]." For this reason, the summations in the dossier prepared by Takai and his staff for submission to the governor did not conclude with the usual recommendation of a punishment; each trailed off without the expected final phrase, "Thus . . ." (document 2). Nor did Takai initially append a separate proposal for punishments in place of the missing proposed verdicts.

The Osaka governor, and subsequently officials in Edo, faced the same problem. Perhaps because the compilers of the Rules for Deciding Judicial Matters did not envision having to deal with Kirishitan as an immediate issue, its list of crimes and punishments did not include anything about such people. The only subversive creeds it referred to explicitly were the banned Nichiren offshoots Sanchō-ha and Fuju Fuse, covered in article 52.[5] The three compilations of the Precedents of Criminal Judgments completed by 1827 took up irregular religious activities under categories such as "deviant practices, strange acts, and deviant theses" (*ihō kikai isetsu*). Under such rubrics the compilers incorporated excerpts from cases of other Buddhist-inspired groups held to be deviant and instances of what might be termed religious charlatanry. These cases often adduce article 52's provisions as a benchmark for evaluating the matter at hand; the combination of references to earlier specific cases with such citations shows how the Precedents of Criminal Judgments functioned to extend and refine the criteria set out in the Rules. None of the three compilations, however, mention Kirishitan.[6] The refrain that the Keihan case was unprecedented would recur repeatedly in the deliberations on it.

PREPARING THE DOSSIER AND ITS REVIEW IN EDO

For several months after Sano's arrest in the first month of 1827 the investigation progressed only slowly. The pace picked up after Mitsugi was remanded to jail in the middle of the sixth month, with the remaining principals being arrested over the course of the next month (in 1827 the addition of an intercalary month meant that there were two sixth months in succession). The final arrests came with the remanding to jail of Yatarō and Makijirō on the eighteenth day of the seventh month.

Throughout this time Ōshio and his colleagues were busy with the interrogations, writing up the testimonies, and securing their confirmation. The poet and scholar Rai San'yō (1780–1832), who happened to visit his friend Ōshio on the fifteenth day of the intercalary sixth month, recorded that the demands of Ōshio's duties at the magistracy had required him to leave his guest to follow up matters there. On the fifth day of the eighth month Ōshio wrote to another friend then in Edo that work at the magistracy was keeping him "inordinately busy" and that he was "going to the jailhouse every day."[7] The dossier on the Keihan Kirishitan case was at length completed some weeks later, and the eastern Osaka magistrate, Takai Sanenori, submitted it to the Osaka governor for review in the ninth month of 1827.

The dossier contained the confirmed testimonies with the various addenda in red, a list of the books and other materials confiscated from Kenzō and Shōni (for this, see appendix 2), and summations of the charges against the principal parties to the incident (document 2). As mentioned, however, the summations did not include the punishments that the investigating magistrate held to be appropriate. Nor did Takai append a separate "proposal for punishments." The Osaka governor thereupon instructed Takai to consult with the western Osaka magistrate, Naitō Noritomo, and to formulate such a proposal for punishments based on comparable cases, even if there were no direct precedents. The governor evidently also allowed Takai to examine the copy of the Precedents of Criminal Judgments kept by the governor (see documents 3 and 5).

Following these instructions and in consultation with the western magistrate, Takai "extrapolated from comparable cases" to come up with a proposal for punishments for the principal figures in the incident, the major secondary figures, and those whose relationship to these figures made them liable to punishment according to the principle of collective responsibility (document 3). He submitted this proposal to the governor somewhat later in the ninth month along with an inquiry about how to apply the principle of collective responsibility to Mitsugi's aged and senile mother (document 4). Takai subsequently submitted a further proposal in the tenth month concerning the more minor secondary figures, whom he expected to receive less-severe punishments (document 5).

At some point after receiving these materials, the Osaka governor for-warded the entire dossier on the investigation to the senior councillors in Edo for their consideration. Exactly when this was or what happened to the dossier between the time it was sent to Edo and the tenth month of the following year, 1828, is not clear. Possibly there was further correspondence between Edo and Osaka that is not available to us. Whatever the reason for the delay, our next information about the case's progress comes from Deliberative Council records, which relate that on 1828.10.22, the senior councillors handed the dossier down to the council with directions to report its opinions on the matter (document 6).

Here the review took a dramatic turn. In the same document 6, which the council submitted to the senior councillors six months later in the fifth month of 1829, the council members expressed reservations about the out-come of the investigation and questioned whether Mitsugi and the oth-ers should properly be considered "Kirishitan" at all. The absence of any specifications in the Rules regarding the punishment of Kirishitan and of any precedents meant that there was no reliable information for gaug-ing what a Kirishitan was. And since Mizuno Gunki had died prior to the investigation, the sources of his practices could not be known.

The council members' reservations were not limited to procedural issues. They also questioned the Osaka Eastern Magistracy's interpreta-tion of the evidence it had gathered. "If it is a matter of using strange arts to startle people with extraordinary things," the council stated bluntly, "devotees of the Kirishitan sect are not the only ones to do so." The council had considered only recently incidents of charlatanry involving fake medi-ums and the use of paper effigies in prayer rituals to release clients from purported possession by vengeful spirits.[8] It would not be surprising if its staff recalled such incidents in reviewing the testimonies of Mitsugi, Kinu, and Sano.

The council pointed also to the problematic implications of Sano's statement that she had visited Nagasaki with the express intent of stepping on a *fumie* and that doing so had strengthened her faith. Underground Kirishitan in the Nagasaki area and other regions of Kyushu had long managed to maintain their faith while accommodating to the necessity to routinely tread on *fumie*. Despite this tacit subversion of the *fumie* system the lack of overt challenges to it from the mid-Edo period on reinforced a supposition that readiness to tread on a *fumie* guaranteed that one was not Kirishitan. In the case of the 1805 investigation of Kyushu villagers, for instance, this readiness served as one of the grounds for sidestepping the possibility that the villagers might be Kirishitan and concluding instead that they simply had engaged mistakenly in the practices of an unnamed "deviant creed."[9] In the eyes of the Deliberative Council, Sano's having actively sought out an opportunity to tread on the *fumie* was further evidence that she and her fellows were not really Kirishitan. At the same time, were her account to be accepted at face value, it would upend the presumption that one who showed no qualms in stepping on a *fumie* could not be Kirishitan and undermine the established mechanism for testing those who might be hiding such inclinations. This in turn would compromise enforcement of the proscription of the pernicious sect.

Confronting these complications, the Deliberative Council made a radical proposal: perhaps the entire dossier should be returned to the Osaka Eastern Magistracy with orders to redo the investigation. Although the council often recommended the adjustment of a proposed sentence, it almost never called into question the original investigators' findings about the facts of the matter. To do so, it was felt, would derogate from the authority of the magistrate responsible, and by extension from that of the shogunal government as a whole.[10]

The unusual suggestion that the senior councillors should order the investigation to be redone had an intriguing subtext: between the time the dossier on the incident had been forwarded to Edo from Osaka and the senior councillors had handed it down to the Deliberative Council, Naitō Noritomo, the Osaka western magistrate at the time of the incident, had been promoted to the Financial and Judicial Affairs Magistracy, and he was sitting on the council when it took up the dossier. Procedural protocol called for regular consultation between the two Osaka magistrates and their staffs regarding the conduct of a criminal investigation, and Takai Sanenori explicitly noted in his proposal for punishments that he consulted Naitō about them (document 3). It seems unlikely that the council would have challenged the Eastern Magistracy's conduct of the investigation had Naitō voiced support for it.

Perhaps Naitō had been dubious from an earlier stage about the investigation, but another factor may have been a sharp flare-up in tension between the two Osaka magistracies following his departure for Edo in the third month of 1829. That same month Ōshio Heihachirō received orders from Takai Sanenori, the eastern magistrate, to investigate corruption within the magistracy. Shortly after Naitō set off for Edo, Ōshio moved to arrest one of the western magistrate's most important and trusted senior staff officials, Yuge Shin'emon (d. 1829). The arrest was averted only by Yuge's preemptive suicide. The specific circumstances behind these events remain uncertain, but Ōshio counted the rooting out of "corrupt and evil officials" as the second of his major accomplishments during his service in the magistracy.[11] Naitō presumably saw the matter differently, and this might well have led him to take a cool view of Ōshio's "first accomplishment," the Keihan Kirishitan investigation.

The senior councillor responsible for overseeing the review of the Keihan Kirishitan case, Mizuno Tadaakira (1762–1834), acknowledged that the Deliberative Council's reservations were "reasonable," but he rejected the idea of ordering the investigation to be redone. Reopening it might cause doubts about government policy and make it more difficult to enforce the proscription of the Kirishitan sect. The council therefore should assume that the principal parties to the incident were indeed Kirishitan, as the investigating officials had decided, and consider appropriate punishments on that basis (document 7). In separate oral instructions, Mizuno added that as a general principle the council should opt for severe punishments (document 8). As a solution to the issue of Sano's having deliberately trodden on the *fumie*, he noted that it could not be known for sure that she had done so since there was no evidence apart from her own statement. All references to this episode should therefore be removed from the record of the investigation. To call for revision of confirmed testimony was highly unusual.[12] On the other hand, investigators were expected to check and corroborate the statements they gathered. The Osaka investigators' failure to provide evidence backing up this aspect of

Sano's story in effect served as a justification for the further irregularity of ordering it excised from the record.

Having received these instructions, the members and staff of the Deliberative Council put aside their reservations and proceeded to formulate recommendations for the sentences of all parties to the incident: the principals, secondary figures, and those caught up in it because of their relationship to people who were directly involved (document 9). The council submitted these recommendations to the senior councillors on 1829.7.8 (documents 10 and 11). First the council dealt with the matter of establishing a proper standard for weighing the crime of being a Kirishitan. Article 52 of the Rules for Deciding Judicial Matters, which specified punishments for various levels of involvement in Fuju Fuse and Sanchō-ha, had set exile to a remote island as the heaviest penalty, and sentences in cases of irregular religious activities usually adhered to this norm. In his proposal for punishments for the principals, Takai Sanenori had recommended adopting a more stringent criterion. Referring to a case where the norm of exile to a remote island had been applied, he had reasoned that the crimes of Mitsugi, Kinu, and Sano warranted "a far heavier punishment." Another case where the sentence had been crucifixion, one of the most severe forms of the death penalty, provided a better model (document 3).

We can assume that once it had been decided to treat the principal parties to the incident as Kirishitan, the Deliberative Council likewise saw crucifixion as the appropriate punishment. The issue now was how to mark out a juridically valid route to that conclusion. The precedent cited by Takai involved shrine priests who purportedly had abetted a popular protest by performing malevolent rites directed at a local official. The Osaka investigators had suspected the Keihan Kirishitan of harboring subversive intentions. They could not, however, find any evidence to support this suspicion and acknowledged that the principals consistently denied having plotted "wicked deeds." Presumably the council saw the case of the shrine priests as too divergent in character from the Keihan incident to serve as the precedent for levying the same penalty. It thus sought an alternative rationale for doing so. It adduced two grounds for pronouncing a more stringent sentence than the norm set out in article 52 of the Rules for Deciding Judicial Matters.

The council first pointed to provisions that had been adopted in the late seventeenth century for special surveillance of the relatives of apostate Kirishitan (*Kirishitan ruizoku*).[13] Those provisions, extending for generations, attested to the enormity of the threat Kirishitan posed and justified adopting a more severe criterion than article 52. Second, the council drew a connection with a crime for which the Rules did specify the punishment of crucifixion: circumventing the barriers set up at checkpoints along the major highways.[14] The council did not explain its reasoning, but we might surmise that it saw an analogy in that the prohibition of circumventing the barriers and the proscription of the Kirishitan sect were both fundamental shogunal laws, made known to all by being posted on signboards throughout the country.[15] Since what the Keihan Kirishitan had done was yet worse than circumventing a barrier, the council recommended that, "to set a warning example," they should receive the additional penalty of being paraded through Osaka prior to crucifixion (the Osaka eastern magistrate had also proposed this additional penalty).

For Mitsugi, Kinu, and Sano, the Deliberative Council affirmed the punishment proposed by Takai, although based on a different rationale. In other instances, however, it called for modification of the recommended sentence. Takai had differentiated between the degree of culpability of the three women and that of the three male principals. The three women not only engaged in pernicious practices that were strictly proscribed but also used them to extract money from their clients. Umon and Heizō, by contrast, were guilty of engaging in proscribed practices, but they had not pursued them for monetary gain. Takai thus proposed to sentence Umon and Heizō to decapitation with display of the head, a form of the death penalty that was a degree less severe than crucifixion. For Kenzō, who had not worshipped the Lord of Heaven and whom the magistracy hesitated to identify as in fact a Kirishitan, he proposed a yet less-severe form of execution (document 3). The Deliberative Council, however, following the senior councillors' instruction to recommend severe punishments in line with the magistracy's conclusion that the five main principals apart from Kenzō were Kirishitan, saw no grounds for treating the men (including Kenzō) leniently. It called for all six principals to receive the same sentence of crucifixion after having been paraded through Osaka (document 10).

The council also devoted much attention to the question of how to deal with those who were now to be defined as "relatives of Kirishitan." The Osaka Eastern Magistracy's proposals regarding the spouses and children of the principals had been based on the general norms of collective responsibility that were an underlying premise of Tokugawa law. Adopting the criteria applicable to "relatives of Kirishitan" meant expanding the scope of people affected and subjecting them to a higher degree of surveillance. The Osaka Eastern Magistracy had proposed levying sentences of varying levels of exile on Gunki's son, Makijirō; the adoptive children of Wasa and Mitsugi; and the wives of Umon and Heizō (document 3). By contrast, the Deliberative Council recommended that they should be kept under close supervision. All should be incarcerated indefinitely and a special enclosure constructed within the Osaka jailhouse in Matsuya-machi to house them. In line with the example of Kirishitan relatives of the early eighteenth century, they might eventually be released from incarceration if nothing untoward was detected in their behavior and instead put into the custody of the village headmen and town aldermen responsible for overseeing the affairs of their locale (documents 10 and 11).

Another knotty issue was what to do about the relatives of the "quasi-Kirishitan"; that is, those friends of Gunki and others whom the Osaka Eastern Magistracy suspected but could not confirm to have received the transmission of Kirishitan practices. As explained at the end of document 11, the council gave considerable thought to how to keep these people, too, under a degree of supervision, while still distinguishing them from those clearly identified as "relatives of Kirishitan."

The senior councillors received the Deliberative Council's recommendations at the beginning of the seventh month. For cases carrying severe punishments of exile to a remote island or one of the forms of the death penalty, the senior councillors typically sought approval from the shogun.[16] They likely followed this procedure in this instance, too. In any event the Deliberative Council's recommendations were accepted without modification, and in the eleventh month the senior councillors sent their orders regarding the sentences to the Osaka governor with directions to transmit them to the Osaka eastern magistrate. The orders, which the Osaka governor conveyed to the magistrate on the first day of the twelfth month, included a command to excise all references to Sano's visit to Nagasaki from the verdicts and to investigate whether there were any other people who might fall within the category of relatives of the Kirishitan and quasi-Kirishitan (document 12). Simultaneously the governor transmitted a memorandum with additional instructions from the senior councillors. Among these instructions was an order to excise references to Sano's Nagasaki visit from not only the verdicts but also all other records concerning the case. The magistracy was to burn the books and other written materials confiscated from Kenzō and Shōni (document 13).

On the fifth day of the twelfth month Takai pronounced the verdicts to the parties to the incident who were still alive at that point. For the principals, these verdicts were the same in content as the summations (document 2), adjusted in the case of Sano and Kinu to remove references to Sano's trip to Nagasaki, but with the addition of the punishment at the end. Two days later the magistrate reported to the senior councillors that the sentences had been carried out and confirmed his compliance with their other orders (documents 14, 15, and 16). He also sent an initial report on the measures he had taken regarding the relatives of Shintarō, one of the quasi-Kirishitan (document 17).

Apart from being announced to those directly concerned, the verdicts as a whole were not made public, as was true of all the records produced by the investigation. There was one important exception, however. Whereas most executions in the Edo period were not public, crucifixions largely were. Reserved for particularly heinous crimes, crucifixion and the ongoing display of the body were intended to serve as a warning and deterrent to others.[17] For the same reason, the verdict in such instances was also displayed. The verdicts handed down to Mitsugi and the other five principals were thus posted on placards at the Tobita execution grounds. Copies of them circulated rapidly and became one of the main sources of information about the incident.

SUBSEQUENT DEVELOPMENTS

The most complete copy of the dossier on the incident available today ends chronologically in the early twelfth month of 1829 with the carrying out of the sentences. A coda of sorts, however, exists in the Precedents of Criminal Judgments, and this enables us to follow the story a little further.

As noted previously, the first three compilations of the Precedents of Criminal Judgments contain no items concerning Kirishitan. Reflecting the impact of the Keihan incident, however, the fourth compilation (put together sometime after 1839) created a new category, "devotion to the Kirishitan sect," in addition to the rubric "deviant practices, strange acts, and deviant theses" under which cases involving irregular religious activities had been subsumed up to that point. The materials listed under "devotion to the Kirishitan sect" all derived from the Keihan incident. It thereby became the defining precedent for identifying and sentencing Kirishitan, should the need to deal with them arise again.

A large part of the materials concerning the Keihan incident in this fourth compilation of the Precedents of Criminal Judgments are excerpts from the summations (document 2) and the Deliberative Council's discussions of the case (documents 6–11). However, the compilation also covers developments that occurred after the early twelfth month of 1829. We have translated the most notable of these additional passages in chapter 10.

The first is a proclamation that served to disseminate wide awareness of the incident. In the memorandum of the fifth or sixth month of 1829 instructing the Deliberative Council to proceed on the assumption that Mitsugi and the others were Kirishitan, the senior councillors had proposed using this as an occasion to call for increased vigilance in checking on and certifying sectarian affiliation (document 7). The Deliberative Council incorporated this point in its overall conclusions about the case (document 11), and as soon as the sentences had been carried out, the senior councillors issued a nationwide proclamation calling for people everywhere to be on the watch for any signs of Kirishitan (document 18).[18]

The remainder of the documents in the Precedents of Criminal Judgments concerning the incident's aftermath are exchanges between Osaka officials and the senior councillors regarding those identified as relatives of the Kirishitan and quasi-Kirishitan. The senior councillors in turn sought the opinion of the Deliberative Council about the reports and inquiries received from Osaka. In the third and intercalary third months of 1830, for instance, the Osaka eastern magistrate reported on additional relatives of the principals who had been located and were presently detained in the Osaka jailhouse or otherwise placed under custody (documents 19 and 20). Many of these were related to Kenzō, whose connections had not been investigated as thoroughly as those of the others. Some had to be summoned from his native domain in Shikoku and also had quasi-warrior status. These circumstances required the Osaka Eastern Magistracy to observe procedural niceties similar to those noted earlier in regard to its dealings with people associated with the court nobility.[19]

Issues arising from the designation of the principals' kin as "relatives of Kirishitan" and the devising of special arrangements for the relatives of the quasi-Kirishitan led to other exchanges. In the first month of 1830 the eastern magistrate inquired about the format to be used for the certificates of sectarian affiliation for those falling into the latter category (document 21). Deaths among the relatives generated a series of inquiries about how to deal with their corpses. The first such inquiry concerned Mitsugi's aged mother, who died late in the twelfth month of 1829 (document 22). They culminated in the sixth month of 1830 with the report of the death of Ito, Wasa's adoptive daughter (document 23).

At the time the sentences were handed down, four identified relatives of the principals were still alive: Ito; Wasa's other adoptive daughter, Toki; Mitsugi's adoptive son, Kamon; and Heizō's wife, Mutsu. All had been ordered to be incarcerated for the time being within a special enclosure in the Osaka jailhouse. The remaining three apart from Ito evidently survived under those conditions for some years thereafter. Our last glimpse of them comes from an inquiry dating from the second month of 1836 in which the Osaka eastern magistrate of the time broached the possibility of their release from incarceration (document 24). The senior councillors consulted the Deliberative Council, which expressed reservations. Precedents from the early eighteenth century concerning relatives of Kirishitan who had been released from incarceration showed that all had been detained for a much longer span of time than the three still confined in the jailhouse. The senior councillors accordingly responded negatively to the Osaka inquiry.

A year later, in the second month of 1837, the Machiya-machi jailhouse burned down in the course of Ōshio's rebellion. Descriptions of its replacement, built in the fourth month of 1838, mention two small separate enclosures for "male and female devotees of the pernicious sect."[20] Were these enclosures intended to house again Toki and the other two? Or were they intended as a preparatory measure, in the event that other Kirishitan appeared in the Osaka area? Their reconstruction points to some of the Keihan incident's ongoing ripples.

The incident's impact on society in general can be seen most clearly in the Buddhist establishment's response. The head temples responsible for supervising the priests caught up in the incident moved quickly to add punitive measures of their own to those imposed by the shogunal authorities. They also sent out instructions to the networks of temples under their authority in which they disseminated the proclamation about being on the watch for Kirishitan and exhorted the temple priests to be vigilant in checking on their parishioners' behavior before certifying their sectarian affiliation. At the same time the head temples urged the priests to impress on their parishioners that the best way to avoid falling under suspicion as a possible Kirishitan was to be enthusiastic in support of their temple of affiliation and to call upon it regularly for the performance of memorial rites and other acts of devotion.[21]

For evidence of the incident's impact on administrative and judicial policy we must rely on more subtle signs. The loss of the fifth compilation of the Precedents of Criminal Judgments means that we cannot know if the category "devotion to the Kirishitan sect" inaugurated by the fourth was carried over into the next, or, if so, how the precedent of the Keihan incident was applied. We can, however, see indications that in the incident's wake officials showed a heightened attentiveness to the possibility that Kirishitan were at large in the land. In 1835, for instance, the Osaka Magistracy investigated another case of women using "rites of a deviant sect" to "delude ignorant and benighted farmers" and obtain offerings of money and clothing from them. The magistrate concluded that this case fit within the usual parameters of "deviant practices." The Deliberative Council concurred, and it was handled as such. But before reaching this decision, the council took care to confirm that there was no evidence of any connection with "the pernicious sect."[22]

A little over a decade later, Kawaji Toshiakira (1801–1868), who was then Nara magistrate but had served previously on the staff of the Temples and Shrines Magistracy, recorded his thoughts on a case handled by the latter magistracy shortly before the Keihan incident. It concerned a woman who adopted a nunlike guise and engaged in strange rites, using a doll that looked like a young boy. At the time, Kawaji had assumed that the woman was influenced by Nichiren practices, and she had been sentenced to banishment. Subsequently when he read the dossier on the Keihan incident, he noted that Mitsugi had used a depiction of Kikudōji, the "Chrysanthemum Child," as one of the substitute images for the Lord of Heaven. Recalling the doll along with the fact that the nunlike woman was originally from Kyoto, engaged in divination, and had remained celibate, he wondered if she was not in fact "the same sort as Mitsugi."

It so happened that sometime after this, the woman reappeared in an area that was supposed to be off-limits to her, still with a doll, and was rearrested. With his suspicions about the possible link to Mitsugi, Kawaji investigated her carefully. He also took the occasion to look into the sources on Christianity preserved in shogunal coffers. In the end he did not turn up any evidence of a Kirishitan link, and the woman was sentenced to exile to a remote island. Writing in 1848 about this episode, Kawaji reflected that the peace of the present age served as a bulwark against the dangers Kirishitan had posed in earlier periods. Nevertheless, using dubious rites to "confound the ignorant" should not be tolerated.[23]

When the Deliberative Council first reviewed the dossier on the Keihan incident in early 1829, it noted the absence of reliable information about Kirishitan and queried whether the incident's principals really should be considered as such. As the council members put it in their initial response to the senior councillors, Kirishitan were not the only ones to use "strange arts to startle people." The two instances here suggest that the decision to deal with the principals as Kirishitan encouraged the reverse proposition: people who engaged in activities similar to those of Mitsugi and her fellows might likewise be Kirishitan. For shogunal officials the incident thus served to endow the notion of "Kirishitan" with a new tangibility and immediacy.

Chapter 7

Submitting the Dossier for Review

1. THE OSAKA EASTERN MAGISTRATE'S REPORT TO THE OSAKA GOVERNOR; NINTH MONTH, 1827

The results of our investigation are as recorded in the preceding dossier. Never before has there been an investigation in this city [of Osaka] of perpetrators of these kinds of evil acts. It appears, however, that the popular mood here is turning unswervingly toward greed. Those who promote pernicious creeds may well take advantage of this. If they conspire to use sorcery to heal illnesses before people's eyes, foresee things that have yet to occur, and make people feel indebted to them, the ignorant farmers and townspeople [who are their clients] most probably will feel grateful and ask to have prayer rituals performed. Quite likely these people will then come up with the misguided idea that if the performers of these rituals can heal illness, they must also be able to conjure up money. Should ordinary people secretly become believers while hiding it even from their parents, children, and siblings, and should these practices spread throughout the world, the situation will become irremediable. I thus had the matter investigated thoroughly. As described in this dossier we have made arrests and brought the investigation to conclusion by having the accused confirm their recorded testimonies. However, as already noted, no such investigations have been conducted previously in this city, and thus there appear to be no appropriate precedents to cite [in recommending punishments]. I therefore ask for your guidance as to what to do about proposing punishments.

Takai Sanenori, ninth month, 1827

2. SUMMATIONS OF THE CHARGES; NINTH MONTH, 1827

Sano

When Sano was living in Kyoto, she forsook her [natural] sentiments as a woman and pursued the fallacious ambition to work miracles that would astound others. She thus attached herself as a disciple to Kinu, who introduced her to the strange arts practiced by Mitsugi. At first, Sano did not realize that this was the pernicious Kirishitan creed, but she became a disciple even though she was already aware that Kinu was not an Inari medium [as she pretended to be]. Pursuing ascetic training to secure an unwavering mind, she doused herself with well water and stood under waterfalls, and at night she went to frightening places in the mountains to harden her mind.

Subsequently, Sano agreed with Kinu to move to Osaka and rent quarters at some distance from Kinu's. She called herself an Inari medium and gathered clients, but because she had not yet received the transmission of the pernicious creed, she found it difficult to heal illness and make divinations. Time and again she sent her son, the late Shinsuke, to Kinu to have her carry out prayer rites and make judgments on Sano's behalf. During this time, Sano mortified her mind and body and through hard training attained an unwavering mind. She pledged never to confess the truth, even should she meet with severe punishment. Finally, she received secret transmissions from Kinu concerning the true deity of this creed, the Lord of Heaven, and the way to chant the mantra for praying to the deity. Kinu initiated her not only into how to perform prayer rites to heal illness and how to amass money but even into how to have knowledge of future events well up in her mind.

According to the transmission Sano received from Kinu, by nature the Lord of Heaven has no shape or form. Sano had heard, however, about the custom in Nagasaki of having people tread [every year] on *fumie*, and she thought the deity must have a likeness. She became consumed by the egregious notion that were she to go there and tread on the image out of faith so as to see this likeness, she would not be subject to [divine] punishment. Planning to arrive [at the beginning of the year] when people would be ordered to tread on the *fumie*, she traveled to Nagasaki and trod on the *fumie* at the inn where she was staying. Seeing the likeness in the image, she became all the more confirmed in her faith.

After Sano returned to Osaka,[1] she was able to predict events at will. She thus began to scheme to seek out like-minded people, live in prosperity, and spread the pernicious creed. She stealthily moved to her present rented quarters, and having made a disciple of Yae, she astounded and converted Kanzō and his wife, Toki, by showing them mysterious feats. She then used these three [to win further followers]. Sano had them say that she was a noblewoman from Kyoto living in retirement who promulgated a practice that could save those who were ill or otherwise troubled and bring prosperity. The three used various means to recommend the "noblewoman" to many people, beginning with Sano's landlord, Yohei. Meanwhile Sano prayed to the Lord of Heaven and performed the practices in the manner transmitted to her. As a result, people took leave of their senses and offered up excessive amounts of money and clothing. Sano appropriated these things and had Yae extract from some of those who made such offerings a secret pledge that they should receive divine punishment as severe as execution if they divulged this. From the money that she appropriated, Sano passed on a share as a token of gratitude to her master, Kinu. The rest she squandered together with Kanzō and Yae. Even worse, to bring about conversions, she disguised her chicanery by saying that the money appropriated would be used henceforth to assist the needy.

In all this, showing not the slightest awe for the shogunal authorities, Sano acted in a manner that was the height of audacity for a woman. She has committed multiple heinous crimes. Thus . . .[2]

Toki

It appears to be true that Toki did not receive transmission of the Kirishitan practices from Sano. However, Yae urged her to have faith in the [Inari] deity Sano worshipped, saying it would surely bring her prosperity. Hearing this and seeing with their own eyes the mysterious feats Sano performed, Toki and her deceased husband, Kanzō, were so impressed that they fell into working on Sano's behalf. They told others that Sano was a Kyoto noblewoman living in retirement and pretended that the noblewoman was lodging with them. Toki and Kanzō divided up the task with Yae, and the three went around urging people to have healing rituals performed to cure illnesses and prayers said for their prosperity and warning them that the noblewoman could mysteriously divine what they were doing. Since in the background Sano secretly worked her pernicious arts, those Toki and the others approached all took leave of their senses and offered up excessive amounts of money and clothing. Appropriating these, Sano had Kanzō take a share as well. Even if Toki did not know how much this came to, she has committed a crime. Thus . . .

Kinu

When Kinu was living in Kyoto, she forsook her [natural] sentiments as a woman and pursued the fallacious ambition to perform remarkable arts. Dissatisfied with being a common Inari medium, she became Mitsugi's follower. At first, Kinu did not realize that Mitsugi was a devotee of the pernicious Kirishitan creed, but she sought to receive the transmission of her secret methods. Pursuing ascetic training to secure an unwavering mind, she doused herself with well water and stood under waterfalls, and at night she went deep into the dark mountains to harden her mind. When at last Kinu attained an unwavering mind, Mitsugi told her about the transmissions of Kirishitan practices that Mitsugi had received from Gunki. Kinu pledged never to confess the truth, even were she to be subjected to the severest punishment. With as solemn a commitment as if she were swearing a sacred oath, she worshipped a drawing of the Lord of Heaven in Gunki's possession and dripped blood on it from her finger. She then received from Mitsugi the secret transmissions of how to chant the mantra for praying to this deity. Mitsugi initiated Kinu into how to perform prayer rites to heal illness and how to amass money; she even initiated her into how to have knowledge of future events well up in her mind.

Kinu continued with her training and recommended it to Sano, whom she accepted as her disciple. Initially she taught Sano only to enter the mountains and perform water austerities, and she did not yet pass on the transmission [of the Kirishitan creed] to her. They agreed to move to Osaka, and Kinu rented quarters some distance away from Sano's. She called herself an Inari medium and attracted clients. Sano's son, the late Shinsuke, constantly visited Kinu to ask her assistance in performing healing rites and divinations for Sano's clients. Kinu acted as Sano's shadow, using pernicious arts to conduct prayer rites and make judgments and receiving a share from the proceeds.

When Kinu observed that Sano's commitment was firm and that she had rigorously followed the training for attaining an unwavering mind, she had Sano make a pledge and passed on to her the secret transmissions as Kinu had received them from Mitsugi. Kinu thought that if she told Sano about her own worship of the drawing of the Lord of Heaven, it might seem as if the level of faith differed depending on whether or not [the practitioner had worshipped] the drawing. She thus told her that by nature the Lord of Heaven has no shape or form. But as a consequence, Sano became consumed by the egregious notion [of finding a way to see the Lord of Heaven's likeness], traveled to Nagasaki, trod on the *fumie*, saw the likeness on it, and became even more confirmed in her faith.[3]

Sano now attained mastery of the pernicious arts. Using Yae and others as her agents, she had them make unfounded claims and urge [prospective clients] to solicit prayer rites and the like. Taking leave of their senses, people came to offer up excessive amounts of money and clothing. Appropriating these, Sano passed [some of the proceeds] on to Kinu through Shinsuke as a token of gratitude to her master. Kinu then passed on a share to Mitsugi. This was in accord with the chicanery she had planned earlier with Mitsugi: Kinu would have her disciples spread the pernicious creed, these would send on the money they extorted [from their clients] to Kinu, and she would send on a share as tribute to her own master.

When Kinu moved to Osaka, she performed healing rites for Tōzō and for Kahei's infant son, and she made use of these connections to deceive Kahei, saying that Tōzō had agreed to act as her household head. Kahei made out that Tōzō was his servant and arranged rental quarters for Kinu, which he had recorded under a false household name for Tōzō. As a result, Tōzō ended up being recorded simultaneously in the population registers of two different blocks.

In all this, showing not the slightest awe for the shogunal authorities, Kinu acted in a manner that was the height of audacity for a woman. She has committed heinous crimes. Thus . . .

Tōzō

It does not appear that Tōzō had faith in the Kirishitan pernicious creed practiced by Kinu or that he agreed to become her household head out of a sense of obligation to her because she had healed his illness. Nevertheless, he visited her constantly, and although he had intimations that her quarters were rented in his name, he acted as if he knew nothing about it and ended up recorded in two different population registers. In this he has committed a crime. Thus . . .

Kahei

It does not appear that Kahei asked Kinu to perform prayer rituals to heal his son's illness out of faith in the Kirishitan pernicious creed that she practiced. Nevertheless, when Kinu told him she wanted to make Tōzō her household head, he should have looked into the matter thoroughly before acting as an intermediary in arranging rental quarters for her. He failed to do so. Instead, feeling obliged to Kinu for healing his son's illness, he arranged the rental without consulting Tōzō. Kahei made it as if Tōzō were his servant and registered a household name for him as if he were setting Tōzō up as a branch house. He also had Kinu added to Tōzō's population register as his grandmother. As a result of these suspect arrangements, Tōzō, who was already registered elsewhere, ended up recorded in the population registers of two different blocks. In this Kahei has committed a crime. Thus . . .

Mitsugi

Mitsugi forsook her [natural] sentiments as a woman and pursued the fallacious ambition to astound others by performing mysterious feats and thereby win fame in both the city and the countryside. She despised the work of Inari mediums as a mere game. Swearing her to silence, the late Gunki, whom she had met at Wasa's house, used sorcery to conjure up the likeness of a woman of whom Mitsugi was jealous, and she was much impressed by this. At the time, she did not realize that these were the pernicious arts of Kirishitan, but she wished to receive their transmission. As Gunki said these were not something to be transmitted lightly, she went at night to stand under waterfalls to make her mind firm. Thereupon she was initiated in what she was told were the secret arts of the Lord of Heaven. After paying a sum of money, she worshipped a drawing of the Lord of Heaven in Gunki's possession. With as solemn a commitment as if she were swearing a sacred oath, she dripped blood from her finger onto this portrait. Gunki then initiated her into how to chant the mantra for praying to this deity as well as how to perform prayer rites to heal illness and how to amass money. She even received the transmission of how to use secret signs in sorcery.

Mitsugi continued thereafter to perform water and mountain austerities to secure an unwavering mind. She set up a new house and began to make a living in the guise of an Inari medium. Following Gunki's instructions, she fabricated an irregular deity title for what she made out to be an Inari shrine, even though it lacked a proper deity body. She decorated the shrine's cloth furnishings with an irregular crest. She also had a set of three drawings mounted on scrolls to be used in place of the drawing of the Lord of Heaven.

Mitsugi's healing rituals and divinations were so successful that she excited the envy of Kinu, who asked Mitsugi to teach her the secret arts. Mitsugi taught her how to perform mountain and water austerities, and when she saw that Kinu had attained an unwavering mind, she had Kinu make a pledge. Mitsugi asked Gunki to allow Kinu to drip blood onto the drawing of the Lord of Heaven, and she initiated her into the secret transmission that she herself had received from Gunki. Kinu, in turn, initiated Sano, who now came to master the pernicious arts. Sano acquired disciples here in Osaka, whom she used as her agents to make unfounded claims [to prospective clients] and urge them to solicit prayer rites and the like. Taking leave of their senses, people offered up excessive amounts of money and clothing. Appropriating these, Sano passed a share of the money on to Kinu, who then sent some of it to Mitsugi as a token of gratitude to her master. In that Mitsugi accepted the money, her claim that she did not know about Sano's having appropriated it cannot be accepted. The arrangement was in accord with the chicanery she had planned earlier with Kinu: Kinu would have her disciples spread the pernicious creed and would send a share of the money they extorted [from their clients] as tribute to her own master.

Apart from this, when Wasa sent her daughter Toki to train with Mitsugi, Toki refused to perform the austerities Mitsugi pressed her to do. Enraged, Mitsugi punished Toki mercilessly. She took [her follower] Kinoshin to waterfalls, where she engaged in water austerities and performed strange feats. She also ignored the difficulties of her mother and elder brother and refused to help them. Instead she continued to pray to the Lord of Heaven year after year and to use pernicious arts to perform healing rituals. She was called a clairvoyant, just as she had hoped, and lived a life of inappropriate splendor.

In all this Mitsugi showed not the slightest awe for the shogunal authorities and acted in a manner that was the height of audacity for a woman. She has committed multiple heinous crimes. Thus . . .

Umon

Out of a fallacious ambition to achieve an undue degree of recognition, Umon studied the spells of the Shingon sect and performed Kangiten rites, but this did not bring any tangible results. Feeling that there must be a faster way, he consulted the late Gunki and was led astray by the pernicious argument that without money it would be difficult to do something exceptional. He paid Gunki some money and further submitted a sacred oath sealed in blood that he would never confess the truth, even were he to be subjected to the severest punishment. He then worshipped the drawing of the Lord of Heaven and received from Gunki the secret transmissions of how to chant the mantra of this deity and how to perform water austerities. He listened to Gunki's expositions of what is written in books by southern barbarians, which are proscribed because they deal with the Kirishitan creed. Even worse, he came up with his own interpretation that this sect "guides people to the true by way of the pernicious."

Umon concealed his faith even from his wife, and when he went periodically to visit Gunki, he pretended that he was going to Kyoto on business as a doctor. He also agreed to Gunki's request that he act as if he were Gunki's master, and under this guise was entertained by Mitsugi with food and drink. Subsequently he ceased to perform water austerities, but he continued to pray to the Lord of Heaven while pretending to invoke Kangiten. It is thus difficult to accept his claim that chronic ailments kept him from engaging in ascetic practices or that he felt remorse in his old age.

In all this Umon showed not the slightest awe for the shogunal authorities, and he has committed multiple heinous crimes. Thus . . .

Heizō

Heizō originally practiced Zen and rose to the rank of senior monk, but he returned to lay life because he found it impossible to keep the precepts.

He was unable to discern true from pernicious and was led astray by a foolhardy temperament. As a consequence, when he heard the late Gunki's expositions on Kirishitan, he found the notions set forth in the proscribed books by southern barbarians to be convincing. He came up with his own interpretation that "neither Confucianism nor Buddhism is equal to this [teaching]." Having pledged that he would never confess the truth, even were he to be subjected to the severest punishment, he worshipped the drawing of the Lord of Heaven in Gunki's possession and dripped blood from his fingers on the portrait. He was initiated into the secret transmissions of how to chant the mantra of this deity and how to perform water austerities.

Because Gunki performed the kind of sorcery Heizō wanted to do himself, Heizō became ever more infatuated with him. Lying to his wife that they should show respect for Gunki because Heizō had received transmissions of *Yijing* divination from him, Heizō always concealed the fact that he was involved with Kirishitan. He went so far as to look after Gunki's wife and child while Gunki traveled to Nagasaki, and when he became aware of the investigation taking place, he burned a picture of Uzume drawn by Gunki as a substitute for that of the Lord of Heaven. It is thus difficult to accept his claims that he ceased performing water austerities because he was preoccupied with trying to scrabble together a living, that his deeply lustful temperament had led to the dissipation of his commitment to praying to the Lord of Heaven, and that he regretted what he had done.

In all this Heizō showed not the slightest awe for the shogunal authorities, and he has committed multiple heinous crimes. Thus . . .

Shōni

It appears to be true that Shōni did not receive secret transmissions of the Kirishitan pernicious arts from Gunki. Nevertheless, after [going through Gunki's belongings] with Masasuke and others following Gunki's death, Shōni took Gunki's papers home with him, and on his own he heedlessly used most of them to make a mat for a floor covering. Among the scraps remaining were some unbound fragments from proscribed works of the Jesus creed. Quite likely other parts of the same works and the pernicious books that Gunki expounded to Umon and others have disappeared because Shōni did not pay proper attention and used them together with other scraps to make the paper mat. This was undoubtedly an act of carelessness [rather than deliberate destruction of evidence]. Nevertheless, in the course of the interrogation Shōni falsely stated that he had not taken charge of these papers. Such deceitful behavior constitutes a crime. Thus . . .

Yatarō

Yatarō claims that he simply studied calligraphy with the late Gunki and did not receive from him transmission of the Kirishitan pernicious creed. If this was the case, he should have immediately reported to the appropriate authorities his discovery of the strange buddha image about which his late father, Shintarō, had left instructions on his deathbed. He failed to do so. Instead, just when Yatarō was hearing rumors about the arrest of disciples who had received Gunki's pernicious creed, his well became infested with insects and the water contaminated. These strange events startled him, and since he and his father had been on close terms with Gunki,[4] he feared what would happen if he were investigated and his house searched. He thus secretly burned the strange buddha image. It seems certain that this was the scroll with the drawing of the Lord of Heaven on which Mitsugi and the others had dripped their blood. Since the father, Shintarō, has died, whether or not he received transmission of the pernicious creed cannot be known, but it is clear that the son took the initiative to burn the drawing that the father had secretly accepted in pawn. Yet in the initial stage of the investigation Yatarō [did not admit this and] falsely stated that both he and his father were only casually acquainted with Gunki. Such deceitful behavior invites suspicion and constitutes a crime. Thus . . .

Makijirō

Makijirō's father, Gunki, transmitted the pernicious arts of the proscribed Kirishitan creed to Mitsugi and others. He had them worship the portrait of the Lord of Heaven, and some of his followers used pernicious arts here in Osaka to cause people to take leave of their senses and to appropriate money from them. Makijirō himself saw Gunki engage in acts of sorcery before his eyes. Even if he was still a child at the time of Gunki's death and did not receive the transmission of the pernicious creed, he is the child of a heinous criminal who violated the government's proscription of this creed. Thus . . .

Kenzō

Kenzō did not have dealings with the late Gunki, nor did he worship the Lord of Heaven or receive books of the Jesus creed from Gunki. Yet, before he absconded Kenzō had a predilection for rare books and sought out works of the Jesus creed in the full knowledge that they are proscribed. He has kept them in his possession even up to now, claiming that they are of use to him in his medical practice. Moreover, he himself secretly composed a book of the Jesus creed, giving it a [misleading] title, and he obtained copies of *fumie* from an itinerant monk of unknown domicile. With intentions that are difficult to fathom, he has ignored the government's proscription [of works of the Jesus creed].

In this Kenzō showed not the slightest awe for the shogunal authorities and has committed a crime. Thus . . .

Daizui

As for Daizui and the priests of his temple group, Daizui's parishioner, the late Gunki, was a devotee of the proscribed Kirishitan pernicious creed and even transmitted it to others. Nevertheless, Daizui remained unaware of this until the present investigation. This was because of dereliction in his duty to look properly into Gunki's behavior before certifying his sectarian affiliation. This constitutes a misdeed. Thus . . .

Shōryū and the Other Priests

As for Shōryū and the four other priests and the priests of their temple groups, Shōryū's parishioner Sano, Zenshō's parishioner Kinu, Zekan's parishioner Mitsugi, Kanryō's parishioner Umon, and Kōhō's parishioner Heizo all received the transmissions of the proscribed Kirishitan pernicious creed and secretly had faith in the Lord of Heaven. That these priests remained unaware of this until the present investigation is because of dereliction in their duty to look properly into their parishioners' behavior before certifying their sectarian affiliation. This constitutes a misdeed. Thus . . .

Ōmi

As for Ōmi, it is true that he succeeded to the position of supervisor of yin-yang diviners only upon the death of his father, Chikugo, which was after Mitsugi's evil deeds had come to light and she had been arrested. Nevertheless, Chikugo had already been incapacitated owing to old age prior to his death, and Ōmi had been acting as his father's deputy. As such, he was aware that Mitsugi's business was prospering, but he did not stop to think that there was anything strange about this and just let it go. He did not realize until the present investigation that Mitsugi was not only a devotee of the Kirishitan pernicious creed transmitted to her by Gunki but was also transmitting it to yet others. This is because of laxness in giving directions to the yin-yang diviners and checking on their behavior. This constitutes a misdeed. Thus . . .

Landlords

As for the landlords and those responsible for matters of the locale, none of them realized until the present investigation that Sano, Kinu, Mitsugi, Umon, and Heizō were devotees of the proscribed Kirishitan pernicious creed and were praying to the Lord of Heaven. In addition, Kinu's landlord and those responsible for matters of the locale also did not realize that her household head, Tōzō, was simultaneously enrolled in the population registers of two different blocks. This is because of laxness in their management of both the certification of temple affiliation and the compilation of the population register. This constitutes a misdeed. Thus . . .

3. THE OSAKA EASTERN MAGISTRATE'S PROPOSED PUNISHMENTS FOR THE PRINCIPAL FIGURES; NINTH MONTH, 1827

When I recently submitted the dossier on the devotees of the pernicious sect to [the Osaka governor] for review, I did not include any proposal for punishments. This was because there are no appropriate precedents to cite as there have been no previous instances [here in Osaka] of punishments meted out to such people. However, I have since received your order to compose a proposal for punishments by taking into consideration other comparable cases. On this understanding, and in consultation with my fellow magistrate, Lord Naitō Noritomo, I have proceeded as follows: As there are no directly applicable precedents, we have extrapolated from comparable cases and have composed a proposal for punishments as attached. I hereby submit these materials for your review.

• Sano, Kinu, and Mitsugi were devotees of the strictly proscribed pernicious creed and prayed to the Lord of Heaven. They additionally used these practices to appropriate money. What they did warrants a far heavier punishment than that levied on Jikū, priest of the temple of Raigōji in Sata, Kawachi province, who was sentenced to exile to a remote island.[5] It may rather be likened to the actions of Kimura Ise, priest of Ichinomiya Shrine in Miyamura, Ōno, Hida province, and his cohorts, who committed the crime of charging money for performing heinous prayer rites while also extracting sacred pledges and affidavits that he had devised to avoid having accusations levied [against himself] in the future. [For this he and his cohorts were sentenced to crucifixion].[6] In light of this example, we propose that Sano, Kinu, and Mitsugi might be sentenced to crucifixion after having been paraded through the three districts of Osaka.

If we receive orders to implement the proposed punishment, copies of the verdict and the execution placard presumably should be sent to the Kyoto Magistracy. In addition, as Mitsugi's adoptive son, Kamon, mentioned in an addendum to Mitsugi's testimony, is implicated [by relationship] in the serious crime of his adoptive parent, he might be sentenced to exile to a remote island.

• Toki was not initiated into the pernicious creed by Sano, but she agreed to the plan to make it out that her late husband, Kanzō, ran an inn [where he put up the "noblewoman" from Kyoto]; she urged others to have [Sano perform] prayer rites for them; and although she does not know the exact amount, she was a party to Kanzō's receiving a share of the money appropriated by Sano. For this, she might be sentenced to distant exile.

• Tōzō put his faith in Kinu's practices without realizing that they were based on the pernicious creed. [But although he himself cannot be said to be a believer,] he ended up listed in two different population registers, and for this he might be sentenced to banishment from the immediate locale.

- Kahei put his faith in Kinu's practices without realizing that they were based on the pernicious creed. [But although he himself cannot be said to be a believer,] without consulting Tōzō, he presented him as being Kahei's own servant and made it appear as though he were setting him up as a branch house. Tōzō was already listed in a population register elsewhere at this time and ended up listed in the population registers of two different blocks as a result. Kahei did something far more egregious than what Tōzō did. He might thus be sentenced to banishment from the three districts of Osaka.

- In contrast to Sano, Kinu, and Mitsugi, Umon and Heizō did not use the practices of the pernicious sect to appropriate money from others, and both have already expressed remorse [for their involvement in it]. However, they worshipped a buddha image of the pernicious sect in the full knowledge that it was strictly proscribed. Keeping the matter concealed even from their wives, Umon submitted a sacred oath [sealed in blood] and Heizō dripped blood directly onto [this image]. Further, both Umon and Heizō listened to Gunki expound what is written in books of the southern barbarians and found this convincing. Heizō, moreover, burned an image that was called Uzume but in fact represented the Lord of Heaven. Both might be sentenced to decapitation after having been paraded through the three districts of Osaka, with subsequent display of their heads.

Umon's wife, Fusa, and Heizō's wife, Mutsu, are implicated [by relationship] in the grave crimes of their husbands. If we receive orders to implement the proposed punishment, both might be sentenced to distant exile.

- Shōni did not receive secret transmissions of the practices of the pernicious sect from Gunki. However, scraps left over from a paper mat that he made appear to be fragments from proscribed books. He may thus have deceitfully pasted other dangerous writings into the mat. In addition he made false statements in his testimony. For this he might be sentenced to exile to a remote island. The [remaining fragments from] the proscribed books might be burned.

- Yatarō did not receive transmissions of the practices of the pernicious sect. However, he burned and disposed of a dangerous drawing of the

Lord of Heaven and made false statements in his testimony. For this he might be sentenced to exile to a remote island.

• Makijirō is presently of insignificant status, [being a dependent in the household of his maternal uncle], but as the son of a man who committed a grave crime, he should be sentenced to exile to a remote island. However, because of his youth he might be kept incarcerated until he reaches the age of fifteen.

• Kenzō not only kept dangerous books of the Jesus creed in his possession but also wrote such a work of his own. These books should be burned and disposed of, and Kenzō might be sentenced to death by decapitation.[7]

• Daizui might be sentenced to expulsion from his temple, and the priests of the temples in his temple group sentenced to fifty days' seclusion.[8] In addition, Gunki committed a grave crime by contravening the strict proscription [of the pernicious creed] and transmitting it to Mitsugi. If he had a grave, it therefore should be destroyed and his remains burned and abandoned. Because there is no grave [this procedure cannot be followed, but] a proclamation to this effect might be made to Daizui and the other parties to the incident.

• Shōryū, Zenshō, Zekan, Kanryō, and Kōhō might be sentenced to expulsion from their temples, and the priests of the temples in their temple groups sentenced to fifty days' seclusion. In addition, Wasa committed a grave crime in choosing to follow Gunki, who contravened the strict proscription [of the pernicious creed]. An order might be issued to Zekan and the other parties to the incident that her grave be destroyed. If, as proposed, we receive your orders for the destruction of Wasa's grave, presumably we should relay these orders to the Kyoto Magistracy and the magistrate should be directed to dispatch an inspector to confirm that [this has been done].

• Wasa's two adoptive daughters, Ito and Toki, mentioned in an addendum to Mitsugi's testimony, have already married, and they clearly did not become believers of the pernicious creed. However, their parent Wasa committed a grave crime. Therefore, if orders are given for her grave to be destroyed, as we propose, Ito and Toki might be sentenced to exile to a remote island, in the same manner as Makijirō and Kamon.

• Because Ōmi acted in place of his father, Chikugo, who was incapacitated owing to old age, he might be sentenced to fifty days' confinement to his house.[9]

• The village headmen and aldermen of Sano and Umon, as well as the town aldermen of Kinu, Mitsugi, and Heizō, have neglected the duties of their positions. Together with the landlords [who rented accommodation to these people] they might be fined ten thousand coppers each, and the members of their five-household groups five thousand coppers each.

I hereby submit the proposed punishments as detailed above for your consideration.

Takai Sanenori, ninth month, 1827

4. INQUIRY ABOUT THE PUNISHMENT OF MITSUGI'S MOTHER; NINTH MONTH, 1827

Inquiry [from the Osaka eastern magistrate to the Osaka governor] concerning the punishment of Eshū, mother of Toyoda Mitsugi, who is a party to the matter of the devotees of the pernicious sect

Mitsugi's mother, Eshū, is the parent of a person who has committed a grave crime, but I have not seen [precedents] where a parent has been punished because of the crime of his or her child. Would it be inappropriate to propose that she be punished in the same manner as Mitsugi's adoptive son, Kamon? As stated in [an addendum to] Mitsugi's confirmed testimony, Eshū is eighty-five years old, senile, and totally uncomprehending of what is happening around her. She clearly was not involved with the pernicious creed that Mitsugi practiced, and I am submitting the inquiry about her punishment only because she is Mitsugi's parent. Given these circumstances, might it be appropriate to propose that she be sentenced to distant exile, which is one grade less severe than exile to a remote island? Since it is difficult to decide on the appropriate punishment, I submit this inquiry separately from the proposed punishments for the parties to the incident. If orders are issued that Eshū be sentenced as here proposed, in my opinion, [the actual sentence should be transmuted to] indefinite incarceration, since, as already noted, she is senile and hardly able to move.[10]

Takai Sanenori, ninth month, 1827

5. THE OSAKA EASTERN MAGISTRATE'S PROPOSED PUNISHMENTS FOR THE SECONDARY PARTIES; TENTH MONTH, 1827

Regarding the persons mentioned in the addenda to [the testimonies of the principal parties involved in] the matter of the pernicious sect, I hereby report [to the Osaka governor] on those who, in my view, should be sentenced to [lesser degrees of] punishment:

Those Mentioned in the Addenda to Sano's Testimony

• Harimaya Uhei and his wife, Soyo, gave money and other items to Sano, which casts suspicion on them. As in this they have been remiss, I propose to sentence them to a strict reprimand when the case is concluded.[11]

• Kenpōya Yohei; his mother, Kiwa; and his wife, Chika, took leave of their senses as a result of Sano's pernicious arts and offered her money and clothing. As in this they were remiss, I propose to sentence all three of them to a strict reprimand when the case is concluded and also to warn them to be careful not to take leave of their senses in this manner again.

• Matsuya Gihei and the eighteen other persons [from whom Sano gathered contributions] likewise took leave of their senses as a result of Sano's pernicious arts and offered her money and clothing. As in this they have been remiss, I propose to sentence them to a strict reprimand when the case is concluded, the same as with Yohei and the others, and also to warn them to be careful not to take leave of their senses in this manner again.

• [The pawnbrokers] Yoshidaya Shinshichi and Namariya Kyūbei did not engage in collusion [to accept illegally pawned items]. Nevertheless, they took leave of their senses as a result of Sano's pernicious arts and accepted large numbers of items in pawn from persons of meager circumstances. As in this they were remiss, I propose to sentence both to a strict reprimand, to confiscate the pawned items, and to order them to pay restitution.

When pawns are confiscated, they should as a rule be returned to their owners, but in light of the particularly evil-natured character of this case, I propose to order that these pawns be turned over to the magistracy.

Those Mentioned in the Addenda to Mitsugi's Testimony

• Harimaya Kinoshin was once Mitsugi's follower, he joined her for water austerities, and he [was aware of her performing] strange acts. Although he did not receive the transmission of the pernicious creed, he appears to be a person who in his inner mind is attracted to such things. Judging by the collection of precedents that you recently allowed me to view, his case may be likened to that of Miyataya Shōjirō [taken up by the] Deliberative Council.[12] I thus propose to sentence him to indefinite incarceration.

Those Mentioned in the Addenda to Shōni's Testimony

• Hōki Masasuke, Teradaya Kumazō, Minoya Kohachi, Matsusakaya Nihei, and Moto, the younger sister of [the present] Kamaya Kyūbei, were not aware that Gunki was a devotee of the proscribed pernicious creed. Masasuke became Gunki's disciple in calligraphy and assisted him in many ways. Kumazō was on friendly terms with Gunki. Kohachi was employed by Gunki and ran errands for him. Nihei helped him in various ways, such as renting temporary quarters for him. Moto went to stay with Gunki at the direction of her father, now deceased. As all were remiss in not realizing what [Gunki was doing], I propose to sentence them to a strict reprimand when the case is concluded. As Kumazō and Kohachi have died [in the meantime], I propose to proclaim to all the parties to the incident that this would have been their sentence.

• Tomitaya Riemon's widow, Kiyo, and the present Kyūbei, son of the deceased Kamaya Kyūbei, knew that Kiyo's deceased husband, Riemon, and Kyūbei's deceased father, the former Kyūbei, were on friendly terms with Gunki, but they remained completely unaware of what was going on. Although the present Kyūbei is deaf, he has proved competent enough to continue his father's household. As both have been extremely inattentive and remiss, I propose to sentence them to a strict reprimand when the case is concluded.

Those Mentioned in the Addenda to Yatarō's Testimony

• Yatarō's mother, Wasa, and his wife, Nobu, were in his household throughout, yet they did not realize that the deceased Shintarō had secretly accepted a drawing of the Lord of Heaven from Gunki as a pawn. In addition they remained unaware that Yatarō had burned and destroyed the scroll with this drawing. As in this they have been remiss, I propose to sentence both of them to thirty days' confinement to their house.

Those Mentioned in the Addenda to Makijirō's Testimony

• Momijiya Jinbei may not have engaged in serious chicanery, but he did once tell Makijirō to remain silent about Gunki's sorcery. Also, although Makijirō is the son of a great criminal, Jinbei took him into his household because he is a relative. In this Jinbei is guilty of a misdeed, but there seems to be no doubt that he was unaware [that Gunki was a devotee of the Kirishitan creed]. I thus propose to sentence him to fifty days' confinement to his house.

I hereby propose the abovementioned [lesser] punishments.

Takai Sanenori, tenth month, 1827

Chapter 8

Deliberations in Edo

6. INITIAL REPORT FROM THE DELIBERATIVE COUNCIL; FIFTH MONTH, 1829

On the twenty-second day of the tenth month of the previous year, 1828, the senior councillors directed the council to deliberate on the dossier submitted for review by [the Osaka eastern magistrate,] Lord Takai Sanenori. We have now considered this dossier on the incident involving Sano and others said to be devotees of the Kirishitan sect.[1]

According to the record of the investigation, Sano and others of the group called themselves Inari mediums but in fact were devotees of the Kirishitan creed and as such engaged in various strange activities. However, there is nothing in the Rules for Deciding Judicial Matters specifying the punishments to be meted out to devotees of the Kirishitan creed, nor are there precedents from previous cases. There are thus also no records detailing the nature of this sect's practices. Further, the yin-yang diviner Toyoda Mitsugi is said to have received the transmission of these practices from Mizuno Gunki, but he had already died before this matter came under investigation. The source of these practices and the manner of their transmission are thus not known. As for the drawing of the Lord of Heaven that Gunki is said to have possessed, it is supposed that the late Shintarō received it in pawn, but subsequently his son, Yatarō, is said to have burned it, and there is no sign of it today.

If it is a matter of using strange arts to startle people with extraordinary things, devotees of the Kirishitan sect are not the only ones to do so. There is [another problem] as well. The record of the investigation states that Sano received the transmission of this sect's practices from Kinu. According to the dossier, when Sano received the transmission, Kinu told her that by nature the Lord of Heaven has no shape or form. Sano had heard previously, though, that in Nagasaki *fumie* are used to ascertain people's beliefs and certify sectarian affiliation and that these carry drawings of this deity. If she went there, she thought, she would be able to see these drawings. She thus went to Nagasaki, trod on the *fumie* at the inn where she stayed, and saw the image on it. Her faith thereupon grew even stronger, and after returning to Osaka, she became clairvoyant into all manner of things and used these powers to confound people and appropriate money and goods from them. Should it become established that Sano trod on the *fumie* out of faith and then continued to be a devotee of the Kirishitan creed as if nothing had happened, the point of requiring people in Nagasaki to tread on *fumie* will be lost, and it may well become difficult to determine if someone is a devotee of the Kirishitan sect.

Nevertheless, those in charge of the investigation have decided that the people involved in this case are unquestionably devotees of the Kirishitan sect and have compiled the confirmed testimonies accordingly. Should it turn out, after the case has been concluded, that the people cannot be determined with certainty to be Kirishitan, [this will cause problems]. Unless the entire investigation is redone it will be difficult to reach an appropriate judgment in this case. Should [the senior councillors] thus order [the Osaka eastern magistrate] to take the above points into consideration, redo the investigation, and resubmit the inquiry regarding it? In confidence we ask your directions on this matter.

Fifth month, 1829

7. THE PRESIDING SENIOR COUNCILLOR'S RESPONSE; FIFTH OR SIXTH MONTH, 1829

The conclusions you have reached through your deliberations in general seem reasonable. However, should the investigation be redone and the accused now be dealt with as not devotees of the Kirishitan sect, it is likely to be even more difficult to dispel questions about this matter in the world at large, and this might well result in laxity in enforcement of the proscription of this sect. Regarding Sano's having trodden on the *fumie* in Nagasaki, there is only her own testimony and no corroborating evidence.

It is therefore difficult to determine with certainty that she did in fact tread on the *fumie*, and there is no need to accept this point [as part of the official record]. References to the matter of the *fumie* thus should be removed from the record of the investigation. Otherwise the parties should be determined to be devotees of the Kirishitan sect, in accordance with the conclusions of the investigating officials. You should deliberate on this basis the appropriate punishments and also how to deal with those related to these Kirishitan.

If punishments are to be levied in the above case, should not directives also be issued to the various [pertinent responsible figures] to take particular care henceforth in checking on and certifying sectarian affiliation? If so, you should look into the form for promulgating such directives and report to us on this.

8. SEPARATE ORAL INSTRUCTIONS FROM THE PRESIDING SENIOR COUNCILLOR; FIFTH OR SIXTH MONTH, 1829

Regarding punishments of devotees of the Kirishitan sect, nothing is specified [concerning cases of this sort] in the Rules for Deciding Judicial Matters, and it is very difficult to locate appropriate precedents. In our view, as a general principle you should lean in the direction of severe punishments in your deliberations. You should pay attention in particular to how to deal with those related to the Kirishitan and inform us of your conclusions.[2]

9. MEMORANDUM FROM THE DELIBERATIVE COUNCIL; TWENTY-EIGHTH DAY, SIXTH MONTH, 1829

We confirm that we have received and will adhere to the directions received [from the senior councillors]. To wit: the matter of the *fumie* is to be deleted from the record of the interrogations concerning the incident; the principals are to be judged as devotees of the Kirishitan sect, in accordance with the conclusions of the investigating officials [of the Osaka Eastern Magistracy]; and we will deliberate accordingly the punishments to be levied and how to deal with those related to the Kirishitan.

The Deliberative Council, acting in unison, twenty-eighth day, sixth month, 1829[3]

10. RECOMMENDATIONS OF THE DELIBERATIVE COUNCIL REGARDING THE PRINCIPAL PARTIES; EIGHTH DAY, SEVENTH MONTH, 1829

We have deliberated on the punishments to be meted out to Sano and the others involved in the case of those said to be devotees of the Kirishitan sect [and have reached the following conclusions]:[4]

Sano

The dossier [submitted by the Osaka eastern magistrate] states that the accused used the methods of the Kirishitan sect to engage in strange activities. However, neither the Rules for Deciding Judicial Matters nor precedents from earlier cases [kept by shogunal offices] include provisions for the punishment of persons who have engaged in the practices of this sect, and it is difficult to know its customary mode of operation. Since we consequently could not firmly determine that Sano was a Kirishitan devotee, we submitted a private inquiry to you as to how to proceed. In response we received your written directions to determine [Sano and the others] to indeed be devotees of the Kirishitan creed, in accordance with the conclusions of the investigating officials, and to deliberate the matter accordingly.

Having looked into and deliberated the matter thoroughly, we have found that in the past [it was ordered that] not only the children but all the relatives of adherents of this sect should be defined as "relatives of Kirishitan." Even now, in places where there are people of the same lineage or related by blood to [people who in the past were once Kirishitan], the local shogunal intendant or domain lord is to check every year on births and deaths among them and report these to the Office for Sectarian Matters.[5] Since this special law was promulgated long ago and has been observed ever since, it is difficult to apply to the case at hand [the less-stringent] provisions in the Rules for Deciding Judicial Matters concerning those who proselytize [banned] teachings such as those of the Sanchō-ha and Fuju Fuse.[6]

Since this is a case involving dangerous crimes, it is essential to deal with it in such a way as to serve as a warning for the future. It may be considered in light of the item in the Rules specifying crucifixion at the site as the punishment for those who circumvent a barrier because they cannot pass through it legally.[7] But what Sano did in fact involves a more heinous crime [than contravention of the law forbidding circumvention of barriers]. To set a warning example, it thus would be appropriate to order that she should first be paraded through the city in addition to the obvious sentence of crucifixion. Subsequent, however, [to the initial submission of the dossier,] it has been reported that Sano has fallen ill and died. In our view you might therefore order that the sentence should be that her corpse preserved in salt should be crucified after having first been paraded through the three districts of Osaka.

However, as for the statement that Sano trod on the *fumie* in Nagasaki, no investigation was conducted in consultation with people there [to corroborate it], and there is only her declaration to this effect. Thus, as you have directed, there is no need to include it in the verdict. In our view, you might order that the verdict [as currently formulated in the summation] be corrected as indicated on the slip we have attached to it. To wit, the following should be deleted: from "According to the transmission Sano received from Kinu, by nature the Lord of Heaven has no shape or form" to "Seeing the likeness in the image, she became all the more confirmed in her faith. After Sano returned to Osaka. . . ."[8] This should be rewritten as "After receiving the secret transmission from Kinu, she was able to predict. . . ."

Toki

According to the dossier, at Sano's request Toki spread stories that Sano was a noblewoman from Kyoto living in retirement who had come to Osaka to disseminate her methods for ensuring prosperity. Toki went around to acquaintances together with her husband, Kanzō, and urged them to have Sano perform prayer rituals for them. Kanzō received a portion of the money and clothes Sano appropriated, although Toki says she does not know the amount. In this way Toki plotted together with Sano from the beginning to deceive many people. Even if she did not receive transmission of the Kirishitan creed, her entire behavior invites suspicion, and she fully deserves the death penalty. Although no specific pertinent precedents can be found, in our view you might order that she should be sentenced to death by decapitation.[9]

Kinu

According to the dossier, Kinu is the same sort as Sano. It thus would be appropriate to sentence her to crucifixion after first having been paraded through the three districts of Osaka, as suggested [by the Osaka eastern magistrate]. Subsequent, however, [to the initial submission of the dossier,] it has been reported that she has fallen ill and died. In our view you might therefore order that the sentence should be that her corpse preserved in salt should be crucified after having first been paraded through the three districts of Osaka.

In accordance with the comment appended to the above deliberations on Sano, in our view you might also order that the verdict for Kinu likewise be corrected as indicated on the slip we have attached to it. To wit, the following should be deleted: from "Kinu thought that if she told Sano about her own worship of the drawing of the Lord of Heaven" to "trod on the *fumie*, saw the likeness on it, and became even more confirmed in her faith." This should be rewritten as ". . . passed on to her the transmissions as Kinu had received them from Mitsugi. Sano now attained mastery. . . ."

Toshimaya Tōzō

Tōzō's actions, as described in the dossier, may be considered in light of a precedent from 1772, when Lord Magaribuchi Kagetsugu was serving as Edo magistrate.[10] After having consulted [the senior councillors], Lord Magaribuchi issued a sentence to Genzaemon, house manager resident in Koami-chō 2-chōme in Edo, of banishment from Edo for the following misdeed:

> Sensuke, of the Ami lineage [of metal craftsmen], who presented himself as a master craftsman of metal decorative fittings, lied that Shinzō, the clerk of Yahei, house manager resident in Koami-chō 1-chōme, was his cousin Akita Kumajirō and claimed that Shinzō was familiar with the skills of this trade. Genzaemon was aware that this was a fabrication, but he went along with the request of Shinzō and Sensuke and took the petition [to have Shinzō be recognized as a craftsman] to the guild members.[11]

Compared with this precedent, the overall character of what Tōzō did is not so egregious [as Genzaemon's action], and in our view you might order that the sentence should be banishment from the immediate locale, as suggested [by the Osaka eastern magistrate].[12]

Harimaya Kahei

Kahei's actions, as described in the dossier, may be considered in light of a precedent from 1767, when Lord Yoda Masatsugu was serving as Edo magistrate.[13] After having consulted [the senior councillors], Lord Yoda sentenced Chūhachi, house manager of Fukagawa Morishita-chō, in Edo, to banishment from the locale for the following misdeed:

> Koto, who lived in the residence of Endō Jinshirō, a warrior in the reserve corps under the supervision of Ichihashi Daizen, was not related to Chūhachi. Nevertheless, at Koto's request, Chūhachi said that she was his younger sister and recorded her as such in the townspeople population register of his block, even though she was at the time resident in a warrior compound and her intent [in seeking to be included in the townspeople population register] was to press for reimbursement or bring a lawsuit over a loan she had made.[14]

The two instances are comparable in that both involve a similar act of deception. However, Kahei arranged rental housing for Kinu, a devotee of the Kirishitan sect. This is far more egregious than what Chūhachi did. In our view, you might thus order that the sentence should be banishment from the three districts of Osaka, as suggested [by the Osaka eastern magistrate]. This is equivalent to banishment from Edo.[15]

Toyoda Mitsugi

As described in the dossier, Mitsugi is the same sort as Sano. It thus would be appropriate to sentence her to crucifixion after first having been paraded through the three districts of Osaka, as suggested by the Osaka eastern magistrate. Further, since she resided throughout in Kyoto and her evil deeds were perpetrated there, in our view you might also direct that the Kyoto magistrate should be instructed to post the execution placard with the verdict there as well, as the Osaka eastern magistrate has further suggested.

Fujii Umon

According to the dossier, Umon engaged in his practice [of the Kirishitan creed] entirely by himself and did not deceive others or appropriate money and such from them. Nevertheless, insofar as he engaged in the practices of the Kirishitan sect, it is difficult to say that his actions are less egregious than Sano's. He is of the same sort as she [and deserves the same sentence].[16] Subsequent, however, [to the initial submission of the dossier,] it has been reported that he has fallen ill and died. In our view you might order that the sentence should be that his corpse preserved in salt should be crucified after having first been paraded through the three districts of Osaka.

Takamiya Heizō

As described in the dossier, the circumstances concerning Heizō are the same as those for the aforementioned Umon. In our view you might order that the sentence should be that he be crucified after having first been paraded through the three districts of Osaka.

Tsuchiya Shōni

According to the dossier, Shōni acceded to a request from Mizuno Gunki and recommended him for a position [in a noble house]. At the time of Gunki's death he also played a leading part in looking after his affairs. He took charge of the diary Gunki had kept as well as works of the Jesus creed and such with the idea of giving them to Gunki's son, Makijirō, when he grew up. Thus, although the investigating officials have concluded that he did not receive transmission of the Kirishitan creed, the overall circumstances invite suspicion. We therefore deliberated the matter thoroughly. In that he looked after Gunki's affairs as one would do for a relative, the following precedent from the materials you handed down to us for reference [would seem applicable]:

> In 1707 the Nagasaki magistrate submitted an inquiry [to the senior councillors] regarding the release from incarceration of relatives of Kirishitan. According to that inquiry, O-kai, the daughter of Chūemon of Mizoo village in the domain of Lord Nakagawa Hisamichi,[17] had testified [at the time of the original investigation prior to her incarceration] that she knew nothing of the pernicious sect and had never been urged to become a devotee. For generations her family had been adherents of the Ikkō sect. But there were devotees of the pernicious sect among her parents,

siblings, and relatives, and she had lived with her parents until she grew up. Without doubt, [the officials investigating her case had asserted,] she must have had water cast on her.[18] Although she had responded that she had no memory of such, given these circumstances, she had been ordered incarcerated. Twenty-seven years having passed since then, [the Nagasaki magistrate] submitted the abovementioned inquiry as to whether it would be appropriate to order her released from incarceration and instead be put under the custody of the locale. In this instance the senior councillors ordered that this arrangement be adopted.[19]

Extrapolating from this case, in our view you might order that Shōni's case be disposed of as follows: [The Osaka eastern magistrate] should proclaim to the parties to the incident that Shōni should have been sentenced to incarceration. As it has subsequently been reported that he has fallen ill and died, [this sentence cannot be carried out, but] they should know that this is the sentence.[20] As for the written materials, in our view you might order that they be burned, as proposed in the inquiry.

Nakamuraya Yatarō

According to the dossier, Yatarō did not receive transmission of the Kirishitan creed from Mizuno Gunki. Nevertheless, after the investigation of the present incident began, he burned the drawing of the Lord of Heaven that his father, Shintarō, had evidently taken in pawn from Gunki. This behavior invites suspicion. In our view you thus might order that his case be disposed of in the same manner as Shōni's. [The Osaka eastern magistrate] should proclaim to the parties to the incident that Yatarō should have been sentenced to incarceration. As it has subsequently been reported that he has fallen ill and died, [this sentence cannot be carried out, but] they should know that this is the sentence.[21]

Makijirō

According to the dossier, Makijirō was fourteen years of age two years ago, in 1827, when he was interrogated, and he was a boy of eleven years of age when his father, Mizuno Gunki, died in 1824. He did not receive transmission of the Kirishitan creed from Gunki. Nevertheless, he is the

son of Gunki, who was a devotee of this creed. The following precedent
from the materials you handed down to us [would thus seem applicable]:

> In 1707 the Nagasaki magistrate submitted an inquiry [to the senior
> councillors] regarding the release from incarceration of the relatives of
> Kirishitan. According to that inquiry, Kichizō, son of Koheiji of Chitose
> village in Hita, Bungo province, in the district of the intendant Muro
> Shichirōzaemon, had testified that his father had cast water on him
> when he was a child. However, the father had not told Kichizō that [in
> so doing] he had made his son into a devotee of the Kirishitan sect, and
> Kichizō did not recall at all being encouraged to follow it. Nevertheless,
> there were devotees of the pernicious sect among his relatives, and
> because the situation was uncertain, he had been ordered incarcer-
> ated. Fourteen years having passed, [the Nagasaki magistrate] submit-
> ted an inquiry as to whether it would be appropriate to order him released
> from incarceration and instead be put under the custody of the locale.
> In that case the senior councillors ordered that this arrangement be
> adopted.[22]

Extrapolating from this case, in our view you might order that Makijirō
be sentenced to incarceration.[23]

Kenzō

According to the dossier, Kenzō purchased books of the Jesus creed and
obtained copies of *fumie* from an itinerant monk. He even composed a
Jesus-creed work himself and kept it in his possession. Given these circumstances, it appears that without question he was indeed a Kirishitan
devotee. Thus, as with the aforementioned Fujii Umon, the appropriate
sentence would be crucifixion after having first been paraded through the
three districts of Osaka. Subsequent [to the initial submission of the dos-
sier], however, it has been reported that he has fallen ill and died. In our
view you might therefore order that the sentence should be that his corpse
preserved in salt should be crucified after having first been paraded
through the three districts of Osaka.[24]

   As for the written materials, in our view you might order that they be
burned, as proposed in the inquiry.

Daizui and the Other Priests

As described in the dossier, the culpability of Daizui, priest of the [Nishi] Honganji branch temple Unseiji, where the deceased Mizuno Gunki was registered, and the priests of the temples in Unseiji's temple group may be considered in light of a precedent from 1792, when Lord Magaribuchi Kagetsugu was serving as financial and judicial affairs magistrate.[25]

Shūken, priest of Ryōshōin, a branch temple with rotating responsibility for the administration of the [main temple] Honkokuji, which is located in Ōami village, Kazusa province, and twenty-nine other priests [failed to exercise proper supervision over their parishioners]. After consulting [the senior councillors], Lord Magaribuchi sentenced Shūken and the other priests to fifty days' seclusion for this misdeed, detailed as follows. The parishioners of these temples gathered together with their family members and people of the same village and [engaged in the following improper activities], which they held to be the traditional mode of expressing faith: they put up a mandala inscribed by Nikkyō, a leader of the Fuju Fuse school, or offered reverence to portraits of priests of the same sect who had been subject to punishment. Shūken and the others nevertheless remained unaware of this, which was a dereliction of duty inexcusable in a priest of a temple in charge of parishioners and responsible for certifying their sectarian affiliation.[26]

Compared with this precedent, the case of Daizui and the priests of the temples in Unseiji's temple group is more serious. He was unaware of the fact that one of his parishioners was a devotee of the Kirishitan sect, which is subject to particularly strict proscription, a situation that bears on the overall preservation of order. In our view, he thus should be punished more strictly than were Shūken and the other Kazusa priests. You might therefore order that Daizui be expelled from the temple and the priests in Unseiji's temple group sentenced to fifty days' seclusion, as suggested by the Osaka eastern magistrate.

Further, were Gunki still alive, he would have been sentenced to the same punishment as Sano and the two other [principal protagonists, Kinu and Mitsugi]. Therefore, despite his having died [before the case came to light], his grave [if he had one] should not be allowed to stand as is. Although there are no cases to serve as a precedent, in our view you might order that [the Osaka eastern magistrate] proceed as he suggests. He should proclaim to those involved in the incident that they should know that although Gunki had no grave, if he had had one, it would be ordered destroyed.

• Shōryū, priest of the Ikkō temple Enkōji, a branch temple of Bukkōji and the temple where Sano is registered, and the priests of the temples in Enkōji's temple group

• Zenshō, priest of the Higashi Honganji branch temple Rentakuji, where Kinu is registered, and the priests of the temples in Rentakuji's temple group

• Zekan, priest of Daijōin, a subtemple of the Nichiren temple Chōmyōji and the temple where Toyoda Mitsugi is registered, and the priests of the temples in Daijōin's temple group

• Kanryō, priest of the [Nishi] Honganji branch temple Jōkōji, where Fujii Umon is registered, and the priests of the temples in Jōkōji's temple group

• Kōhō, priest of the Rinzai Zen temple Kanzanji, a branch temple of Myōshinji and the temple where Takamiya Heizō is registered, and the priests of the temples in Kanzanji's temple group

As described in the dossier, the circumstances concerning these priests and temples are the same as with the aforementioned Daizui of Unseiji and the priests of the temples in Unseiji's temple group. In our view you thus might order that Shōryū, Zenshō, Zekan, Kanryō, and Kōhō should all be expelled from their temples and the priests of the temples in their temple groups sentenced to fifty days' seclusion, as suggested by the Osaka eastern magistrate.

Further, were Wasa still alive, she would have been sentenced to the same punishment as Sano and the four others,[27] and her grave should not be allowed to stand as is. In our view you might thus order that the Osaka eastern magistrate should proclaim to Zekan and the others involved in the incident that Wasa's grave should be destroyed, as he suggests. He also should convey directions to the Kyoto magistrate to send an inspector [to make sure this has been done]. In addition, according to the record of the investigation, Wasa died in the middle of the eighth month of 1818. If Zekan had taken up service as the priest of Daijōin prior to this, he would have been responsible for the negligent handling of the certification of [Wasa's] sectarian affiliation. In our view, you might thus order that in the verdict [concerning the priests], Wasa's name should be inserted after Mitsugi's as also Zekan's parishioner.

Takeuchi Ōmi

As described in the dossier, a number of retainers of the Tsuchimikado house are responsible for supervising the yin-yang diviners. Toyoda Mitsugi was under the supervision of Takeuchi Ōmi's father, Chikugo, but at the time Ōmi had taken over his father's duties, as Chikugo was old and feeble. Nevertheless, Ōmi remained unaware that Mitsugi was a devotee of the Kirishitan creed and thought simply that her business was flourishing. To be sure, the nature [of his responsibility regarding her] is different from that of a temple charged with certifying sectarian affiliation. His negligence in checking on her is therefore much less serious [than that of the temple where she is registered]. Nevertheless, this case [concerns Kirishitan], and it thus differs from other matters and bears on the preservation of order henceforth. In our view, the circumstances may be considered in light of the precedent of Shūken, which we took account of above in the deliberations on Daizui of Unseiji and the priests of Unsei-ji's temple group. Following that precedent, you might order that Ōmi should be sentenced to fifty days' confinement to his house.

Landlords and Headmen

The landlords, village headmen, and village aldermen of the rural districts where Sano and Fujii Umon resided

The landlords, block aldermen, and five-household groups of the urban districts where Kinu and Takamiya Heizō resided

The block alderman and five-household group of the town block where Toyoda Mitsugi resided

[The culpability of the above people], as described in the dossier, may be considered in light of the stipulations in the Rules for Deciding Judicial Matters pertaining to devotees of [banned] groups such as the Sanchō sect and Fuju Fuse. These state that even if village officials do not themselves receive the transmission of such teachings or adhere to them, nor allow people who propagate such teachings to reside in their locale, the village headman should be sentenced to a heavy fine and the village aldermen to a light fine if they remain unaware that there are large numbers of devotees among the villagers [for whom they are accountable].[28] Kinu's landlord, the landlord's five-household group, and the block alderman committed an [additional] misdeed in not being aware that Tōzō, her official household head, was enrolled in two population registers, but this is not so serious a matter as to warrant a sentence more severe than that given the other landlords, five-household groups, and aldermen. More significant, all remained unaware that [people for whom they were accountable] were devotees of the Kirishitan creed, which has long been subject to especially strict proscription. This is something that bears on the preservation of overall order. In our view you might thus order that the sentences handed down are to be more severe than those specified in the provision of the Rules [concerning Sanchō-ha and Fuju Fuse]. Namely, the village headmen and the block aldermen in urban districts should be stripped of their duties and fined five thousand coppers each. The landlords and village aldermen in rural districts should be stripped of their duties and fined three thousand coppers each. The members of the five-household groups should be fined three thousand coppers each.

11. THE DELIBERATIVE COUNCIL'S RECOMMENDATIONS REGARDING THE SECONDARY FIGURES; EIGHTH DAY, SEVENTH MONTH, 1829

What follows pertains to the people taken up in the addenda to the confirmed testimonies [of the main figures].[29]

• The addendum regarding Uhei and Soyo indicates that they cannot really be said to have committed a misdeed. Nevertheless, their testimony has been confirmed as part of the conclusions reached by the investigating officials. It would therefore be appropriate to sentence them to a strict reprimand, as proposed [by the Osaka eastern magistrate]. However, the record of the interrogation indicates that they were confounded by Sano in 1820. [Their gullibility on that occasion] is consequently a past offense that happened more than twelve months ago. In our view, in line with the specifications of the Rules for Deciding Judicial Matters [regarding past offenses], you might thus order the Osaka eastern magistrate to proclaim that they are pardoned and not subject to punishment.[30]

• The addendum regarding Yoshichi indicates that his wife, Yae, plotted together with Sano to confound numerous people. Even if she did not receive the transmission of the Kirishitan creed, her behavior invites suspicion. She was the same sort as Toki among the parties to the incident, and were she alive, she would not be able to escape a sentence of death. Properly speaking, Yoshichi should also thus be interrogated strictly. However, he has been essentially insane for more than ten years and at present has suffered a stroke. It is therefore difficult to interrogate him. In our view you might order that since he is the husband of Yae, who cooperated with Sano and committed a crime, he should be put under the custody of relatives and the interrogation completed once he has fully recovered.[31]

• The addendum regarding Yohei, Kiwa, and Chika indicates that they were simply remiss. Nevertheless, the money that Yohei received from Yae was obtained through dishonest means. It thus would not be proper to leave it in his possession. In our view, you might order the Osaka eastern magistrate to confiscate the money and sentence the three to a strict reprimand.

As to whether the three should be told to be careful not to take leave of their senses henceforth [as proposed by the Osaka eastern magistrate], the officials in charge [may include this in the reprimand] if they think it appropriate. In our view, however, there is no need to issue an official order for them to do so.

• The addendum regarding Gihei and the eighteen others who were deceived by Sano and her followers and handed money and clothing over to her indicates that their situation is similar to that of Yohei, Kiwa, and Chika. However, when Yae and Sano were arrested, some of them evidently did not come forward to inform the Osaka eastern magistrate because they had given Yae a pledge in which they declared that they should be struck down by divine punishment if they told anyone about their donations. Those who gave this pledge cannot be said to have been simply remiss. In our view you might thus order as follows: A statement should be added to the verdict that those among Gihei and the eighteen others who gave such a pledge committed a misdeed. As noted in the above recommendations regarding Yohei, Kiwa, and Chika, it would not be proper to leave the money these people received in their possession, and therefore it should be confiscated. The Osaka eastern magistrate should sentence [those who gave such a pledge] to a fine of three thousand coppers or, depending on their circumstances, confinement to their house for thirty days. He may sentence all those who did not give a pledge simply to a strict reprimand.[32]

As to whether these people should be told to be careful not to take leave of their senses henceforth, this should be handled in the same manner as we suggested in the recommendations regarding Yohei, Kiwa, and Chika.

• The addendum regarding [the pawnbrokers] Shinshichi and Kyūbei states that Sano's son, Shinsuke, pawned clothing, naming himself as the primary depositor and Kenpōya Yoshichi of Kawasaki village and Iseya Kanzō of Shinchi Ura-machi in Dōjima, Osaka, as the joint endorsers. Shinshichi and Kyūbei were thus not negligent [in observing the procedures for] accepting items in pawn and should not be held culpable in this regard.[33] However, because the items pawned were obtained dishonestly, it would not be proper to leave them in Shinshichi's and Kyūbei's possession. In addition, as specified in the Rules for Deciding Judicial Matters, "In a case where [a pawnbroker] does not know that items are stolen, but there is a guarantor and [the pawnbroker] takes the items in pawn in the usual manner, if it is determined upon investigation that the pawnbroker was unaware that the items were stolen, the guarantor should be made to recompense the pawnbroker for the sum [given in exchange for the pawned items], and the stolen items should be confiscated and returned to the owner."[34]

Based on this provision, it would be appropriate to confiscate the pawned items and require Yoshichi and Kanzō to recompense [the two pawnbrokers]. However, Kanzō died in the course of interrogation. Yoshichi, being essentially insane and having suffered a stroke, should, as noted previously, be put under the custody of relatives with the intent of interrogating him once he has fully recovered. It is thus difficult to order the guarantors to recompense [the pawnbrokers]. In our view, therefore, the further provision of this article in the Rules would be applicable. Namely, "If the guarantor is also subject to punishment and it is not possible to obtain from him the requisite sum, the pawnbroker should be made to suffer the loss."[35] Based on this provision, you might order that Shinshichi and Kyūbei should not be subject to punishment and that the pawned items be confiscated.

The above pawned items are things that Sano and the others appropriated from Matsuya Gihei and the eighteen others who are party to this incident. In that Gihei and the others have committed a misdeed and all should be subject to punishment, it seems questionable whether the confiscated items should be returned to them, as would usually be the case. We have examined this matter closely and deliberated upon it in light of multiple precedents [involving swindling]. According to these, in a case [of simple deception] where a person has been cheated out of goods by a swindler, the goods should be returned and the person cheated not held culpable. If, however, a person hands over goods to a blackmailer and agrees to keep the matter secret [instead of reporting it to the authorities], that person, too, should be held culpable and the items should not be returned. In this case, although Gihei and the eighteen others were cheated by Sano and her followers, none came forward to report the situation to the magistrate when Sano was arrested. Some among them are further culpable of the misdeed of giving a pledge that they should be struck down by divine punishment if they told anyone else about donating clothes and money to her. In our view it thus would be appropriate to follow the example of the situation where a person has been complicit in blackmail, and not return the items to Gihei and the others. You might order that the pawned items be transferred to the Osaka Eastern Magistracy, as proposed in the magistrate's report.

• The addendum concerning [the Inari medium] Koto, also known as Mitsugi,[36] and [her son,] Jōsuke, indicates that Koto did not become Kinu's disciple, despite Kinu's urging, and subsequently they broke off relations. It appears true that neither Koto nor Jōsuke received the transmission of the Kirishitan creed. Neither Koto's behavior in this regard nor the fact that she changed her name to Mitsugi out of envy for Toyoda Mitsugi's ability are such as to warrant punishment. Nevertheless, if she repeatedly found Kinu's urging her to become a disciple to be strange, she should have reported this to the magistracy. It was remiss on her part to simply let the matter go, and both she and Jōsuke should [in principle] be sentenced to a strict reprimand for this. However, the date of this act of remissness cannot be ascertained from the record of the investigation. If it happened more than twelve months ago, Koto and Jōsuke should be pardoned, in our view, in line with the specifications [regarding past offenses] in the Rules for Deciding Judicial Matters. You might thus order the Osaka eastern magistrate to proclaim that they are not subject to punishment.[37]

- The addendum concerning [Wasa's adoptive daughters] Ito and Toki indicates that they did not receive transmission of the Kirishitan creed. If their adoptive mother, Wasa, were alive, however, she would have been subject to the same punishment as Sano and the other four. In our view you might thus order that both should be sentenced to incarceration, just as with Mizuno Gunki's son, Makijirō.[38]
- The addendum concerning [Mitsugi's disciple] Kinoshin indicates that he did not receive transmission of the Kirishitan creed. Nevertheless, he was impressed by what Toyoda Mitsugi was able to accomplish through her practice and once became her disciple. He went with her to the place where she engaged in austerities and subsequently accompanied her on a trip [to Konpira]. His behavior invites suspicion, and as his situation among the parties to the incident is comparable to that of Shōni, in our view his case might be disposed of in the same manner. That is, you might order the Osaka eastern magistrate to proclaim to the parties to the incident that Kinoshin should have been sentenced to incarceration. As it has subsequently been reported that he has fallen ill and died, [this sentence cannot be carried out, but] they should know that this is the sentence.
- The addendum concerning [Mitsugi's mother,] Eshū, indicates that she is of an extremely advanced age and cannot understand what is going on around her. Further, the record of the investigation of Toyoda Mitsugi and the others contains no evidence that Eshū received transmission of the Kirishitan creed from Mitsugi. It therefore does not seem appropriate to impose punishment on her on the grounds of her daughter Mitsugi's crime, particularly in that, as noted, she is of an extremely advanced age and it is not possible to interrogate her. In our view you might thus order the Osaka eastern magistrate to direct that she be put under the custody of relatives.[39]
- The addendum concerning [Mitsugi's adoptive son,] Kamon, indicates that he did not receive transmission of the Kirishitan creed. Nevertheless, he is the adoptive son of Toyoda Mitsugi, who is a devotee of this creed. As such, he is in a position similar to that of Mizuno Gunki's son, Makijirō. In our view you might thus order the Osaka eastern magistrate to sentence him to incarceration.[40]
- The addendum concerning [Umon's wife,] Fusa, indicates that she did not receive transmission of the Kirishitan creed. Nevertheless, she is the wife of Umon, who was a devotee of this creed. Her position is therefore similar to that of Mizuno Gunki's son, Makijirō. In our view you

might thus order [the Osaka eastern magistrate] to proclaim to the parties to the incident that Fusa should have been sentenced to incarceration. As it has subsequently been reported that she has fallen ill and died, [this sentence cannot be carried out, but] they should know that this is the sentence.[41]

• The addendum concerning [Heizō's wife,] Mutsu, indicates that her position is similar to that of Fusa. In our view you thus might order the Osaka eastern magistrate to sentence her to incarceration.[42]

• The addendum concerning [Gunki's calligraphy student] Hōki Masasuke indicates that he did not receive transmission of the Kirishitan creed from Gunki. Nevertheless, Gunki's wife, Soe, and son, Makijirō, went to Masasuke and told him that they were reluctant to continue troubling Heizō, with whom they were staying while Gunki traveled to Nagasaki. They thus asked Masasuke to make other arrangements for them. Unable to refuse this request, he rented quarters within the city [of Kyoto] on their behalf. This was tantamount to acting as a guarantor for someone of uncertain background and falls under the following provision in the Rules for Deciding Judicial Matters: "One who does not know that a person was previously sentenced to banishment but failed to check his origins before agreeing to act as his guarantor should be sentenced to a fine."[43]

However, as Masasuke was Gunki's calligraphy student, he may well have been unable to avoid assisting Gunki's wife and child and renting housing for them. It thus would seem appropriate to reduce the punishment in the provision in the Rules for Deciding Judicial Matters by a degree and sentence Masasuke to a strict reprimand, as proposed by the Osaka eastern magistrate. According to the record of the investigation, however, these events took place in 1822. Masasuke's action is therefore a past offense that occurred more than twelve months ago.[44] In our view, in line with the specifications in the Rules for Deciding Judicial Matters, you might thus order the Osaka eastern magistrate to proclaim to the parties to the incident that Masasuke is pardoned and not subject to punishment. As it has subsequently been reported that he has fallen ill and died, [the pardon cannot be enacted, but] they should know that this is the sentence.

• The addendum concerning [Gunki's friend] Kumazō indicates that he did not receive transmission of the Kirishitan creed from Gunki. However, at the time Gunki absconded from the Kan'in princely house,

Kumazō allowed him to stay overnight at his place and sent him off in a palanquin. This corresponds to the following provision in the Rules for Deciding Judicial Matters: "One who is not an absconder's guarantor but nevertheless shelters him shall be sentenced to a fine."[45] Based on this provision, Kumazō should be liable to a fine of three thousand coppers.[46] According to the record of the investigation, however, these events took place in 1818. Kumazō's act is therefore a past offense that occurred more than twelve months ago. In our view, in line with the specifications in the Rules for Deciding Judicial Matters, you thus might order the Osaka eastern magistrate to proclaim to the parties to the incident that Kumazō is to be pardoned and not held subject to punishment. As it has subsequently been reported that he has fallen ill and died, [the pardon cannot be enacted, but] they should know that this is the sentence.

• The addendum concerning [the palanquin bearer] Kohachi indicates that he did not receive transmission of the Kirishitan creed from Gunki. However, when Gunki absconded, he hired Kohachi to transport his household belongings [to Kyūbei's house for safekeeping]. This act [may be considered in light of] the following provision in the Rules for Deciding Judicial Matters: "If an absconder's possession of a house that should be subject to confiscation is kept concealed, the headman of the locale should be stripped of his duties and fined five thousand coppers, the landlord should be sentenced to a heavy fine, and the members of the five-household group should be sentenced to a fine."[47] Kohachi's culpability is comparable to that of a member of the five-household group, and thus he should be sentenced to a fine of three thousand coppers.[48] According to the record of the investigation, however, these events took place in 1818. Kohachi's act is therefore a past offense that occurred more than twelve months ago. In our view, in line with the specifications in the Rules for Deciding Judicial Matters, you might thus order the Osaka eastern magistrate to proclaim to the parties to the incident that Kohachi is to be pardoned and not held subject to punishment. As it has subsequently been reported that he has fallen ill and died, [the pardon cannot be enacted, but] they should know that this is the sentence.

• The addendum concerning [Gunki's friend] Nihei indicates that he did not receive transmission of the Kirishitan creed from Gunki. Nevertheless, when Gunki asked Nihei [to find temporary lodgings] for him, Nihei did so without checking Gunki's origins. This falls under the following provision in the Rules for Deciding Judicial Matters: "One who does not know that a person was previously sentenced to banishment but failed to check his origins before agreeing to act as his guarantor should be sentenced to a fine."[49] Based on this provision, Nihei should be sentenced to a fine of three thousand coppers.[50] But as over ten years have passed since this took place, it is a past offense that occurred more than twelve months ago. In our view, in line with the specifications in the Rules for Deciding Judicial Matters, you might thus order the Osaka eastern magistrate to declare that Nihei is to be pardoned and not held subject to punishment.

• The addendum concerning Moto, the daughter of [Gunki's friend] Kyūbei, indicates that her father put her in Mizuno Gunki's custody, and it appears that during that time she neither received transmission of the Kirishitan creed nor engaged in any other activities that would invite suspicion. Nevertheless, at the time Gunki absconded, Kyūbei took charge of Gunki's possessions, and he subsequently put Gunki up in his house. It was remiss of Moto to have just let this go without trying to stop him. For this it would be appropriate to sentence her to a strict reprimand, as proposed by the Osaka eastern magistrate. However, the record of the investigation also indicates that Kyūbei often went to visit Gunki together with the late Nakamuraya Shintarō, and two others. They would all go into a secluded room that no one else was allowed to enter and sometimes would engage in secret discussions there. Since Moto is the daughter of Kyūbei, who engaged in activities of this sort that invite suspicion, it does not seem appropriate simply to let her remain [in her present locale]. The following precedent would seem applicable:

> In 1811 the senior councillors asked the Deliberative Council to discuss an inquiry submitted by the Nagasaki magistrate concerning how to deal with castaways who had returned to this country after drifting to China and other countries. The magistrate proposed that if interrogation did not turn up evidence of questionable activities, the castaways should be handed over to their original domain lord or fief holder. The lord, in turn, should be ordered to see that they stayed within their home locale and did not move freely to some place outside his jurisdiction. After discussing this matter, the Deliberative Council recommended that it be handled in the manner proposed in the inquiry, and the matter was decided thus.

In our view, based on this precedent, you might direct the Osaka eastern magistrate to sentence Moto to a strict reprimand. In addition, however, he should order her to move somewhere within the province of Yamashiro outside the city limits of Kyoto; he should issue instructions as well that she is not free to live elsewhere. He should also inform the Kyoto Magistracy about this order.[51]

• The addendum concerning Kiyo, [the widow of Gunki's friend Riemon,] indicates that she did not receive transmission of the Kirishitan creed; nor did she engage in any activities that invite suspicion. Arranging for Mizuno Gunki to stay in the rental housing owned by her husband, Riemon, was Riemon's doing, and she simply followed his decision. She thus has not committed any misdeed. Nevertheless, the record of the investigation also indicates that Riemon met secretly with Gunki together with Itoya Wasa and two others,[52] and they sometimes held secret discussions in a secluded room that others were not allowed to enter. Since Kiyo is the wife of Riemon, who engaged in activities of this sort that invite suspicion, it does not seem appropriate simply to let her remain [in her present locale]. In our view, in the same manner as with Moto, you might direct the Osaka eastern magistrate to order her to move somewhere within the province of Yamashiro outside the city limits of Kyoto; he should issue instructions as well that she is not free to live elsewhere. He should also inform the Kyoto Magistracy about this order.[53]

• The addendum concerning the present Kyūbei, [the son of Gunki's deceased friend Kyūbei,] indicates that he did not receive transmission of the Kirishitan creed; nor did he engage in activities that invite suspicion or appear to have been involved in any other misdeed. Nevertheless, as noted in the above recommendations regarding Moto, his father, the former Kyūbei, was friendly with Mizuno Gunki and did engage in activities that invite suspicion. Since the present Kyūbei is the son of a person of this sort, it does not seem appropriate simply to let him remain [in his present locale]. In our view, in the same manner as with Moto, you might direct the Osaka eastern magistrate to order him to move somewhere within the province of Yamashiro outside the city limits of Kyoto; the magistrate should issue instructions as well that he is not free to live elsewhere. The Osaka eastern magistrate should also inform the Kyoto Magistracy about this order.

• The addendum concerning Yazobei,[54] [the nephew by marriage of Gunki's friend Shintarō and cousin of Shintarō's son, Yatarō,] indicates that

that he neither received transmission of the Kirishitan creed nor engaged in any activities that invite suspicion. To be sure, Yatarō, [who upon his father's death had taken the latter's name, Shintarō,] requested Yazobei not to say anything about [the new] Shintarō's having previously gone by the name Yatarō. When, however, the Osaka Magistracy had Yazobei arrested and interrogated him under the impression that he was Yatarō, he stated the true situation. In our view there are not sufficient grounds to hold him culpable.[55]

• The addendum concerning [Shintarō's wife,] Wasa;[56] [Yatarō's wife,] Nobu; [Yatarō's concubine,] Tsugi; and [Shintarō's and Yatarō's clerk] Tsunehachi indicates that they did not receive transmission of the Kirishitan creed. Nevertheless, the record of the investigation includes evidence that Wasa's husband, the former Shintarō, visited Gunki together with Itoya Wasa and two others and held secret discussions in a secluded room. He also accepted in pawn from Gunki a strange buddha image and kept it in his possession. Yatarō burned this drawing in accordance with his father's deathbed instructions. Even if Wasa did not know the details of Shintarō's secret discussions with Gunki, it was her son who took care of matters after her husband's death. For her not to be aware of activities that invite suspicion, such as taking the strange drawing in pawn and then burning it, is more egregious than ordinary negligence. In our view, her behavior deserves a sentence of thirty days' confinement to her house.

Nobu's culpability regarding the doings of her father-in-law and husband is of a lesser degree than Wasa's. It would be appropriate to sentence her to a strict reprimand. As Tsugi and Tsunehachi are both servants, they cannot really be accused of committing a misdeed.

However, the aforementioned four people are the wives and servants of Shintarō and Yatarō, who engaged in activities that invite suspicion of the sort described. It therefore would not be appropriate to let them remain in their present locale. Their situation in this regard is the same as that of Moto. In our view you might thus order the Osaka eastern magistrate to sentence Wasa to thirty days' confinement to her house, as he has proposed, and to sentence Nobu to a strict reprimand. He should also order all four, including Tsugi and Tsunehachi, to move somewhere within the province of Yamashiro outside the city limits of Kyoto; he should issue instructions as well that they are not free to live elsewhere. The magistrate should also inform the Kyoto Magistracy about this order.[57]

• The addendum concerning [Shintarō's adopted son-in-law] Shinbei and [daughter] Mume indicates that they did not receive transmission of the Kirishitan creed; nor did they engage in activities that invite suspicion or appear to have been involved in any other misdeed. Nevertheless, as with the foregoing recommendations regarding [Shintarō's wife,] Wasa, and the three others, they are the adoptive son and the daughter of Shintarō, who was friendly with Mizuno Gunki and engaged in activities that invite suspicion. It consequently would not be appropriate to let them remain in their present locale. In our view, in the same manner as with Moto, you might direct the Osaka eastern magistrate to order them to move somewhere within the province of Yamashiro outside the city limits of Kyoto; he should issue instructions as well that they are not free to live elsewhere. The magistrate should also inform the Kyoto Magistracy about this order.[58]

• As described in the addendum concerning [Makijirō's uncle,] Jinbei, his culpability may be considered in light of a precedent from 1802, when Lord Suganuma Sadayoshi was serving as financial and judicial affairs magistrate.[59] After having consulted [the senior councillors], Lord Suganuma pronounced the following sentence:

> When a band of conspirators broke into and smashed the house of the Shugen priest Honjuin Eiren of Yamaguchi village in Dewa province, among the items lost were a sword, a short sword, and items of clothing. These were carried off by Kinji and others from [the nearby] Kawarago village. Subsequently Chōroku and Ichirobei of Kawarago village brought these items back, and Eiren secretly accepted them. He surmised that if he told the truth about this when the matter was investigated, it would cause trouble for [Chōroku and Ichirobei]. Thus he told his son Shikibu, whom he repeatedly sent to serve as his representative [at the interrogation], to say that Eiren did not know what had happened to the lost items. For committing the misdeed of having Shikibu testify falsely, he is sentenced to thirty days' seclusion.

Since the circumstances surrounding Jinbei's actions were more egregious than those figuring in this precedent, in our view you might order [the Osaka magistrate] to sentence him to wearing handcuffs for fifty days.[60]

• The addendum concerning [Riemon's friend] Bunsuke indicates that he acceded to Riemon's request and nominally registered [Soe, Gunki's wife,] as a member of his own household under the name of Suma, whom he was told had absconded. In so doing he cooperated with Riemon in what was a total fabrication. His culpability may be considered in light of a precedent concerning a comparable misdeed from 1798, when Lord Murakami Yoshiaya was serving as Edo magistrate.[61] After having consulted [the senior councillors], Lord Murakami disposed of this misdeed as follows:

> Bunkichi, a house owner in the townspeople block adjacent to the temple of Tentokuji in Nishikubo, knew that his tenant Denjirō in fact served in a daimyo house under the name Sugimoto Denjirō. Nevertheless he agreed to Denjirō's request to arrange matters concerning the status of Tani, [a female samisen teacher,] by having the two of them recorded on the town population register as "the samisen player Denjirō and his wife, Tani." As this was a particularly serious misdeed for one with the status of a house owner, Lord Murakami sentenced Bunkichi to a fine of five thousand coppers.[62]

Since Bunsuke's degree of culpability is much less than that of Bunkichi, a sentence of a strict reprimand would be appropriate. However, the record of the investigation indicates that Riemon arranged for Bunsuke to take "Suma" nominally into his household at the time when Mizuno Gunki was dismissed from the service of the Kan'in princely house. Since this dismissal occurred in 1818, Bunsuke's action is a past offense that occurred more than twelve months ago. In our view, in line with the specifications in the Rules for Deciding Judicial Matters, you might thus order [the Osaka eastern magistrate] to declare that Bunsuke is to be pardoned and not held subject to punishment.

Because it appears [from the record of the investigation] that Bunsuke did no more than take "Suma" nominally into his household, we have proposed dealing with the matter as stated. If, however, her name has continued to be listed in the population register for Bunsuke's household up to the present, it would be difficult to treat this as a past offense. In that case, in our view, you might order the Osaka eastern magistrate to sentence Bunsuke to a strict reprimand.[63]

We have reported on our deliberations in the form of comments attached [to the pertinent items in the dossier of materials submitted by the Osaka eastern magistrate]. For Uhei of Shinchi Ura-machi in Dōjima and the others [interrogated for lesser misdeeds], we have attached comments regarding the sentences and the procedures to be followed to the addenda wherein their testimony is recorded.[64]

In addition, in our view [attention should be given to the following matters:]

- Those who are devotees of the Kirishitan creed—namely, Sano, Kinu, Toyoda Mitsugi, Umon, Heizō, and Kenzō, as well as Mizuno Gunki and Itoya Wasa, who died before the present investigation began—may have recognized kin, sons-in-law, or fathers-in-law apart from those who came to light in the present investigation.[65] If so, these persons all should be questioned and the procedures for dealing with relatives of Kirishitan applied to them as well.

- The negligence of the priest of the temple with which Kenzō is registered and of the priests of its temple group in failing to look into his behavior properly before certifying his sectarian affiliation should be thoroughly clarified through interrogation.[66] If the circumstances are the same as those recorded in the testimony of Daizui of Unseiji and the other temple priests involved in the incident, they should receive the same sentences.

- The dossier indicates that Riemon, Kyūbei, and Shintarō, who were deceased before the investigation began, all had been friendly with Gunki when they were alive and had engaged in numerous suspicious activities. Apart from them, Kanzō and his wife, Toki, and Yoshichi's wife, Yae, arranged with Sano to confound people and behaved in a manner that also invites utmost suspicion. Unlike the case with [Itoya] Wasa, however, it cannot be definitely ascertained that they were in fact devotees of this sect. It thus is not appropriate to define those connected to Riemon and the other five as relatives of Kirishitan. But since all six engaged in suspicious activities, if they have other recognized kin, sons-in-law, or fathers-in-law apart from those already investigated, these should all be questioned. Even if these kin and in-laws have not done anything suspicious, those residing in Osaka should not be permitted to live freely anywhere outside the three districts of Osaka. Those residing in Kyoto should be ordered to move somewhere within the province of Yamashiro outside the city limits of Kyoto and instructed that they are not free to live elsewhere. In Kyoto, because of the proximity to the imperial palace, a sentence of banishment beyond the city limits is imposed in place of physical punishments such as flogging and tattooing.[67] This instance does not involve such physical punishments, but we have suggested [a comparable arrangement] because it would be inappropriate to allow these people to continue to live within the Kyoto city limits.[68]

• Orders should be given to those connected to Riemon and the other five that the [restrictions on residence] apply for only one generation but are to remain in effect as long as they live.[69] If they move [elsewhere within the permitted area] or die, this should be reported to the Osaka eastern magistrate.

• As for Makijirō and the others sentenced to incarceration, since it would be inappropriate to put them together with those jailed for other reasons, orders should be given to construct a separate enclosure for them within the jailhouse and to keep strict watch to make sure they do not engage in strange activities. If, upon thorough investigation, there is no evidence after several years of anything suspicious, [the Osaka eastern magistrate] should submit an inquiry as to whether they might be released from incarceration and placed under the custody of the locale. In addition, once the sentences have been carried out, in our view, it would be advisable to issue general proclamations regarding the necessity to take particular care in looking into people's behavior before certifying their sectarian affiliation, as specified by shogunal law.

The Deliberative Council, acting in unison, seventh month, 1829

Chapter 9

⟡

The Senior Councillors' Orders and Their Implementation

12. THE SENIOR COUNCILLORS' ORDERS REGARDING SENTENCES; FIRST DAY, TWELFTH MONTH, 1829

Order [from the senior councillors] conveyed [to the Osaka eastern magistrate by the Osaka governor, Lord Ōta Sukemoto]: The following sentences are to be pronounced in the incident that has been investigated under the supervision of [the Osaka eastern magistrate,] Lord Takai Sanenori:[1]

Sano (Deceased)

The corpse, preserved in salt, is to be paraded through the three districts of Osaka and crucified.

However, in the verdict to be proclaimed, the following phrase is to be deleted: from "According to the transmission Sano received from Kinu, by nature the Lord of Heaven has no shape or form" to "Seeing the likeness in the image, she became all the more confirmed in her faith. After Sano returned to Osaka. . . ." This is to be rewritten as "After receiving the secret transmission from Kinu, she was able to predict. . . ."

As for the figures mentioned in the addenda to Sano's testimony, [the following measures are to be taken]:

- Harimaya Uhei and his wife, Soyo, should be sentenced to a strict reprimand, but as it is a past offense [the statute of limitations applies, and] they are not be subject to punishment.

- [Yae's husband] Kenpōya Yoshichi is to be put under the custody of relatives and be interrogated fully if he recovers from illness.

- [Sano's] landlord Yohei; his mother, Kiwa; and his wife, Chika, are to be sentenced to a strict reprimand and the money that Yae brought Yohei confiscated.

- Among Gihei and the eighteen others [who entrusted money and clothing to Sano], some gave a pledge that they would not tell others about this on pain of being struck down by divine punishment if they did. Those who did so cannot be said to have been simply remiss. A statement is to be added to the verdict that this behavior constitutes a misdeed and they are to be fined three thousand coppers or, depending on their circumstances, ordered confined to their house for thirty days. Those who did not give such a pledge are to be sentenced to a strict reprimand. As above [with Yohei], the money they received is to be confiscated.

- The pawnbrokers Shinshichi and Kyūbei were not negligent in [observing the procedures for] accepting items in pawn. They thus are not to be held culpable, but the items they took in pawn are to be confiscated and handed over to the magistracy.

Toki

Death by decapitation.

Kinu [Deceased]

The corpse, preserved in salt, is to be paraded through the three districts of Osaka and crucified.

However, in the verdict to be proclaimed, the following phrase is to be deleted: from "Kinu thought that if she told Sano" to "even more confirmed in her faith." The phrasing is to be rewritten as ". . . passed on to her the transmissions as Kinu had received them from Mitsugi. Sano now attained mastery. . . ."

• As for Koto, who is mentioned in the addenda to Kinu's testimony, it is clear that she did not receive any transmission of the [Kirishitan] creed. Nevertheless, on more than one occasion she thought that what Kinu was encouraging her to do was strange. If Jōsuke heard from his mother about this, both of them should have reported the matter to the magistracy. As it was remiss of them simply to let the matter go, both should be sentenced to a strict reprimand. However, it is difficult to ascertain from the record of the investigation the exact date of this act of remissness. If it is a past offense that occurred more than twelve months ago, they should be declared not subject to punishment.

Toshimaya Tōzō

Banishment from the immediate locale.

Harimaya Kahei

Banishment from the three districts of Osaka.

Toyoda Mitsugi

To be paraded through the three districts of Osaka and crucified.

The Kyoto magistrate is to be directed to erect there as well an execution placard with the verdict.

As for the figures mentioned in the addenda to Mitsugi's testimony, [the following measures are to be taken]:

• Ito and Toki, the adoptive daughters of the deceased Itoya Wasa, and Kamon, the adoptive son of Mitsugi, are to be sentenced to incarceration.
• The deceased Harimaya Kinoshin should have been sentenced to incarceration, were he still alive. This is to be proclaimed to the parties involved in the incident.
• Mitsugi's mother, Eshū, is of an extremely advanced age and does not understand what is going on around her. Since it is not possible to

interrogate her, no sentence is to be levied and she is to be ordered put under the custody of relatives.

Fujii Umon (Deceased)

The corpse, preserved in salt, is to be paraded through the three districts of Osaka and crucified.

• Umon's deceased wife, Fusa, who is mentioned in the addendum to his testimony, should have been sentenced to incarceration, were she still alive. This is to be proclaimed to the parties involved in the incident.

Takamiya Heizō

To be paraded through the three districts of Osaka and crucified.

• Heizō's wife, Mutsu, who is mentioned in the addendum to his testimony, is to be sentenced to incarceration.

Tsuchiya Shōni (Deceased)

Were Shōni still alive, he should have been sentenced to incarceration. This is to be proclaimed to the parties involved in the incident.

Additionally, the written materials kept by Shōni are to be burned.

As for the figures mentioned in the addenda to Shōni's testimony:

• The deceased Hōki Masasuke should have been sentenced to a strict reprimand, were he still alive, but as this is a past offense, he is not to be subject to punishment. This is to be proclaimed to the parties involved in the incident.
• Matsusakaya Nihei should be sentenced to a fine of three thousand coppers, but since this is a past offense, he is to be declared not subject to punishment. The same applies to Teradaya Kumazō and Minoya Koha-chi, but as both have died, this disposition is to be proclaimed to the parties involved in the incident.

- Moto, the younger sister of the present Kamaya Kyūbei, is to be sentenced to a strict reprimand; Kyūbei and Kiyo, the widow of Tomitaya Riemon, are not to be held accountable. The three are to be ordered to move somewhere within the province of Yamashiro outside the city limits of Kyoto and instructed that they are not free to live elsewhere. The Kyoto Magistracy is also to be informed of this order.

Nakamuraya Yatarō (Deceased)

Yatarō should have been sentenced to incarceration, were he still alive. This is to be proclaimed to the parties involved in the incident.

As for the figures mentioned in the addenda to Yatarō's testimony, his mother, Wasa, is to be sentenced to thirty days' confinement to her house, and his wife, Nobu, to a strict reprimand. They also are to be ordered to move somewhere within the province of Yamashiro outside the city limits of Kyoto and instructed that they are not free to live elsewhere. This order applies as well to Shinbei, the adoptive son-in-law of [Yatarō's father,] the elder Shintarō; Shinbei's wife, Mume; Yatarō's concubine, Tsugi; and his servant Tsunehachi. The Kyoto Magistracy is also to be informed of this order.

Makijirō (Deceased)

Makijirō should have been sentenced to incarceration, were he still alive.[2] This is to be proclaimed to the parties involved in the incident.

As for the figures mentioned in the addenda to Makijirō's testimony:

- Momijiya Jinbei is to be sentenced to wearing handcuffs for fifty days.
- Minoya Bunsuke agreed to Riemon's request that he falsely register Suma, whom he was told had absconded [and who was actually Gunki's wife, Soe,] as a member of his household. For this act of remissness he should be sentenced to a strict reprimand, but because it is a past offense, he is to be declared not subject to punishment.
- However, if this was not just a temporary arrangement and Suma's name is still recorded in Bunsuke's population register, it cannot

properly be treated as a past offense, and he should be sentenced to a strict reprimand.

Kenzō (Deceased)

The corpse, preserved in salt, is to be paraded through the three districts of Osaka and crucified.

The written materials kept by Kenzō are to be burned.

Daizui, Priest of Mizuno Gunki's Temple, Unseiji

Expulsion from the temple.

If there had been a grave for Mizuno Gunki, it should have been ordered destroyed. As there is no grave, it is to be proclaimed to those involved in the incident that they are to know [that it would have been destroyed].

The Priests of Unseiji's Temple Group

Fifty days' seclusion.

Shōryū, Priest of Sano's Temple, Enkōji

Expulsion from the temple.

The Priests of Enkōji's Temple Group

Fifty days' seclusion.

Zenshō, Priest of Kinu's Temple, Rentakuji

Expulsion from the temple.

The Priests of Rentakuji's Temple Group

Fifty days' seclusion.

Zekan, Priest of Toyoda Mitsugi's Temple, Daijōin

Expulsion from the temple.

Zekan and those involved in the incident are also to be ordered to destroy Wasa's grave and the Kyoto Magistracy directed to dispatch an inspector to oversee this. If Zekan took up service as priest of the temple prior to 1818, [he would be responsible for] the negligent handling of the certification of Wasa's sectarian affiliation. Thus, if that is the case, Wasa's name is to be inserted after Mitsugi's [as also Zekan's parishioner] in the verdict [concerning the priests].

The Priests of Daijōin's Temple Group

Fifty days' seclusion.

Kanryō, Priest of Fujii Umon's Temple, Jōkōji

Expulsion from the temple.

The Priests of Jōkōji's Temple Group

Fifty days' seclusion.

Kōhō, Priest of Takamiya Heizō's Temple, Kanzanji

Expulsion from the temple.

The Priests of Kanzanji's Temple Group

Fifty days' seclusion.

Takeuchi Ōmi

Fifty days' confinement to his house.

Those Culpable Under the Principle of Residential Mutual Responsibility

• In the rural districts where Sano and Fujii Umon resided: their land-lords, the village headmen, and the village aldermen
• In the urban districts where Kinu and Takamiya Heizō resided: their landlords, the block aldermen, and the [landlord's] five-household group
• In the town block where Toyoda Mitsugi resided: the block aldermen and the five-household group

The village headmen and block aldermen are to be stripped of their duties and fined five thousand coppers each. The landlords and village aldermen in rural districts are to be stripped of their duties and fined three thousand coppers each. The members of the five-household groups are to be fined three thousand coppers each.

Other Directions

• A special enclosure within the jailhouse is to be set aside for those newly sentenced to incarceration; they are to be kept under watch and their behavior observed. If, after several years, there is no evidence of anything suspicious, an inquiry should be submitted [to the senior councillors] about releasing them from incarceration and placing them under custody of the locale.
• No specific directions have been issued as to whether the Osaka eastern magistrate should instruct, as he has proposed, Yohei; his mother, Kiwa; and his wife, Chika, as well as Gihei and the other eighteen people [who offered money and clothing to Sano] not to take leave of their senses henceforth.
• Sano, Kinu, Toyoda Mitsugi, Umon, Heizō, and Kenzō, as well as Mizuno Gunki and Itoya Wasa [are to be punished as Kirishitan]. If they have any recognized kin, sons-in-law, or fathers-in-law apart from those who have already been investigated, they are to be dealt with as relatives of Kirishitan. Orders are thus to be issued that they be sought out and questioned.
• Kanzō and his wife, Toki; Yoshichi's wife, Yae; Riemon; the former Kyūbei; and Shintarō cannot be said to have been devotees of the Kirishitan creed. Nevertheless, they engaged in various suspicious activities.

Thus if they have other recognized kin, sons-in-law, or fathers-in-law apart from those already investigated, these are all to be sought out and questioned. Even if there is nothing suspicious about their behavior, those residing in Kyoto are to be ordered to move somewhere in the province of Yamashiro outside the Kyoto city limits and those residing in Osaka instructed that they are not free to reside outside the three districts of Osaka.

All the recipients of this order are to be instructed that [the restrictions on residence] apply for only one generation but are to remain in effect as long as they live. If they move [elsewhere within the permitted area] or die, this is to be reported to the Osaka Eastern Magistracy.

• The negligence of the temple with which Kenzō is registered and its temple group in failing to look properly into his behavior before certifying his sectarian affiliation is to be investigated thoroughly and clarified. If the circumstances are the same as those recorded in the testimony of Daizui of Unseiji and the others, the priests of Kenzō's temple and its temple group are to be sentenced to the same respective punishments as Daizui and the others.

Eleventh month, 1829

13. OTHER DIRECTIONS FROM THE SENIOR COUNCILLORS; FIRST DAY, TWELFTH MONTH, 1829

[Memorandum transmitted by the Osaka governor to the Osaka eastern magistrate] informing him of the following further instructions received from the senior councillors:[3]

During the time Lord Matsudaira Muneakira was serving as Osaka governor,[4] [the Osaka eastern magistrate] Lord Takai Sanenori submitted to him two ledgers and other materials concerning the investigation of people who were devotees of the proscribed pernicious sect and appropriated money and goods or who possessed books of the Jesus creed. In response to Lord Takai's query about appropriate punishments for those involved, [Lord Matsudaira] directed him to look into comparable cases and, in consultation with [the Osaka western magistrate] Lord Naitō Noritomo, to propose punishments appropriate to the facts of the matter as he saw them. Lord Takai thus submitted a proposal for punishments.[5]

In addition, we have heard that in response to further queries [from Lord Matsudaira], Lord Takai responded that the principals were without question devotees of the pernicious sect.

Thereupon the matter was reviewed [in Edo by the senior councillors and the Deliberative Council]. They concluded that even if those involved were not actual devotees of the pernicious sect and had simply bruited about strange things as if they were adherents of the pernicious sect so as to extort money and goods, what they did was far more heinous than the actions of those who propagated the teachings of the [banned] Sanchō-ha and Fuju Fuse sects. Punishing them severely for having promoted the strictly proscribed pernicious creed would also serve to prevent [subversive practices] from developing henceforth.

As it thus [has been officially determined] that these people without doubt are devotees of the pernicious creed, their relatives are to be dealt with severely as well. Although [at present] there seem to be no others of the same sort apart from those reported in the record of the investigation, this cannot be known for sure, since such people try to keep their activities secret. Orders thus will be issued that authorities everywhere, not just those in the provinces under the supervision of the Osaka Magistracy,[6] are to search unremittingly for people of this sort and are to discuss and settle upon appropriate measures for preventing [subversive activities].

Regarding the dossier submitted by Lord Takai, including the report on the investigation [with the confirmed testimonies] and memoranda, and the inquiries about appropriate punishments transmitted [to the senior councillors] by Lord Matsudaira, we have issued formal orders separately.[7] The following points are also to be noted:

Regarding the matter of Sano's treading on a *fumie* in Nagasaki, there is no evidence apart from her own testimony. It thus cannot be treated as judicially verifiable. Such a matter, [if allowed to stand as part of the official record,] will be detrimental to the investigation and certification of sectarian affiliation. All references to Sano's treading on the *fumie* are thus to be deleted without exception from the record of the investigation and from all other materials pertaining to the incident.

The corpses of those who have died while detained in the jailhouse, apart from those sentenced to having the pertinent punishment inflicted on their dead bodies, are to be discarded.[8]

As there is no need to examine further the books and written materials kept by Shōni and Kenzō, they are to be ordered incinerated directly.

Once the sentences have been pronounced and carried out, the senior councillors are to be informed immediately.

Twelfth month, 1829

14. THE OSAKA EASTERN MAGISTRATE'S ACKNOWLEDGMENT OF COMPLIANCE; SEVENTH DAY, TWELFTH MONTH, 1829

Report on the pronouncing of the sentences as directed by Edo for the parties to the incident of those who worshipped a buddha image of the proscribed pernicious sect, transmitted its creed, and appropriated money and goods, or who kept books of the Jesus creed.[9]

I hereby confirm the receipt of your order to pronounce the sentences as directed. Two days ago, on the fifth, I pronounced the sentences. In addition, I report below on the [several further issues raised in your order]:

• Among Gihei and eighteen others mentioned in the addenda to Sano's testimony, four submitted a pledge stating that they should be struck down by divine punishment if they told anyone [about their donations]. These four are Kawachiya Manjirō and his wife, Tora, as well as Ōshimaya Kiroku and his wife, Toku. This misdeed has been added to the verdict concerning them. Manjirō and Kiroku have been sentenced to pay fines of three thousand coppers each, and Tora and Toku have been sentenced to thirty days' confinement to their homes. As the others did not submit such a pledge, they have been sentenced to a strict reprimand. We have confiscated what remains of the money that they received from Yae.

• An addendum to Kinu's testimony includes a statement by Koto, also known as Mitsugi, mother of Edoya Jōsuke, noting that she had heard strange things from Kinu and that after discussing this with Jōsuke, she had broken off relations with Kinu. This occurred thirteen years ago, in the tenth month of 1817.[10] Koto fell ill and died this month, after I received the order from Edo. Consequently, I have proclaimed to Jōsuke and the other parties to the incident the order's specifications concerning Koto and Jōsuke. To wit, "If Kinu told Koto strange things, Jōsuke and Koto should have reported this to the magistracy. They were remiss to simply let the matter go. If Koto were alive, she and Jōsuke [in principle] should have been sentenced to a strict reprimand, but since this is a past offense, they will not be subject to punishment."

• As for Minoya Bunsuke, an addendum to Makijirō's testimony indicates that twelve years ago, in 1818, at Riemon's request, Bunsuke briefly reported [Soe, under the name of] Suma, as being a member of his household. Soon after, however, he had Suma's registration transferred to the former Kamaya Kyūbei. She was registered as a member of Bunsuke's household only for that period, and her name is no longer listed in Bunsuke's population register. I have thus proclaimed [to the parties concerned] that although [in principle] Bunsuke should be sentenced to a strict reprimand, as it is a past offense, he will not be subject to punishment.[11]

• Zekan became the priest of Daijōin, the temple where Toyoda Mitsugi is registered, after [Itoya Wasa's death] twelve years ago in the eighth month of 1818. Specifically, he came to the temple ten years ago, in the ninth month of 1820.[12] Wasa's death occurred during the tenure of Ijō, two generations before Zekan. In pronouncing Zekan's verdict, I therefore did not include any charge regarding negligence in the certification of Wasa's sectarian affiliation.

• We interrogated Ryōnen, the priest of Enshōji, a branch temple of [Nishi] Honganji and located in Aburakake-machi in Osaka, where Kenzō is registered, and the priests of the other temples in Enshōji's temple group. In the same manner as Daizui and the others, they stated that they were not aware of the fact that Kenzō bought and wrote books of the Jesus creed. I ordered their testimony recorded and sentenced Ryōnen to expulsion from his temple and the priests of the temples in Enshōji's temple group to fifty days' seclusion.

• Kōhō, the priest of Kanzanji, the temple where Takamiya Heizō is registered, fell ill and died on the twenty-second day of the eleventh month of this year.[13] I hereby report this, and since Kōhō would have been sentenced to expulsion from his temple if he were alive, I pronounced this sentence to the parties to the incident.

• I pronounced to Zekan and the other parties to the incident that Wasa's grave was to be destroyed and informed the Kyoto magistrates Lord Matsudaira Sadatomo and Lord Odagiri Naoaki that they should send inspectors to check on this.[14] On the seventh day of this month I received confirmation from Lord Matsudaira and Lord Odagiri that they had immediately dispatched inspectors and that the grave has indeed been destroyed. I thus report that these orders have all been carried out.

• In addition to the above, a separate enclosure within the jailhouse grounds has been prepared for those who have been ordered to be incarcerated, and they have been interned there. If after several years there is no evidence of anything suspicious, [the Osaka eastern magistrate serving at that time] will submit an inquiry as to whether they might be released from incarceration and placed under the custody of the locale.

• In pronouncing the sentences of Yohei; his mother, Kiwa; and his wife, Chika; as well as of Gihei and the eighteen others, I did not include a special caution about not taking leave of their senses henceforth.

• We will investigate whether there are any other recognized kin, sons-in-law, or fathers-in-law of Sano, Kinu, Toyoda Mitsugi, Umon, Heizō, and Kenzō, as well as Mizuno Gunki and Itoya Wasa, and will subsequently report our findings to you. We will further investigate to see if Kanzō and his wife, Toki; Yoshichi's wife, Yae; Riemon; the former Kyūbei; and Shintarō have any other recognized kin, sons-in-law, or fathers-in-law. If there are such persons, even if they have done nothing suspicious, I will issue orders to them in accord with the directions received from you and will report to you about this.[15]

• As for the son and daughters of Yatarō whose names appear in his testimony, their status as recognized kin of Shintarō is already known. I will report separately about the orders I issued to them on the occasion of pronouncing sentences in this incident.[16]

Takai Sanenori, seventh day, twelfth month, 1829

15. THE OSAKA EASTERN MAGISTRATE'S RESPONSE TO THE SENIOR COUNCILLORS' OTHER DIRECTIONS; SEVENTH DAY, TWELFTH MONTH, 1829

I hereby confirm the receipt of the [additional] orders [from the senior councillors].[17] As for the matter of Sano's treading on a *fumie* in Nagasaki, all references to this have been deleted from the record of the interrogation and other documents, and we have ensured that no traces of it remain. As for those who died while detained in the jailhouse, I have proclaimed to the parties to the incident that apart from those sentenced to having the pertinent punishment inflicted on their dead bodies, their corpses will be discarded. The written materials kept by Shōni and Kenzō have all been burned.[18] Thus I report.

Takai Sanenori, seventh day, twelfth month, 1829

16. REPORT ON THE INCINERATION OF THE CONFISCATED WRITTEN MATERIALS; FIFTH DAY, TWELFTH MONTH, 1829

In accordance with the orders from Edo about the written materials [confiscated from Shōni and Kenzō], it has been reported that they were incinerated in front of the waiting area for parties to a suit [located outside the main gate of the Osaka Eastern Magistracy]. The incineration took place in view of those waiting and was done under the supervision of Ōshio Heihachirō and Seta Tōshirō, the senior staff officials in charge of the case.[19]

17. THE OSAKA EASTERN MAGISTRATE'S REPORT ON SHINTARŌ'S KIN; SEVENTH DAY, TWELFTH MONTH 1829

Report on the order about moving their residence issued to the recognized kin of the elder Nakamuraya Shintarō.

Sutejirō, nine years old, son
Kyō, six years old, daughter
Ai, sixteen years old, daughter with concubine
    children of Nakamuraya Yatarō

Sutejirō, Kyō, and Ai are grandchildren of the late Shintarō. In accordance with the recent shogunal order, [in pronouncing sentences on the parties to the incident,] I ordered [Shintarō's wife and] Yatarō's mother, Wasa; Yatarō's wife, Nobu; and Yatarō's concubine, Tsugi, to move somewhere in the province of Yamashiro outside the Kyoto city limits and instructed them that they are not free to reside elsewhere. I consequently have also ordered Sutejirō, Kyō, and Ai to move together with them and have instructed them as well as Wasa, Nobu, and Tsugi that they are not free to reside elsewhere even after they have reached adulthood. I hereby report on this matter.

It is not easy to determine whether the late Shintarō has any other recognized kin. We will pursue the matter further, but as Sutejirō and the other two were mentioned in Yatarō's testimony, I have for the moment issued orders to them as above. I have further ordered that they are to know that [the restrictions on residence] apply for only one generation but are to remain in effect as long as they live. If they move [elsewhere within the permitted area] or die, this is to be reported to the Osaka Eastern Magistracy.

Takai Sanenori, [seventh day,] twelfth month, 1829

Chapter 10

Aftermath

18. PROCLAMATION WARNING AGAINST KIRISHITAN; TWELFTH MONTH, 1829

The Kirishitan sect has long been proscribed. Nevertheless, recently in the Kyoto–Osaka area, people said to belong to this sect have been found engaging in deviant practices. They have been severely punished. An even more rigorous search than heretofore should be made for any signs of this sect. People everywhere should be constantly on watch, and if they see something suspicious, they should immediately report this to the appropriate authorities. Depending on the circumstances they may be granted a reward, and orders will be issued to ensure that the person who has been reported does not seek revenge. If it should come out that people kept quiet despite being aware of [suspicious activities], not only they but also those of the same locale will be subject to punishment.[1]

19. REPORT BY THE OSAKA EASTERN MAGISTRATE ON ADDITIONAL RELATIVES OF THE PRINCIPALS TO THE INCIDENT; THIRD MONTH, 1830

In the twelfth month of last year, 1829, the senior councillors ordered that if Sano, Kinu, Toyoda Mitsugi, Umon, Heizō, and Kenzō, as well as Mizuno Gunki and Itoya Wasa, had any recognized kin, sons-in-law, or fathers-in-law apart from those we have already investigated, they should be dealt with as relatives of Kirishitan. I thus was to look into this matter and report my findings to [the senior councillors].[2] I hereby report the results to date of my investigation of this issue.

[The following additional relatives have been identified:]

Kō

Residing together with Kanaya Uhachi, tenant of a rental property managed by Hikawaya Uhei in Tenma 8-chōme in Osaka.

This Kō is Kinu's niece.[3]

Hisae

Heizō's adoptive daughter, who lived together with him.

Tame

Kenzō's adoptive mother, who lives together with Kumedayū in the village of Sumiyoshi, Sumiyoshi county, Settsu province, in the domain of Lord Ōkubo Tadazane.[4]

Tame is eighty-one years of age as of this year. She is extremely elderly.

Shū[5]

Kenzō's wife.

Ryōzō

Kenzō's son by birth.

The above Tame, Shū, and Ryōzō originally resided along with Kenzō together with Zenbei in rented quarters in Funadaiku-machi in Dōjima managed by Matsumotoya Yuzō, who was represented at the magistracy by Okamotoya Tamizō, and they were listed on the population register there. However, Kenzō arranged for them to be transferred to Kumedayū's register. Kumedayū has no direct connection with Kenzō but states that he took Tame and the others into his population register because he was on friendly terms with him.

Fujita Chūtatsu

Retainer of the Kajii imperial cloister,[6] presently residing temporarily with Fushimiya Kyūbei of Moto Tenma-chō in Osaka.

According to the testimony taken from Chūtatsu, he is the son of Hanbei, the elder brother of Kenzō's adoptive father, who was the doctor Fujita Kyōan. Kyōan and Hanbei maintained separate residences, but when Chūtatsu was six years of age, Hanbei died, and so Chūtatsu was taken in and raised by his uncle Kyōan. At the age of twenty-four, Chūtatsu established a separate residence, and when he was twenty-seven, Lord Hachisuka of Tokushima in Awa took him on as a retainer, and he moved to Awa. During this time Kenzō became Kyōan's adoptive son and married his daughter Shū. Lord Hachisuka subsequently released Chūtatsu from service, and he became a ronin. He is at present a retainer of the Kajii imperial cloister. Kenzō and Chūtatsu are thus adoptive cousins.

Suehiroya Kahei

Resident in Kyōgoku-machi south of Gojō Bridge in Kyoto.

Kahei is the husband of Wasa's adoptive daughter Toki, and as it appeared that he might be Wasa's son-in-law, I investigated the situation. He stated as follows: "Prior to Wasa's death thirteen years ago in the eighth month of 1818, I became involved in an affair with Toki. Following Wasa's death, I took Toki as my wife eleven years ago in the first month of 1820, with Minoya Sahei, resident on Higashi-no-tōin street north of Nijō street, acting as her nominal parent." [Kahei thus was never actually Wasa's son-in-law.] Because Toki and Kahei had an affair while Wasa was still alive and he might be thought to be Wasa's son-in-law, I have nevertheless reported his situation here.

Minoya Ichimatsu

Resident on Higashi-no-tōin street north of Nijō street.

Ichimatsu is the son of Wasa's adoptive daughter Ito, who is presently incarcerated. He thus is the [adoptive] grandson of Wasa. His father was a man named Karakiya Mansuke, who reportedly died some time ago.

The circumstances being as stated, I have ordered Kō, Hisae, Shū, Ryōzō, Kahei, and Ichimatsu to be detained for the moment in the jail-house. Because Tame is extremely elderly, I have ordered her put under the custody of the locale, and I have ordered Chūtatsu put under the custody of the associate who accompanied him [to the magistracy].[7] Sano, Umon, Gunki, and Heizō seem to have no recognized kin whatsoever. I will investigate further to see if Kenzō had additional blood relatives in distant provinces, but I report here initially on what has been ascertained so far.

The Deliberative Council's Recommendation

Although Kō and the seven others may be considered as the relatives of Kirishitan, in our view their relationship [to the principals to the case] is not such as to require that they be incarcerated. [The senior councillors] thus might direct [the Osaka governor] to inform Lord Takai that he should order Kō and the five others presently detained in the jailhouse to be released and put under the custody of the locale. Once he has investigated the names of all the relatives of those party to the incident, Lord Takai should submit a comprehensive list.[8]

20. REPORT BY THE OSAKA EASTERN MAGISTRATE ON ADDITIONAL KIN OF KENZŌ; INTERCALARY THIRD MONTH, 1830

I hereby report on the following relatives of a devotee of the pernicious sect:

Resident in the Village of Yamazaki, Oe County, Awa Province [in Shikoku], in the Domain of Lord Hachisuka

- Aoyama Shin'emon: Kenzō's nephew
- Shin'emon's younger brother, Isogorō: likewise Kenzō's nephew

- Shin'emon's elder sister, Sata: Kenzō's niece

Resident in the Village of Chiejima, Awa County

- Seto Kashichirō: Kenzō's maternal uncle
- Kashichirō's son, Shunpei: Kenzō's cousin

As I reported to you last month, having learned that these people appeared to be Kenzō's recognized kin, I sent a notice about this matter to Lord Hachisuka's Osaka representative. I requested him to check on their circumstances and whether or not they indeed were Kenzō's recognized kin and, [assuming that they were,] to order them to appear at this office. He consequently reported that they had arrived [in Osaka] and sent them here. The representative's office notified me subsequently that Kenzō's nephew Shin'emon serves in the Inokura guard post; he receives a stipend from Lord Hachisuka and is not a farmer. I asked for further details of the situation, and the representative's office submitted a report, a copy of which I append here.[9] On the basis of this report and questioning [Shin'emon and the others], it was confirmed that they are indeed Kenzō's recognized kin, as noted at the head of the present report. I thus ordered Shin'emon; his younger brother, Isogorō; and his elder sister, Sata, put in the custody of Lord Hachisuka's Osaka representative. As Kashichirō is eighty-two years of age and extremely elderly, I had him put in the custody of a person from his village of Chiejima who is staying temporarily in Osaka. I have had Shunpei detained for the moment in the jailhouse.[10]

The Deliberative Council's Recommendations

As with [Kinu's niece] Kō and the seven others whom Lord Takai reported on separately,[11] Aoyama Shin'emon and the others are to be considered relatives of Kirishitan, but their circumstances are not such as to call for incarceration. In our view, the senior councillors might thus direct [the Osaka governor] to instruct Lord Takai that he should release Shunpei from detention in the jailhouse and put him in the custody of the locale. Once the investigation of all the relatives of parties to the incident is complete, Lord Takai should submit a comprehensive list of their names.[12]

21. INQUIRY FROM THE OSAKA EASTERN MAGISTRATE ABOUT THE CERTIFICATES OF SECTARIAN AFFILIATION FOR RELATIVES OF PARTIES TO THE INCIDENT; FIRST MONTH, 1830

The recognized kin, sons-in-law, and fathers-in-law of the eight principal parties to the incident of the pernicious sect—Sano, Kinu, Toyoda Mitsugi, Umon, Heizō, and Kenzō, together with Mizuno Gunki and Itoya Wasa—have been determined to be relatives of Kirishitan. Since it has been decided to deal with them as such, I have continued to look into [matters pertinent to this situation]. As for those among these relatives who have previously been ordered incarcerated at the jailhouse, there is no need at present for their certificates of sectarian affiliation. In their case it thus will not cause any problem if no immediate decision is reached about how to deal with this matter. However, among the recognized kin, sons-in-law, and fathers-in-law of Kanzō and his wife, Toki; Yoshichi and his wife, Yae; Riemon; the former Kyūbei; and Shintarō, many of those residing in Kyoto have been ordered to move somewhere in Yamashiro province outside the Kyoto city limits. It thus is necessary to decide the format for the certificates of sectarian affiliation for them [to take to their new place of residence].[13]

If I direct that the format should follow that of the certificates of sectarian affiliation used in previous times here in Osaka for the relatives of apostate Kirishitan (see the attached copy), this will be tantamount to indicating that they are indeed, without any qualification, relatives of Kirishitan. Will this be contrary to the senior councillors' intent? Further, since they have moved their place of residence, should the circumstances of this move also be recorded on the certificate? As I am unable to reach a conclusion about these points, I hereby submit an inquiry seeking the senior councillors' directions.

In addition, if the circumstances of these persons' move of residence is to be recorded on the certificate of sectarian affiliation, should the earlier protocol for handling the [natural] deaths of relatives of apostate Kirishitan also be applied, and the deaths of these people accordingly reported annually to the Office for Sectarian Matters in the seventh and twelfth months? I hereby seek your directions on this issue as well. . . .

[Attached example of model certificate from 1760][14]

The above man and woman, two persons in total, are without question parishioners of this temple. As its priest, I am thereby responsible for their affiliation with it. Since they are the relatives of apostate Kirishitan, I will be sure to keep watch over their comportment and activities. Should they be involved in anything connected with the Kirishitan sect, I should be held guilty of the same crime. For future witness, I hereby certify their affiliation with this temple.[15]

The Deliberative Council's Recommendation

The situation of the recognized kin, sons-in-law, fathers-in-law, and mothers-in-law of Kanzō and the others is different from that of those identified as the relatives of Kirishitan. [The restrictions imposed] apply only to them and not to their descendants. Matters concerning them are to be handled by the Osaka Eastern Magistracy, and there is no need to inform the Office for Sectarian Matters of their names or to report their deaths. It thus is not necessary to record the circumstances of the moving of their residence on their certificates of sectarian affiliation. However, in our view, the senior councillors might direct [the Osaka governor] to inform Lord Takai that in instances where the person in question is under a different jurisdiction, Lord Takai should instruct the pertinent authority to report that person's death to the Osaka Eastern Magistracy.[16]

22. THE DELIBERATIVE COUNCIL'S RESPONSE TO AN INQUIRY ABOUT HOW TO HANDLE THE CORPSE OF MITSUGI'S MOTHER; FIRST MONTH, 1830

On the twenty-ninth day of the twelfth month of last year, 1829, the senior councillors instructed us to deliberate and submit our views on the following inquiry from the Osaka governor:

Eshū, the birth mother of Toyoda Mitsugi, one of the parties to the incident involving devotees of the pernicious creed, was of an extremely advanced age and did not understand anything happening around her. It thus was not possible to interrogate her conclusively. In accordance with the shogunal order from the senior councillors, [the Osaka eastern magistrate] therefore pronounced that she would not be subject to punishment and should instead be placed in the custody of her relative

Yorozuya Tōbei of Uchino Niban-chō in Kyoto.[17] However, [Tōbei] submitted a notice to the Kyoto Magistracy that Eshū's condition had suddenly deteriorated and that she had died. The magistrate dispatched a staff official [to investigate the circumstances]. After examining the corpse, the official confirmed that indeed Eshū's death was the result of illness [and not unnatural]. [The Kyoto magistrate] has thus sent notice [to the Osaka eastern magistrate] that he has ordered the corpse to be kept provisionally, [subject to further instructions].

Although Eshū was declared to be not subject to punishment, she is the parent of a major criminal, and thus Lord Takai has submitted an inquiry to me as to whether the corpse should be discarded. Although no pertinent precedents can be found among the materials at hand, would it be appropriate to direct him to order the corpse discarded, as proposed in his inquiry?

The Deliberative Council's Recommendation

Since Eshū's extremely advanced age made it impossible to interrogate her conclusively, she was declared to be not subject to punishment and placed in the custody of a relative. Nevertheless, she is the mother of Mitsugi, who was a devotee of the Kirishitan creed. She thus falls in the category of relatives of a devotee of this sect. The proclamation of 1687 specifies as follows:

> When a relative or descendant of a Kirishitan dies, the corpse should be examined, and if there are no unusual circumstances, it should be handed over to the temple where the person was registered. These points should be recorded in the roster [to be kept by local authorities in areas where there are people identified as relatives of Kirishitan and] submitted twice annually in the seventh and twelfth months to the office responsible for Kirishitan matters. The name of the person concerned should thereupon be removed from the roster.[18]

Considered in light of this proclamation, in our view the senior councillors might direct [the Osaka governor] to convey the following order to Lord Takai: He should inform the Kyoto magistrate that the latter at his discretion may hand Eshū's corpse over to the temple where she was registered. In line with the import of the above proclamation, Lord Takai should also see that this matter is reported to the Office for Sectarian Matters.[19]

23. THE DELIBERATIVE COUNCIL'S RESPONSE TO AN INQUIRY ABOUT HOW TO HANDLE THE CORPSE OF WASA'S ADOPTIVE DAUGHTER ITO; SIXTH MONTH, 1830

On the tenth day of this month the senior councillors instructed us to deliberate and submit our views on an inquiry from the Osaka governor concerning measures taken by Lord Takai in regard to those involved in the incident of devotees of the pernicious sect. To wit, Ito, who [previously] lived together with [her son] Minoya Ichimatsu, was the former adoptive daughter of Itoya Wasa, one of the parties to the incident. In accordance with the shogunal order, she was confined under strict watch within a separate enclosure in the jailhouse, with the understanding that if after several years there was no evidence of suspicious behavior, an inquiry should be submitted as to whether she might be released from incarceration and placed under the custody of the locale. However, she developed a sudden high fever, following which her condition deteriorated rapidly, and she has died. Lord Takai dispatched staff officials from both the Eastern and Western Magistracies to the jailhouse, and upon their having examined the corpse, he has ordered that it be kept provisionally, [subject to further instructions].

This matter concerns the adoptive daughter of Itoya Wasa, who is said to have been a devotee of the Kirishitan creed. [Because of this relationship,] Ito was ordered to be confined within a separate enclosure in the jailhouse. Now that she has died, however, there is no further issue of concern and no reason to keep her corpse within the jailhouse precincts. The situation is the same as with [ordinary] Kirishitan relatives. In our view it therefore would be appropriate to handle it in light of the proclamation of 1687, to which we referred in our deliberations in the first month of this year on how to deal with the corpse of Eshū, the birth mother of Toyoda Mitsugi. The senior councillors might direct the Osaka governor to instruct Lord Takai as follows: At his discretion, he may order that Ito's corpse be handed over to the temple where she was registered. He should also inform the Office for Sectarian Matters about the matter, as specified in the above proclamation. Henceforth, in case of the death of one of the Kirishitan relatives kept confined within the jailhouse, the corpse should be inspected, and so long as there are no matters of concern, no inquiry need be submitted [to Edo]. The matter should be handled in the same manner as Ito's corpse on this occasion and reported once resolved.[20]

24. THE DELIBERATIVE COUNCIL'S RESPONSE TO AN INQUIRY FROM THE OSAKA GOVERNOR ABOUT RELEASING THE INCARCERATED RELATIVES OF THE PRINCIPAL PARTIES; SECOND MONTH, 1836

On the fourteenth day of this month we were ordered [by the senior councillors] to deliberate and report on the following inquiry from the Osaka governor:

> Among the parties to the incident of devotees of the pernicious sect, a shogunal order was handed down in the twelfth month of 1829 regarding Toyoda Kamon, the adoptive son of the yin-yang diviner Toyoda Mitsugi; Mutsu, the wife of Takamiya Heizō; and Toki, the [adoptive daughter of Wasa and] wife of the deceased Suehiroya Kahei. To wit, they were to be confined under strict watch in a separate enclosure within the jailhouse, with the understanding that if after several years there was no evidence of suspicious behavior, an inquiry should be submitted as to whether they might be released from incarceration and placed under the custody of the locale. [The Osaka eastern magistrate] Lord Ōkubo Tadazane reports that close attention has been paid to their behavior since then, and nothing suspicious has been heard regarding any of them.[21] As a number of years have passed, he asks whether it would now be appropriate to order all of them released from incarceration and placed under the custody of the locale.

Kamon and the other two are the adoptive son, wife, and adoptive daughter of people who were devotees of the Kirishitan sect. None of them were themselves involved with this sect. Nevertheless they are the kin of people who committed a heinous crime. When the Deliberative Council considered this matter in 1829, it therefore proposed that they should be confined in a separate enclosure within the jailhouse. If after several years there was no evidence of suspicious behavior, [the Osaka eastern magistrate] was to submit an inquiry as to whether they might be released from incarceration and placed under the custody of the locale.

At that time the Deliberative Council received [from the senior councillors] various materials to use as precedents, including decisions made in the Genroku [1688–1704] and Hōei [1704–1711] eras about the relatives of devotees of the same sect. One was the inquiry from 1707 regarding Tō, son of Sukebei of Hita Chitose village in Bungo province. [According to this inquiry,]

> [At the time of the original investigation several decades ago,] Tō declared that he had never known anything about the Kirishitan sect and did not recall ever being encouraged to follow it. Both from observations of him and from what he said, there did not appear to be evidence of his having received [the practices and teachings] of the pernicious sect. However, as his parents, siblings, and relatives were devotees of the Kirishitan sect, he was ordered incarcerated. As twenty-eight years had passed since his incarceration, the Nagasaki magistrate of the time submitted an inquiry [to the senior councillors] about releasing him from detention and placing him in the custody of the locale. The senior councillors directed the magistrate to permit this, but to ensure that Tō was not left unsupervised.[22]

In the above instance there were many other relatives [of Kirishitan] apart from Tō who had been kept incarcerated, all of them for more than twenty or thirty years, and some of these continued to be detained. Compared with these precedents, Kamon and the two others have not yet been incarcerated for a particularly long period. In our view, the senior councillors might thus direct the Osaka governor to inform Lord Ōkubo not to proceed as proposed in the inquiry.[23]

Second month, 1836

Draft of the Response to Be Issued to the Osaka Governor

To Lord Doi Toshitsura, [Osaka governor][24]

We have received and acknowledge the purport of the report by [the Osaka eastern magistrate] Lord Ōkubo Tadazane that you have forwarded to us. The report proposes the release from incarceration and placing under the custody of the locale the following relatives of devotees of the pernicious sect: Toyoda Kamon, the adoptive son of the yin-yang diviner Toyoda Mitsugi; Mutsu, the wife of Takamiya Heizō; and Toki, the wife of the deceased Suehiroya Kahei.

Although Lord Ōkubo's proposal is based on the orders issued in 1829, Kamon and the others have not as yet been incarcerated for a particularly long period. It thus would be difficult to proceed as proposed. You should inform Lord Ōkubo accordingly.

Joint signature [of the senior councillors], second month, 1836[25]

Part III

RUMORS AND RETELLINGS

The shogunate prohibited the publication of straightforward accounts of current events. Information circulated anyway, of course, but with varying degrees of reliability, elaboration, and outright fabrication. The Keihan Kirishitan incident is a good example. We are fortunate that two inveterate collectors of news of what was going on in the world separately recorded the information about the incident that they had garnered from multiple sources. One, based in Osaka, was the anonymous author of a massive work known as *The State of the Floating World* (*Ukiyo no arisama*). The other was Matsura Seizan (1760–1841), the former daimyo of Hirado domain, who for most of his long retirement kept an extensive record of things of interest that he had read and heard; he titled this miscellany *Night Tales from the Kasshi Day* (*Kasshi yawa*). *The State of the Floating World* and *Night Tales* add to our picture of the incident. They also show how information about events such as this was obtained and transmitted, both at the time it happened and later.

Ōshio's uprising in the second month of 1837 brought renewed attention to the Keihan Kirishitan incident. The uprising, which left a substantial part of Osaka in ashes, spawned large numbers of so-called true accounts (*jitsuroku*): imaginative retellings of current events intended for a broad audience. *The State of the Floating World* and Seizan's *Night Tales* were private works. As collectors of information, the author of *The State of the Floating World* and Seizan likely also passed on to their acquaintances what they learned, but they did not directly seek a larger audience. By contrast *jitsuroku* were often commercial enterprises. The ban on writing about current events using actual names meant that they could not be published, but hand copies circulated in substantial numbers through book dealers and book lenders (*kashihon'ya*).[1] *Jitsuroku* about Ōshio and his uprising often drew a connection to his earlier investigation of the Kirishitan. The intertwining of the two events added to the notoriety of both.

The State of the Floating World, *Night Tales*, and *jitsuroku* about Ōshio all approached the Keihan incident as a newsworthy event. However slanted the perspective, their aim was to record information about what had happened. The incident also figured, however, in writings with a specifically ideological aim: the anti-Christian literature that took on new life in the context of Japan's reluctant reopening under pressure from the Western powers. Here it stood as a warning of the need to be on guard against the dangers posed by Kirishitan.

THE STATE OF THE FLOATING WORLD

The author of *The State of the Floating World* indicates that he was born in 1785, began his compilation in 1806, and concluded it forty years later in 1846. In a modern print edition it occupies well over one thousand pages of a large-format volume with two tiers of print to the page. The author is commonly held to have been a physician who lived in Saitō-machi in Osaka.[2] This area was close to Shirokoura-machi, the location of Jōkōji, the temple where Fujii Umon was registered, and the author counts the priest's wife as one of his informants. In his reportage of the incident, translated in chapter 11, he describes the background and activities of each of the main protagonists, beginning with Mizuno Gunki. This section, which comes quite early in the compilation, is one of a succession of surveys of happenings in different parts of the country in the same period. The sections preceding that on the Keihan incident take up the arrival of Russian ships in Sakhalin and Matsumae in the north and later in Shikoku, peasant uprisings in various regions, and an array of natural disasters that occurred in 1828 and 1829. The section following the

Keihan incident deals at length with the mass pilgrimages to the Ise Shrines in 1830.

Occurrences involving the Osaka Magistracy also drew the author's interest. Later sections cover Ōshio's uprising extensively, as might be expected, but the author writes as well about earlier events in which Ōshio figured, apart from the Keihan incident. Indeed, even if not always reliable, *The State of the Floating World* is one of our few sources of information about Ōshio's activities as an official. For instance, its account of Ōshio's ouster in early 1829 of his counterpart in the western division of the Osaka Magistracy, the leading senior staff official Yuge Shin'emon, appears to be the only extant contemporaneous account of this murky episode.[3]

As the author tells it, Ōshio first arrested some of the outcast leaders who worked closely with Yuge as his "hands" and extracted evidence from them of the senior staff official's engagement in extortion and malfeasance. One member of the gang would trick people into setting up gambling dens; the others would then move in to make arrests and share the proceeds. The gang was also involved in robbery and outright murder. With this evidence in hand, Ōshio took swift advantage of the opportunity provided by the transfer of Yuge's superior, Naitō Noritomo, to a new position in Edo in the spring of 1829. This left Ōshio's superior, the eastern magistrate, Takai Sanenori, temporarily in sole charge of the Osaka Magistracy. The night Yuge returned from seeing Naitō off for Edo, Ōshio sent a summons for him to appear the next morning for a hearing at the Eastern Magistracy. Fearing that it would mean the extinction of Yuge's house were he arrested and investigated, family members pressured him to commit suicide.[4]

Sawayanagi Masumi, who has made a survey of references to the Keihan Kirishitan in accounts of Ōshio, notes that almost all date from after his 1837 uprising. Often they introduce Ōshio's association with the Keihan Kirishitan as an explanatory factor for the rebellion itself, or for Ōshio's initial success in evading arrest after its collapse. Ōshio is said to have become Mitsugi's disciple in Kirishitan sorcery, or to have confiscated books of the Jesus creed from the Kirishitan he arrested and made a thorough study of them. In this way he learned secret ways to confound people, to hide from view and escape mysteriously, or to extinguish fire. *The State of the Floating World* is unusual in that even before the uprising, it already identified Ōshio as the official responsible for the Kirishitan

investigation.⁵ At this point, the author was thoroughly impressed by
Ōshio. In his account of Yuge's downfall, he praises Ōshio as upright and
honorable, and he stresses that Ōshio deserved all the merit for the investigation and execution of the Kirishitan.⁶

In later sections on the rebellion (not translated here), the author pres-
ents a more critical view. There he reports rumors of Ōshio's having used
Kirishitan sorcery to escape, although he does not appear to subscribe to
such speculation himself.⁷ He also gives the synopsis of a kabuki play that
incorporated a variety of references to Ōshio, reportedly staged to full
houses in Kyushu and Shimonoseki (in western Honshu) not long after
the uprising. In a dramatic denouement a woman named Mitsu, who
exercises influence in the shogunal court, reveals herself to be the Ōshio
character's true mother. She hands him a scroll full of Kirishitan sorcery;
then, after some parting words, she collapses on the stage, turning into
a heap of bones. "This," the author comments, "is an allusion to the
Kirishitan Toyoda Mitsugi whom Ōshio brought to judgment some years
ago." He notes the cleverness with which the playwright weaves in references to Ōshio and Takai Sanenori but also criticizes the temerity of putting on such a production, "barely changing one or two graphs in the
characters' names," even before authorities in Edo had pronounced the
sentences on Ōshio and his fellows.⁸

The author bases his account of the Keihan incident on several different types of information. Immediately before he takes up the incident
proper, he copies out the full text of an anti-Christian chapbook called
Origins of the Kirishitan (*Kirishitan kongenki*).⁹ It relates the multiple evils
of the Kirishitan: their aim to "seize the country" by seducing the populace with the ways of their sect, their proficiency in sorcery, and their prop-
agation of morbid practices such as bloody self-flagellation. Presumably
the author saw the chapbook as providing a preview of what might be
expected from the Keihan Kirishitan.

For his description of the Keihan incident as such the author turns to
rumors that he heard in the wake of the executions, supplemented with
information that he sought out from acquaintances. Apart from the wife
of the Jōkōji priest and others evidently residing in Osaka, he cites a certain Takashima Unmei (perhaps another physician), who claimed to have
known of Gunki's efforts to extort money while still in the employ of the
Kan'in princely house. Unmei also passed on information from "a private
secretary [yōnin] of the magistrate." In addition to hearsay evidence of this

sort, the author includes transcriptions of the execution placards and the proclamation that the shogunate issued about watching out for Kirishitan. He notes that many curiosity seekers gathered to copy the placards, drawing the ire of the authorities. He himself borrowed a friend's copy.[10]

The State of the Floating World unquestionably has a hit-or-miss character. Examples are the author's acceptance of a story that Mitsugi had originally been a prostitute in Osaka called Taka who married a wealthy townsman, the tales he relates of Sano's activities in Fukuwatari in Bizen (modern Okayama prefecture), and the even more far-fetched account of the exploits of another woman in Harima province. The exaggerations and distortions give a sense of the rumors about the incident that circulated in Osaka at the time, and of the embroidery the story acquired in the course of retelling.

NIGHT TALES FROM THE KASSHI DAY

Matsura Seizan became daimyo of Hirado domain, located in Kyushu, while still in his teens. He retired in 1806 at the age of forty-seven and took up residence in the domain's lower compound in the Honjo district of Edo. At the urging of his friend Hayashi Jussai (1768–1841), the shogunal Confucian scholar, in 1821 he began to keep an account of matters of interest that he called *Night Tales from the Kasshi Day*. The title referred to the day on which he began this miscellany, the seventeenth day of the eleventh month, equivalent to the *kasshi* day in the sexagenary cycle.[11] The compilation, which he continued for twenty years until his death in 1841, paralleled *The State of the Floating World* in its broad scope. Among other things, Seizan recorded what he heard in Edo about the Keihan Kirishitan. Unlike the author of *The State of the Floating World*, however, Seizan does not seem to have gathered information about the incident in a systematic manner. Rather, he reported bits and pieces of news as they came into his purview over a span of years. In chapter 12 we have gathered the most notable of these fragmentary comments.

With a wide network of contacts among the political elite, Seizan had access to news about the incident from a quite early stage. He initially heard about it in the tenth month of 1829, after the Deliberative Council had submitted its recommendations to the senior councillors but before the latter had issued orders regarding the sentences. He understood the information to originate from Naitō Noritomo, the former Osaka western magistrate who had been transferred to Edo in the third month (item 1). A few months later, Seizan noted that a proclamation calling for watchfulness against Kirishitan had been issued in the wake of the sentencing of the Keihan group and copied it into his miscellany. He then continued with an account of rumors heard from a visitor from Osaka who had been staying with one of the sumo wrestlers in his employ (item 2). Because sumo wrestlers traveled to different parts of the country to take part in tournaments, they were a useful conduit for gathering information, and Seizan frequently referred to things he had heard from one or another of the wrestlers he housed at his residence.[12]

A month or so later, in the spring of 1830, Seizan noted that the crucifixions had been carried out at the Tobita execution grounds and that he had received copies of the execution placards from someone in Osaka. He transcribed the verdicts into the miscellany, noting, "The devotees of the pernicious creed were uncovered five years ago. They were arrested one after the other and finally punished last winter."[13] He then added what appears to be a copy of a broadsheet or some other written account that he "obtained from somewhere, I have forgotten where" (item 3).

At this stage Seizan does not seem to have associated the investigation of the Keihan Kirishitan with Ōshio. That changed after Ōshio's uprising seven years later, in 1837. As soon as word of the uprising reached Edo, Seizan began to record the news. In this context, he also took note of Ōshio's earlier involvement in the Keihan Kirishitan investigation. One entry blames Ōshio for the harshness of the treatment meted out to Kenzō as a scholar of Western learning (item 4). Seizan himself had an interest in Western studies and went so far as to acquire Dutch commentaries on some chapters of the Old Testament. He arranged secretly with one of his retainers to view the *fumie* tablets that the Hirado domain borrowed from the Nagasaki Magistracy every year for the annual confirmation that the domain harbored no Kirishitan. He even had the domain painter draw exact replicas of the different kinds of tablets used.[14] Seizan must have felt some alarm at what had happened to Kenzō as a result of his indulgence in similar activities.[15]

Somewhat later, but evidently before receiving news that Ōshio had been found, Seizan recorded rumors that Ōshio had become a Kirishitan himself; Mitsugi's vengeful spirit might have possessed Ōshio and driven him to rebellion, he speculated (item 5). By the time of his last comment on Ōshio and the Keihan group sometime in 1837, however, Seizan had concluded that Mitsugi and the others were not really Kirishitan but probably followers of the Buddhist cult of Dakiniten.[16] Ōshio, Seizan observed, undoubtedly had recognized this but used the arts of Dakiniten he had obtained from Mitsugi to pursue his own misbegotten dreams of worldly glory (item 6). Seizan thus seems to have been somewhat skeptical about the Kirishitan character of this incident, much like the Deliberative Council in its initial stance in 1829. At the same time, he was clearly ready to believe in the possibility of sorcery and possession.

LATER RETELLINGS

The suggestion that Ōshio had fallen under the sway of the Kirishitan he investigated was developed most fully in the many *jitsuroku* about him. It was undoubtedly through such works that a wider audience became familiar with the name of Mitsugi and her association with Ōshio. Works of this sort continued to be read into the Meiji period, when some were eventually published. In chapter 13 we translate an excerpt from one such piece, put out in 1882 by the Tokyo publisher Eisensha under the title *A Biography of Ōshio Heihachirō* (*Ōshio Heihachirō denki*), or, alternatively, *The Water Margin at Tenma* (*Tenma suiko den*, after the famous Chinese novel *Shuihu zhuan*).[17] It likely reproduces an Edo-period manuscript. Here, Mitsugi casts a curse on both Ōshio and his superior, the Osaka eastern magistrate, Takai Sanenori. Through her Kirishitan dark arts she corrupts Ōshio, famous for his moral probity. When Ōshio questions her, she threatens that he, too, will "end up on a cross," just like her—a prophecy that is fulfilled. Mitsugi and her Kirishitan sorcery, then, were ultimately responsible for Ōshio's rebellion.

Mitsugi and the Keihan incident also came to figure in late Edo anti-Christian writings. In the aftermath of the incident, as we have seen, the shogunate proclaimed the need for greater vigilance in watching out for Kirishitan, and the possibility of Kirishitan activity took on a new immediacy in the eyes of officials such as Kawaji Toshiakira.[18] For Kawaji the situation called for caution rather than alarm. Others, however, saw a clear and present danger, especially as the Western powers brought increased pressure in the 1850s for access to Japan. A focal point of the alarmist camp was the Mito domain, already associated with an anti-Christian intellectual tradition fostered by domain scholars such as Aizawa Seishi-sai (1782–1863) and encouraged by the domain lord Tokugawa Nariaki (1800–1860).

Nariaki firmly believed that the Western powers would use the "poison of the pernicious creed" to subvert the Japanese populace and facilitate incursions into the country. This belief was a key reason for the hardline stance he took in 1853, when Commodore Matthew Perry of the United States confronted shogunal leaders with the demand that they open the country to foreign intercourse. Nariaki addressed several memorials on this issue to the senior councillors in which he called on them to reject the demand resolutely. As one of the grounds for his position he alluded to the Keihan incident, where Kirishitan had been discovered only recently "secretly spreading their creed." Since this had occurred despite the strict proscription of Christianity, were the shogunate to accept Perry's demand and enter into relations with the United States, "as a matter of course there is sure to be a resurgence of this creed."[19]

Although Nariaki saw opening the country as an invitation to the spread of Christianity, he was also an advocate of the principle "know your enemy." As such, he questioned the ban on the dissemination of information about Christianity; it was essential for the elite, at least, to be familiar with the dangers it posed. When the senior councillors disregarded his advice and acceded to Perry's demand, Nariaki put his efforts into other ways of calling attention to Christianity's evils and the need to take action against them. One was a project to put out a Japanese edition of a Ming collection of anti-Christian writings titled *A Collection for Destroying the Pernicious* (*Poxieji*, Jp. *Hajashū*; 1639). In 1855, Nariaki obtained permission from the shogunate for the Mito domain to publish a reprint of this work. It appeared the following year.

Nariaki also planned a parallel compilation that would focus on the history of the problems Christianity had caused in Japan. He thus directed the scholars in his service to make a comprehensive collection of all materials related to this issue beginning with the time of Oda Nobunaga (1534–1582) and to organize them appropriately. The result was *Compilation to Put an End to the Pernicious* (*Sokkyo hen*).[20] Finally completed in 1860, this work had four sections, two of which drew attention to the Keihan incident. The first section consisted of edicts and proclamations that showed the decisive actions taken in the past to counter the Christian threat. It began with Toyotomi Hideyoshi's 1587 proscription of

Christianity and ended with the proclamation calling for vigilance against Kirishitan issued in the wake of the Keihan incident. The second section brought together records of events that "clarified the nefarious plans of the barbarian bandits." The execution placards of Mitsugi and the five others were the next to the last item, immediately preceding an account of Westerners who had tried to open relations with Japan in the first decades of the nineteenth century.[21]

Nariaki died the month after the compilation was completed. His death and the turmoil that beset Mito during the last years of Tokugawa rule meant that the plan to publish *Compilation to Put an End to the Pernicious* was never realized, and it remained in manuscript form. It exerted substantial influence even so, and it firmly ensconced the Keihan Kirishitan incident as recent evidence of the ongoing Christian threat to Japan. Mito thinkers continued to reinforce the point in other writings as well. Aizawa, for instance, referred to the incident in a short piece that he wrote in the same period about the dangers arising from the foreign presence in the newly opened ports. "The old hag from Yasaka" (Mitsugi) had "propagated pernicious ideas,. . . bewitched people, gathered devotees, and formed a band." Since she had been caught and swiftly executed, the evil had not spread, but the incident showed how easily people could be led astray.[22] For the Mito thinkers the Keihan incident thus served to illustrate both the problems that could be expected to escalate further with the opening of the country and the kind of measures needed to deal with them.

Ōshio and his fellow investigators had suspected the Keihan Kirishitan of "plotting wicked deeds" (in other words, seditious activities) but had been unable to find evidence of this. Nor could they get the accused to admit to such. Popular association of Mitsugi with Ōshio's own act of sedition lent credence, ironically enough, to this suspicion. In the writings and compilations of the Mito thinkers such suppositions became incontrovertible.[23] In this way, rumors and retellings steadily reshaped the story even as they transmitted it to new audiences.

Chapter 11

~

The State of the Floating World

THE KIRISHITAN AFFAIR OF 1829

The arrest of a group of Kirishitan in 1827 and their execution on the fifth day of the twelfth month of 1829.[1]

Mizuno Gunki

The roots of this Kirishitan incident go back to a retainer of the Kan'in princely house called Mizuno Gunki. People say he was born in Shimabara in Hizen province (some say Amakusa) and came to Kyoto, where he entered the service of the princely house. He was by nature an evildoer, who bought up no longer valid documents [to use for extortion] and engaged in other kinds of chicanery.[2] Around 1802 or 1803,[3] he joined Lord Sasaki Tango, a retainer of the noble Kujō house, on a trip to Niwase and Matsuyama in Bitchū province and Katsuyama and Tsuyama in Mimasaka province. (At this time, [my friend] Takashima Unmei was traveling in the region and happened to be in Niwase. He tells me that the two had concocted an elaborate plot and caused people in Niwase much trouble.) The smaller daimyo houses in the area were at a loss as to how to deal with these people, who were throwing their weight around as retainers of an imperial prince and regent, and the domain officials ended up spending large amounts of money on the two. Only in Tsuyama did the local daimyo representative come out and confront them; it is said that he immediately chased them away.[4] This happened when I was in Kyoto, and Noguchi Kurando and I had a good laugh at the absurdity of these daimyo houses' being overawed and spending such a lot of money on these two.

Gunki probably did a lot of other things of the same sort. He died four years ago. His temple of affiliation was Unseiji in Samegai in Kyoto. (I'm not sure about the characters; the same goes for the temples mentioned below. Forgive me if the characters are wrong![5] Unseiji is a branch temple of Nishi Honganji.) Because he was interred [rather than cremated], evidently he was buried in a Nichiren temple. (I don't know the further specifics of this temple's name.)[6] It's said that this man transmitted the pernicious creed to Toyoda Mitsugi, Takamiya Heizō in Osaka, and others, too.

In Shirokoura-machi in Osaka there is a temple called Jōkōji that is affiliated with Nishi Honganji.[7] One of its parishioners was a man known as Dai-I, who managed a branch of the Yamatoya Jūbei firm. (His real name may have been Ihei or Iemon.)[8] The temple of Muryōkōji in Kisabe in Kawachi province was closely connected to Jōkōji. (The priest was the older brother of the priest of Jōkōji.) The priest of Muryōkōji was an exceptionally good talker who made his living by cheating people out of their money. He put his talent for evil deception to use on behalf of the head temple, [Nishi Honganji,] too. This priest duped Dai-I into lending ten thousand *monme* in silver to the head temple. Greedily deceiving people and taking their money is a common practice in that sect. Because the money was not returned even after the due date had passed, Dai-I repeatedly pressed the Muryōkōji priest, but to no avail. Dai-I was furious but did not know what to do.

At that time, a person who knew Mizuno Gunki told Dai-I that if he relied on Gunki, he could get his money back without further ado, so Dai-I arranged with this person to ask for Gunki's help. Gunki readily accepted his request, and from this point onward he began to frequent Dai-I's house and curry favor with him. Dai-I was so angry with the head temple and the Muryōkōji priest, and so happy that Gunki had agreed to get his money back for him, that he got carried away and feted Gunki lavishly. At some point, Gunki offered to show Dai-I the imperial palace.[9] Accompanying Dai-I to Kyoto, Gunki arranged for him to enter the palace precincts. Dai-I believed that he had met the emperor face-to-face and even been presented with a cup of sake from him. He was so delighted that he put up even more money. How Gunki managed to dupe him in this manner I don't know; it all must be because of the pernicious arts of the Kirishitan.

After this, Dai-I was cheated out of his money again and again, without getting back any of the money he had already lent to Nishi Honganji. Gradually he realized that he was being swindled. "People who appear friendly at first turn out to be the worst—that must be how I got cheated," he thought. "People told me that this must be one of those so-called swindlers, and they made various efforts to stop me, but I didn't listen and just went on until things got to this state." Bitterly regretting what he had done and filled with shame and anger, Dai-I felt he could no longer face the world. He was struck by a sudden illness and died not much later. I record this here just as I heard it from the wife of Jōkōji's priest. "Because of this affair," she told me, "some years ago the temple lost this important parishioner. And now, it has been made to suffer terribly because of those Kirishitan! It is really too cruel."

The wife and son of Gunki were arrested and remanded to jail. I've been told both that they died in the jailhouse and also that they were decapitated on the day when the executions took place; I don't know the specifics. Takashima Unmei heard from a private secretary of the magistrate's that more than a hundred people were executed on the fifth day of the twelfth month [of 1829], and that among them two children were decapitated, so perhaps Gunki's son was one of these. I haven't heard their names, so I'm not certain. A man who makes his living running errands for town residents is said to have delivered a letter for Gunki just once. I heard that even this man was arrested and fined three thousand coppers. From this one can imagine what happened to people who were close to Gunki.

The priest of Unseiji was sentenced to expulsion from his temple on that same day, the fifth of the twelfth month. He was handed over to the head temple, which was instructed to deal with him according to temple regulations. The head temple sent down the same order [of expulsion] and declared in addition that the priest was not to have any contact with his relatives and that his wife was to be returned to Muryōkōji, which is her parental home. Because he has been punished by the shogunal authorities, nobody in the capital region will rent him a place to stay, and since he can't go to his relatives' either, he has been in great trouble ever since that day. I record here what I heard at Jōkōji, whose [current] priest is related to the priest [of Muryōkōji].[10] It's said that the priest of the Nichiren temple where Gunki's body was buried was also expelled from his temple on the same day. There are various other rumors as well, but the details are too complicated and can't be confirmed, so I've omitted them here.

Toyoda Mitsugi

This woman was born in Echizen province. Her father was from a lineage of shrine priests, but because of extreme poverty the whole family moved to Kyoto, where her father and elder brother got by roaming the streets to perform purifications for people or conducting rites for a fee. Mitsugi was born with reasonably pleasing looks. She became the wife of a samurai in the service of a noble house and gave birth to a daughter. However, this man was involved in all kinds of bad business and spent more money than his status allowed. He ended up selling his wife as a prostitute to a brothel called Yoshidaya in Kita Shinchi in Osaka.[11] (At this time, Mitsugi was called Taka.)

A block alderman called Hyakumonjiya Goroemon, who was in charge of two blocks in this area (1-chōme and 2-chōme), put up twenty ryō to redeem her contract and made her his wife.[12] However, she proved to have a haughty temperament. She spent her days sitting at her desk practicing calligraphy and studying, amused herself playing the koto or samisen, or sat around making small decorative objects like pouches for toothpicks or for paper tissues. Whenever she left the house, even if it was just to visit the neighbors, she covered her head [like a noblewoman], ordered a servant to dress up in a crested jacket and carry a short sword,[13] and walked around in a fashion unbecoming of a townsperson. She showed no sign of rejoicing over the fact that she had been redeemed from prostitution. She not only spoke haughtily to the servants but even talked back to her husband, as if to say, "My status is beyond that of a mere townsman's wife." Goroemon himself was a crook who later ended up in the jailhouse for some corrupt scheme; yet, he was not up to the task of controlling this woman. At the time, work was being done on the Midori Bridge over the Shijimi River,[14] and she demanded that he arrange for her to do the calligraphy [for the bridge's name sign]. She got her way, but after this Goroemon had had enough and divorced her. She then rented a house in Shinchi Ura-machi [in the Dōjima area] and set up a school for children; but she was not content with this either, and it appears that she returned to Kyoto.

The man who told me all this is Tobaya Gihei of Fukushima Masagobashi, who knows about these matters because he used to live close to the Hyakumonjiya house. The wife of Nakaya Zenbei (the owner of a

cloth shop in Hon-machi), who was born in Dōjima and often visited
the Hyakumonjiya house when she was twelve or thirteen years old, con-
firms Tobaya's story. She has told me that "Taka" [that is, Mitsugi] was
very pretty, with a white complexion, pink cheeks, and a straight nose,
but that she behaved in a cold, unfriendly manner.

After this, Mitsugi moved around from one place to another in Kyoto, until
she finally became another man's wife. (There are various rumors, such
as that she became a geisha in Ponto-chō, had her contract there redeemed,
became someone's wife, and later ended up as Gunki's concubine.) But
after a while, that man became involved with another woman. Angry over
this infatuation, Mitsugi left him. He immediately went ahead and took
the other woman in, soon making her his new wife. Mitsugi was furious
about this and was constantly looking for ways to take revenge. After this,
she made her living on her own as an Inari medium. (Such mediums worship foxes as "something-or-other Inari." There are many such persons
in Kyoto and here in Settsu province.)

It was around this time that she met Gunki. She heard that Gunki
knew mysterious arts and repeatedly asked him to teach her, but Gunki
refused, saying that his arts were very difficult to learn and that it wouldn't
do her any good to know them. Yet she continued to importune him,
pleading that she didn't care what kind of miserable death his teaching
might bring upon her. In the end, he agreed to show her his methods.
She pledged that she would keep her eyes closed and not open them until
he told her to, and that she would not lose her composure, whatever
strange events might occur. When he finally said that she could open her
eyes, she saw the woman she resented with such jealousy, the woman for
whom that hateful man had abandoned her, standing right in front of
her, laughing. She jumped at the woman in a rage, but in the same instant
the woman disappeared, leaving Mitsugi to grasp at thin air.

Although she was ashamed to have broken her pledge not to become
flustered, she now set her mind all the more firmly on learning these mysterious arts. She performed various austerities to obtain an unwavering
mind, and in the end evidently received the transmission of those arts. I
don't know anything about the image that those people worshipped as the
main icon of their practice, but I've heard that in addition they also worshipped an image of a woman with her hair hanging loose, dangling an
infant upside down. When one joins that sect, one must cut all one's

fingers vertically, press out some blood, and let it drip onto that painting. This icon is used to take pledges from initiates that they will reveal nothing to others and that they will never break their vow, even if it costs them their life.

It so happened that an infant from a rich household in Kyoto had lost all sight in both eyes. Even the pupils had shriveled and turned white.[15] Since it was a rich household, the parents had tried all kinds of treatments, irrespective of the expense, but it was all to no avail, and the child had now become blind. Someone told the child's mother that Mitsugi had mastered mysterious arts and urged her to ask Mitsugi to perform a prayer rite. The mother approached Mitsugi through this person, even though she did not expect such a rite to have any effect. Mitsugi said that she would reply to the request as soon as she had consulted the deity. Soon she sent word that since the deity found that a prayer rite would be effective, she would perform one. She asked for a piece of clothing that the blind infant had worn directly on its skin and said that she would pray over it for seventeen days. The infant's eyes would clear up by a little after dawn on the sixth day.

Even though she had accepted the advice to ask for this rite, the mother didn't expect any miracle and put the matter out of her mind. Yet, true to Mitsugi's word, shortly after dawn on the sixth day both eyes made a popping sound, and it looked as if fire had shot out of them toward the ceiling. The mother heard the sound and looked up, wondering absentmindedly what was going on. Then the child said, "I can see the sliding doors! I see you, Mother!" The mother was astounded. Only then did she remember that she had asked Mitsugi to perform a prayer rite. Overcome by faith, she immediately went to Mitsugi to tell her the news and thank her profusely. Since this was a rich household, she gave Mitsugi tens of gold ryō, but Mitsugi refused and would accept no payment at all.

[Mitsugi evidently continued to have close relations with this household thereafter.] Takashima Unmei told me he had heard from one of the [Osaka] eastern magistrate's private secretaries that Mitsugi declared [after her arrest] that the woman had continued to show great regard for her and thus would be very sad to hear that Mitsugi had been arrested. When Mitsugi was executed, this mother and child were both sentenced to indefinite incarceration. All the property of the household was confiscated. The shop manager and two shop clerks were forbidden to live anywhere in the country outside Okazaki and two other areas of Kyoto, and they were ordered to report to the authorities as soon as they had settled in one of these three areas.

Ichimonoya Kihachi serves as block assistant in Komeya-machi in Osaka, on the west side of Naniwabashi street. He originates from Miyagawa-chō in Kyoto, where he lived a comfortable life and even owned quarters to rent out, but in recent years he has suffered bad fortune and ended up in his present circumstances. According to this Kihachi, until some twenty years ago Mitsugi rented a house from him. She was an arrogant woman who worshipped Inari and held certification from the Yoshida house.[16] She wore red *hakama* and had a servant holding a red umbrella accompany her even on everyday errands [just as if she were of noble birth]. At that time, however, she was still poor, and at one point she was a full year in arrears on her rent. At other times she seemed to be earning large amounts of money, and on one occasion she not only cleared a year of unpaid rent but even paid a full year ahead. Already at that time, people found this strange and talked about her. Later, he said, she was much in demand and moved to Yasaka.

Mitsugi continued to thrive, and people began to call her a clairvoyant. She grew even more conceited, and she always moved around in palanquins. To pull people in, she performed prayer rites but never took large fees. She threw gold and silver around, helping out the poor. As for the source of all that money, I've been told that even though outwardly she did not accept payment, the people she prayed for often developed a desire to give her money and would take it to her. A rich retired man suffered a severe illness that was untreatable, but to his delight he recovered thanks to Mitsugi's prayers. After this Mitsugi became very close to that man. She recommended a concubine to him, to whom she gave thorough instructions: whenever she was in need of money, she would have this concubine wring it out of the man, and then she spent it lavishly. (She had other means of obtaining money as well; I discuss those in the section about Sano of Kawasaki.)

A soy-sauce dealer called Nakamuraya lived on Higashi-no-tōin street [in Kyoto]. A branch house of this dealer, called Nakamuraya-something, owned what I believe was a dry goods business on Matsubara street. (Others told me it was a pawnshop.) This man was close to Mitsugi, and she would borrow money from him. (There are various rumors, including one that he secretly studied Kirishitan books that Mitsugi had pawned in his shop.) It's said that this shopkeeper, too, secretly delved into the pernicious creed, but he died three or four years ago, so his fourteen- or fifteen-year-old son, Makijirō, was arrested and jailed. Some say the son was decapitated, others that he was sentenced to indefinite incarceration. All the household property was confiscated, and even the shop clerks were punished in various ways, so I'm told.[17]

> Above I've recorded what I've heard from the priest's wife at Jōkōji and from Yamatoya Rinzō and others, just as they told it. Yamatoya Rihei told me another tale about Nakamuraya. A few years ago, a large crowd of guests gathered at Nakamuraya's place, and although he had some sake, he had no other special treats to offer. "Let me catch some carp in the River of Heaven [that is, the Milky Way] and make some soup," he said.[18] Nakamuraya put some water into a bucket and lit a paper lantern, which he tied to the bucket. When he lifted the bucket onto the roof, it immediately rose up and disappeared into the clouds. After a short while it came down again and landed back on the roof. When he took the bucket down, it held two large carp. With these he made a soup that he served to all, causing a lot of merriment.

Mitsugi, evil and crooked though she was, fell in love with the son of a certain household in Kyoto. Because he was more than twenty years younger than she, she hid her amorous feelings. Instead, for the sake of appearances, she went through an acquaintance and proposed to adopt him as her son. However, the boy was the household's only son and the parents would not allow it. Then she cast a serious illness on the boy, causing terrible sores to break out all over his face and making him look grotesque. The parents had no idea what might have caused this, and they were distraught with worry. Mitsugi thereupon offered to perform prayer rites for the boy, and since the sores were so bad that even the doctor had refused to treat them, the parents asked her to do so. She took the boy into her own house and prayed over him. One or two days later there seemed to be some improvement, and the parents were delighted. She then took up the matter of his adoption once again: "This boy is so ill that he can hardly be saved. If I do manage to save him and he recovers because of my prayers, you should let me have him." The parents agreed: "His life is now in your hands. If you can save him, you can do with him what you want." Soon the sores were healed, and the boy recovered his old looks. Mitsugi held the parents to their promise and took the boy as her adoptive son. His name was Kamon. Only thirty days later he was arrested together with Mitsugi and remanded to jail. He appears to have been completely unaware of the fact that Mitsugi was engaged in such a pernicious creed, but since they were now mother and son he could not escape punishment. People say that he was decapitated, or that he was sentenced to indefinite incarceration. I haven't heard any definitive confirmation of this.[19] (People tell various rumors about this; I've recorded here just as I heard from Yamatoya Rinzō, Kashimaya Shōsuke, and others.)

Mitsugi's mother and elder brother led miserable lives in the Kitano area [in Kyoto], but even though Mitsugi was a celebrated clairvoyant and threw money around like dirt, she made no effort to help them. She behaved in a most unfilial way. In the beginning her mother used to visit her, but there were many things about Mitsugi's behavior that she did not approve of. She feared that if she were to keep connections with such a person, who might end up doing who knows what, the entire family might meet a bad end, so she broke off relations some years ago. Mitsugi's brother did not pay heed to such things and occasionally went to see her, ignoring his mother's admonitions. Once he stayed at her house for two or three days, and he noticed many things that gave him pause. He thought that if his aged mother had turned her back on her only daughter, it must have been for a good reason. His fears aroused, he, too, evidently broke off relations. Even so, being close relatives, they could not escape punishment. As soon as Mitsugi was arrested her brother was also remanded to jail, and he apparently died in the jailhouse soon after. Her mother was eighty years old, and because of her extreme age she was placed in the custody of her locale in Kyoto. When Mitsugi was executed, all persons involved were summoned to hear the sentences, but her mother was ill, so someone else was sent to represent her. I don't know what orders were issued at this time or what sentences were handed down [to those who were not principals]. (This is what I heard from Yamatoya Rinzō.)

When Sano from Kawasaki village was arrested and confessed that she had practiced the pernicious creed together with Mitsugi, the criminal investigation section [of the Osaka Magistracy] dispatched Nagata Satsuemon to Kyoto to arrest her. However, Mitsugi was constantly visiting high-ranking court nobles, saying that she had official duties in their service. In her comings and goings she was always carried in a palanquin and accompanied by a large entourage. Since she did not appear to be at all fazed [by Sano's detention], Nagata became concerned about how the court would react if he arrested her, and so he retreated to Osaka. To replace him, Ōshio Heihachirō immediately came up to Kyoto. He disguised himself as a townsman, feigned an illness, and visited Mitsugi to ask for prayer rites. She accepted, so he moved in and stayed in her house. When Mitsugi was out of the house, he investigated the inside of her shrine and found that the shrine furnishings were all made of silk decorated with a strange crest. Outwardly, it appeared to be dedicated to Inari, in accordance with its name; but there was no deity body inside, only a mask of Otafuku. It seems that Ōshio took this mask, waited for Mitsugi to come home, confronted her with his suspicions, and then arrested her. Mitsugi was a wily woman and she tried to talk herself out of this, but to no avail. (My source for this is Tamaya Kyōan from Tenma [in Osaka].)

In the jailhouse Mitsugi was handled with special care until her execution because her crimes were so serious, and especially because she was the ringleader. Since Sano, Kinu, Umon,[20] Kenzō, and others had all died while detained in the jailhouse, she was treated with all the more care. The magistracy employed a lowly woman from the Osaka slum of Nagamachi to look after Mitsugi in the jailhouse for a daily wage of some two hundred coppers. This woman attended to her needs, served her food, and gave her massages. Mitsugi would hit and kick this woman whenever something displeased her, and when she didn't like the seasoning of her food she would throw it at her. After a while there was no one willing to care for Mitsugi. Even when the jailhouse offered eight hundred coppers per day, no one could put up with this work for a whole day, such was the hardship involved. In the end, it seems, persons of low status were enticed by the high pay and did what they could, with five or six persons taking turns.

There was another rather absurd matter in this connection. [A mother and son] in Kitano here in Osaka worshipped Inari but failed to make even a miserable living in that way. These people heard that in Kyoto there were clairvoyants called Toyoda Mitsugi and her son, Kamon, who enjoyed great fame, earned lots of money, spent that money like water, and were flourishing. Envious of their success, the mother took the name Toyoda Mitsugi and her son renamed himself Kamon so as to swindle people and make a profit. They raised suspicion because of those identical names, and they were arrested immediately and remanded to jail. I've heard it said that both mother and son died in the jailhouse. Although these people evidently had nothing to do with the Kirishitan, they suffered an untimely death because of their unbecoming greed.[21] (This is something that was said at a house owned by Kashimaya Kōshichi, an outcast leader of Funa-machi. Such outcast leaders act as chiefs of the other outcasts and are dispatched [by the magistracy] as "hands" to make arrests, so they know much about what goes on in the jailhouse.)[22] These are things that Kashimaya Shōsuke told me.

On the fifth day of the twelfth month the sentences of the Kirishitan were pronounced, and it was announced that they would be paraded through the three districts of Osaka. Because they were criminals so wicked as to practice the pernicious creed, which has been strictly banned since the beginning of the present realm, crowds of people lined up from the jailhouse at Matsuya-machi all along the route to the execution grounds, just to catch a glimpse of them. When Mitsugi was dragged through the jailhouse gate, she hummed the following poem as she saw the mass of spectators:

They have come from the west, the east, the north, and the south
Just waiting to see me—at Matsuya-machi[23]

Even in this dire situation she was perfectly composed. In spite of the fact that she'd spent three years in the jailhouse, where many of her fellows had died, she didn't appear in the least malnourished; her complexion was glowing white and her body plump. Her eyes were sharp, her nose straight, and even though she was fifty-six years old, she looked as though she had not even reached fifty. She was triumphant, and here and there she shouted, "I'm the old lady who is the general of the Kirishitan! Take a good look at my face!" When she arrived at the execution grounds and was pulled off the horse, she nodded to each of the officials and said something to them with a broad smile on her face. The pariahs told her to stop chattering and say the *nenbutsu*, but she replied, "The *nenbutsu* is not for Kirishitan. I'm returning to the Plain of High Heaven!" She was still laughing when she was tied to the post. In the beginning she kept both hands closed, but when she was pierced by the first spear she laughed and opened one hand. After the second spear she merely closed that hand and retained her composure. In that way, she took eleven spears, I'm told. Someone had written out five of her death poems on pieces of paper and put them next to the placard proclaiming her crimes.

I've heard all this from Wada Shūsuke, Tamaya Kyōan, and others who witnessed these events.

Daijōin (Jōdo Sect)

This temple belongs to the Jōdo sect.[24] It is the temple where Mitsugi was registered. [Its priest] has been expelled.

Takamiya Heizō

This man lived in Matsuyama-machi in the Ue-machi area. Originally he was a Zen monk and priest of a temple in Harima province. However, he had illicit relations with a widow who was one of his parishioners, and because of this misdeed, he [left the temple and] came to Osaka. Since he was close to the priest of Kanzanji in Kitano, he relied on his help. Kanzanji accepted him as a parishioner, and [with the temple papers in hand] he rented a house in Kitano; he moved to Matsuyama-machi later. He made his living as a storyteller of military tales. He became Gunki's disciple and was initiated in the pernicious creed. Some years ago, when Gunki was away on a journey to Nagasaki, this man purportedly took in Gunki's wife and son and looked after them.

Once when Heizō was partying in a place called Shin-machi or something like that, he got carried away by the merriment and announced that he would demonstrate some interesting things. He performed a few strange tricks that people found mysterious, and since that time people began to talk about him as a "mysterious" figure, so "Mysterious" [Kimyō] became his nickname. When he performed as a storyteller, he styled himself Kitayama Kinai; "Kinai" then got changed to "Kimyō." Those tricks had made Heizō suspect; it came out that he was a Kirishitan, and he was arrested. (I was told this by Kinuya Shichibei.) On the fifth day of the twelfth month he was paraded through the town to the execution grounds and crucified together with Mitsugi. He was dripping tears along the entire route, and when he was taken off the horse at the grounds, his legs gave way and he was unable to stand. His face was as gray as dust. As soon as he took the first spear, he writhed in pain. Leaking urine and making a miserable spectacle, he took nine spears. (This, too, is based on the accounts of Wada, Tamaya, and others.)

Kanzanji

This temple belongs to the Zen sect, Myōshinji branch. The priest of this temple failed to detect that someone he had accepted as a new parishioner was an adherent of the banned Kirishitan creed and went ahead and certified him as affiliated with his temple. Therefore the priest was treated in a particularly severe manner. As with the other priests, he was provisionally confined to the temple [while the incident was being investigated]. He became ill while the judicial procedures were under way and died, so the magistracy sent an inspector, who ordered that the body be covered [and not be buried or cremated]. On the day of the sentences, representatives from the temple were summoned to the magistracy. Because this priest had died in circumstances where, if he had been alive, he would have been sentenced to expulsion from the temple, his body was to be kept as it was for the time being. No funeral was to be held, and further orders would follow.[25] The priests of the temples that belonged to the same group as Kanzanji were reprimanded and sentenced to fifty days' house confinement. (Some people say that they closed the temple gates and secluded themselves on their own initiative [as an expression of remorse].) The other temples in Kanzanji's group are Kushōji, Zuikōji, Myōchūji, Gentokuji, and Baishōin. In addition, the priests of Jōkōji, Enkōji, Rentakuji, Unseiji, and Daijōin,[26] all of which had Kirishitan parishioners, have been sentenced to expulsion. In total, more than fifty temples belonging to the same temple groups received some form of punishment. (I heard about the handling of Kanzanji from the Kushōji priest.)

Fujii Umon

This person was registered in the block as Irakoya Keizō. He was a medical doctor by profession. His real name was Fujii Umon. He lived on a back alley, about fifty yards west of the rear of the theater in Kita Shinchi. Although he had reached the age of sixty, he lived in great poverty. He had moved here from Kyoto some ten years earlier. He's said to have been Mizuno Gunki's disciple. At Jōkōji they say he was Sano's disciple. (It's also said that those people had a strict rule that one should take only one

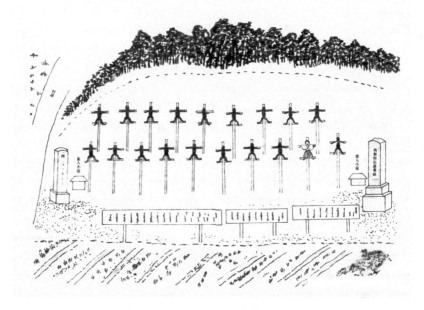

Figure 11.1 Mass crucifixion at Tobita execution grounds, showing the 1838 crucifixion of Ōshio Heihachirō and his followers after his rebellion the previous year. Only one of those crucified on that occasion was still alive at the time (*first row, second from right*); all the rest (including Ōshio) were already dead and their corpses had been preserved in salt. The scene, including the execution placards in the foreground proclaiming the verdicts, must have been much the same at the time of the crucifixion of Mitsugi and the others at the end of 1829. Redrawing of Matsura Seizan, *Kasshi yawa, kan* 55, "Tobita oshiokiba no ryakuzu." Shimura Kiyoshi.

disciple, because the risk of detection would increase if one took on a larger number.) Umon was arrested together with Mitsugi and the others but died in the jailhouse. His body was preserved in salt and crucified with the others. The dead were pierced by just two spears, one from the right and one from the left; after that, the executioners merely pretended to continue piercing the body.

Jōkōji

This temple belongs to the Nishi Honganji branch. It is the temple where Fujii Umon was registered. In this case, too, the priest was first summoned, given a severe reprimand for the heinous crime of having an adherent of the prohibited pernicious sect among his parishioners, and provisionally confined to the temple precincts. On the day sentences were pronounced, he was summoned again and told that, by rights, he should be defrocked and banished. As an act of extraordinary mercy, however, his sentence was merely expulsion from the temple. He should be thankful for this leniency and was to vacate the temple immediately. The regional head temple representative was also called in on the same day and given a severe reprimand.[27] He was instructed that the subsequent handling of the matter of the Jōkōji priest was to be left to the head temple, [Nishi Honganji,] which was to deal with him according to temple regulations. That same day the Jōkōji priest went back to the temple briefly in the early afternoon; he left the temple permanently an hour or so later. Sonkōji in Kajiki-machi took him in, since its priest was related to him. He had his family remain in Jōkōji on the assumption that this would not be a problem, but the head temple ordered the family members to leave immediately and move to Sonkōji. This caused great consternation. (Since the previous month, the priest's wife had been bedridden with an illness that caused her to cough up blood.) There was nothing they could do, though, so the family left Jōkōji together with a certain woman.[28]

This woman is extremely licentious; she had already been married twice before she became the wife of the previous priest of Jōkōji. (She is the daughter of the priest of Eiōji in Akō in Harima province.) As she, too, is related to the priest of Sonkōji, she had gone to stay there, whereupon she evidently became involved in an illicit affair with the previous Jōkōji priest, whom she then married. Some twelve or thirteen years ago [the previous priest died and] she became a widow; she then started sleeping with her late husband's younger brother. Her behavior was extremely lascivious, and soon she became pregnant with a child by this brother. Her daughter [by her late husband] was already grown up [when the former priest died], and one would have expected her to adopt a husband [who could become the next priest] for the daughter. However, because she was such a licentious woman, she did not do so until seven or eight years ago, when she adopted the man who has now been expelled from Jōkōji. At the time he was the priest of a temple called Kōzanji on Rokujō street [in Kyoto], which is of a rank that allows its priests to sit in one of the side rooms of Nishi Honganji. Jōkōji has a higher rank, allowing its priests to sit in the main hall. Because both the rank and the parishioner base of Jōkōji are superior, the Kōzanji priest became this woman's adoptive son-in-law out of greed, while at the same time he adopted someone else to serve as the priest of Kōzanji. Everybody now ridicules him for ending up in such a wretched fashion [despite having gone through all these machinations].

Umon moved down from Kyoto some ten years ago and became a parishioner of this temple. At that time, his temple registration must have been transferred from a Kyoto temple [to Jōkōji]; also, there must have been a guarantor here in Osaka, and a document must have been drawn up to record this transfer. However, even though this was only ten years ago, no one at Jōkōji has any clue who facilitated Umon's registration or who acted as his guarantor. One can only call it a severe misdeed that nobody has any idea how he became a parishioner of this temple, and that there is nothing about any of this in Jōkōji's roster of parishioners. Because the previous priest had died a few years earlier and the transfer occurred at the time when his widow was running wild, everything in the temple was in disorder. It is in the nature of that sect to desire money more than anything else, and they may well have brought this misfortune on themselves out of greed for some silver. Because this temple was closely caught up with this Kirishitan incident, most of my information about these events is based on what I've heard at Jōkōji.

Fujita Kenzō

([Kenzō's adoptive father] Kyōan was deceived by Kenzō's evil cunning and suffered the shame of posthumous obscurity; [because his line has been terminated,] the rites to his ancestors are also now discontinued.)[29]

A native of Awa province in Shikoku, Kenzō became a disciple of the physician Fujita Kyōan, who resided a short distance west of Ōe Bridge along the Dōjima waterfront [in Osaka]. Kyōan regarded Kenzō as a man of talent, and although he had both a son and a nephew, he discarded these as his heirs and adopted Kenzō. Kyōan had a considerable amount of custom and had become quite wealthy. However, after Kenzō succeeded to Kyōan's practice, he was not called upon as much as his adoptive father had been, so he took up the office of alderman of one of the Dōjima blocks alongside the family medical profession. (The leading residents of the Dōjima riverfront area are all brokers, and they were too busy with their businesses [to take on an alderman's duties].)[30] Dōjima being the kind of place it is, Kenzō soon began to speculate in rice bills. He loved trinkets and spent much money collecting such things. He ran up large losses on the rice market and ended up having to pawn even his house. Taking advantage of his position as alderman, he in fact double pawned his house.[31] At the same time he was also borrowing money from other people; it's said he was involved in countless illegal dealings. The man to whom Kenzō had pawned his house the first time lived within the block. He found out that Kenzō had double pawned it and sued him for this. The magistrate held that given Kenzō's status as both a physician and a block alderman, he had committed a serious misdeed, and he was banished from the city of Osaka. (Others say that this lawsuit ended with a private settlement but that he was driven out of the block because of his misdeeds.) After this he moved to Sumiyoshi.

Kenzō owned some Kirishitan books, which, it's said, he sold to Sano in Kawasaki. When this came out, he was arrested and remanded to jail. (This is based on what I've been told at Jōkōji and on popular rumors. Kinuya Shichibei has a different account. According to him, Kenzō was friendly with a priest of the Hiraoka Shrine, to whom he lent Kirishitan books. This priest had illicit relations with a widow in a nearby village. When he was arrested for some wrongdoing and his house was searched, these books came to light. From this investigation it became clear that the books belonged to Kenzō, who was then arrested.)[32]

Kenzō died in the jailhouse, so his body was preserved in salt and the sentence carried out on the same day [that the other Kirishitan] were executed. His eighty-year-old adoptive mother, wife, and child had been placed in the custody of their locale. (The child is said to be an eight-year-old boy.) On the day the sentences were pronounced, they were summoned and sentenced as well. Kenzō's aged mother was returned to the place where she had been staying and placed in the custody of that locale. His wife and son received sentences of indefinite incarceration. (Others say the wife was decapitated and the son incarcerated.) Even Kenzō's elder brother was ordered to come up to Osaka from Awa and was incarcerated indefinitely.[33] The households of the relatives of those who practice the Kirishitan creed are all to be terminated.

Fujita Kyōan adopted the son of a certain Naniwaya Tahei from Dōjima, a prominent townsman, as the husband of a younger sister of Kenzō's wife. However, this son failed to please his adoptive parents and was soon divorced. He returned to his parents' household but lived in a separate house. As Kenzō's sister-in-law yearned for [her former husband], she ran away to live with him as husband and wife. Kenzō was furious about this and evidently cut off relations with them. Even so, this sister-in-law continued to be listed in the Fujita household register, and because of this connection both she and Tahei's son were arrested and sentenced to indefinite incarceration.[34]

Some people gossip about how cruel it was for Kenzō's sister-in-law and her former husband to meet such a fate merely because of the woman's household registration. However, some six years ago this son of Tahei was enjoying a party at the Horie pleasure quarters, calling in lots of geisha. Tipsy from drink, he said, "Let me show you a funny trick," and made some gestures. Then he turned to the geisha, who were playing the samisen and singing together, and said, "I've just snatched away your underwear, and there you go singing on without noticing anything! What a joke!" None of them believed him, so he said, "You can't tell from my words alone whether it's true—you'd all better check your underclothes!" When they checked for themselves, they were shocked to find that their underwear had indeed disappeared. They had no idea how he could have taken it. They told him to return their clothes immediately, so he said, "Right, let me get them out, then," pulled them out of his sleeve, and gave them back. They were all stunned at this, and it became the talk of the town. I recall hearing from Yoshikawaya Kichibei of Doshō-machi how "that son of Naniwaya Tahei, who was adopted by Fujita, did a very strange trick in Horie the other day." He went on to tell me this and that about what had happened in Horie. Thinking about it now, I'm convinced that Tahei's son also must have learned that pernicious creed. Because people talked so much about what he did in Horie, it must have reached the ears of the authorities. One can only say that he brought his fate down upon himself.

Enshōji

Enshōji is a branch temple of Nishi Honganji; it is located in Shin Utsubo, Aburakake-machi, [Osaka]. This is the temple with which the Fujita household is affiliated. The magistrate sentenced its priest to expulsion from the temple and the priests of the other temples in Enshōji's group to strict seclusion; subsequent measures regarding these priests were to be decided by the head temple. In contrast to other sects, priests of this sect have a wife and children. The Enshōji priest evidently assumed that the sentence of expulsion applied to himself alone and that there would be no problem if his wife and children stayed on at the temple, but the head temple then ordered his family to leave Enshōji as well. This priest was bedridden with a severe illness and unable to use his arms and legs; therefore he apparently had to be carried out lying on a wooden door.

It seems that this is the second expulsion this temple has experienced because of Fujita. When Kyōan died a few years ago, Kenzō sent someone to inform the temple. He requested that the priest conduct the funeral, which would be held midafternoon the following day. This Kyōan was an extremely stingy man who never worshipped at the temple. Whenever the temple asked for contributions, he turned a deaf ear. The priest must have thought that this was a good occasion to extort some money from the Fujita household, so he replied that the next day was inconvenient for the temple and that he would send an assistant priest instead. When Kenzō heard this he was livid. He sent a runner with the message that it was unacceptable to leave this to an assistant, as though Kyōan had been some pauper living in a hut in a back alley, and that the priest should by all means preside in person. The temple refused: "In fact, the heart of the matter is that the implements necessary for such a service have been pawned for thirty-five *ryō*. You will have to put up this sum so that these implements can be retrieved from pawn. At the moment, the temple has no cash whatsoever and can't do this by itself." Kenzō sent many runners, but all to no avail.

The next day, as the time for the funeral was approaching, Kenzō finally sent a runner with the money. Soon the priest appeared and performed the funeral service. Kenzō was furious at the priest's outrageous behavior and just glared at him, speechless. Not even waiting out the month of mourning, he confronted the priest to retrieve the sum he had advanced, but the temple had planned to keep it right from the start and would not return any of it. Kenzō thereupon decided to press the temple severely. The priest had no option but to discuss the matter with the temple's confraternity, which offered Kenzō five *ryō*. "Since the matter concerns the temple," [the confraternity representative] said, "please bear with this and accept this amount." Kenzō, however, said that he could make no such allowances, and in the end he brought a lawsuit about the matter before the authorities. [The magistrate] deemed it a serious offense for a priest to go so far as to extort money from a parishioner over the body of a dead man and it is said that he sentenced the priest to expulsion from the temple.

To be sure the temple acted outrageously, but people evidently also considered Kenzō's conduct immoderate. I've heard this tale from Mōri Kōan. As Kyōan's close friend he was present at the funeral, so he knows exactly what happened. He told me that while the temple was clearly at fault, he was also appalled by Kenzō's character and had made sure to keep his distance from him after that.

Sano

Sano lived in Kawasaki in Tenma. (Kawasaki is located about three hundred yards to the east of the gate of Taiyūji in Kitano.) She was Kinu's disciple. It's said that she fasted and retreated at night to Inari mountain in Kyoto or to other desolate places to perform severe austerities in order to attain an unwavering mind. When she had accumulated enough merit in this manner she was initiated in the pernicious creed. She cloaked her activities by calling herself an Inari medium, and she cheated people with prayer rites while raking in money. In due course this escalated, and she swindled her landlord, Kenpōya Yohei, as well as people around Dōjima.

"I can make money increase by means of my miraculous powers," she allegedly told them. "To try me out, just deposit ten thousand coppers with me, or only as little as a thousand!" Since this is a place full of greed, people were taken in by this, and they all deposited money with Sano. To every ten thousand coppers she took, Sano would add interest of three thousand at the end of the month and take this sum along to show to the person [who had made the deposit]. "In a single month, you have made a profit of three thousand coppers," she'd say. "Put that into your ledger as incoming funds." After she'd got her clients to note this down, she'd tell them, "Even with just ten thousand coppers you make this much in a month. If I take these three thousand back with me and circulate them together with the original deposit, your profit will increase even more." She'd merely show the interest to her clients and then take it home with her again. The next month, she again showed the interest, had it recorded in the ledger as incoming funds, and took the money home with her.

At this point, Sano would say, "Even with an outlay of only ten thousand coppers, you're making this much interest. To earn more, the bigger your investment, the better." Her clients, the landlord among them, dredged up all the money they could get their hands on. The landlord, Kenpōya Yohei, even took out a short-term loan of a horse load of cotton, to be repaid at the end of the month, which he entrusted to Sano. She merely gave her clients oral reports, saying, "The deposit has grown by so much this month, adding up to this much. Make a record of the interest." The clients would note this down in their ledgers, but that was all. They didn't get even three coppers in cash from her.

Because Yohei had to pay back the money he'd borrowed he asked Sano to hand over three thousand *monme* in silver of the interest to solve his cash problem. But from the very beginning, her claim that she had lent out this money and made large profits had been a scam. Together with the evil company she kept, she'd squandered all the money that had been deposited with her, and the money was not going to appear from anywhere else, either.

Yohei kept pressing Sano. In the beginning she held him off by saying that Inari had worked so hard to increase this money that it would go against the deity's will to make such a demand now. She even intimidated him with suggestions that this would invite divine retribution and bring him no good. Yohei, however, was in financial straits and dunned her again and again. The others who'd entrusted money to her became suspicious and also began to press her to pay it back, threatening to make a legal complaint to the authorities. Finding it difficult to withstand this pressure, Sano went to Yohei. "For some time," she said,

you've been asking me to take out some of the profits, but since the deity has taken such special care to increase the money, it would be an insult to demand that the money must be taken out now, and this would surely call down divine punishment. Please wait for a short while longer. I've received many invitations from Fukuwatari in Bizen province (fifteen miles inland from the castle town), asking me to spread my creed there. If I stay there for forty or fifty days to spread the creed, I'll gain a great deal of money, and I'll then be able to use that to cover your needs. In that way the deity will not be angered and the money will increase greatly, bringing you immense riches. Please be patient for just a little while longer.

In this way she deceived Yohei. He was a man foolish enough to have trusted her so much that he ended up in this fix, so he said, "In that case, I'll get my lenders to wait a little longer. Be sure to get your hands on some money as soon as you can!" "I'll pack up my things and prepare to leave tomorrow," she replied. To alleviate Yohei's doubts, she left all her possessions in his care and asked him to look after her affairs; she then quickly made her escape to Fukuwatari.

Some twenty days after this all her fellows were arrested, and it became clear that she was a Kirishitan. Because she was not in her lodgings, Kenpōya Yohei was summoned [to the magistracy] and reprimanded: "Sano, who has been renting quarters from you, belongs to the Kirishitan sect proscribed by the government. Whether or not you knew that this person was a Kirishitan when you took her in as a renter, this amounts to serious neglect of your duty [to investigate your renters]. This is a heinous misdeed!" Yohei had hardly expected anything of the kind and was taken completely by surprise. In shock he said, "How could I have taken her in as a renter if I'd known such a thing?" "That stands to reason," the officials said. "But where has Sano gone?" "She's gone to a place in Bizen called Fukuwatari." "Are you sure about that? If you're deceiving us, you'll be held culpable of the same crime as she is." "She's sent two letters since she left for that place, so it can't be a lie," Yohei replied. The officials declared that they would immediately dispatch someone to arrest her. "I have unfinished business with that old hag," Yohei said, "so please let me go there myself and fetch her back. There's no reason why the authorities should be inconvenienced with this task. Please allow me to take care of this." "That's splendid," said the officials, "but how do you think you are going to get her to come back? She is a major criminal!" "I will have to trick her," Yohei replied. "I'll definitely bring her back with me!" "You need to make plans right away. When will you be setting off? Are you going to travel by land or by ship?" "Because this is an important matter," Yohei responded, "and since it's impossible to know how many days a journey by ship would take, I'll travel by land, leaving tomorrow morning." After this he left the magistracy, made preparations, and set off immediately the following day.[35]

When Yohei arrived in Fukuwatari and met the old woman, he put on a show of great sincerity and begged her for help: "The reason I've come here is none other than this: earlier I'd told a friend who lives nearby that you had increased my money with the help of Inari. After you left for this place, a rich man heard about this. He wants me to ask you to accept a deposit of thirty thousand *monme* in silver and increase it. He came to me with this request and has visited me many times, asking me again and again if you aren't back yet. As I've already told you, I'm also being pressed for three thousand *monme* in silver and am in great trouble because of this. Therefore I'd like you to return to Osaka, take this deposit, and pass three thousand *monme* of it on to me. Because it would be difficult to explain this matter properly in a letter, I've come here to see you. Please help me out of this fix!"

Sano had been performing prayer rituals in Fukuwatari ever since she had arrived and had secretly begun to spread her creed, but it was a very rural place and she had not made much progress. She had gone there merely to escape those who were demanding repayment of the money they had deposited with her, so she quickly agreed. She said she'd take care of some matters first and then head back to Osaka together with Yohei the following morning. "I've done it!" Yohei thought, and he continued to sweet-talk her so as to keep up the deception. The next day they left Fukuwatari together. When they were only five miles away from Osaka, a large group of people dressed as officials stepped out into the road, asking, "Are you Kenpōya Yohei? Is the person with you Sano?" When Yohei affirmed this, they instantly pulled Sano away and told Yohei that they had no business with him and that he should go home.

Both Sano and Yohei were greatly taken aback, and Yohei, who was let go, fled home immediately. From there he went directly to the magistracy. "As I was returning from Bizen with Sano," he said, "she was stolen away from me by some people dressed as officials—I don't know who they were. After bringing her all the way here, there was nothing I could do to stop them. I pray you to investigate this promptly." "Thank you for your trouble," he was told. "We'd already been discussing dispatching someone to arrest Sano, and we decided it was time to haul her in." Yohei was ordered to leave, so he went home. There was no longer any hope that Sano would return his money if only he waited a little more. Left with no other option, he sold his house and repaid his debts. He then used the remainder together with some additional borrowed money to buy the guild share of the Onoe bathhouse in Kita Shinchi and became a bathhouse manager. (Later, all persons who had had dealings with the Kirishitan were placed in the custody of their locale and banned from leaving the block. In those circumstances, it would have been impossible for Yohei to sell his house and buy a new place, but since this was at the very beginning of the affair, he had managed to do this before that ban was issued.)

After the execution of the Kirishitan, Yohei was also summoned to the magistracy and sentenced to a fine of two million coppers. Greatly shocked, he complained about this, only to be severely reprimanded: "You have lent money to a Kirishitan and made illegitimate profits from this. By rights, this warrants a sentence of decapitation, and it's only by special grace that you are merely being ordered to pay up the profit you have gained. You should be grateful for this! It's payment in return for your life." Those "great profits" were entirely nominal, and Yohei had not made even three coppers [out of his dealings with Sano]. Things came to this pass because his greedy wish for ill-gotten gain had led him to lend her so much money that he destroyed his household finances and was even forced to sell his house. Yohei was friendly with Tobaya Gihei, who lives in the Fukushima area of Osaka, and Gihei says that Yohei told him some of what had happened. Here I've recorded just as I heard it from Gihei.

There is a man called Bizen'ya Shinshichi who moved here from the town of Saidaiji in Okayama. When his aunt visited Osaka, I asked them about the situation in Fukuwatari. They told me that Sano had many followers there. Few of them were townspeople or farmers; most were so-called hill people. They lived in a village of some one hundred households under the supervision of an outcast chief who worked as a hand for the domain office in charge of criminal investigations. Because everyone in this village had been converted, the domain tried to use pariahs to arrest the outcasts. This task proved to be quite beyond them: sixteen pariahs were killed, while just one outcast suffered a slight injury. In the end the outcasts were crushed by the retainers of the domain. They were arrested one by one and the leaders were all exiled to remote islands.[36]

Enkōji

Enkōji is a temple of the Bukkōji branch of the Ikkō sect. This is the temple where Sano was registered. The priest was sentenced to expulsion from the temple on the same day as the others, but he was a child of only twelve or thirteen years old. His mother reckoned that it wouldn't be a problem if he remained there that night, so she paid no heed to the warnings of others and let the young priest stay. News of this reached [the magistracy]. Holding that this lack of awe for shogunal authority constituted a grave misdeed, the magistrate sentenced the priest to exile to a remote island and ordered the temple property confiscated.[37]

Kinu

Just like Sano, this woman made use of the pernicious creed to bewitch people and rob them of money, clothing, and anything else that they might possess. It's said that she deceived many by promising them that she would increase their money.

Rentakuji

Rentakuji belongs to the Higashi Honganji branch. Its priest was expelled.[38] The temples in the same group were ordered to remain strictly secluded in the same manner as with the group temples mentioned above.

[I learned that the following fines were imposed on people implicated in this case:]

2,700,000 coppers	Masuya Yasubei (sake brewer, Kohata-machi in Tenma)
2,000,000 coppers	Kenpōya Yohei
200,000 coppers	Ise-machi in Tenma
7 *ryō* in gold	Block officials in Dōjima[39]

I'm told that in addition to the above, fines were imposed on many others, in some cases as little as three thousand coppers. There have been exaggerated rumors of many people being sentenced to decapitation or exile. For what I've recorded here, however, in every case I've investigated the source. On Mitsugi and Gunki, I've heard Unmei's report of what a magistrate's private secretary told him. In addition, I've learned much at Jōkōji. I heard detailed reports on the way Kanzanji was dealt with from Yamatoya Rinzō and the priest of Kushōji. I received information about events in Tenma from Akashiya Kihei in Kitano. I checked the sources also for other matters and left out what I found to be dubious.

A masseur who lived in rental housing owned by Taiyūji lived close to Sano and visited her often. For every massage she paid him one hundred coppers, treated him to drink and snacks, and let him eat his fill. He became greatly obliged to her, and on his rounds he talked up her mysterious powers and recommended her warmly to others. Because he had deposited seventeen thousand coppers with her in the hope that she would increase his money, he was provisionally confined to his locale. On the day the sentences were pronounced he was summoned and sentenced to a strict reprimand. Akashiya Risuke told me that he accompanied this man [to the magistracy].

Kashimaya Shōsuke told me that he has heard the following elsewhere: The detection of the Kirishitan started when one of them (although I asked, he doesn't know the name; I suppose it must be Kinu or Yae) cajoled a lot of people into making deposits by promising them to increase their money, winning them over by doing the things I've described above. A sake dealer and a water drawer deposited borrowed sums of money with her that exceeded their means. They were told that this money was increasing, but they never received any actual cash. The water drawer was a lowly laborer and was often dunned by his lender. Therefore he visited the woman many times, asking her to pay him some of the interest, but she always talked her way out of this and never handed him anything. The sake dealer, too, became suspicious and went to see her many times to get his money back. [The Kirishitan] had all come together to use up this money, so she had none at hand. When she ran out of reasons to refuse, she had no other option but to run away and go into hiding.

The sake dealer grew ever more angry: "No matter in what province she is hiding, I'll track her down!" He threw his business to the wind, traveled around looking for her, and learned that she was in fact hiding with some relatives in Harima province. He wanted to go there right away, but he realized that if the relatives kept her hidden and refused to hand her over, there would be nothing he could do. He mulled this over for some time. Nearby lived a man who in recent years had been a retainer employed by a senior staff official of the magistracy but had since withdrawn from service. Now he rented a hut and led a humble life. The sake dealer went to talk to this man, assuming that he would know about matters of this sort. The man said, "That is easy enough. If we dress up as officials and go there to carry out an investigation, the local people won't be able to keep her hidden. We can then seize her and bring her back." The sake dealer was very happy with this idea, so they both made themselves out to be officials and went to the place where she was hiding. They told the village officials that they were acting on orders from Osaka. The village officials then had the village searched and found the woman. Since the two had made themselves out to be shogunal officials, they immediately tied her up and took her back with them to Osaka. But as this was all a hoax, there was not much they could do after that. Although they threatened her in various ways, she insisted that she didn't have a single copper. There's no way to get the best of an evildoer, and the sake dealer had not obtained a written contract, so he could hardly file a lawsuit against her. All he could do was to continue to dun her fruitlessly.

Since this woman was so unexpectedly "arrested" in Harima province, she had left there the fox that she called her deity. This fox possessed a girl in the household where the woman had stayed and went into a frenzy: "She went to Osaka without me, so now I've no one to worship me. What am I to do!" This fox possessed another person as well and was beyond anybody's control. The local people talked this over, and the village officials traveled to Osaka to make an appeal at the magistracy: "The person called something-or-other whom you arrested recently left behind a fox. This fox has gone wild, causing trouble in the village. Therefore we entreat you to order the arrested person to take charge of this great fox as soon as possible." The officials at the magistracy told them that no such arrest had taken place. Thereafter, however, this matter was investigated, and the circumstances behind the sake dealer and the former retainer posturing as shogunal officials came out. All were arrested. A confession was obtained from that woman, and thus, quite unexpectedly, this Kirishitan affair came to light. It is said that the impostor who had traveled down [to Harima] to "arrest" her died in the jailhouse shortly afterward. Kinuya Shichibei also told me this story, saying that he had heard it somewhere.

The execution of Kirishitan is a rare occasion, seldom to be seen since the beginning of the realm. Onlookers gathered in throngs, and because they believed that the condemned would be paraded along the road to Sakai, the area around Shimanouchi and the Nippon Bridge [where the road to Sakai crosses the Dōtonbori River] was so crammed with people that all traffic stopped. However, apparently for the reason that the Nakamuraya firm in Kyoto had some connection with Nakabashi street, the parade progressed along that route instead, and the tens of thousands of onlookers all rushed pell-mell to get to Nakabashi street.[40] According to what I've heard, a nursemaid carrying a child on her back was knocked down, and the child was trampled to death. Two or three others died as well and there were countless injuries.

Chapter 12

Night Tales from the Kasshi Day

Matsura Seizan

ITEM 1 (CIRCA TENTH MONTH, 1829)

At the beginning of the tenth month [of 1829], I had the following discussion with a certain person I met:

"Last year, or maybe this year, a person in Osaka was found practicing the Jesus creed and was finally arrested."

"How does one recognize that 'Jesus creed'?" I said.

"A girl had been lying ill for a long time, and neither medicine nor prayer rites had any effect. She was near death, and her parents were much distressed. At that time, a townsperson skilled in incantations managed to heal this girl. That townsperson had received the secret transmission of the Jesus creed. He passed it on to people with sick family members and in this way gained many believers."[1]

"What kind of transmission is that?" I asked.

"In origin, it was passed down by survivors of the fall of Osaka Castle who hid themselves among the townspeople.[2] The members of that group are said to have gradually increased in number."

When I asked what kind of group it was, he said, "There must be over twenty or thirty members. Three or four among them are men, and the rest are all women."

"If they've broken the shogunal proscription, they'll certainly be punished severely," I responded.

"Of course, they'll be crucified."

"That sort will be only too glad to be crucified," I said. "That's the very idea of that sect."

"Indeed. According to the person who told me about this, the magistrate declared during the investigation, 'You must convert! Don't you fear punishment for having [turned to] an evil creed that the shogunal authorities have proscribed throughout the land?' The woman being interrogated answered, 'I have offered my life to my god from the moment I began this practice, so why should I change it just because you say it's an evil creed and threaten me with execution?' She showed no fear at all."

"What sort of god was she serving?" I asked.

"Nothing that much out of the ordinary. One was a so-called Okame mask of an unsightly woman, with some material attached to it to look like clothing.[3] The other was a figurine of an old man. The investigators became suspicious and broke the figurine, but they found nothing strange inside it. What might have been the main object of her prayers?"

We talked more about this, but I've forgotten what was said. Apparently, the source of this tale is the Osaka magistrate, who talked about it when he came to Edo. If that's true, there must be some substance to it.[4]

ITEM 2 (TWELFTH MONTH, 1829)

I'd heard rumors that [Kirishitan] had been caught in the capital region, but now it's confirmed. A Confucian scholar who has been staying among my retainers recently returned from a visit to Kyoto, so I asked him about this. "Here in Edo," he said, "I've heard rumors that people of that sect were discovered in Kyoto and Ōmi and have been arrested, but I heard nothing about this when I was in Kyoto."

A visitor from Osaka has been staying in the house of a wrestler who resides in my retirement retreat. When the wrestler asked this visitor whether he knew anything about this turn of events, he said,

An old woman in her sixties who lived in the Yasaka neighborhood in Kyoto installed a main icon of some sort in a roadside shrine and brought about various miracles by performing prayer rites there. She was very effective at healing the sick and reviving the dead, and there was no wish she could not fulfill; she did many other mysterious things as well. That old woman won everybody's faith and prospered, never lacking in money or goods.

A young man lived in that old woman's house, and people assumed that he was her lover. At one time she took him with her on a pilgrimage to Ise. His clothing was so dashing that he attracted everybody's attention. The couple aroused the suspicions of an official [from Kyoto], too. He waited for them to return, whereupon he arrested them at the Fushimi crossroads [at the entrance to the city limits]. During the ensuing investigation, it came out that they were Kirishitan, so they were immediately taken to Osaka and jailed there.[5] For some reason the old woman received severe treatment in the jailhouse, and even had her teeth and fingernails pulled out. Many of those who had turned to her and whose wishes she had fulfilled had converted to this sect, and I've heard that more than eight hundred were arrested and remanded to jail, though that number must include relatives of followers of that sect. Such relatives, wives, and children were placed in the custody of their locale.

This man said that this practice had spread some three years ago, and that the arrests were evidently made last spring. Purportedly, that old woman was completely unaffected by torture. Rumors say that by practicing the pernicious Kirishitan creed, she had become impervious to all pain.

Let me copy here a written report that the wrestler in my service also [obtained]:

In Yasaka, in the eastern part of Kyoto, an old woman who lived in rented quarters worshipped some deity or buddha in an inner room and performed divinations. Her predictions often proved accurate, and many clients visited her every day. Perhaps she made arrangements with like-minded people—in any case, in 1827 she made a pilgrimage to Ise, and I saw her myself on the road. She was wearing an undergarment made of joined pieces of scarlet and purple silk crepe and an overgarment of Nishijin silk.[6] She was accompanied by a young man twenty-four or twenty-five years old, wearing the same attire and carrying two swords. This old woman was some sixty years of age. People said she spent large amounts of money at every post station [on the road]. She brought as a servant a maid about thirty years of age who carried a bundle on her back. I later heard that their appearance had aroused suspicion and they had been arrested. Evidently that man revealed everything, and a number of Kyoto townspeople were arrested one after the other. For some reason, though, the Osaka Magistracy took charge and had all these townspeople brought to Osaka. This was the year before last, and the case is not yet resolved, even now. Most of the townspeople were jailed, and even their wives, children, and relatives were placed in the custody of their locale. According to rumor, last spring some seven hundred or eight hundred people were jailed in Osaka. I've heard that many of them died in the jailhouse, while others have been handed over to their locale. I've also heard that the old woman did not give in, no matter what kind of torture was inflicted on her, but I don't know the truth of this.

Previously tales of this sect or of the Amakusa uprising were copied and circulated as rental books [without any particular problem]. But now the possessors are punished whenever such works are found. I've heard that as a result bookdealers have burned all books of this sort. There were many rumors about this matter in the streets of Kyoto from 1827 until last spring, but nothing has been heard about it since then. It appears, though, that this case has yet to be brought to a conclusion.

According to the account passed on by the visitor from Osaka, the teeth and nails of that old woman were pulled out. Would this have been done as some kind of torture? If this is true, it must be based on some old precedents. *Record of the Heavenly Punishment Visited upon Followers of the Jesus Creed* mentions the following:[7]

• In the Kan'ei years [1624–1645], men and women of the Kirishitan sect were rounded up in all provinces and taken to Edo. They were strung up while still alive head down on the shore at [the execution grounds at] Suzugamori outside Shinagawa. When the tide came in, their heads were swallowed by the waves, and they couldn't breathe; when the tide went out, it was as though they had come back to life. This is similar to what the Buddhist sutras call a temporary reprieve from the torments of hell.[8]

• In the Kan'ei years, more than a hundred beggars were rounded up in Edo for being Kirishitan (the theory that they were lepers rather than beggars is completely wrong). They were herded into a fenced enclosure in Asakusa Torigoe, denied food, and starved to death. A hole was dug on the spot, and they were buried there.[9]

ITEM 3 (CIRCA SPRING 1830)

I obtained a snippet of news about this incident from somewhere, I've forgotten where. I append a copy of it here. Some parts of the text are unintelligible, and there are many copying mistakes.

The Kirishitan Incident

Some say that Mizuno Gunshun came from the Amakusa area in Kyushu; others say that his native province cannot be known for sure. (Gunshun is a mistake for Gunki; the *ki* [記] of Gunki is pronounced the same way as the character *ki* [喜], the cursive form of which looks like *shun* [春]. The same mistake recurs below.) While undergoing training as a Kirishitan, he stayed for a time in Ōtsu in Ōmi province, and also in [nearby] Ishibe along the [Tōkaidō] highway. He went repeatedly to Kyoto and also traveled to Nagasaki, and as a result became an accomplished scholar. In Kyoto, there was a woman called Mitsugi, possibly originally the daughter of a court noble. She had come to work in the pleasure quarters, until a man who had become her steady customer paid off her contract. He was a man of learning, and since Mitsugi was talented and intelligent, he showered favors on her, even letting her engage in scholarship, so she became knowledgeable in many fields. He even allowed her to become a disciple of the master of an academy. However, for some reason she lost her connection to that house—some say that this man died. After this, she came to dislike the "floating world"; she sought the company of scholars and eccentrics and went around wearing something like a poet's cloak. Even though she was a woman, she had superior mental capabilities. Abstaining from carnal relations and living as a true eccentric, she happened to meet this Mizuno Gunshun. They soon became close to each other. Mitsugi told [Gunshun] that she still pined for the man who had died. [Gunshun] said that he could show the man to her, but she would not be able to exchange words with him. [Mitsugi] asked [Gunshun] to use his arts to show her the man. The man's living figure appeared before her, right where she was sitting, but disappeared when Mitsugi spoke to him. After this, Mitsugi had faith in this practice.

Mizuno Gunshun was growing old, so he wanted to pass on [his practice] to a good disciple. However, that practice does not work if one indulges in intimacy as husband and wife. Gunshun was enamored with Mitsugi's spirit and bearing, and after this he allowed her to begin training and transmitted everything to her. In the meantime, a well-informed story-teller called Kimyō likewise became his disciple.[10] Because Kimyō was a man, he honed his skills more quickly than Mitsugi. He caught people's attention and made plenty of money, which he then spent frequenting teahouses. He was knowledgeable about the practice and even had books about it, but he was weak and lazy. As a result, people said he was not as proficient a practitioner as Mitsugi was.

After Gunshun's death, Kimyō and Mitsugi gathered followers of the same inclination. One of Mitsugi's disciples was an old grandmother in Tatsuta-chō in Tenma [in Osaka]. She revived a person in Harima province who had died, and she got a large amount of money for doing this. It was after this that the matter came to light. Three or four years ago, there was a surge in people who acted as Inari mediums, and the authorities began to hunt these people down. Some of them turned out to be in fact secretly worshipping a deity called Daiusu Buddha,[11] and these, it was found, were Mitsugi's disciples. This then led to Mitsugi's arrest. I'm told that according to the testimonies taken in the jailhouse, these people engaged in various kinds of mysterious arts. From all this it became clear that they were Kirishitan.

If a theater audience, tipsy with wine, cheers a scene showing the dark arts and calls it "today's Kirishitan," they will simply be reprimanded, and it won't become a serious judicial matter, even though the arts depicted in such plays are said to draw from those of the Amakusa rebels of two hundred years ago. In this case, however, the perpetrators were crucified, and the members of their households and their close blood relations have been condemned to indefinite incarceration. It was ordered that even [more distant] relatives are to be registered and that all illnesses, deaths, and the like among them must be reported to the shogunal authorities; an inspector will then be dispatched to confirm the circumstances. Within the household of Mizuno Gunshun, every single servant was questioned, so the investigation became an enormous undertaking. As for Mitsugi, her house was destroyed, and it's said they even dug up and removed three feet of soil from the plot. The priest of the temple where she was registered was [found guilty of] dereliction of duty, and the priests of the [other temples in the same] temple group were let off with a sentence of thirty days' strict seclusion.

Mitsugi had no disciples in Kyoto, but many in Osaka. Another person of the same persuasion was also discovered. The matter came to light because this person said that execution would in fact lead to a better afterlife. "Although the Ikkō sect, with which I am affiliated, is flourishing," this person further declared, "it only teaches about future rebirth after death. Because I put my faith totally in Daiusu Buddha, he will bestow good fortune on me not only in the past and future but also in this life. I will not give up this faith even if am put to the cross!" The temple with which this person was registered thus had no choice but to report the matter to the authorities. The head temple—Nishi Honganji, it seems—earned praise from the authorities for its prompt action. This case is still under investigation.[12]

ITEM 4 (CIRCA THIRD MONTH, 1837)

A neighbor told me the following:

Ōshio has long been a Confucian of the school of Wang Yangming.[13] He was responsible for the investigation of that old woman who was executed in Osaka some years ago as a follower of what was called the "teaching of Heaven." At that time, works in Chinese, including *Hydraulic Methods of the Great West* and *Illustrated Guide to Western Machinery*, were discovered in the house of a scholar of Western learning who was said to be a member of the same group. (These works are by the Ming scholar Li Madou [Matteo Ricci], who was an adherent of Jesus learning.)[14] Ōshio branded these as works of the pernicious creed and, after investigating the matter, concluded that this scholar must be executed. This seems excessively cruel. When Lord Takai Sanenori was the magistrate, Ōshio won his favor because of his assessment of this incident and came to be put in charge of the criminal investigations section. Lord Takai, too, was convinced by Ōshio's views on this matter. It's said that there are records of this investigation in the Osaka Magistracy. . . .[15]

ITEM 5 (EARLY 1837)

One day, Ogino Baiu showed me some Chinese poems that the rebel Ōshio had once sent to Mogami Tokunai.[16]

. . . [As for these poems], according to a certain person, "Wang Yangming had a follower named Luo Rufang. The rebel Ōshio is said to have long revered Wang Yangming. Probably he was influenced by the ideas of this Luo." A biography of Luo can be found in *Draft History of the Ming Dynasty*. It seems from this that he combined the Way of the Sages with Buddhism.[17] When the rebel says [in one of the poems], "I will not cease the quest for 'transmission of the heart,' even unto death," what does he mean? Thinking about it from the vantage point of what has happened, it would seem that the vengeful spirit of that old woman of the Jesus creed whom Ōshio had investigated must have taken possession of him and used her sorcery to make him commit [this heinous crime]. . . .

[Another poem ends,] "This morning, with the full tide, the boat sets off. For ten leagues I sleep soundly; having realized my dream, I am at ease." Many of the other rebels were captured right away, but the whereabouts of Ōshio and his son have not been discovered. Some say he must have stolen a boat and fled. Was it as a portent of this that he wrote these lines? Even if his plot failed, the traitor has been able to flee without any concern for others; this must be the implication of "For ten leagues I sleep soundly." As for "having realized my dream, I am at ease," it is rumored in Osaka Castle that this crook is a follower of Jesus, just like that old woman some years ago. In that case, his true wish should be to be executed for the sake of others. Why then doesn't he express remorse for his crime? He should go himself to the cross and seek to rise up to heaven in the same manner as the founder [of that creed]!. . .

[Ogino] also said, "Will the rebel Ōshio kill himself, or realize his wish as a follower of Jesus? If the latter, we should style him 'a wolf in priest's robes' after he is crucified. He may make himself out to be like a priest, but his true nature is that of a wolf."[18]

ITEM 6 (LATE SPRING 1837)

As seen above, one often encounters claims that Ōshio Heihachirō was a Kirishitan. Such claims are not entirely groundless. Some years ago, there was an old woman in Kyoto who was a devotee of that pernicious sect. Because of his learning, Ōshio was assigned to investigate her. He told the magistrate, "If I were to receive instruction in that creed for a while before I investigate her, I would be able to learn that sect's deepest secrets, and she would not be able to keep anything hidden from me." The magistrate agreed with this idea and privately granted Ōshio permission to go ahead with it. Ōshio entered this sect and became a follower of that old woman, and in the end he was able to hear just what that creed was all about. As a result, the members of this woman's group all had their crimes exposed.

When Ōshio delved into the Way they pursued, he found that it was not Kirishitan but the arts of Dakiniten. He nevertheless accused them all of being devotees of the Jesus creed and found them guilty as such. But since he had already acquired the Dakiniten arts himself, he used these as a pathway for seeking promotion in Edo. He used the Dakiniten method to offer up prayers with the aim of achieving his inner ambition. The world doesn't know this and calls him a Kirishitan because that's the way it looks, but the claim that he entered the Jesus sect is not the actual truth of the matter; it is merely what he told the magistrate. In the end, he must have been possessed by Dakiniten and through that gained a fleeting reputation. But because it was wrong from the start, all he did was to ruin himself.[19]

Chapter 13

A Biography of Ōshio Heihachirō

People respected and revered Ōshio, saying, "In a world bedazzled by money, only Ōshio Heihachirō is incorruptible! This is truly a man who lives for his duty!" Then, however, Ōshio discovered a group of devotees of the banned Kirishitan sect. Strangely, from that moment onward he exuded a sense of pride and self-conceit, and later he came to conceive of a grave plot. However surprising this turn of events may seem, it could not be helped. According to the rumors circulating in the town, it was all the doing of the wrathful spirit of Toyoda Mitsugi, one of the Kirishitan whom Ōshio exposed.

ON MIZUNO GUNKI OF THE KIRISHITAN SECT

A ronin from Karatsu in Hizen province called Mizuno Gunki lived in Yasaka Kami-chō. He worshipped the Inari deity in his house and engaged in strange practices of healing, divination, and many other things. His divinations hit the mark so precisely that everyone found it astonishing, and people flocked to him. Later it came out that what Gunki worshipped was in fact the banned Kirishitan creed; it was because he used its pernicious practices that whatever he tried worked well and he flourished day upon day.

Nearby lived a poverty-stricken man called Hachibei. He was happily married, and he and his wife worked side by side to eke out a meager existence without complaining about their impoverished circumstances. Every once in a while, Gunki engaged Hachibei for some work, and his wife would go along to help out. One day Hachibei left early in the morning, saying that he was going out to work; but night fell, and Hachibei failed to return. His wife stayed awake all night, waiting for him anxiously, but at dawn he still had not come home. Distraught with worry, the wife asked others for help and went around the neighborhood looking for Hachibei. No trace could be found of him, and his wife was beside herself with grief. She visited Gunki and asked him to perform prayer rituals to bring Hachibei home. Gunki immediately agreed, since Hachibei was a close friend. Straightaway he began to worship in front of his altar, and the wife, too, prayed that her husband might return. She worshipped together with Gunki every day.

When the rites were complete, Gunki said, "I've prayed to the best of my ability, but your husband is no longer of this world and you'll have to give up your hopes." Overcome by sorrow, the wife wailed with grief as though she had gone mad: "If he is no longer of this world there is nothing I can do, but our parting was so unexpected that he must have some last words that he wants to say to me. I wish I could meet him just once more! Please, somehow arrange for me to meet him! If that can't be done, I want to die, too!" Gunki was at a loss what to do, but the situation was so unusual that he felt he had to help: "If you miss your husband so dearly, I'll do as you wish and send for him by means of a method that I know so that you can meet him one last time. But this is a dangerous method, and you must not tell anybody about it." He had her promise him solemnly that she would keep this a secret. Thereupon they went into another room, where he performed a most strange ritual.

How mysterious! The husband, who was said to have already left this world, suddenly appeared in front of his wife and said, "Since I am no longer of this world, you can't rely on me anymore to provide for you in your daily life. Henceforth you must depend on the head of this house as your master and pray for me with the help of his blessed practices. If you do that, I'll soon be reborn in heaven and escape the torments of hell. I beg you to help me in this!" As soon as he had finished speaking, he disappeared.

His wife was both astounded and distraught, but after a while she dried her tears and turned to Gunki: "My late husband asks me to depend on you as my master and pray for him morning and night with the help of your practices so that he can escape from hell and be reborn in heaven. Please accept me as your disciple. I'll serve you every day so that I can become accomplished in your practice and help my husband to escape from his suffering." She begged him tearfully. Gunki was moved by the depth of her sincerity and agreed to accept her. She swore an oath, became his disciple, and devoted herself single-mindedly to learning what Gunki taught her. Gunki found her worthy of his trust, so he told her that he would allow her to receive all the secret transmissions and practices that she wished for. He brought out a drawing of the Lord of Heaven, and she cut her finger and dripped some blood onto the drawing as a sacred oath. He transmitted to her the mantra [of the Lord of Heaven], the prayer rituals, the method to collect money, and all the gestures and spells of his sorcery. Thereafter every night she loosened her hair, doused herself with water, and went out into the hills. She dedicated herself so wholeheartedly to austerities that she became able to achieve anything she wanted.

She now joined with Gunki in his practice, changed her name to Toyoda Mitsugi, and began swindling people out of large sums of money. To cloak her activities, she set herself up as a yin-yang diviner at Yasaka Kami-chō and conducted divinations and prayer rituals under that guise, but the hidden truth was that she practiced pernicious Kirishitan arts. She continued in this way for some time, engaging in various suspect activities. Then Gunki fell ill and died, and now Mitsugi was alone. She took the money that Gunki had stored up and distributed it among people who put their faith in her, luring them into her creed. That creed appeared to be something marvelous to foolish benighted people who cannot resist the temptation of easy money, and the number of devotees grew rapidly.

Mitsugi drew in Sayo, the mother of Kyōya Densuke of Kawasaki village (Nishinari county, Settsu province), and Kinu, who was living with Harimaya Tōzō in Tatsuta-machi in Tenma in Osaka, and encouraged them to collect money by engaging in her practices.[1] She took a portion of this money as gratitude payments to herself as their master, and she distributed it among the poor so as to spread the pernicious creed. Many were deceived by the extraordinary things that were conjured up before their eyes and joined the group. People who embraced this faith abounded in Kyoto, Osaka, and even places beyond; who knows where this might have ended. How appalling that people could believe that these pernicious arts, engaged in by people arrogantly living lives of luxury, were the most superior creed of all!

HOW ŌSHIO HEIHACHIRŌ EXPOSED THE PERNICIOUS CREED
THANKS TO HIS SUPERIOR INTELLIGENCE

The disciples of Toyoda Mitsugi were spreading the pernicious creed not only in Kyoto but also in Osaka. Lowly people foolishly placed their faith in it and worshipped the disciples as though they were living gods or buddhas; so many believers lined up before their gates that it was as bustling as a market. Ōshio Heihachirō heard about this and found it most suspicious. As the saying goes, "There are no mysteries in the correct Dharma," but this practice was all too mysterious. Privately, he reported about this to the magistrate, Lord Takai Sanenori. Ōshio then disguised himself in the garb of a townsman and left for Kyoto. He went to Mitsugi's house in Yasaka, made up a story [pretending that he needed her services], and begged her to perform prayer rituals for him. Mitsugi readily agreed and began the rituals. Ōshio already had a plan, so he paid her a generous sum. After this he went to Mitsugi's house every day and observed her practice closely. He found it to be indeed highly suspect and continued to probe into what she was doing. Mitsugi had no idea that he was spying on her; she believed that Ōshio was a sincere believer. When she tested him, he appeared to have an earnest desire to join her creed, so she lowered her guard and encouraged him to learn various pernicious arts. She showed him the drawing of the Lord of Heaven and taught him in detail about the Kirishitan practice.

As soon as he heard these things Ōshio signaled the magistracy staff officials to arrest Mitsugi, and they hauled her off to Osaka. This old woman now found herself in the jailhouse. She was livid that all her concerted efforts to spread that creed had come to nothing now that Ōshio had exposed her secrets. In a rage, she shrieked, "Just watch, just watch! My grudge will cling to you, Ōshio, and soon I'll make sure that you, too, end up on a cross, just like me!" The fury with which she cursed him was a horror to behold.

The persons implicated in this incident were interrogated one after the other, and all of them confessed. Toyoda Mitsugi was guilty of the heinous crime of spreading a creed that is strictly banned by shogunal law, so she was punished severely. She was paraded through Osaka and crucified. The others who had faith in this creed were also sentenced to various punishments. The ringleader, Mizuno Gunki, had already died, but because of his central role, his grave in Kyoto was destroyed and his remains

Figure 13.1 Illustration from *A Biography of Ōshio Heihachirō* showing Ōshio and subordinate officials arresting Mitsugi. *Ōshio Heihachirō denki: Kinko jitsuroku*. Eisensha, 1886. National Diet Library Digital Collection.

exposed before being discarded. All credited the smooth conclusion of this incident to Ōshio's superior intelligence and praised him highly. The sentences were pronounced in 1829.

ON THE WORKINGS OF MITSUGI'S WRATHFUL SPIRIT

After this, strange things began to happen in Ōshio's house. On rainy nights, the lamenting voice of an old woman was heard on the roof. At times, a ball of fire would roll into the house. At night the women in his household sometimes saw the figure of an old woman. All these strange goings-on made people very afraid, but the stout Ōshio was unaffected. Then the magistrate, Lord Takai, suddenly fell ill. Mitsugi's wrathful spirit troubled him every night, so he soon retired from the post of magistrate. People said that all this was owing to the grudge of that old woman.

The author of this work has been told the following. Mine, the daughter of Chūbei in Hannyaji village, was adopted by Ōshio when she was
fourteen years old. He said he planned to marry her in due course to his
[adoptive] son Kakunosuke, but in the end he made her into his own concubine. When she was seventeen, in the eleventh month of 1836, she
gave birth to a son, who was given the name Imagawa Yumitarō. Ōshio
often told people that Imagawa was the original name of the Ōshio house
and that they were descended from the famous Imagawa Yoshimoto.[2]
Also, Ōshio had a room at the back of his house that not even his friends
were allowed to enter.

To turn the prospective wife of one's son into one's own concubine is
a bestial act. How could such a person achieve great things? Ever since
his childhood Ōshio had been raised according to the teachings of the
Confucian masters, and he had never committed an immoral act of this
sort. What could have led him astray in this manner? Was this another
effect of the grudge of that evil old woman Toyoda Mitsugi? All the Kirishitan books that Mitsugi owned were supposedly burned, but some say
that Ōshio secretly set aside the books that appealed to him, hid them,
and studied them carefully. However this may be, many rumors about
these strange matters went around after [Ōshio's death].

It is also said that Ōshio told his beloved concubine Yū to shave her
head and become a nun so as to evade the wrathful spirit of Toyoda
Mitsugi. Others say that he did this to pacify the spirit of Yuge Shin'emon
of the Western Magistracy, whom he cornered into committing sep-
puku. There are grounds for each of these rumors; I must leave it to the
reader to decide which is true or not.[3]

[When Ōshio Heihachirō and his son disappeared without a trace after
the failed rebellion of 1837,] there were rumors that he must have learned
the mysterious arts of the Kirishitan from the books he had taken from
Mitsugi, so that now he was able to hide in deep mountains and remote
valleys and sustain himself by drawing in qi and sipping mist.[4]

Appendix 1

‿

Mitsugi's 1822 Arrest

INTRODUCTION

As mentioned in chapter 3, Mitsugi was arrested in 1822, several years before the Kirishitan incident came to light, as a result of trouble that arose when she undertook a pilgrimage to the Konpira shrine complex in Shikoku on behalf of the noble Yamanoi house. The Kyoto magistrate evidently consulted the senior councillors about the case, perhaps because it involved a noble house, and a fragment of the records concerning it was preserved in the Precedents of Criminal Judgments Organized by Category.[1] A translation of this fragment follows.

SUMMATION BY THE KYOTO MAGISTRATE

Toyoda Mitsugi, a yin-yang diviner resident in Yasaka Kami-chō, acted in a high-handed manner while traveling in Sanuki province. Calling herself Toyoda Tango, she declared that she was making a pilgrimage [to Konpira] on behalf of the noble Yamanoi house. At Minami Takinomiya village, she tried to hire palanquins and coolies using a ledger of requisition slips and receipts bearing the seal of the Yamanoi house. She did not go so far as to attempt requisitioning them without charge, but she sent her servant, Mitsuemon, with the ledger to negotiate the hiring.[2] No coolies were available there, however, and a mutual misunderstanding occurred as a result of the absence of the village officials. This then led to a dispute. At the inn Mitsugi struck the village aldermen Hanbei and Heizaemon with her fan, and when they raised doubts about her status, she challenged them to follow her back to Kyoto [to see that she was indeed acting on behalf of the Yamanoi]. She also deliberately abandoned the luggage pannier [carrying the Yamanoi crest], leaving it behind at the inn as evidence of the authenticity of her relationship [to the Yamanoi].

As Mitsugi was extremely remiss in all of this and committed a misdeed, she should be sentenced to confinement to her house for a period of one hundred days. However, she has already been remanded to jail for some days and thus is to be exempted from further punishment.[3]

THE DELIBERATIVE COUNCIL'S RECOMMENDATIONS

This case can be considered in light of an earlier case about which the Kyoto magistrate consulted the senior councillors, who handed it down to the Deliberative Council to discuss in 1814. In this earlier case, Bun'iku, a priest of the temple of Seirinji in Negi village, Mino province, went [to Kyoto] to call on Lord Kujō. With the aim, according to him, of avoiding delays on the road, he wrongly prepared a ledger of requisition slips and receipts for coolie services inscribed with the title "temple designated to perform prayer rites for Lord Kujō." In addition, he hired coolies at Musa post station in Ōmi province and recorded that in the ledger. He said that he was late and would pay subsequently and continued on to Kyoto without settling the account. Instead he simply left the ledger at the post station [as a pledge]. In Kyoto he asked Murakami Hayato to take care of the matter.[4]

Bun'iku did not go so far as to use the name and title of Lord Kujō to requisition horses and coolies without charge. Nevertheless it was a misdeed for one who is a priest to behave in a manner that invites trouble. The Kyoto magistrate proposed sentencing Bun'iku to one hundred days' confinement to his house. The Deliberative Council recommended a lesser sentence of fifty days' confinement to his house, and this recommendation was followed in handing down the judgment.

Considered in light of this precedent, [the following points are pertinent]: Bun'iku used a ledger inscribed at his instigation with the title "temple designated to perform prayer rites for Lord Kujō," claiming that he did so with the aim of calling expeditiously upon Lord Kujō. By contrast, Mitsugi made use of a ledger that she had in fact received from the Yamanoi house. In this regard she is not culpable of a misdeed [in the same sense as Bun'iku was]. However, she struck the village aldermen

Hanbei and Heizaemon. Although she is a woman, the gravity of what she did is not so different from Bun'iku's case.[5] It thus would be appropriate to sentence her to fifty days' confinement to her house, the same as Bun'iku. But as she already has been remanded to jail for some days, she should be exempted from further punishment.

Appendix 2

Disposition of the Proscribed Books

The category of books defined as "proscribed" (*kinsho*) evolved over the course of the Edo period; how books in that category should be dealt with was also subject to varying interpretation. By origin, proscribed works related to Christianity were writings in Chinese or translated into that language by Jesuit missionaries active in China and their associates. According to Itō Tasaburō, the core of such proscribed books in Chinese were thirty-two works whose import was banned in 1630. The adoption of a more stringent policy in 1685 added further works to the category. Reflecting this expansion, in 1698 the Osaka Magistracy distributed a list of thirty-eight proscribed books to the city's bookdealers and ordered them to post it in their stores. Two decades later, the shogunate shifted to a somewhat more lenient stance. Under the shogun Yoshimune, in 1720 it directed the Nagasaki Magistracy, which was responsible for overseeing the inspection of books imported from China, to allow the import and sale of works that did not explicitly promote Christianity. Nineteen works, primarily of a mathematical, astronomical, or technological nature, were exempted from proscription.

This change in policy, however, was not publicly proclaimed. It remained private knowledge among the officials directly concerned with the import and inspection of books, and many in intellectual circles as well the broader range of officials continued to assume that works once labeled as proscribed remained forbidden. The printing by the Kyoto bookdealers' guild in 1771 of a list of thirty-eight proscribed books that largely coincided with the 1698 Osaka list reinforced this assumption.[1]

For those who investigated the 1827 Kirishitan incident, the local precedent of the 1698 list was paramount. Using it as their criterion for evaluating the works found in Kenzō's possession and the scraps remaining from Gunki's papers, the investigators divided these items into two categories: works on the 1698 list and other works that "invite suspicion." The former included several mathematical works (among them two copies of Matteo Ricci's translation of Euclid) that had in fact been exempted from proscription a century earlier, as well as expositions of Christian doctrine that continued to be banned. The items that "invited suspicion" included a translation by Shizuki Tadao (1760–1806), a scholar of Western learning, of Western travel accounts and a work by Maeno Ryōtaku (1723–1803), another scholar of Western learning, that extolled the superiority of Western scientific theory over Chinese. Also listed in the category of works that "invited suspicion" were Kenzō's own summation of what he had learned about Christianity from the proscribed books in his possession ("The Torch of Rhinoceros Horn, Draft"); a number of pieces of unclear provenance, with titles indicating that they dealt with cosmological (although not necessarily Christian) theories or matters concerning the West; and four drawings of *fumie* that Kenzō had acquired.[2]

As mentioned in the introduction to part 3, Kenzō was not exceptional in taking an interest in proscribed works on Christianity in Chinese. Itō Tasaburō cites examples of a number of scholars contemporary to Kenzō who owned or read the same Christian writings as he did, and the testimonies indicate that others in Kenzō's circle of intellectual acquaintances were also familiar with such works. Both Itō Tasaburō and Peter Kornicki point out that lists of proscribed works such as the 1698 Osaka list and that printed by the Kyoto bookdealers' guild in 1771 had a dual effect. On the one hand they endowed the listed works with an aura of fear and danger. On the other they piqued interest in those works. Kornicki suggests that while the display of such lists may have outwardly signaled compliance with shogunal policy, it also served to hint at what might be discreetly provided to select customers.[3] As noted in the introduction to part 3, the news of Kenzō's sorry fate must have sent a frisson of concern through those who shared his interests. It evidently did not, however, put a stop to the quiet circulation of the works whose possession brought him disaster.

Appendix 3

~

Manuscript Versions of the Keihan Kirishitan Incident Dossier

Three different manuscript copies of the documents concerning the investigation and judgment of the Keihan Kirishitan case are known to exist. The translations of the dossier in parts 1 and 2 are based on a collation and combination of the first two of these three copies, which are described in the following.

1. The best-known and overall the most complete copy is what we refer to as the Kōda-bon manuscript. Carrying the title "Jashūmon ikken kakitome" (Record of the case of the pernicious sect), this manuscript was once owned by the modern scholar Kōda Shigetomo (1873–1954). The original is today kept by Keiō University Library, while the Historiographical Institute of the University of Tokyo holds a modern traced facsimile.[1] Evidence suggests that this copy derives from Uchiyama Hikojirō (1797–1864), a senior staff official in the Osaka Western Magistracy. This manuscript has two notable characteristics. First, it reproduces not the dossier sent to Edo in late 1827 but a revised version made after the sentences had been handed down at the end of 1829. One of the issues that caused officials in Edo great concern was how to deal with Sano's statement that she had gone to Nagasaki with the intent of treading on the *fumie* (see the introduction to part 2). The senior councillors eventually directed the Osaka eastern magistrate to have all mentions of Sano's trip struck from the official record. The Kōda-bon manuscript was copied after this had

been done and so does not include any information about Sano's trip or the reasons for it.

The Kōda-bon's second distinctive feature is that it contains important materials apart from the dossier proper. Specifically, it incorporates a record of the deliberations in Edo in 1829 concerning the incident (the documents translated in chapter 8). The transcription of this part of the Kōda-bon is in the hand of Uchiyama Hikojirō. Unlike the orders subsequently issued by the senior councillors regarding the sentences and the disposal of other matters (see chapter 9), the record of the deliberations in Edo was not communicated officially to the Osaka Magistracy and must have reached Osaka and Uchiyama by an unofficial private route. The source was plausibly Naitō Noritomo, who had served as Osaka western magistrate until the third month of 1829. At that point Naitō was promoted to financial and judicial affairs magistrate and moved to Edo. In that capacity he sat on the Deliberative Council and participated in its discussions of the incident. Quite likely Naitō gave a copy of the record of those discussions to his successor as Osaka western magistrate, Shinmi Masamichi (1791–1848), when he met Shinmi in Edo prior to the latter's departure for Osaka in the middle of the seventh month of 1829 to take up his duties there.[2] At some point during his tenure as Osaka western magistrate, which lasted until the eighth month of 1832, Shinmi in turn presumably showed the materials to Uchiyama, who made a copy for his own reference.

In the eighth month of 1830 Takai Sanenori, the Osaka eastern magistrate who had presided over the incident's investigation, received permission to retire from his duties for health reasons and return to Edo. The new eastern magistrate arrived in Osaka several months later, in the second month of 1831. In the interim the western magistrate, Shinmi Masamichi, was responsible for overseeing the operation of the Eastern as well as the Western Magistracy. This circumstance, we can surmise, gave Uchiyama the opportunity to have a copy made as well of the revised version of the dossier on the incident kept in the Eastern Magistracy. The transcriber of this copy cannot be determined, but Uchiyama evidently kept it together with the copy he himself made of the record of the deliberations in Edo, so the two form a single set of related documents.

2. A second copy of the dossier of materials forwarded to Edo and some of the correspondence exchanged between Osaka and Edo regarding the incident is preserved today at the Center for Modern Japanese Legal and

Political Documents attached to the University of Tokyo Graduate School for Law and Politics. Titled "Jashūmon ginmisho" (Dossier on the investigation of the pernicious sect), it was owned previously by the scholar and thinker Yoshino Sakuzō (1878–1933). We thus refer to it as the Yoshino-bon manuscript. This manuscript derives from a copy of the dossier kept by Matsudaira Muneakira (1782–1840), who served as Osaka governor from 1826 to the eleventh month of 1828, when he was transferred to the post of Kyoto governor. He was thus the highest shogunal authority in Osaka at the time of the incident's investigation. Takai Sanenori, the Osaka eastern magistrate, had consulted Matsudaira about the incident, and in his capacity as Osaka governor Matsudaira had overseen the initial back-and-forth with Edo regarding it. He evidently retained a private copy of the dossier as originally submitted to him.

The Yoshino-bon manuscript, which hitherto has not received attention from researchers, does not contain the discussions by the Deliberative Council and some other documents found in the Kōda-bon. Yet it has the great merit of reproducing the content of the testimonies and summations as originally drafted by the Eastern Magistracy and forwarded to Edo in 1827 under Matsudaira's supervision. In particular it includes the passages about Sano's trip to Nagasaki that were subsequently erased from the records of the case kept at the Osaka Magistracy and that do not appear in the Kōda-bon. Comparison of the Yoshino-bon and Kōda-bon makes it possible to reconstruct exactly what was excised from the original version of the dossier.[3]

3. A third manuscript is owned by the library of the University of the Sacred Heart (Seishin Joshi Daigaku) in Tokyo and was presumably owned previously by Ebisawa Arimichi. We refer to it as the Seishin-bon manuscript. This manuscript is of uncertain provenance and also is abridged as well as corrupt in various regards. It is of interest primarily because, in contrast to the Kōda-bon, it contains an account of Sano's trip to Nagasaki. The fuller and more reliable version of these passages to be found in the Yoshino-bon diminishes its value in this regard, however.[4]

The translation of the dossier and the deliberations in Edo in chapters 1 through 9 makes use of both the Yoshino-bon and the Kōda-bon. It follows the Yoshino-bon for the passages about Sano's Nagasaki trip, indicating in notes what has been excised in the Kōda-bon. It uses the Kōda-bon for the account of the Edo deliberations and other materials not included in the Yoshino-bon. In the Kōda-bon the section on the Edo deliberations is appended at the manuscript's end, but we have given priority to the sequence of the case's development and embedded this section between the documents in the dossier that preceded and followed it chronologically.[5]

GLOSSARY

accusation (of crimes apart from those admitted) — *satto* 察度

addendum — *shugaki* 朱書き

alderman — *toshiyori* 年寄

arts beyond the ordinary — *ijutsu* 異術

ascetic training — *shugyō* 修行

banishment from the immediate locale — *tokorobarai* 所払

banned — *gohatto* 御法度

branch house — *bunke* 分家

branch temple — *matsuji* 末寺

brothel — *okiya* 置屋

buddha image — *butsuga* 仏画, *butsuzō* 仏像

buddha's punishment — *butsubachi* 仏罰

certificate/certification of sectarian affiliation — *shūshi aratame* 宗旨改, *shūmon aratame* 宗門改, *shūshi tegata* 宗旨手形, *shūshi ukeai* 宗旨請合, *teraukejō* 寺請状

chicanery — *takumi* 巧

city limits of Kyoto — *rakuchū rakugai* 洛中洛外

clairvoyant, clairvoyance — *mitōshi* 見通, *mitōsu* 見通す

clairvoyant powers — *tsūriki* 通力, *myōtsū* 妙通

clerk	*tedai* 手代
confirmed testimony	*ginmi tsumari no kuchigaki* 吟味詰之口書
crime	*futodoki* 不届
criminal investigation section	*tōzoku ginmi yaku* 盗賊吟味役, *tōzokugata* 盗賊方
cross-examine together	*tsukiawase ginmi* 突合吟味
custody of the locale	*tokoro azuke* 所預
dark arts	*majutsu* 魔術
decapitation	*shizai* 死罪
decapitation with display of the head	*gokumon* 獄門
deity body	*shintai* 神体
deity title	*shinshi* 神謚
Deliberative Council	*hyōjōsho* 評定所
dereliction of duty	*tōkan* 等閑
detached room	*hanare zashiki* 離座敷
deviant creed	*ishū* 異宗
deviant practices	*ihō* 異法
disciple	*deshi* 弟子
distant exile	*jūtsuihō* 重追放
divine image	*miei* 御影
divine punishment	*shinbatsu* 神罰
drawing of the Lord of Heaven	*Tentei gazō* 天帝画像
Edo Magistracy	*machi bugyō* 町奉行
effigy	*hitogata* 人形
execution placard	*sutefuda* 捨札
exile to a remote island	*entō (ontō)* 遠島
expulsion from temple	*taiin* 退院
extraordinary things, feats	*kimyō* 奇妙, *kikai* 奇怪, *kii* 奇異
fellow devotees, fellows of the same mind	*dōshi* 同志
Financial and Judicial Affairs Magistracy	*kanjō bugyō* 勘定奉行
fine	*iryō* 違料, *karyō* 過料
five-household group	*goningumi* 五人組
fox witchery	*kitsune tsukai* 狐遣ひ
handcuffing	*tejō, tegusari* 手鎖
hands (informal investigation agents)	*tesaki* 手先
head temple	*honzan* 本山
healing rituals	*kaji* 加持
holding	*chigyōsho* 知行所
house confinement	*heimon* 閉門, *oshikome* 押込
house manager (in Edo)	*ienushi* 家主
house name	*yagō* 屋号

household head	*namaenin* 名前人
Inari medium	*Inari myōjin sage* 稲荷明神下げ
incarceration	*rōsha* 牢舎
indefinite incarceration	*nagarō* 永牢
inspector	*kenshi* 検使
intendant	*daikan* 代官
interrogate	*ginmi* 吟味
interrogate severely	*kibishiku ginmi* 厳敷吟味
jailhouse	*rō* 牢, *rōyashiki* 牢屋敷
Jesus creed	*Yaso* 耶蘇
Keihan (Kyoto–Osaka area)	京坂
Kirishitan creed (sect)	*Kirishitan shūmon* 切支丹宗門
Kyoto governor	*Kyōto shoshidai* 京都所司代
Kyoto Magistracy	*Kyōto machi bugyō* 京都町奉行
landlord	*ienushi* 家主
lax	*orosoka* 疎
Lord of Heaven Buddha	*Tentei nyorai* 天帝如来
main house	*honke* 本家
main icon, sacred icon	*honzon* 本尊
manager (of a shop)	*bantō* 番頭
mantra	*darani* 陀羅尼
master	*shishō* 師匠
members (as yet undiscovered) of a group	*yorui* 余類
miracle, miraculous	*kizui* 奇瑞, *fushigi* 不思議, *shintoku* 神徳
miraculous event	*reigen* 霊験
miraculous powers	*jinzū* 神通, *myōhō* 妙法, *jinriki* 神力
misdeed	*furachi* 不埒
mysterious arts	*fushigi no jutsu* 不思議之術, *kimyō no jutsu* 奇妙之術, *myōjutsu* 妙術
negligent	*bunen* 不念, *fuyukitodoki* 不行届
Office for Sectarian Matters	*shūmon bugyō* 宗門奉行, *shūmon aratame yaku* 宗門改役
off-limits (place)	*okamaiba* 御構場
oral transmission	*kuden* 口伝
Osaka Eastern/Western Magistracy	*Ōsaka higashi/nishi machi bugyō* 大坂東/西町奉行
Osaka governor	*Ōsaka jōdai* 大坂城代
pardon	*yūmen* 宥免
pariah	*eta* 穢多
parishioner	*danna* 旦那, *danka* 檀家
past offense	*kyūaku* 旧悪
pernicious arts	*jajutsu* 邪術, *jahō* 邪法

pernicious creed (sect)	*jashūmon* 邪宗門, *jahō* 邪法, *jadō* 邪道
population register	*ninbetsu(chō)* 人別(帳)
practice austerities	*shugyō* 修行
prayer rituals	*kaji* 加持, *kaji kitō* 加持祈祷
Precedents of Criminal Judgments Organized by Category	*Oshioki reiruishū* 御仕置例類集
princely house	*miya* 宮, *miyakata* 宮方, *miyake* 宮家
private secretary (of magistrate)	*yōnin* 用人
proclamation	*ofuregaki* 御触書
profession	*gyōtei* 業体
proposal for punishments (of misdeeds)	*otogamezukegaki* 御咎附書
proposal for punishments (of serious crimes)	*oshiokizukegaki* 御仕置附書
proscribed	*goseikin* 御制禁, *gogenkin* 御厳禁
provisionally confined	*tasandome* 他参留
punishment (for misdeed)	*otogame* 御咎
punishment (for serious crime)	*oshioki* 御仕置
recognized kin	*imigakari no shinrui* 忌掛之親類
relatives of Kirishitan	*Kirishitan ruizoku* 切支丹類族
remanded to jail	*jurō, nyūrō* 入牢
remarkable arts	*kijutsu* 奇術
remarkable things	*kizui* 奇瑞
remiss	*futsutsuka* 不束
rental quarters, rented quarters	*shakuya* 借屋, 借家
represent (someone) before the magistrate	*daihan* 代判
representative (of daimyo)	*rusui(yaku)* 留守居(役)
reprimand	*shikari* 叱
retainer	*kerai* 家来, *samurai bōkō* 侍奉公, *kashi* 家士, *on'uchi* 御内
Rules for Deciding Judicial Matters	*Kujikata osadamegaki* 公事方御定書
sacred oath	*shinmon* 神文
sacred pledge	*shinganjō* 神願状
scribe	*yūhitsu* 祐筆
scriptures	*kyōmon* 経文
seclusion	*enryo* 遠慮
senior councillors	*rōjū* 老中
senior monk	*chōrō* 長老
senior staff official (of the magistracy)	*yoriki* 与力
Shinto diviner	*shinshoku* 神職
sign	*inmon* 印文
sorcery	*yōjutsu* 妖術, *yōdō* 妖道
spell	*jumon* 呪文

staff official (of the magistracy)	*dōshin* 同心
statement	*mōshiguchi* 申口
storyteller specializing in military tales	*gunsho kōshaku* 軍書講釈
strange	*fushigi* 不思議, *ayashi* 怪, *kii* 奇異, *kikai* 奇怪
strange arts	*ijutsu* 異術
strict reprimand	*kitto shikari* 急度叱
strict seclusion	*hissoku* 逼塞
subtemple	*tatchū* 塔中
summation	*kigami* 黄紙
supervision	*shihai* 支配
teaching of the Lord of Heaven	*Tenshukyō* 天主教
teahouse	*chaya* 茶屋
temple group	*kumidera* 組寺
temple of affiliation, temple where registered	*dannadera* 檀那寺, *bodaiji* 菩提寺, *tanomidera* 頼寺
Temples and Shrines Magistracy	*jisha bugyō* 寺社奉行
temporary lodging	*kashizashiki* 貸座敷
testament	*yuigon* 遺言
testimony	*kuchigaki* 口書
those responsible for matters of the locale	*tokoro no mono* 所之者
true deity	*honzon* 本尊
unregistered person	*mushuku* 無宿
unwavering mind	*fudōshin* 不動心
verdict	*kasho, togagaki* 科書
village headman	*shōya* 庄屋
water austerities	*yokusui* 浴水, *suiyoku* 水浴
wicked deeds	*karukarazaru gi* 不軽儀
Yijing divination	*Ekidō* 易道
Yijing diviner	*Eki uranai, Ekisen* 易占
yin-yang diviner	*onmyōji* 陰陽師

NOTES

The place of publication of all Japanese-language works cited in the notes is Tokyo unless otherwise indicated.

INTRODUCTION

1. In the Urakami case the authorities ultimately accepted the villagers' denial of being adherents of a "deviant creed." Resolution of the Amakusa case was achieved by the villagers' admitting that they had previously engaged in deviant practices and promising that they would no longer do so. See Ōhashi Yukihiro, *Kirishitan minshūshi no kenkyū* (Tōkyōdō Shuppan, 2001), 147–75, 206–39; Peter Nosco, "Secrecy and the Transmission of Tradition: Issues in the Study of the 'Underground' Christians," *Japanese Journal of Religious Studies* 20, no. 1 (1993): 21–24.
2. David L. Howell, "Foreign Encounters and Informal Diplomacy in Early Modern Japan," *Journal of Japanese Studies* 40, no. 2 (2014): 295–327; Bob Tadashi Wakabayashi, *Anti-Foreignism and Western Learning in Early-Modern Japan: The New Theses of 1825* (Cambridge, Mass.: Council on East Asian Studies, Harvard University, 1986); for the 1824 incident, see 86–90.
3. Fujita Yūkoku, "Kōshin teisho," in *Yūkoku zenshū*, ed. Kikuchi Kenjirō (Yoshida Yahei, 1935), 723; Howell, "Foreign Encounters," 314.

4. The biography was subsequently reprinted in different formats, including a 1977 paperback edition. See Kōda Shigetomo, *Ōshio Heihachirō* (Tōadō Shobō, 1910; repr., Chūōkōronsha, 1977), 30–48.

5. Miyagi Kimiko touches on this issue in summarizing the incident in her biography of Ōshio, *Ōshio Heihachirō* (Asahi Shinbunsha, 1977), 103–8.

6. Researchers today increasingly favor the term "underground Christian" (*senpuku Kirishitan*) over the earlier standard "hidden Christian" (*kakure Kirishitan*).

7. Worship of Inari, a popular deity associated with prosperity and good harvests, fused elements of Buddhist and folk origin. Inari mediums (*Inari sage* or *myōjin sage*) conducted divinations and healing rituals by entering into a trance in which they invited (*sage*) Inari to take possession of them.

8. Ebisawa Arimichi, *Ishin henkakuki to Kirisutokyō* (Shinseisha, 1968), 11–61. The abbreviation "Keihan" derives from alternative readings of the first character in "Kyoto" and the second in "Osaka." We use it as a convenient acronym.

9. The major representative of the former approach is Ōhashi Yukihiro, the contemporary researcher who has written most extensively on the incident; see *Senpuku Kirishitan: Edo jidai no kinkyō seisaku to minshū* (Kōdansha, 2014), 126–55; *Kinsei senpuku shūkyō ron: Kirishitan to kakushi nenbutsu* (Azekura Shobō, 2017), 91–132. Hayashi Makoto exemplifies the second approach; see "Kinsei kōki ni okeru Tsuchimikado-ke, onmyōji," *Ningen bunka* 24 (2009): 1–12; "Tenshūkyō to onna onmyōji," *Aichi Gakuin Daigaku Bungakubu kiyō* 41 (2011): 212–20; "The Female Christian Yin-Yang Master," trans. Elizabeth Tinsley, *Cahiers d'Extrême-Asie* 21 (2012): 223–39. In English Nakagawa Sugane and Helen Hardacre follow the latter approach in brief discussions of the incident. See Nakagawa Sugane, "Inari Worship in Early Modern Osaka," trans. Andrea C. Damon, in *Osaka: The Merchants' Capital of Early Modern Japan*, ed. James L. McClain and Wakita Osamu, 180–212 (Ithaca, N.Y.: Cornell University Press, 1999), and Helen Hardacre, *Shinto: A History* (New York: Oxford University Press, 2017), 275.

10. On the image of Kirishitan and the works that generated and perpetuated it, see George Elison, *Deus Destroyed: The Image of Christianity in Early Modern Japan* (Cambridge, Mass.: Harvard University Press, 1973), 213–21, 319–74; Jan C. Leuchtenberger, *Conquering Demons: The "Kirishitan," Japan, and the World in Early Modern Japanese Literature* (Ann Arbor: Center for Japanese Studies, University of Michigan, 2013). The term "Kirishitan," transcribed by varying combinations of characters used phonetically, comes from the Portuguese *cristão*. Applied originally to Catholic missionaries and their followers, it took on the further connotations mentioned here in conjunction with the proscription of Christianity in the early seventeenth century. Regarding the circulation of popular tales about Kirishitan and the Shimabara-Amakusa uprising, see Kikuchi Yōsuke, *Kinsei jitsuroku no kenkyū: Seichō to tenkai* (Kyūko Shoin, 2008), 119–49.

11. Mark Teeuwen and Kate Wildman Nakai, eds., *Lust, Commerce, and Corruption: An Account of What I Have Seen and Heard by an Edo Samurai* (New York: Columbia University Press, 2014), 399 (slightly modified).

12. See chapter 7, document 1.

13. The officials consistently used a different term, "the Jesus creed" (Yaso), to refer to Christian texts in Chinese. The officials saw Kirishitan (= "the pernicious sect") and "the Jesus creed" as connected, but they nonetheless systematically distinguished one from the other.

14. Researchers in Japan today commonly use the term "Kirishitan" to distinguish Japan's encounter with Catholicism in the sixteenth and seventeenth centuries from the forms of Christianity introduced beginning in the 1860s. They also frequently refer to the underground Christian communities that survived in Kyushu throughout the Edo period as Kirishitan. They identify post-1860s Christianity in Japan, together with Christianity in general, as Kirisutokyō. We follow this convention to some extent in speaking of the Keihan group as Kirishitan. This should not, however, be taken to imply any connection between it and the underground Kyushu communities.

15. The Kan'in princely house was one of four cadet branches of the imperial line. Emperor Kōkaku, who reigned from 1779 to 1817, ascended the throne from this house.

16. For examples of the mantra and sorcery, see Leuchtenberger, *Conquering Demons*, 16, 176, 194–96. For the term "Tentei," see Ebisawa Arimichi, ed., *Nanbanji kōhaiki, Jakyō taii, Myōtei mondō, Ha Deusu* (Heibonsha, 1964), 25–29; "Kirishitan shūmon raichō jikki," MS copy dated 1783, Bunko 07 00885, Waseda Daigaku Toshokan.

17. The type of divination performed by yin-yang diviners under the supervision of the Tsuchimikado (known in Japanese as *onmyōdō*, "the Way of yin and yang") was based on the *Yijing*. Securing a license from the Tsuchimikado house provided prestige and also protection from interference from government officials, who periodically cracked down on the welter of popular practitioners who engaged in some sort of divination and healing or incantatory rites.

18. The practice of ferreting out Christians by forcing suspects to tread on images of Christ or Mary was first introduced in the 1620s in Nagasaki. Initially the images were made of paper, but beginning in 1629 it became customary to use metal ones. Such *fumie* plates were kept under strict guard by the Nagasaki Magistracy. Domanial or shogunal officials elsewhere could apply to borrow them when the need arose, but treading on *fumie* as a general requirement was confined to Nagasaki and adjacent areas. In Nagasaki, all locals and visitors were expected to tread on *fumie* at the beginning of the year. Over time this requirement took on the character of an annual celebratory event specific to Nagasaki; see Yasutaka Hiroaki, *Fumie o funda Kirishitan* (Yoshikawa Kōbunkan, 2018).

19. Reflecting the difference in his situation, Kenzō's testimony appears toward the end of the dossier; see chapter 6. At the time of the incident, Kenzō had gone bankrupt as a consequence of speculating on the Osaka rice exchange, but he and his adoptive father before him were prominent enough as physicians to repeatedly receive a high ranking in popular listings of doctors in the Osaka area. See Nakano Misao, *Ōsaka ishi banzuke shūsei* (Kyoto: Shibunkaku, 1985), 155, plates 6, 9, 10; Nakano Misao, *Ōsaka meii den* (Kyoto: Shibunkaku, 1983), 86–89.

20. The officials' reports on their investigation of these three—Riemon, Kyūbei, and Shintarō—appear in chapter 5. A considerable part of the subsequent discussions among officials about the incident revolved around how to handle those connected to persons suspected but not confirmed to be Kirishitan— what we have termed quasi-Kirishitan.

21. Reports on the investigation of these associates appear in chapter 5. Reports on associates of Sano, Kinu, and Mitsugi whom the officials suspected might have become Kirishitan devotees appear as addenda to the testimonies of the three women.

22. Sone Hiromi, "Josei to keibatsu," in *Mibun no naka no josei*, ed. Yabuta Yutaka and Yanagiya Keiko, vol. 4 of *Edo no hito to mibun* (Yoshikawa Kōbunkan, 2010), 68, 94.

23. Gunki had both a wife and a concubine and a son by the latter. The son's testimony appears in chapter 5.

24. Seki Tamiko, " 'Jashūmon ikken' ni miru danjo no shosō," in *Esunishitī, jendā kara miru Nihon no rekishi*, ed. Kuroda Hiroko and Nagano Hiroko (Yoshikawa Kōbunkan, 2002), 210–12.

25. Ebisawa, *Ishin henkakuki to Kirisutokyō*, 35, sees an echo of the sacrament of baptism in the group's emphasis on water austerities, but his argument fails to convince. For a critique of Ebisawa's view, see Yamane Chiyomi, "Kirishitan kinsei-shi ni okeru Keihan Kirishitan ikken no igi," *Ōshio kenkyū* 19 (1985): 20–43.

26. Kōda, *Ōshio Heihachirō*, 17–18. In Ōshio's case, his father died young, and he succeeded his grandfather. On the organization of the Osaka Magistracy and Ōshio's activities as senior staff official, see Yabuta Yutaka, *Bushi no machi: "Tenka no daidokoro" no samurai tachi* (Chūōkōronsha, 2010), 53–100, 145–71; Yabuta Yutaka, "Shinmi Masamichi to Ōshio Heihachirō: 'Shinmi Masamichi nikki' ni yoru kōsatsu," in *Ōshio Heihachirō no sōgō kenkyū*, ed. Ōshio Jiken Kenkyūkai, 1–17 (Osaka: Izumi Shoin, 2011); Yabuta Yutaka, "Ōsaka machi bugyō to 'Keihan Kirishitan jiken' " (forthcoming).

27. Ōshio shared responsibility for the Keihan Kirishitan investigation with another senior staff official, Seta Tōshirō (d. ca. 1837).

28. Kōda, *Ōshio Heihachirō*, 188.

29. Kan'o Mototaka served as Kyoto eastern magistrate from 1825.6.17 to 1828.11.22.

30. The complications involved in negotiating arrangements to investigate someone with court connections can be seen in the description of the arrangements the Osaka officials made to interrogate Takeuchi Ōmi, the retainer

of the Tsuchimikado house who had been responsible for overseeing Mitsugi's activities as a yin-yang diviner. See chapter 6.

31. The Osaka governor, a post usually held by a daimyo of significant standing, was responsible for the defense of Osaka and supervision of the entire western half of the country. A parallel high shogunal official in Kyoto, the Kyoto governor (*Kyōto shoshidai*), was charged with guarding that city and also represented the shogunate in relations with the court. The two governors ranked immediately below the senior councillors (*rōjū*) in Edo, and the posts were often stepping-stones to a subsequent appointment as senior councillor.

32. An advisory body, the Deliberative Council represented the main repository of judicial expertise in the shogunal administration. For further information about its organization, see part 2, pp. 142–44. Regarding the distinction between the competence to investigate and competence to sentence and the features of the shogunal system of criminal justice summarized here, see Hiramatsu Yoshirō, *Kinsei keiji soshōhō no kenkyū* (Sōbunsha, 1960), 458–60, 494–95, 499–507, 518–22. For the situation in Osaka and Kyoto, see Ogura Takashi, *Edo bakufu kamigata shihai kikō no kenkyū* (Hanawa Shobō, 2011), 63–117, and Yabuta, "Ōsaka machi bugyō." For an overview of the mechanisms of criminal jurisprudence, see Daniel V. Botsman, *Punishment and Power in the Making of Modern Japan* (Princeton, N.J.: Princeton University Press, 2005), chapter 1.

33. Torture usually consisted of beating with a stick or forcing those accused to sit with their legs folded under them while successively heavier weights were placed on their thighs. In principle it was to be carried out according to a specified protocol, including the presence of officials other than those involved in the direct interrogation; see Hiramatsu, *Kinsei keiji soshōhō*, 785–818; Botsman, *Punishment and Power*, 35–37. Hiramatsu points out that the Osaka Magistracy normally did not use torture in interrogating women (801).

34. As noted, many other parties to the incident died before the sentences were handed down, but apart from Sano's son and the two associates mentioned here, they all died after their testimonies had been confirmed, not before. One indication of the importance of confirmed testimony in Tokugawa criminal jurisprudence is that although unconfirmed testimony was not admissible, sentences could be handed down on the basis of testimony that had been confirmed even if the person in question was no longer alive; see Hiramatsu, *Kinsei keiji soshōhō*, 886–87. This is what happened with the parties to the incident who died in the period between the confirmation of their testimony and the handing down of the sentences at the end of 1829.

TRANSLATION STRATEGIES

1. Publication of the collated transcription of the dossier is forthcoming. The documents translated in chapter 10 are not part of this dossier; for details, see

part 2, pp. 152–54. For information about the records of rumors concerning the incident that are translated in part 3, see pp. 231–37.

2. The list of protagonists that follows this section includes the most important of these alternative names.

1. SANO AND HER ASSOCIATES

1. Kawasaki, where Sano lived, was located on the outskirts of the city of Osaka proper. Technically it was classified as "rural," and it thus came under the administrative jurisdiction of an intendant rather than the Osaka Magistracy. The Osaka Magistracy had wide-ranging judicial authority over the region surrounding the city, however, and the intendant does not seem to have played any role in the ensuing investigation.

2. In the Edo period, the Buddhist Pure Land branch known today as the Jōdo Shin (True Pure Land) sect was commonly referred to as the Ikkō (Single-Minded) sect, and we have followed this custom in the translation.

3. There was a Honpukuji in Kyoto, but it was not situated on Imadegawa street; this may be a copying error for Honmanji, which is located there.

4. As mentioned under "Translation Strategies," we have used italics in parentheses to indicate brief interpolations written in red ink by the investigating officials.

5. This section of Kyoto was widely known as a slum area. Many of its inhabitants were too poor to rent anything more than temporary lodgings. See Sugimori Tetsuya, *Kinsei Kyōto no toshi to shakai* (Tōkyō Daigaku Shuppankai, 2008), 344–52. Sano and her husband, however, evidently lived in regular rental quarters.

6. This area was adjacent to that in front of the Kyoto Daibutsu where Sano had lived with her husband.

7. Tenma was the name of one of the three administrative districts of Osaka, but in place-names such as this it indicated not the district as a whole but a subsection of it, the general area around the Tenmangū Shrine (also known as the Tenma Tenjin Shrine; item 26 on the Osaka map), whose origins long antedated the rise of the early modern city of Osaka.

8. If these effigies (*hitogata*) were similar to those used standardly in purification rituals, they probably were simple paper cutouts.

9. The Fushimi Inari mountain, located to the southeast of Kyoto, was and is dotted with shrines and altars dedicated to the different manifestations of the Inari deity. It has continued to the present to be a major center of Inari worship.

10. Nyakuōji, located in the Higashiyama hills on the eastern outskirts of Kyoto, was the tutelary shrine of a temple associated with mountain asceticism. As with many such sites in the area, Nyakuōji had several "falls" (in actuality

springs channeled through a spout to fall freely), which a variety of religious practitioners used for water austerities.

11. Dōjima was the name given to the stretch of blocks along the Yodo River west of the Tenma area; it encompassed the area on the Osaka map where items 1, 3, 14, and 15 were located.

12. Mediums often enshrined the deity they worshipped by wrapping material around a piece of wood to look like clothing and give the object a doll-like appearance. Presumably this is what Sano did.

13. Sano described the candle as a "500-*monme* candle"; in other words, one weighing about four pounds, much larger than the candles in everyday use.

14. Kinu and the others referred to the deity as *Tentei nyorai*, or Tentei (Lord of Heaven) Buddha. The terminology suggests that they understood the deity as a supernatural being akin to a buddha and explains expressions such as "the buddha's punishment."

15. As mentioned in the introduction, the mantra *Zensu Maru paraizo*, or a variant of it, was a common feature of descriptions of Kirishitan in chapbooks and popular literature. The elements derived from the Portuguese equivalents of "Jesus, Mary, paradise."

16. We have not been able to identify the specific purification prayer; Sano refers to it as the *misogi rikugō no harae*.

17. The preceding paragraph and the first three sentences of the following paragraph, with their account of Sano's wish to travel to Nagasaki, would eventually be ordered deleted from the transcript of Sano's testimony (see part 2, documents 7, 12, and 13). What we refer to as the Kōda-bon MS, which was prepared after the deletion, thus does not include them. For the translation of these later deleted passages we rely on what we term the Yoshino-bon MS, which preserves the transcript's original form. A third MS, the Seishin-bon MS, has a slightly abbreviated version. For the characteristics and provenance of these MSS, see appendix 3.

18. Shinsuke was born in 1803; in 1820, when Sano traveled to Nagasaki, he would thus have been seventeen.

19. This sentence, the following two paragraphs, and the first sentence of the paragraph thereafter, all of which concern Sano's trip to Nagasaki, were excised in the Kōda-bon MS. The Seishin-bon MS contains them in a somewhat truncated form.

20. The shogunate officially recognized the guild of commercial rental-house guarantors for Osaka (*sangō ie ukenin*) in 1732. Members of the guild acted as guarantors for people who did not have personal access to an appropriate guarantor for renting rooms or property, charging a fee in return.

21. This is the first of the extended addenda written in red. As here, we have used subheadings to indicate these longer addenda.

22. The Kōda-bon MS omits the preceding four sentences.

23. The Kōda-bon MS omits the preceding reference to Sano's trip to Hizen.

24. According to the exchange rate between gold and silver current at the time, this would come to approximately 2,200 *monme* in silver, a little over the 2,000 *monme* Sano had proposed.

25. The contributors recruited by Yae, Toki, and Kanzō lived almost entirely in the blocks around Shinchi Ura-machi in the Dōjima area, where Toki and Kanzō resided; in the adjacent Tenma area; in Kawasaki village, where Yae and Sano resided; or in other nearby villages on the northern outskirts of Osaka. A number of women evidently contributed on their own, but because women in Osaka could not be listed as householders in their own name, they are identified by their relationship with the male household head.

26. In an effort to reduce the possibility that people would use pawnshops to unload stolen or otherwise irregularly obtained goods, the shogunate issued repeated edicts warning pawnbrokers to be sure the pawner had a joint endorser. It also directed pawnbrokers to be on guard about people pawning goods in a quantity or quality at odds with their means or status. See *Ofure-gaki Kanpō shūsei*, ed. Takayanagi Shinzō and Ishii Ryōsuke (Iwanami Sho-ten, 1934), 1002, 1012–13, 1015–16, 1021–22; *Ofuregaki Tenmei shūsei*, ed. Takayanagi Shinzō and Ishii Ryōsuke (Iwanami Shoten, 1936), 871. Shinsuke may have divided up the items between pawnshops so as to avoid arousing suspicion because of the large number of items.

27. This would have been equivalent to 1,136 *ryō* in gold according to the exchange rate of the time. It has been estimated that the yearly income of a carpenter in this period might have been 1,587 *monme* in silver (26 *ryō* in gold), and that of a midlevel warrior 9,000 *monme* in silver (150 *ryō* in gold); see Takeuchi Makoto and Ishikawa Hiroaki, *Hitome de wakaru Edo jidai: Chizu, zukai, gurafu de miru* (Shōgakukan, 2004), 15. Sano thus succeeded in collecting a substantial total sum, although judging from what we learn about the instance of her landlord, Yohei, she gave a considerable amount of this back to her clients as "interest."

28. Sano appears to have given Yohei back about 80 percent of what he had donated. Yohei was an early investor and donated more than the others. Assuming that Sano followed the practices common in pyramid schemes, she may well have given him a better rate of return than she gave to the others.

29. The deity of the Fushimi Inari complex was known as the deity of the three peaks, and different manifestations of it were worshipped at three main shrines. The manifestation of the third "peak," Ōichihime, was a female deity, which may account for the decision to associate Sano with it. In fact, these shrines are not located on three different summits but rather on three different levels along the pilgrims' route to the top of this 764-foot mountain.

30. The Inari deity was associated with foxes and snakes, but animals in general were regarded as potential sources of pollution at many shrines. Inari mediums had a particular animosity against dogs because dogs were seen as enemies of foxes.

31. As mentioned in the introduction, the investigators state repeatedly that they interrogated the accused "severely," but this is the only explicit reference to torture.

32. The Kōda-bon MS omits the preceding sentence.

33. The Kōda-bon MS omits the preceding two sentences. Instead it substitutes a different one: "I swear that there are no other members of this sect apart from those presently being interrogated."

34. The term "filled with remorse" (*ayamari iri sōrō*), which appears at the end of the confirmed testimonies of many of the main figures, was a coded set phrase that in the eyes of the investigators indicated that the testifier acknowledged committing a serious crime that warranted severe punishment. The parallel phrase "repent deeply" (*osore iri sōrō*) generally indicated acknowledgment of lesser wrongdoings. See Hiramatsu Yoshirō, *Kinsei keiji soshōhō no kenkyū* (Sōbunsha, 1960), 764–66.

35. Stomach massage was supposed to improve digestion, blood circulation, and elimination.

36. This is our tentative interpretation of an otherwise cryptic phrase. Suitengū shrines were believed to be efficacious for ensuring safe childbirth, and they often used dog symbols, since dogs were seen as being blessed with easy deliveries. As previously noted, Inari mediums had strong taboos against things associated with dogs.

2. KINU AND HER ASSOCIATES

1. The Kōda-bon MS omits the phrase "the Lord of Heaven has no shape or form."

2. Kinu and the others seem to have thought of the Lord of Heaven as something comparable to the supernatural beings they knew as buddhas. Kinu thus speaks here of *butsubachi* (buddha's punishment or karmic punishment). Similarly she and others often refer to the drawing of the Lord of Heaven as a "buddha image" (*butsuzō, butsuga*).

3. This sentence and the following phrase about Sano's return to Osaka are found in both the Kōda-bon and Yoshino-bon MSS. Their retention in the former was perhaps inadvertent, as all references to Sano's trip to Nagasaki have otherwise been carefully removed from its record of the incident.

4. Mashita Michiko, "Kinsei Ōsaka no onna namae: Hō kisei to jittai," *Josei shigaku* 10 (2000): 1–15, suggests that officials in Osaka were more restrictive in this regard than their counterparts in Kyoto and Edo because they were afraid that well-to-do townsmen would try to disguise their wealth by putting some of their property in the names of their female relatives. Officials also feared that houses rented by women of low status might be used as illegal brothels.

5. Kinu probably changed her name from Kikue for the purposes of registration because Kinu sounded more appropriate as the name of a commoner woman

than Kikue, the name she had adopted as an Inari medium. It thus better befitted her claimed status as the grandmother of a low-ranking townsman.

6. The preceding four sentences appear only in the Yoshino-bon MS. They were removed in the Kōda-bon version presumably because of their connection to Sano's trip to Nagasaki.

7. The Kōda-bon MS omits this phrase.

8. People purchased charcoal bundled in straw bales to use for heating and cooking. They typically kept these in a storehouse or in an earthen-floored part of the house such as the kitchen.

9. In other words, unlike Sano, Toki, and Kinu, who were remanded to jail for intensive interrogation, Tōzō was put under the charge of the commoner officials of his block and summoned together with them and his landlord to the magistracy for interrogation. Instead of appearing before the magistrate himself, the landlord relied on someone else, probably a professional lawyerlike agent, to represent him.

10. *Tengu* were demonic creatures believed to live in the hills or mountains. In the early modern period they were often depicted either as beings resembling mountain ascetics with a red face and long nose or as hobgoblin-like figures with a bird's beak, human limbs, sharp claws, and feathered wings. Their nature was ambiguous: at times they caused harm, but they could also act as protectors.

11. Kan'o Mototaka served as Kyoto eastern magistrate from 1825.6.17 to 1829.5.3.

3. MITSUGI, MIZUNO GUNKI, AND WASA

1. This note about Mitsugi's earlier arrest for a different case was presumably attached to the file on a separate piece of paper. The earlier case had been forwarded to Edo and considered by the Deliberative Council, and a record of it is preserved in *Oshioki reiruishū*, ed. Ishii Ryōsuke, 16 vols. (Meicho Shuppan, 1971–1973), 10:55–56. For a translation of this record, see appendix 1.

2. A teahouse (*chaya*) was not only a place where tea and refreshments were served; customers could also order female company. In more upscale establishments, teahouses summoned such women from nearby brothels (*okiya*) that kept the women under contract. The women lived in the brothel but received customers at teahouses rather than at the brothel. Teahouses of a lower standard had their own women under contract. Those in Nijō Shinchi were of the latter kind. See *Kyōto-fuka yūkaku yuisho*, in vol. 9 of *Shinsen Kyōto sōsho* (Kyoto: Rinsen Shoten, 1986), 112–24.

3. Mitsugi uses a slightly different term for the purification prayer (*jingi rikugō misogi*), but we have taken it to be the same formula described by Sano as *misogi rikugō no harae*. See chapter 1, note 16.

4. Miyagawa-chō, located east of the Kamo River off Shijō street, was another teahouse district. Katsura was likely one of the women who worked there.

5. The payment to Gunki came to about half the thirty *ryō* in gold that Mitsugi said she had when she moved in with Wasa.

6. Otafuku (Good Fortune; also known as Okame) is the name of a woman depicted comically as having a round face, a small nose, exaggerated red cheeks, and a large forehead. Masks of Otafuku were often used in *kagura* shrine dances and *kyōgen* humorous plays. She was also often identified with Ame no Uzume, the maiden who in the ancient myths helped to restore light to the world by dancing in front of the cave in which the sun goddess Amaterasu had hidden. For Gunki one reason for using Uzume as the stand-in for the Lord of Heaven was that Uzu- in Uzume hints at -usu in Deusu, one Japanese rendering of the name of the Christian God. Shōki (Ch. Zhong Kui) is a Chinese general who was commonly depicted on roof tiles or slips of paper as a guardian of the house against demons. Kikudōji (Chrysanthemum Child; also known as Kikujidō, or Chrysanthemum Child of Mercy) refers to a boy in the service of King Mu of Zhou (Jp. Bokuō) who was sent into exile and became an immortal by drinking only the dew that gathered on chrysanthemum flowers. The character of Kikudōji was well known from noh and kabuki.

7. Toyotomi Hideyoshi (1537–1598) had risen from lowly origins to great power and wealth as the unifier of the country, and upon his death the court granted his deified spirit the title Hōkoku Daimyōjin. After the Tokugawa destroyed the Toyotomi house in 1615, the shogunate asked the court to retract this title, and it continued until the end of the Edo period to prohibit the reconstruction of the Hōkoku Daimyōjin Shrine (also known by the alternative reading Toyokuni Daimyōjin Shrine). People thus came to associate the deity title Hōkoku (which means "prosperous land") with prosperity in general rather than Hideyoshi in particular. It was only in 1868 that Hideyoshi's status as a deity regained official recognition from the new Meiji government. See Miki Seiichirō, "Toyokuni-sha no zōei ni kansuru ichi kōsatsu," *Nagoya Daigaku Bungakubu kenkyū ronshū shigaku* 33 (1987): 196–209.

8. Inari was regarded as having multiple manifestations. Many Inari mediums took one of these as their personal guardian deity, obtaining its specific name through an oracle from the deity. See Anne Marie Bouchy [Busshī Annu Mari], "Inari shinkō to fugeki," in *Inari shinkō no kenkyū*, ed. Gorai Shigeru (Okayama: San'yō Shinbunsha, 1980), 207–9.

9. The Seishin-bon manuscript, which does not include the addenda, instead has a note that does not appear in the two main manuscripts: "Personal comment: According to Mitsugi, Gunki told her that there is no sacred icon [for the Lord of Heaven], and that the one he had was devised in the lands of the southern barbarians. The meaning behind the drawing of a woman with her hair hanging loose, a child, and a sword should be further investigated."

10. An indentured adoptive daughter (*futsū yōjo*) was one whose true parents entered into a contract with the adoptive parent in which they agreed to renounce any say over what was done with their daughter henceforth. Such

an arrangement was often an intermediate step toward other forms of inden-
ture, including the adoptive parent's sale of the girl into prostitution.

11. In fact Kyōgoku-chō was located north of Gojō Bridge.

12. In the Edo period, Gionsha consisted of a shrine and multiple temple halls.
Many of the Buddhist structures were torn down in the early Meiji period,
when Gionsha was refashioned as a Shinto shrine and named Yasaka Jinja.
Two famous teahouses were located in front of the main gate, on both sides
of the road. Nakamura-rō, now a fashionable traditional restaurant, was originally one of these teahouses.

13. See chapter 5, note 7, for the possible background to Gunki's irregular financial dealings.

14. Mitsugi gives only a vague description of Shintarō's address here; subsequently
he is identified as living south rather than north of Matsubara street.

15. The Yamanoi were a minor court noble house of middle rank. Konpira, located
on Shikoku in modern Kagawa prefecture, was an important shrine-temple
complex that attracted pilgrims from all over the country.

16. Mitsugi presumably thought this name was more suitable for a retainer associated with a noble house.

17. Takinomiya is located in present-day Ayagawa-chō, Kagawa prefecture, a little east of Konpira.

18. In a mutual credit group (tanomoshikō), the members agreed to pay regular
installments, in return for which they gained the right to receive in turn
(or by drawing lots) the amount accumulated up to that point. Shogunal
authorities regarded such arrangements as a private matter among the parties concerned and typically refused to adjudicate any disputes that might
arise.

19. The Inari deity was believed to use fox or snake spirits to run errands for it.
Many Inari mediums today assume their personal guardian deity to be a fox
or snake deity. See Bouchy, "Inari shinkō to fugeki," 210–21.

20. There appears to be some confusion in the date of this meeting. Mitsugi
undertook her pilgrimage to Konpira in 1821, and according to the other testimonies that follow, Gunki returned from Nagasaki in 1822.

21. The Washinoo were a middle-ranking house of court nobility.

22. The location of Gunki's temporary lodgings on Kiyamachi street is given var-
iously in different testimonies as "north" or "south" of Matsubara street.

4. GUNKI'S MALE DISCIPLES UMON AND HEIZŌ

1. The temple of Kannonji in Ōyamazaki, between Kyoto and Osaka, was famous
for its icon of Kangiten and the cult associated with it. Kangiten is a Buddhist
divinity whose antecedents lie in the Hindu deity Gaṇeśa. It combines both
destructive and protective characteristics and is associated with rites to ensure
prosperity and guard against disaster.

2. In the late Edo period the Sanbongi area located on the western side of the Kamo River was known as an unofficial pleasure district.

3. Sacred oaths (*shinmon*) were often written on special paper printed with the insignia of a deity and included the name of the deity who could be expected to inflict punishment if the oath were not kept. In this case no deity is explicitly named.

4. In *The True Principles of the Lord of Heaven* (*Tianzhu shiyi*, Jp. *Tenshu jitsugi*) Matteo Ricci (1552–1610) explained the basic principles of Christian doctrine through the medium of a fictitious dialogue between a Chinese scholar and a Christian theologian. The work, which includes a critique of Buddhist ideas but argues for the compatibility of Christianity and Confucianism, was published in Beijing in 1603. *Ten Pieces Transcending Common Sense* (*Jiren*, Jp. *Kijin*, or, more correctly, *Jiren shipian*, Jp. *Kijin jippen*) was another explanation of Christian doctrine by Ricci published in Beijing in 1608. These works circulated in Japan in both printed and copied forms; they were proscribed by the shogunate in 1630 because they dealt with Christianity.

5. The Hiraoka Shrine was an important shrine with a long history. Mizuhaya Hida (also known as Mizuhaya Heikō [1753–1815]; the surname is sometimes transcribed as Mizuhashiri) studied medicine in Osaka and wrote a number of medical works. He was also active as a poet.

6. *Comprehensive Compendium of Healing* (*Shengji zonglu*, Jp. *Seisai sōroku*) is a large and rare early twelfth-century Chinese medical lexicon.

7. The manuscripts vary as to whether this woman's name was Fusa or Fuki; we have opted to refer to her consistently as Fusa.

8. The Ue-machi area extended along the western side of Osaka Castle; it encompassed the area between the blocks south of items 12 and 13 on the Osaka map to item 22 in the north.

9. Monks of the Zen sect who had completed an initial stage of training then spent a period as itinerant monks (*unsui*) in which they traveled in quest of a further master and a higher stage of enlightenment.

10. In the modern city of Kobe.

11. Books about famous battles and military heroes, such as *Records of the Pacification of the Realm* (*Taiheiki*), a tale of the wars of the fourteenth century, and *Romance of the Three Kingdoms* (*Sangokushi engi*), which recounted the exploits of the generals of the Three Kingdoms period in China, were a major source for tales related by storytellers in small theaters that drew a popular audience.

12. As noted in the introduction, Kirishitan elements figured prominently in the Shimabara-Amakusa uprising of 1637–1638, and its suppression required a major effort by the recently established Tokugawa shogunate. The uprising spurred the implementation of further anti-Christian measures and continued to loom large in both the popular and official imaginaries of the dangers posed by Christianity.

13. In this way it was possible for Soe and Makijirō to avoid having to register as a separate household.

14. As mentioned earlier, a coded wordplay lay behind Gunki's use of images of Otafuku/Ame no Uzume as a stand-in for the Lord of Heaven (see chapter 3, note 6). The characters for Uzu 宇須 in Uzume could also be used for the phonetic transcription of -usu in Deusu (Deus). The same was true of the character for Usu 臼 in Recluse of Mount Usu (Usuyama Sanjin), which Gunki says he has adopted as his own name.

15. From their names, Kimoto Kazuma and his daughter appear to be of warrior background. Kazuma may have been the retainer of a Kyoto court family, as Gunki had been. Perhaps for this reason the Osaka officials evidently did not try to summon them for questioning, unlike adoptive relatives of the other principals and a number of Gunki's other associates. For one further reference to Hisae, see chapter 10, document 19.

5. GUNKI'S ASSOCIATES AND SON

1. The Kōda-bon MS gives the date as "intercalary sixth month," but we follow here the Yoshino-bon MS. Its dating of Shōni's remanding to jail to 1827.6.21 is more plausible in terms of the overall sequence of arrests.

2. North of Gionsha was an open area that offered various entertainments, including horses that could be rented for pleasure riding, archery and food stalls, and sumo bouts. See Demura Yoshifumi and Kawasaki Masashi, "Kinsei no Gionsha no keikan to sono shūi to no rensetsu ni kansuru kenkyū," *Doboku keikakugaku kenkyū ronbunshū* 21 (2004): 393–98.

3. Although Takada Shibazaki (Shōni's native village) and Nagasu were located in adjacent provinces, they were only a few miles away from each other. Both were under the jurisdiction of Shimabara domain but were not contiguous with its main holdings, which were situated in Hizen province on the other side of Kyushu.

4. The Nijō house was one of the five houses of nobility from which the imperial regent was selected. It thus stood at the apex of court society.

5. Although Gunki had a "live-in" (*sumikomi*) position at the Kan'in princely house, from repeated references in the testimonies, it appears that during these years he actually lived primarily in the rental quarters owned by Riemon. Retainers of Kyoto noble houses received only meager stipends (scribes employed by the Nijō house in the late Edo period, for instance, received annual stipends of ca. eight *ryō* in gold). Retainers of this sort often lived in the town and concurrently pursued other occupations, such as a teacher of one of the arts, as an additional source of income. See Nakamura Yoshifumi, "Sekke no keishi tachi," in *Chōtei o torimaku hitobito*, ed. Takano Toshihiko, vol. 8 of *Mibunteki shūen to kinsei shakai*, 73–105 (Yoshikawa Kōbunkan, 2007). Since Gunki took in calligraphy students, he would have needed some sort of quarters in the town as a place to offer lessons.

6. Such temporary lodgings (*kashi zashiki*) seem to have been a more casual arrangement than rental quarters (*shakuya* or *shakutaku*).

7. Since loans by noble houses received special consideration in shogunal courts, others often tried to protect their own financial dealings by funneling them nominally through such houses. Gunki's irregular machinations may well have been linked to arrangements of this sort.

8. Noh songs (*koutai*) were excerpts from noh plays typically performed by amateurs as table entertainment or for festive occasions.

9. Shōni testified that he made *shibugami* out of the recycled paper. *Shibugami* is made by coating layers of Japanese mulberry-fiber paper with persimmon tannin for reinforcement and waterproofing.

10. The investigators presumably asked Shōni whether the materials he recycled for the mat included copies of Chinese books, and he responded in this way to indicate that they did not appear to be written in Chinese.

11. *Refutations of the Pernicious Sect* (*Hekijashū*, Ch. *Pixieji*) is a collection of late Ming anti-Christian writings compiled by Ouyi Zhixu (1599–1655). Although its purpose was to refute Christian ideas, the fact that it discussed them in the process led to its incorporation in post-1685 lists of proscribed works, including the list of thirty-eight such works that the Osaka Magistracy distributed to the bookdealers of the city in 1698. See Itō Tasaburō, "Kinsho no kenkyū," part 1, *Rekishi chiri* 68, no. 4 (1936): 341. For the investigators, the 1698 list was a key point of reference. See appendix 2.

12. She did piecework tying knots in the fabric prior to its being dyed in a dappled pattern.

13. Located on the Uji River south of Kyoto, Fushimi offered easy access to Osaka by river transport. Gunki presumably intended to hide out in Osaka or points beyond.

14. Both the Yoshino-bon and Kōda-bon MSS give the name Toki here, but it seems likely that this is a mistake for Moto, and we have translated the passage accordingly.

15. There may be some confusion about the date when Shintarō was sent to Edo, as even at the end of Meiwa (1764–1771) he would have been only four or five.

16. This Wasa should not be confused with Mitsugi's and Gunki's friend of the same name; the two women had no connection with each other.

17. Yatarō is referred to as Shintarō in what follows, but to avoid confusion we use the name Yatarō throughout.

18. If the Jirobei mentioned here were Wasa's father, as in the earlier part of Yatarō's testimony, Wasa would be Yazobei's niece. The Jirobei described here as Yazobei's elder brother presumably was instead the third-generation successor to Wasa's father. Typically the younger Jirobei would have inherited both the business and the name.

19. Izutsuya was a famous teahouse that featured prominently in illustrated guides to Kyoto, such as *Karaku meishō zue* of 1864.

20. The daimyo Katō Akikuni (1808–1856) was lord of Minakuchi domain from 1815 until 1845.

21. The text gives a date equivalent to 1825, but Gunki died in the twelfth month of 1824.

22. A six-mat room in the Kyoto–Osaka area would be approximately 12.5 by 9.5 feet, hardly large enough to freely manipulate a twelve-foot spear.

23. "Distant exile" (*jūtsuihō*) was a severe form of banishment, though less stringent than "exile to a remote island" (*entō* or *ontō*).

6. KENZŌ AND OTHERS IMPLICATED IN THE INVESTIGATION

1. Both the Yoshino-bon and Kōda-bon MSS give the name of Kenzō's adoptive father as Kōan 幸庵. *Ukiyo no arisama* (*The State of the Floating World*), translated in chapter 11, gives it as Kyōan 杏庵, as do a series of popular listings of physicians in Osaka. The judicial records translated in chapter 10 use other characters that also are read Kyōan 恭庵. We have thus unified throughout as Kyōan.

2. See the testimony of Fujii Umon, chapter 4, p. 85.

3. Dōjima was the nation's largest rice market and was known for its extensive trade (and speculation) in rice futures.

4. Lists from 1811–1812 and 1820 ranking notable doctors in the Osaka region (in the format used for ranking sumo wrestlers for a tournament) include Kenzō in a prominent position; see Nakano Misao, *Ōsaka ishi banzuke shūsei* (Kyoto: Shibunkaku, 1985). Rumors in the incident's wake have him serving as a block alderman in the Dōjima area and also relate details about his losses from speculation in rice bills. See chapter 11, pp. 256–57.

5. When people absconded, their names were put on the list of absconders kept by the magistracy, and their relatives and those responsible for the affairs of the locale where they resided were charged with searching for them.

6. "House arrest" (*chikkyo*) was a punishment levied on those of warrior status; the person subject to it was expected to remain confined within one room of his residence.

7. The title Kenzō gave his booklet, *Nensairoku kō*, refers to an episode in the Chinese *History of the Jin Dynasty* (*Jinshu*, Jp. *Shinjo* [648]), where two wise men search for strange sea creatures by using a burning rhinoceros horn for light. Rhinoceros horn was believed to have the unique property of burning underwater.

8. Regarding the works confiscated, see appendix 2.

9. The Ikkō sect, or Jōdo Shinshū (True Pure Land) sect as it is known today, was divided into several branches, including two Honganji lineages referred to as Honganji and Higashi (East) Honganji. The names derived from those of their head temples in Kyoto. To distinguish the two, Honganji

is often identified as Nishi (West) Honganji, and we have followed that practice here.

10. Both the Nishi and Higashi Honganji lineages of the Ikkō sect developed sites of worship in the Ōtani area in the eastern hills of Kyoto linked to what were purported to be graves of the founder, Shinran (1173–1262). To express their faith, believers often sought to have a fragment of their remains placed in the ossuary maintained by the lineage with which they were affiliated. In this instance, Shōni and the others presumably hesitated to follow to the letter Gunki's directions to abandon his bodily remains and instead had the throat bone put in the ossuary as a token burial. What Shōni and the investigators referred to as the "throat bone" (nodo no hone) was presumably what today is popularly known as nodobotoke. Nodobotoke (throat buddha) is also the Japanese term for the English "Adam's apple," but the bone in question, which continues to be singled out today in Japanese crematory and burial practices, is in fact one of the neck vertebrae, the second Vertebra cervicalis.

11. The supervisors of court personnel (kinrizuki) were shogunal officials under the Kyoto governor. They were responsible for keeping watch over a variety of matters affecting the court, including the behavior of the court nobility. As they were supposed to consult the court liaison officers (buke tensō), who represented the court, and report to the Kyoto governor, they functioned as an interface in the delicate balance between shogunal authority and court autonomy. For the other people from Kyoto caught up in the case, the Osaka Eastern Magistracy went through the Kyoto Magistracy, responsible for matters concerning town administration and commoners, but Takeuchi Ōmi and the Tsuchimikado house came under the jurisdiction of the court rather than the magistracy. As can be seen from the account here, this circumstance added further complications to the process of summoning and questioning Ōmi.

12. In insisting that they sanctioned only divination based on the Yijing, the Tsuchimikado retainers presumably sought to reduce their implication in Mitsugi's crime. In fact the Tsuchimikado house did not require the yin-yang diviners under its supervision to conduct divination solely on the basis of the Yijing. So long as the recipients promised to revere "the Way of yin and yang" and paid the Tsuchimikado house a fee, it issued licenses to a wide variety of religious figures engaged in divination. See Hayashi Makoto, Kinsei onmyōdō no kenkyū (Yoshikawa Kōbunkan, 2005), 85; Hayashi Makoto, "The Female Christian Yin-Yang Master," trans. Elizabeth Tinsley, Cahiers d'Extrême-Asie 21 (2012): 225–27.

13. This report is not to be found among the extant documents concerning this case.

14. The investigators do not indicate where they obtained the fumie. Possibly they borrowed it from the Nagasaki magistrate, as daimyo in the Kyushu area did when necessary.

PART II. THE JUDICIAL REVIEW PROCESS

1. Yabuta Yutaka, "Ōsaka machi bugyō to 'Keihan Kirishitan jiken'" (forthcoming).
2. The Deliberative Council's recommendations were generally submitted as the unanimous view of the council members (*hyōjōsho ichiza*), but on occasion the main members failed to agree and submitted multiple opinions.
3. For an English translation of the Rules for Deciding Judicial Matters, see John Carey Hall, "Japanese Feudal Law: The Tokugawa Legislation (Part IV: The Edict in One Hundred Sections)," *Transactions of the Asiatic Society of Japan* 41, no. 5 (1913): 683–804.
4. Hiramatsu Yoshirō, *Kinsei keiji soshōhō no kenkyū* (Sōbunsha, 1960), 547–52; Ogura Takashi, *Edo bakufu kamigata shihai kikō no kenkyū* (Hanawa Shobō, 2011), 108–9.
5. See *Tokugawa kinreikō*, ed. Ishii Ryōsuke, 11 vols. (Sōbunsha, 1959–1961), *bekkan*: 93–94. For the complicated history of the lengthy conflict between state authorities and Fuju Fuse leaders and between those leaders and their opponents within the Nichiren sect, see Jacqueline Stone, "When the Lotus Went Underground: The Nichiren *Fuju fuse* Movement and the Kanbun-era Persecution" (forthcoming). Fuju Fuse was proscribed definitively in 1665–1666. Sanchō-ha, a separate movement that emerged in the 1680s, was the target of concerted repression in the early 1700s; see *Nichirenshū jiten* (Nichirenshū Shūmuin, 1981), 508; *Oshioki reiruishū*, ed. Ishii Ryōsuke, 16 vols. (Meicho Shuppan, 1971–1973), 12:183–91. Thereafter it seems largely to have disappeared, but because it was conjoined with the more persistent Fuju Fuse in article 52 of the Rules for Deciding Judicial Matters, its name was perpetuated as epitomizing banned religious practices. Article 52 simply specified the punishments for people who contravened the ban in one manner or another; it did not go into the reasons for the ban.
6. For further discussion of these points, see Kate Wildman Nakai, "'Deviant Practices' and 'Strange Acts': Late Tokugawa Judicial Perspectives on Heteropraxy" (forthcoming).
7. Aiso Kazuhiro, *Ōshio Heihachirō shokan no kenkyū* (Osaka: Seibundō Shuppan, 2003), 1:97–104; Yabuta, "Ōsaka machi bugyō."
8. See *Oshioki reiruishū*, 12:115–16.
9. Ōhashi Yukihiro, *Kirishitan minshūshi no kenkyū* (Tōkyōdō Shuppan, 2001), 167–69.
10. Hiramatsu, *Kinsei keiji soshōhō*, 862–63, 867n3; see also Daniel V. Botsman, *Punishment and Power in the Making of Modern Japan* (Princeton, N.J.: Princeton University Press, 2005), 35–36.
11. Kōda Shigetomo, *Ōshio Heihachirō* (Tōadō Shobō, 1910; repr., Chūōkōronsha, 1977), 24–28; Fujiwara Arikazu, "Ōshio Heihachirō to 'jashūmon ikken,'" *Kansai Daigaku Jinken Mondai Kenkyūshitsu kiyō* 13 (1986): 206–10; Aiso,

Ōshio Heihachirō, 1:143–47. Regarding Ōshio's move against Yuge, see part 3, p. 233.

12. Hiramatsu, *Kinsei keiji soshōhō*, 849–50, 867n3.

13. The shogunate issued an edict in 1687 requiring daimyo as well as local shogunal officials to regularly collect information about the behavior of relatives, descendants, and in-laws of apostate Kirishitan and report it to Edo. In 1695 it further specified the range of relatives affected. Identification as the relative of a Kirishitan continued for up to five generations, but the specific number varied, depending on whether descent was through a male or female child. Descent in the male line meant more generations of liability. See *Ofuregaki Kanpō shūsei*, ed. Takayanagi Shinzō and Ishii Ryōsuke (Iwanami Shoten, 1934), 634–36; Shimizu Hirokazu and Shimizu Yūko, eds., *Kirishitan kankei hōsei shiryō* (Sōkyū Shuppan, 2002), 255–57; Tamamuro Fumio, *Sōshiki to danka* (Yoshikawa Kōbunkan, 1999), 162–77; Nam-lin Hur, *Death and Social Order in Tokugawa Japan: Buddhism, Anti-Christianity, and the Danka System* (Cambridge, Mass.: Harvard University Asia Center, 2007), 100–102.

14. Article 20; *Tokugawa kinreikō, bekkan*: 66.

15. It may be noted that the Deliberative Council made no reference to the cases that had arisen in Urakami and Amakusa in the 1790s and early 1800s. Although those are seen today as having involved underground Kirishitan, they did not figure as potential precedents because they were not dealt with as such at the time.

16. Hiramatsu, *Kinsei keiji soshōhō*, 520–21, 565–68.

17. See Botsman, *Punishment and Power*, 18–20.

18. The proclamation appears in various compilations, including *Ofuregaki Tenpō shūsei*, ed. Takayanagi Shinzō and Ishii Ryōsuke (Iwanami Shoten, 1937), 2:716–17.

19. See pp. xxxi, 136, 315n11.

20. Fujii Yoshio, *Ōsaka machi bugyō to keibatsu* (Osaka: Seibundō Shuppan, 1990), 105–6. See also *Tekagami, Tekagami shūi*, vol. 6 of *Ōsaka-shi shi shiryō* (Osaka: Ōsaka-shi Shiryō Chōsakai, 1982), 44–45.

21. See Hirata Atsushi, *Shinshū shisōshi ni okeru "shinzoku nitai" ron no tenkai* (Kyoto: Ryūkoku Gakkai, 2001), 118–21; Matsukane Naomi, "Shiryō shōkai: Shūmon okite (kōgi yori jashūmon ofureshimeshi): Keihan Kirishitan ikken-go ni okeru Higashi Honganji gakusō no enzetsu," *Dōhō Daigaku Bukkyō Bunka Kenkyūjo kiyō* 32 (2012): 107–14; Matsukane Naomi, "Keihan 'Kirishitan' ikken ni taisuru Bukkōji kyōdan no taiō," *Rekishi no hiroba: Ōtani Daigaku Nihonshi no Kai kaishi* 19 (2016): 3–16; "Kirishitan jato ikken," MS copy, 2019-1, Tōkyō Daigaku Shiryō Hensanjo. Some villages also submitted pledges to adhere strictly to the proclamation's provision. For an example, see Fujiwara, "Ōshio Heihachirō," 223–24.

22. *Oshioki reiruishū*, 15:116–18. This case appears in the same fourth compilation as the materials on the Keihan incident.

23. Kawaji Toshiakira, *Neifu kiji*, in *Kawaji Toshiakira monjo* (Nihon Shiseki Kyōkai, 1932–1934), 4:168–72. Kawaji Toshiakira would subsequently play a central role in negotiations with the Western powers in the last years of Tokugawa rule.

7. SUBMITTING THE DOSSIER FOR REVIEW

1. The preceding paragraph and this phrase would subsequently be removed and were not included in the execution placard inscription. They appear only in the Yoshino-bon MS and in the records concerning the case found in *Oshioki reiruishū*, ed. Ishii Ryōsuke, 16 vols. (Meicho Shuppan, 1971–1973), 12:161–62. A somewhat abbreviated version appears in the Seishin-bon MS.

2. Here and subsequently, as noted in the preceding introduction to part 2, the Osaka eastern magistrate omitted the proposed sentence that normally came at the end of the summation of charges. In the original dossier each individual summation was attached separately to the pertinent testimony. The Yoshino-bon MS reproduces this format. The Kōda-bon MS combines the separate summations into a single continuous document, however, and we have followed its arrangement here.

3. The wording in this paragraph from "Kinu thought" was later deleted and does not occur in the Kōda-bon MS or the execution placard inscription.

4. The first part of this sentence appears only in the Yoshino-bon MS and in *Oshioki reiruishū*, 12:168.

5. In this case, which occurred in 1788, Jikū, the head priest of a main temple of the Yūzū Dainenbutsu sect, transmitted to lay believers practices for attaining salvation in this life that deviated from the sect's established teachings. He also swore them to secrecy. The Osaka magistrate who investigated the case proposed that Jikū be sentenced to expulsion from the temple after having submitted an oath recanting his wrongful views. The Deliberative Council recommended a more severe punishment, however, and he was sentenced to exile to a remote island; *Oshioki reiruishū*, 3:420–24.

6. This case arose in the context of a large-scale popular protest in 1774 against the shogunal intendant in Hida. The priests of the Ichinomiya Shrine were held culpable of abetting the protest by performing prayer rituals directed against the intendant; see *Oshioki reiruishū*, 6:267–69. "Kimura Ise," the name of the priest given here, is presumably a mistranscription of "Mori Ise," the actual name of the priest involved. The view today is that the priests did not specifically target the intendant in the rituals they performed. The shrine served as a gathering place for the protestors and the priests conducted prayers at their request for the protest's success. However, it is now believed the prayers did not include a curse against the intendant. See *Gifu-ken shi: Tsūshi-hen, kinsei, jō* (Gifu: Gifu-ken, 1968), 1167–68.

7. "Decapitation" (*shizai*) was a middle-level death penalty. According to the specifications in article 103 of the Rules for Deciding Judicial Matters, the decapitation took place within the jailhouse, the condemned person was not paraded through the streets beforehand, nor was the head subsequently displayed. It was thus held to be a less-severe punishment than the death sentence proposed for Umon and Heizō, which incorporated the latter two elements. The recommendation of it for Kenzō reflected the investigators' conclusion that Kenzō could not be identified as properly a "Kirishitan," unlike Umon and Heizō. As with other severe forms of the death penalty, a sentence of decapitation also meant that the corpse was ordered to be abandoned and used for sword practice, and the condemned person's property was confiscated; *Tokugawa kinreikō*, ed. Ishii Ryōsuke, 11 vols. (Sōbunsha, 1959–1961), *bekkan*: 129.

8. Seclusion (*enryo*) and strict seclusion (*hissoku*) were part of a group of similar punishments levied for relatively minor misdeeds. The gates to the house were to be kept closed, guests were not to be received, and the household members were to refrain from ordinary social activities. They were, however, permitted to leave the house discreetly under cover of darkness.

9. As with seclusion and strict seclusion, a sentence of house confinement (*oshikome* or *heimon*) meant that the gates to the house were to be kept closed, guests were not to be received, and the household members were to refrain from ordinary social activities. It was somewhat more severe than other similar forms of punishment in that the household members were not to leave the house even at night.

10. Incarceration, which was not a routine punishment, was sometimes used as a substitute for exile to a remote island when that was held to be impractical or otherwise inappropriate.

11. "Reprimand" (*shikari*) and "strict reprimand" (*kitto shikari*) were the mildest punishments levied on commoners. In effect the magistrate simply pronounced to the miscreants in court the fact of the reprimand.

12. Since the Osaka governor was provided with a copy of the Precedents of Criminal Judgments Organized by Category, quite likely the Osaka eastern magistrate refers here to a case included in that compilation. We have not, however, been able to identify it. This is true as well for the precedents mentioned in the following unless otherwise specified.

8. DELIBERATIONS IN EDO

1. Here and subsequently records concerning the incident frequently reiterate the information about the place of residence that served in the testimonies to identify each party. We have omitted the repetition.

2. These "oral" (i.e., private) instructions from the senior councillors were a kind of appendix to the preceding document and were handed down to the Deliberative Council at the same time.

3. A note attached to the dossier explains the processing of documents 7, 8, and 9 as follows: "[The presiding senior councillor] Lord Mizuno Tadaakira directly handed the two preceding documents [7 and 8] to [the temples and shrines magistrate] Lord Tsuchiya Yoshinao, [Edo magistrate] Lord Tsutsui Masanori, and [the financial and judicial affairs magistrate] Lord Naitō Noritomo, and these [three members of the Deliberative Council] forwarded notice of their receipt of the documents [to the senior councillors]."

4. The Osaka eastern magistrate had divided his proposal for punishments for the figures involved in the incident into two main parts: an inquiry regarding those he expected to receive severe punishments (document 3) and a report on those whom he proposed to sentence to lesser punishments (document 5). The Deliberative Council approached the matter from a somewhat different angle. It addressed first those for whom there were individual confirmed testimonies (document 10) and then those whose testimony was incorporated in an addendum to the confirmed testimony of the figure with whom they were associated (document 11). A heading attached to the recommendations notes that they were handed directly to the presiding senior councillor, Mizuno Tadaakira, on the eighth day of the seventh month, 1829, by three members of the Deliberative Council acting jointly: Tsuchiya Yoshinao, temples and shrines magistrate; Sakakibara Tadayuki, Edo magistrate; and Soga Sukemasa, financial and judicial affairs magistrate.

5. This office, *shūmon bugyō* (known also as *shūmon aratame yaku*), was established in the 1640s to enforce anti-Christian measures. It evolved as a concurrent appointment, held jointly by one inspector general (*ōmetsuke*) and one construction works magistrate (*sakuji bugyō*).

6. As noted in the introduction to part 2, the provisions in the Rules for Deciding Judicial Matters concerning Sanchō-ha and Fuju Fuse served as the normal benchmark for deciding sentences in cases involving irregular religious practices. These provisions had been applied, for example, in the case involving the Raigōji priest Jikū to which the Osaka eastern magistrate referred in document 3.

7. Article 20; *Tokugawa kinreikō*, ed. Ishii Ryōsuke, 11 vols. (Sōbunsha, 1959–1961), *bekkan*: 66.

8. The reference is to the summations submitted by the Osaka eastern magistrate (document 2). The revised wording would appear in the execution placards based on the summations.

9. The Deliberative Council thus recommended a sentence a couple of degrees more severe than that of distant exile proposed by the Osaka eastern magistrate.

10. Magaribuchi Kagetsugu (1725–1800) served as Edo northern magistrate from 1771 to 1787.

11. Genzaemon was presumably serving as Sensuke's guarantor in his capacity as the manager of the property where Sensuke lived.

12. We can surmise that the Deliberative Council members saw Tōzō's case as analogous to that of Genzaemon because both involved misrepresentation of a relationship. They judged Tōzō to be less at fault than Genzaemon, however, and thus instead of adopting the exact punishment as in the precedent, they suggested reducing it by a degree. Through this process they reached the same conclusion as the Osaka eastern magistrate regarding the appropriate punishment.

13. Yoda Masatsugu served as Edo northern magistrate from 1753 to 1769.

14. Presumably it would have been difficult to pursue the lawsuit so long as she was included in a warrior household.

15. In this case the recommendation was to increase the punishment a degree from that meted out in the precedent used as an analogy.

16. As mentioned in the introduction to part 2, the Osaka eastern magistrate had seen Umon and Heizō as somewhat less culpable than Sano, Kinu, and Mitsugi because the two men had not tried to extort money from others and had expressed remorse. The magistrate consequently had proposed to sentence them not to crucifixion but decapitation with subsequent display of the head. The Deliberative Council, emphasizing the common involvement with Kirishitan practices, called for levying the same sentence on the two men as on the women.

17. Nakagawa Hisamichi (1663–1710) was daimyo of the Oka domain in Bungo.

18. In other words, undergone a ceremony of baptism.

19. The Deliberative Council concluded that Shōni could be considered comparable to Gunki's relative because he had assumed the role in making the funerary and other arrangements after Gunki's death that a relative would normally play. For a precedent it turned to one of several "Kirishitan relative" cases from the early eighteenth century that dealt with people who denied being Kirishitan themselves but were the relatives of Kirishitan. These cases concerned not the original decision to incarcerate these relatives but whether they should continue to be incarcerated some decades on (something that points up the paucity of judicial records concerning Kirishitan). From the comment indicating that the senior councillors had provided the council with these materials, it appears that they were not part of the body of precedents stored in the council's archives. They subsequently would be appended to the record of the council's discussions of the Keihan incident that was incorporated in the fourth compilation of *Oshioki reiruishū*. For the case of O-kai cited here, see *Oshioki reiruishū*, ed. Ishii Ryōsuke, 16 vols. (Meicho Shuppan, 1971–1973), 12:182.

20. The Osaka eastern magistrate had proposed a sentence of exile to a remote island, the most severe form of banishment. As previously mentioned (see chapter 7, note 10), incarceration was sometimes used as a substitute for exile to a remote island. Adopting the precedent of O-kai and holding that those connected to the Keihan incident principals should be kept under supervision, the Deliberative Council opted for this substitution.

21. As with Shōni, the Deliberative Council recommended changing to incarceration the sentence proposed by the Osaka eastern magistrate of exile to a remote island.

22. The case of Kichizō is included among the Kirishitan relative cases in the materials consulted by the Deliberative Council (*Oshioki reiruishū*, 12:182). There, however, he is described as having been incarcerated for thirty-four years.

23. The Osaka eastern magistrate had proposed that Makijirō be incarcerated until he became an adult, at which time he should be exiled to a remote island. The Deliberative Council recommended that as a Kirishitan relative he be incarcerated indefinitely rather than exiled.

24. The Deliberative Council recommended a considerably more severe sentence than that of ordinary decapitation proposed by the Osaka eastern magistrate.

25. This is the same figure whose handling of a case as Edo magistrate was cited earlier as a precedent for deciding the appropriate sentence for Tōzō. Magaribuchi subsequently served as financial and judicial affairs magistrate, responsible for judicial matters, from 1788 to 1797.

26. Honkokuji was a main temple of the Nichijū lineage of the Nichiren sect. In 1609 the shogunate had punished Nikkyō (1560–1620), a leader of this lineage, for propagating Fuju Fuse teachings. Despite the ban on Fuju Fuse, the parishioners of the branch temples affiliated with Honkokuji had evidently continued to show devotion to sacred objects associated with Nikkyō and other Fuju Fuse priests. The punitive action by Magaribuchi cited as a precedent here was directed at the priests of the branch temples for failing to pay heed to their parishioners' activities and put a stop to them.

27. The "four others" are Kinu, Mitsugi, Umon, and Heizō. Earlier, the Deliberative Council likened Gunki to Sano, Kinu, and Mitsugi, the three principals who had actively propagated their practices to others. Here the council expands the framework of comparison to include Umon and Heizō, who had received transmission of the practices but had not propagated them.

28. These provisions are included in article 52 of the Rules for Deciding Judicial Matters. See *Tokugawa kinreikō, bekkan*: 93–94.

29. The Osaka Eastern Magistracy did not make recommendations regarding several tangential figures mentioned in the addenda. By contrast, working methodically through the addenda, the Deliberative Council took note of everyone who had been drawn into the investigation.

30. Article 18 of the Rules for Deciding Judicial Matters set a statute of limitations of twelve months for "past offenses" (*kyūaku*), unless the offense was subject to the death penalty, or the perpetrator was involved in some other crime or had absconded and been placed on permanent search (*nagatazune*); see *Tokugawa kinreikō, bekkan*: 65. The Deliberative Council recommended adopting this statute of limitations in several following instances as well. The Osaka eastern magistrate and his staff undoubtedly were aware of this provision but did not raise the possibility of applying the statute of limitations in

the proposals for punishments that were submitted to the Osaka governor and subsequently forwarded to Edo. This was perhaps because, officially speaking, the Osaka magistrates did not have access to the Rules and thus could not refer explicitly to its provisions.

31. Because Yae died in the course of the investigation of the incident, there was no confirmed testimony for her, and the Osaka eastern magistrate had not made any specific recommendation regarding what to do with Yoshichi.

32. The Osaka eastern magistrate had not made distinctions among this group of people, but the Deliberative Council put added weight on the act of giving a pledge of secrecy and proposed that those who had done so should receive a more severe sentence than the rest.

33. The Deliberative Council thus recommended treating the pawnbrokers more leniently than proposed by the Osaka eastern magistrate.

34. Article 57; *Tokugawa kinreikō, bekkan*: 101.

35. Article 57; *Tokugawa kinreikō, bekkan*: 101.

36. Not to be confused with Toyoda Mitsugi, whose name Koto adopted.

37. The Osaka eastern magistrate had not made any recommendation as to what to do with Koto and Jōsuke.

38. The Osaka eastern magistrate had recommended a sentence of exile to a remote island. As with the other defined as "relatives of Kirishitan," the Deliberative Council suggested a sentence of incarceration instead.

39. The Deliberative Council recommended less-stringent treatment than that proposed by the Osaka eastern magistrate, which had been incarceration in place of a sentence of distant exile.

40. The Osaka eastern magistrate had proposed a sentence of exile to a remote island.

41. The Osaka eastern magistrate had proposed a sentence of distant exile.

42. The Osaka eastern magistrate had proposed a sentence of distant exile.

43. A subsection of article 85; *Tokugawa kinreikō, bekkan*: 122.

44. According to Heizō's testimony, these arrangements were more likely made in 1821 (see chapter 4, p. 95), but the difference would not have borne on application of the principle of exemption from punishment for a past offense.

45. Article 44; *Tokugawa kinreikō, bekkan*: 86.

46. The Osaka eastern magistrate had recommended a lighter sentence of a strict reprimand.

47. A subsection of article 44; *Tokugawa kinreikō, bekkan*: 86.

48. The Osaka eastern magistrate had recommended a lighter sentence of a strict reprimand.

49. See note 43.

50. The Osaka eastern magistrate had recommended a lighter sentence of a strict reprimand.

51. Moto and many of the others discussed in the remainder of document 11 were relatives of people who had associated with Gunki but whom the investigation had not explicitly identified as Kirishitan. At the end of this document

the Deliberative Council explains the rationale for its proposals regarding people who fell into this category as compared with those identified as the relatives of Kirishitan, for whom it recommended incarceration. The Osaka eastern magistrate had recommended a sentence of strict reprimand for Moto but had not raised the issue of restrictions on her place of residence henceforth. The Deliberative Council presumably saw the arrangement concerning the castaways as pertinent because they, like Moto, had been exposed to a subversive environment. Although they themselves evidently had not engaged in proscribed activities, this exposure was held to warrant keeping them under supervision. Unlike the castaways, however, Moto and others taken up in the remainder of document 11 were not to stay in their "home locale" strictly speaking, which would have been the city of Kyoto. Instead they were to move outside the city proper but remain somewhere in the surrounding province of Yamashiro. At the end of this document the Deliberative Council explains subsequently that this was because of the special circumstances of Kyoto as the emperor's seat (see pp. 201–2).

52. This refers to the elder Kyūbei and Shintarō.
53. The Osaka eastern magistrate had proposed sentencing both Kiyo and the present Kyūbei to a strict reprimand. In both cases the Deliberative Council did not follow the proposal for an explicit sentence of strict reprimand but recommended instead putting restrictions on their place of residence henceforth.
54. The Kōda-bon MS gives the name as Yahei.
55. The Osaka eastern magistrate had not included Yazobei in the list of people to whom he proposed to mete out sentences.
56. Not to be confused with Itoya Wasa, mentioned a few lines later.
57. The Osaka eastern magistrate had proposed to sentence both Wasa and Nobu to thirty days' confinement to their house and had not made any proposal regarding Tsugi and Tsunehachi.
58. The Osaka eastern magistrate had not made any proposal regarding what to do with Shinbei and Mume.
59. Suganuma Sadayoshi served as financial and judicial affairs magistrate from 1797 to 1802.
60. The Osaka eastern magistrate had proposed a sentence of fifty days' confinement to his house. Handcuffs were a more onerous penalty than house confinement for the same number of days. See Sone Hiromi, "Josei to keibatsu," in *Mibun no naka no josei*, ed. Yabuta Yutaka and Yanagiya Keiko, vol. 4 of *Edo no hito to mibun*, (Yoshikawa Kōbunkan, 2010), 82.
61. Murakami Yoshiaya served as southern Edo magistrate from 1796 to 1798.
62. This case is included in *Senjutsu kakurei* (Selected precedents), a collection of precedents compiled prior to *Oshioki reiruishū*. See "Senjutsu kakurei: Shohen," 68 vols., MS copy, 818-1/ndljp/pid/2610580, National Diet Library Digital Collection, vol. 3, no. 3; vol. 8, no. 3. See also Owaki Hidekazu, "Kinsei no mibun idō, nijūka to 'ninbetsu' no toriatsukai," *Nihon rekishi* 839 (2018): 22.

63. The Osaka eastern magistrate had not made any proposal as to how to deal with Bunsuke.

64. This remark indicates that the preceding recommendations were originally appended separately, item by item, to the dossier submitted by the Osaka Eastern Magistracy. The Kōda-bon copy of the Deliberative Council's discussions, which is our fullest source of information about them, combines the individual recommendations into a continuous record, and we have followed that format here.

65. The specific term used for "recognized kin" is "relations for whom one should observe avoidances related to death pollution" (*imigakari no shinrui*). The term indicated a degree of legal kinship—and in this case, judicial liability—comprising one's spouse, siblings, and a finely calibrated range of both paternal and maternal ascendant and descendant blood relations. For a chart of the scope of "recognized kin" as interpreted by the shogunate from the end of the seventeenth century, see Atsuko Hirai, *Government by Mourning: Death and Political Integration in Japan, 1603–1912* (Cambridge, Mass.: Harvard University Asia Center, 2014), 59. Although the category "recognized kin" served as the foundation for the category "relatives of Kirishitan," the latter was of broader scope than the former. Fathers-in-law and sons-in-law did not fall within the category of "recognized kin," which is why they are additionally specified here.

66. The section of the dossier dealing with temples and the Osaka eastern magistrate's recommendations for sentences did not include Kenzō's temple.

67. See Hiramatsu Yoshirō, *Kinsei keiji soshōhō no kenkyū* (Sōbunsha, 1960), 953, 956.

68. In both instances the concern seems to have been to avoid exposing the palace to a contaminating action or presence. In early 1830, following the pronouncing and carrying out of the sentences on the parties to the incident, the Deliberative Council elaborated somewhat further on its thinking about this matter. It noted that the proclamation of 1687 concerning "relatives of Kirishitan" had specified that they were not to be allowed to move to another jurisdiction; if such a move were unavoidable, the authorities of the locale to which such a relative moved should be informed. The council continued that the definition of "relatives of Kirishitan" underlying this proclamation presumed that the Kirishitan in question had "once been a devotee of that sect but subsequently apostatized and converted to a recognized sect" and that the relative had been born after the conversion. These presumptions did not apply to the case at hand. Nevertheless, restrictions in their freedom of movement should be imposed on the relatives of those whose behavior had invited suspicion, and in the case of those who had resided hitherto in Kyoto, it "would not be appropriate to allow people of this sort to continue to live within the Kyoto city limits"; *Oshioki reiruishū*, 11:495–96.

69. By this specification (*ichidai kagiri*) the Deliberative Council sought to distinguish the treatment of those linked to people who could not be clearly

identified as Kirishitan from that of those put in the category "relatives of Kirishitan." For the latter, the restrictions would be expected to continue for multiple generations.

9. THE SENIOR COUNCILLORS' ORDERS AND THEIR IMPLEMENTATION

1. As with the Deliberative Council's recommendations, the orders reiterate the addresses and information about status used to identify the principals. We have again omitted the repetition.
2. The Deliberative Council had dealt with Makijirō as if he were still alive when it formulated its recommendations in the seventh month of 1829. Evidently he had died in the interim.
3. Document 12 is the formal order regarding the disposition of the case issued by the senior councillors in the name of the shogun. Together with this formal order, the senior councillors also conveyed instructions in a less-official form about how to deal with various delicate matters presented by the case. Document 13 sets out these accompanying instructions.
4. Matsudaira Muneakira (1782–1840) served as Osaka governor from 1826.11.23 to 1828.11.22; at the time these directions were issued, in 1829.12, he was serving as Kyoto governor; he would remain in that office until 1831.
5. See document 3.
6. The Osaka Magistracy had supervisory authority over the four provinces of Settsu, Kawachi, Izumi, and Harima.
7. In the form of the preceding document 12.
8. In other words, the corpses were to be disposed of by the outcasts serving at the magistracy, most likely through a cursory burial in the cemetery adjacent to the execution grounds. Only the corpses of those expected to be subjected to the public execution of crucifixion were to be preserved in salt; Hiramatsu Yoshirō, *Kinsei keiji soshōhō no kenkyū* (Sōbunsha, 1960), 965. During the course of the nearly three years that it took to process the case, many of the lesser figures detained in the jailhouse had died. It is not clear what had been done with their corpses, but likely they had already been provisionally disposed of.
9. On 1829.12.7 the Osaka eastern magistrate sent three separate reports to Edo confirming that he had carried out the senior councillors' orders and responding to issues they had raised. As the three reports (documents 14, 15, and 17) contain some repetition and also repeat some of the language of the orders from Edo (documents 12 and 13), we have condensed them and omitted the repetitions. In document 14 the magistrate responded to the main formal order from Edo (document 12).
10. The order from Edo (and before that the Deliberative Council's recommendations) had noted that the addendum on Koto had failed to indicate when her

interaction with Kinu had occurred; it thus was not clear whether or not this constituted a past offense.

11. The order from Edo had noted that it was not clear what had happened to Soe/ Suma's registration subsequently. If she were still listed in Bunsuke's population register, his action in nominally listing her could not be treated as a past offense. He thus would not be exempt from punishment.

12. The testimony had stated that Zekan had become priest of Daijōin "only in 1823" but had left vague what his status at the temple might have been before that. The further information here clarifies that he had entered the temple in 1820, presumably as a novice or in another junior capacity. This was still after Wasa's death in the eighth month of 1818.

13. A temple of Nishi Honganji lineage located in Sakai, near Osaka, kept an account of the disposal of the Kirishitan incident and particularly its impact on the temples involved. According to this account, Kōhō in fact hung himself before the sentences were handed down. See "Kirishitan jato ikken," MS copy, 2019-1, Tōkyō Daigaku Shiryō Hensanjo.

14. Matsudaira Sadatomo (1773–1856) served as Kyoto western magistrate from 1827.8.9 to 1835.5.20; Odagiri Naoaki (dates unknown) replaced Kan'o Mototaka as Kyoto eastern magistrate on 1829.5.15 and served in that capacity until 1831.7.12.

15. The orders received from Edo had indicated that any pertinent relatives of the first group, who had been defined as Kirishitan, were to be treated as "relatives of Kirishitan." For the second group, who were suspect but could not firmly be identified as having received transmission of the Kirishitan creed, any pertinent relatives were to be subject to restrictions on their residence. See document 12.

16. See document 17.

17. This document is a response to document 13. The first part, omitted here, repeats the directions from Edo transmitted in that memorandum.

18. Another record in the collection of documents pertaining to the incident, included as document 16, indicates that the materials had been burned two days previously.

19. In the Kōda-bon MS, document 16 is appended to the list of confiscated books (see appendix 2). Document 15, sent to Edo two days later together with documents 14 and 17, simply notes that the confiscated materials were incinerated. We thus have included here the further details about the incineration contained in document 16.

10. AFTERMATH

1. *Oshioki reiruishū*, ed. Ishii Ryōsuke, 16 vols. (Meicho Shuppan, 1971–1973), 11:494–95.

2. See document 12. This and the following documents all come from records kept by the Deliberative Council. They typically consist of excerpts from an inquiry by the Osaka Eastern Magistracy and the Deliberative Council's recommended response to the inquiry. The dates given in the document titles usually refer to the date when the Deliberative Council submitted its recommendation to the senior councillors. After receiving document 12 in the twelfth month of 1829, the Osaka eastern magistrate had sought a clarification of the scope of relationship presumed in the specification "recognized kin, sons-in-law, or fathers-in-law." Did "sons-in-law" include "not only the husband of a daughter but also the husband of a sister, aunt, or niece, or the son-in-law of a nephew?" The Deliberative Council had responded that it was limited to the husband of a daughter; *Oshioki reiruishū*, 11:495–96.

3. In her testimony Kinu stated that when she first moved to Osaka she had lived with a relative, since deceased, named Harimaya Bunjirō in Nōjin-chō in Tenma. Bunjirō's exact relationship to her, and his relationship to Kō, are unclear, but it seems possible that he was Kinu's brother and Kō's father.

4. Ōkubo Tadazane (1778–1837) was daimyo of the Odawara domain, located in eastern Japan, but his landholdings included seven villages in Sumiyoshi county. Coincidentally he was also a long-serving senior councillor.

5. *Oshioki reiruishū* gives her name as Chū; we have amended it here in line with the name as given in the testimonies.

6. Known since Meiji as Sanzen'in, this was one of five Tendai-related cloisters traditionally headed by an imperial prince.

7. Chūtatsu was given more deferential treatment than Kenzō's other relatives presumably because of his quasi-warrior or noble status as a retainer of the Kajii imperial cloister. The associate who assumed custody over him was likely another retainer. Chūtatsu's name appears in thirteen lists of doctors in the Osaka area dating from 1833 to 1850, and most likely he was already a doctor in 1829; see Nakano Misao, *Ōsaka ishi banzuke shūsei* (Kyoto: Shibunkaku, 1985). The listings suggest that he came through the incident relatively unscathed, despite the connection with Kenzō.

8. *Oshioki reiruishū*, 11:496–98. The Deliberative Council's position that Kenzō's son and wife need not be incarcerated contrasts with the treatment specified for the wives and children of the other principals. Despite the Deliberative Council's recommendation that it was not necessary to keep Kō and the others incarcerated, it appears that they continued to be detained in the jailhouse rather than being released to the custody of the locale. An inquiry from the Osaka governor discussed by the council in the fourth month of 1832 indicates that Shū, Ryōzō, and Ichimatsu had been "detained for the moment in the jailhouse but suddenly fell ill and died one after the other" (*Oshioki reiruishū*, 11:359).

9. The report is not included in the excerpts from these documents preserved in *Oshioki reiruishū*. We have not been able to confirm the location of the guard post; it is possible that the name has become garbled.

10. In other words, the Osaka eastern magistrate differentiated between relatives of Kenzō's who might be considered to be of warrior status (putting them in the custody of officials of their domain) and relatives who were commoners.

11. See document 19.

12. *Oshioki reiruishū*, 11:501–2. In fact, as with Shū, Ryōzō, and the others mentioned in note 8, Shunpei evidently continued to be detained in the jailhouse, since his name is included with theirs in the report of the fourth month of 1832, recording that they had died while being provisionally detained; see *Oshioki reiruishū*, 11:359.

13. When people moved, they had to take a certificate of sectarian affiliation from the temple where they were currently registered to the village officials or town aldermen of their intended new place of residence. Only then could they be properly included in the population register of that locale. The Osaka eastern magistrate's query concerned the format of such a certificate for those treated as quasi-Kirishitan relatives. Would an ordinary format suffice, or should it incorporate the further details required for those defined unequivocally as Kirishitan relatives?

14. We have omitted the details of the people named and give only the most pertinent point: compared with ordinary certificates of sectarian affiliation, a temple where relatives of apostate Kirishitan were registered had to acknowledge a heightened degree of responsibility for keeping watch over them.

15. The two people certified in this instance were residents of the outcast (*hinin*, *kaito*) community. For the connection between apostate Kirishitan of the seventeenth century and the Osaka outcast community, see Tsukada Takashi, *Ōsaka no hinin: Kojiki, Shitennōji, korobi Kirishitan* (Chikuma Shobō, 2013); Tsukada Takashi, "Early Modern Osaka *Hinin* and Population Registers," in *Japan's Household Registration System and Citizenship: Koseki, Identification and Documentation*, ed. David Chapman and Karl Jakob Krogness, 21–42 (London: Routledge, 2014). A list from 1775 of outcast descendants of apostate Kirishitan alive in Osaka at the time includes fifty-four people, considerably fewer than comparable lists from earlier years. Since descendants were to be removed from the roster of relatives of Kirishitan after five generations for descendants in the male line and three for descendants in the female line, presumably quite a number of outcasts descended from apostate Kirishitan had been deleted from the roster in the interim. Most of those remaining were of the third and fourth generation of descent; see Tsukada, *Ōsaka no hinin*, 104–11. Another fifty years later, there likely would have been still fewer, if any, descendants of the specified degree of relationship, and it is not clear whether the Osaka Magistracy at the time of the Keihan Kirishitan incident had any actual experience dealing with persons defined as Kirishitan relatives.

16. *Oshioki reiruishū*, 11:500–501. The Deliberative Council's recommendations are dated the intercalary third month, 1830.

17. According to the addendum about Mitsugi's relatives attached to her testimony, Eshū had been placed under the custody of the locale during the

course of the investigation (see chapter 3, p. 74). The Deliberative Council had recommended that she be placed under the custody of a relative instead of incarcerated (see chapter 8, p. 193). Yorozuya Tōbei's name has not previously been mentioned; presumably his relationship to Mitsugi was not so close as for him to be regarded as "recognized kin" and thus subject to restrictions himself as the relative of a Kirishitan.

18. For this proclamation, see *Ofuregaki Kanpō shūsei*, ed. Takayanagi Shinzō and Ishii Ryōsuke (Iwanami Shoten, 1934), 635. "The office responsible for Kirishitan matters" mentioned in this proclamation is the same as the Office for Sectarian Matters. As noted, typically the outcasts serving in the magistracy would dispose of the corpse of someone who died while detained at the jailhouse (see chapter 9, note 8). In principle no funeral or memorial service was to be held in such cases; see Hiramatsu Yoshirō, *Kinsei keiji soshōhō no kenkyū* (Sōbunsha, 1960), 964–67. The Osaka eastern magistrate presumably wondered whether Eshū's corpse should be handled in the same fashion. The Deliberative Council pointed out, however, that such restrictions did not apply to the relatives of Kirishitan. Since Eshū came under this category, they recommended that the stipulations in the 1687 proclamation be followed and Eshū's corpse released to the temple where she had been registered.

19. *Oshioki reiruishū*, 11:494.

20. *Oshioki reiruishū*, 11:503. Between the death of Eshū in the first month and that of Ito in the sixth, the Deliberative Council had considered three other inquiries from the Osaka eastern magistrate about disposing of the corpses of the relatives of parties to the incident: Suehiroya Kahei, the husband of Wasa's adoptive daughter Toki; Yoshichi, the incapacitated husband of Yae; and Haiya Gen'emon, the son-in-law of Gunki's friend Kyūbei. In all three cases the same procedures were followed as with Eshū. The documents do not otherwise mention Gen'emon, who presumably came to the magistrate's attention in the ongoing search for further "recognized kin, sons-in-law, and fathers-in-law" (Gen'emon is described as having died before acting on the order to move outside the Kyoto city limits). These circumstances suggest that there may have been others apart from those explicitly named in the extant documents who were also required to move outside the Kyoto city limits because of a link to the parties to the incident. For the reports on the three deaths, see *Oshioki reiruishū*, 11:499–500, 502–3.

21. Ōkubo Tadazane (dates unknown) served as Osaka eastern magistrate from 1834.7.8 to 1836.3.8. A bannerman holding the title Settsu no kami, he is to be distinguished from the Ōkubo Tadazane mentioned in document 19, a daimyo with the title Kaga no kami.

22. This case is included in an inquiry from the Nagasaki magistrate in 1707 about releasing a number of incarcerated Kirishitan relatives into the custody of the locale. See *Oshioki reiruishū*, 12:182.

23. In 1829 the Deliberative Council had quoted as precedents two other cases submitted by the Nagasaki magistrate in 1707, those of O-kai and Kichizō (see

document 10, pp. 183–84). Perhaps in this instance the Deliberative Council instead picked up Tō as the most pertinent precedent because the records submitted by the Nagasaki magistrate presented him as the least implicated personally in Kirishitan activities and thus the most "innocent" among the Kirishitan relatives. Since even as blameless a person as Tō had been kept incarcerated for over two decades, the council appears to have reasoned, there were no grounds for the early release of Kamon and the others, even if they, too, were not personally culpable.

24. Doi Toshitsura (1789–1848) served as Osaka governor from 1834 to 1837. He was responsible for suppressing Ōshio's rebellion early in 1837 and served subsequently as Kyoto governor and senior councillor.

25. *Oshioki reiruishū*, 11:387–88.

PART III. RUMORS AND RETELLINGS

1. See Peter F. Kornicki, "Manuscript, Not Print: Scribal Culture in the Edo Period," *Journal of Japanese Studies* 32, no. 1 (2006): 23–52; Kikuchi Yōsuke, *Kinsei jitsuroku no kenkyū: Seichō to tenkai* (Kyūko Shoin, 2008).

2. See *Ukiyo no arisama*, ed. Harada Tomohiko and Asakura Haruhiko, vol. 11 of *Nihon shomin seikatsu shiryō shūsei* (San'ichi Shobō, 1970), 3.

3. See the introduction to part 2, p. 148.

4. Harada and Asakura, *Ukiyo no arisama*, 204–5.

5. Sawayanagi Masumi, "Bakumatsuki no 'Kirishitan' imēji ni tsuite: Ōshio no ran kanren shiryō ni okeru Keihan Kirishitan ikken jōhō o chūshin ni," *Kokushikan shigaku* 14 (2010): 24–29, 36.

6. Harada and Asakura, *Ukiyo no arisama*, 205.

7. Sawayanagi, "Bakumatsuki no 'Kirishitan' imēji," 25; Harada and Asakura, *Ukiyo no arisama*, 435–36.

8. Harada and Asakura, *Ukiyo no arisama*, 495–97. The name Ōshio (Great Salt), for instance, was changed to Oshio (Small Salt).

9. This work appears to combine passages from the earlier *Kirishitan monogatari* (Tales of Kirishitan), published in 1639 and reprinted in 1665, and the later *A True Account of the Coming of the Kirishitan Sect to This Country*; see Jan C. Leuchtenberger, *Conquering Demons: The "Kirishitan," Japan, and the World in Early Modern Japanese Literature* (Ann Arbor: Center for Japanese Studies, University of Michigan, 2013), 203–8.

10. Harada and Asakura, *Ukiyo no arisama*, 67–69. We have omitted these materials from the translation in chapter 11 since they duplicate the passages concerning the six principals in documents 2 and 18.

11. As the first element of the sexagenary cycle, *kasshi* was also considered propitious.

12. For Seizan's fondness for sumo and the wrestlers he patronized, see Ujiie Mikito, *Tonosama to nezumi kozō: Rōkō Matsura Seizan no sekai* (Chūōkōronsha, 1991), 101–4.

13. As with *The State of the Floating World*, we have omitted the transcription of the proclamation and verdicts since they duplicate materials translated in part 2. Seizan added brief comments to several of the verdicts he transcribed, noting, for instance, that Mitsugi was said to have originally been a prostitute who then became Gunki's concubine; *Kasshi yawa*, ed. Nakamura Yukihiko and Nakano Mitsutoshi, 20 vols. (Heibonsha, 1977–1983), *zokuhen*, 3:212, 214–15.

14. Yasutaka Hiroaki, *Hirado Matsura-ke no meihō to kinkyō seisaku: Tōei sareta daikōkai jidai to sono hate ni* (Fukuoka: Seinan Gakuin Daigaku Hakubutsukan, 2013), 24–25, 34–35, 47–50.

15. Nakano Misao remarks on a similar reaction among scholars in Osaka (*Ōsaka meii den* [Kyoto: Shibunkaku, 1983], 86–89).

16. Dakiniten is a divinity of Hindu and Buddhist origin that in Japan became closely associated with Inari and fox worship. Rites to Dakiniten were seen as a means to ensure victory in battle and worldly success.

17. Digital versions can be viewed via both the National Diet Library Digital Collection (http://dl.ndl.go.jp/info:ndljp/pid/1939594) and the National Institute of Japanese Literature (http://school.nijl.ac.jp/kindai/NIJL/NIJL-00120.html). The National Diet Library version dates from 1886, indicating that the biography was sufficiently popular to be reprinted.

18. See the introduction to part 2, pp. 155–56.

19. "Tokugawa Nariaki jūjō goji kengisho," in *Bakumatsu seiji ronshū*, vol. 56 of *Nihon shisō taikei* (Iwanami Shoten, 1976), 9–10; Kirihara Kenshin, "Haiya to jōi: Bakumatsu shūkyō shisō ni okeru kōki Mitogaku no isō," in *Kami to hotoke no bakumatsu ishin*, ed. Iwata Mami and Kirihara Kenshin (Kyoto: Hōzōkan, 2018), 167–68.

20. The work's title comes from a phrase in Mencius 3.2:9: "I also wish . . . to put an end to pernicious doctrines and to oppose twisted actions" (James Legge, trans., *The Chinese Classics* [Hong Kong: Hong Kong University Press, 1960], 2:284; modified).

21. "Sokkyo hen," 22 vols., MS copy, C60:73, Tōkyō Daigaku Sōgō Toshokan; Itō Tasaburō, "Bakumatsu ni okeru Yasokyō haigeki," *Rekishi chiri* 65, no. 3 (1935): 22–27; *Mito-shi shi*, vol. 2, pt. 3 (Mito: Mito-shi Yakusho, 1976), 1082–85. The third section of *Sokkyo hen* brought together a wide range of anti-Christian writings, while the fourth focused on records of the Shimabara uprising and such. For the Mito anti-Christian compilation and publishing projects, see Kiri Paramore, *Ideology and Christianity in Japan* (New York: Routledge, 2009), 121–23; Kirihara, "Haiya to jōi," 179–84.

22. Itō, "Bakumatsu ni okeru Yasokyō haigeki," 37; Aizawa Seishisai, *Gyobusaku*, in *Hekijahen, Gyobusaku* (No pub., no date), ndljp/pid/754814, National Diet Library Digital Collection, folio 5b.

23. Ōhashi Yukihiro points out that the Meiji period saw a further twist on these associations when Mitsugi's name was invoked in connection with media

campaigns against female leaders of new religious groups; *Kinsei senpuku shūkyō ron: Kirishitan to kakushi nenbutsu* (Azekura Shobō, 2017), 154. An 1896 newspaper article claimed, for instance, that Nakayama Miki (1798–1887), the founder of Tenrikyō, was in fact Mitsugi's daughter. Perhaps drawing on another *jitsuroku*, this article has Mitsugi and Miki escape from Ōshio's investigation. As they roamed through Yamato province they were taken in as servants by the Nakayama household. They worked hard and the household head let his son marry Miki. Miki, the journalist maintained, wanted to revive the Kirishitan creed of her parents and devised Tenrikyō as a cover for that evil teaching; *Chūō shinbun*, May 12, 1896.

11. THE STATE OF THE FLOATING WORLD

1. *Ukiyo no arisama*, ed. Harada Tomohiko and Asakura Haruhiko, vol. 11 of *Nihon shomin seikatsu shiryō shūsei* (San'ichi Shobō, 1970), 58–67.
2. The testimonies make clear that Gunki engaged in some sort of irregular financial dealings while employed by the Kan'in princely house. It is possible that these involved loans made nominally by the princely house, which would fit with the story here that he tried to use canceled loan receipts or something of the sort to extort additional money; see chapter 5, note 7.
3. Amended; the original has "Kyōhō 2 or 3," which would be 1717–1718; presumably, the author meant "Kyōwa 2 or 3," which corresponds to 1802–1803.
4. Tsuyama was the only larger domain in this area, which had many small fiefs.
5. The author does have the characters wrong and gives the name of Gunki's temple as Unsenji 雲仙寺 rather than Unseiji 雲晴寺. To facilitate comparison with the testimonies and judicial records, we have corrected such errors.
6. Gunki was not buried in a Nichiren temple. The story that he was may have originated from the fact that his friend Itoya Wasa had been buried in a Nichiren temple; Mitsugi became a parishioner of the same temple.
7. As mentioned in the introduction to part 3, the author of *The State of the Floating World* lived near Shirokoura-machi, and he obtained various pieces of information about the incident from the wife of the Jōkōji priest. For the different Honganji lineages of the Ikkō (Jōdo Shinshū) sect, see chapter 6, note 9. Jōkōji, which belonged to the Nishi Honganji lineage, was the temple of affiliation of Fujii Umon, and its priest was sentenced to expulsion from the temple for dereliction in its duty to keep proper watch over him.
8. "Dai" is another reading of the first character of Yamatoya, and "I" corresponds to the first character of this man's name—which, as the author speculates, may have been something like Ihei or Iemon. "Branch firms" (*bekke*) were run by relatives or trusted employees who were allowed to set up a new store as a branch of their master's main store. The author subsequently mentions a Yamatoya Rinzō and Yamatoya Rihei as two of his sources.

9. In the medieval and early modern periods, commoners were allowed on certain occasions to enter the imperial palace and observe some rites performed in the palace courtyard; see Kishi Yasuko, *Kinsei no kinri to toshi kūkan* (Kyoto: Shibunkaku Shuppan, 2014), 154–75. In the late Edo period, these observers had to obtain passes to enter the palace. It was not easy for ordinary townspeople to secure such passes, but a court retainer like Gunki would have had ready access to them.

10. In other words, according to the author, not only did Unseiji in Kyoto and Jōkōji in Osaka alike belong to the Nishi Honganji lineage but also their priests were linked by common family ties to another Nishi Honganji temple, Muryōkōji in Kawachi, which was near Osaka. The fact that the Ikkō sect, unlike other premodern Japanese Buddhist sects, allowed its priests to marry and have families facilitated the forging of marital and blood ties between temples. The author relates in the following still further connections of this sort involving Jōkōji; see pp. 255–56.

11. The *okiya*, the term translated here as "brothel," managed the prostitutes indentured to it but did not receive customers, instead dispatching them to teahouses that acted as the intermediary between the customer and the brothel; see chapter 3, note 2. Kita Shinchi was another name for Sonezaki Shinchi, where one of Osaka's brothel districts was located.

12. Aldermen (*machi toshiyori*) in Osaka played a role comparable to that of *nanushi* in Edo. Landholding townspeople themselves, they were responsible for managing a variety of administrative tasks concerning the commoner urban population. In Osaka, usually each block had its own alderman, who performed his administrative duties alongside his ordinary occupation (in the late Edo period Osaka had a little over six hundred blocks); see Kōda Shigetomo, *Edo to Ōsaka* (Fuzanbō, 1934; repr., 1995), 47–51. Since an alderman was responsible for supervising the residents of his block, he could be held accountable for failing to keep proper track of their doings, as seen in parts 1 and 2.

13. The garment mentioned is a *kanban*, a short jacket typically worn by samurai servants that displays on its back the crest or name of the house.

14. The text gives the bridge's name as Fuchi, likely because of a transcription mistake.

15. The following story appears to attribute to Mitsugi events that the investigation linked to Kinu and to the child's father rather than its mother; see chapter 2, pp. 40–41.

16. A noble house that licensed shrine priests.

17. This story appears to attribute to Mitsugi the connection that instead existed between the Kyoto townsman Nakamuraya Shintarō and Gunki. Makijirō was Gunki's son, not Shintarō's.

18. According to popular legend, carp that show their strength by climbing a waterfall ascend to heaven and become dragons.

19. According to Mitsugi's testimony, the background to her adoption of Kamon was her curing of his mother's illness, not his, and when he fell ill after the

adoption, he was sent back to his parents. Whereas this story, like many of those about Mitsugi, portrays her as deeply lustful, her testimony stresses her disdain for sexual relations.

20. The text refers to Umon as Uezō 植蔵, a mistranscription of Umon's alternative name, Keizō 桂蔵. We have unified as Umon.

21. This is a somewhat embellished story about the woman named Koto whom Kinu tried to recruit as a disciple (see chapter 2, pp. 43–45; chapter 8, document 11; chapter 9, documents 12 and 14). There is no evidence in the testimonies or judicial records that Koto's son adopted the name Kamon.

22. The author uses the term *kaito* for what we have translated as "outcast leader" and *hinin* for ordinary outcasts. In early modern Osaka *kaito* was often used to indicate the areas inhabited by outcasts and, by extension, the outcast population in general, rather than as a term specific to the outcast leadership.

23. This poem puns on the homonym *matsu*, "wait" and "pine tree" (in the place-name Matsuya).

24. Daijōin was a Nichiren temple, not a Jōdo temple.

25. The official version of events was that Kōhō, the priest of Kanzanji, fell ill and died on 1829.11.22 (chapter 9, document 14). As noted there, however, his death gave rise to various rumors, including that he committed suicide before the officials had pronounced their sentence; see chapter 9, note 13.

26. As with Unseiji, the names and characters of several of these temples have become garbled.

27. In Osaka, one "main hall" (*midō*) was responsible for overseeing all temples in the region belonging to the Nishi Honganji branch of the Ikkō sect. Another oversaw temples belonging to the Higashi Honganji branch. The *midō* were nominally under the immediate direction of the branch heads in Kyoto, but their actual business was conducted by representatives (*rusui*), who performed the task in rotation. The author refers here to this representative (*midō rusui*).

28. In what follows the author explains that this "certain woman" was the widow of the previous priest of Jōkōji and the adoptive mother of the priest at the time of the incident, the man who had just been sentenced to expulsion from the temple.

29. Since descendants were responsible for performing ancestral rites, the effects of termination of a line extended back to the ancestors.

30. As mentioned in chapter 6 in regard to Kenzō's testimony, Dōjima was the nation's largest rice market and exchange.

31. One of the tasks of the aldermen was to prevent double pawning. If Kenzō in fact served as an alderman, it would have made it easier for him to get away with such malfeasance.

32. There is no evidence that Kenzō had any contact with Sano or that she was familiar with the Chinese works he owned. The testimonies of both Fujii Umon and Kenzō confirm that they each were acquainted with the priest of Hiraoka Shrine and that he knew about the proscribed Chinese books that

Kenzō owned. However, it was Umon's testimony that led the investigators to Kenzō, not a separate investigation of the Hiraoka priest, who had died over a decade before the Kirishitan incident came to light. See chapter 4, p. 85; chapter 6, p. 129.

33. Kenzō's adoptive mother, wife, son, and other relatives (although not his elder brother) were investigated subsequent to the pronouncing and carrying out of the sentences on 1829.12.5. None of them, however, was sentenced to indefinite incarceration. See chapter 10, documents 19 and 20.

34. The judicial records do not provide any corroboration of this.

35. There is no evidence that Yohei made such an arrangement with the officials of the Osaka Eastern Magistracy. His quarrel with Sano was the immediate cause for her arrest, and suspicions that she might be a Kirishitan arose only in the course of her interrogation.

36. This appears to refer to an incident that occurred in 1814. A preacher called Kōjun was found to have converted outcasts from an area on the outskirts of the castle town of Okayama to the doctrines of the banned Nichiren offshoot Fuju Fuse. (Although known in the Okayama area as hill people, the outcasts did not live in Fukuwatari, which is quite a distance from the Okayama castle town.) The chief of these outcasts, who did indeed work for the criminal investigations office, was banished, while the converted outcasts were reprimanded and ordered to submit oaths that they would adhere to the teachings of their original temple. See Yoshida Tokutarō, ed., *Ikeda-ke rireki ryakki* (Okayama: Nihon Bunkyō Shuppan, 1965), 2:1202; *Shisei teiyō* (Okayama: Fukutake Shoten, 1974), 2:753.

37. The priest of Enkōji was in fact forty-four years old. The judicial records give no evidence that he was exiled, and the temple continues to exist to this day. Matsukane Naomi has used documents from Enkōji's head temple, Bukkōji, to trace the circumstances of the priest's family and arrangements concerning the management of the temple and its parishioners following the priest's expulsion; "Keihan 'Kirishitan' ikken ni taisuru Bukkōji kyōdan no taiō," *Rekishi no hiroba: Ōtani Daigaku Nihonshi no Kai kaishi* 19 (2016): 3–16.

38. Rentakuji was Kinu's temple of affiliation.

39. Masuya Yasubei is the name of one of the people who entrusted money to Sano; the judicial record does not indicate that either he or Yohei were fined. Another of Sano's clients lived in Ise-machi, but again there is no evidence that the block was fined. The block aldermen, landlords, and members of the landlords' five-household groups were indeed fined, but for sums considerably less than seven *ryō*.

40. The Nakamuraya was the business of Shintarō, one of Gunki's associates in Kyoto. Shintarō died before the incident came to light, but his son, Yatarō, and other family members and employees were held to be culpable. No mention is made elsewhere in the documents of a possible connection between the Nakamuraya and a house along Nakabashi street. The road to Sakai led directly

to the Tobita execution grounds and was the route normally used for parading those condemned to be crucified there.

12. NIGHT TALES FROM THE KASSHI DAY

1. This story would seem to be a variant and expansion of the account of Kinu's curing the eye disease of Kahei's son; see chapter 2, pp. 40–41.
2. Those who joined in the defense of Osaka Castle against the Tokugawa forces in 1614 and 1615 are said to have included a substantial number of Kirishitan ronin.
3. Okame is the same as Otafuku, which Gunki used as a disguised alternative to the scroll with the drawing of the Lord of Heaven; see chapter 3, pp. 61–63. In a parenthetical note, Seizan describes "Okame" as having a face with "three flat parts and two full"; in other words, a low forehead, flat nose, and sunken chin along with two plump cheeks.
4. Matsura Seizan, *Kasshi yawa*, ed. Nakamura Yukihiko and Nakano Mitsutoshi, 20 vols. (Heibonsha, 1977–1983), *zokuhen*, 1:154–55.
5. The story reported here of the old woman's pilgrimage to Ise accompanied by a young man and their arrest upon returning to Kyoto perhaps derives from Mitsugi's pilgrimage to Konpira in Shikoku on behalf of the Yamanoi noble house in 1821. Her arrest on that occasion, however, did not lead to discovery of her involvement with the Kirishitan group. See chapter 3, pp. 69–70, 72; and appendix 1.
6. A high-quality silk fabric that was both costly and decorative.
7. Seizan refers here to *Yaso tenchūki*, an undated work by Murai Masahiro (1693–1759) about the Shimabara uprising. An Edo-based military scholar, Murai served a daimyo who was subsequently allocated the Shimabara domain.
8. The name of the festival of the dead, Urabon, when the souls of the deceased return temporarily home, was translated in Chinese Buddhist scriptures as "reprieve from being suspended upside down."
9. Matsura, *Kasshi yawa*, *zokuhen*, 3:111–13.
10. According to *The State of the Floating World*, Kimyō was the nickname of Heizō, who was indeed a storyteller.
11. Characters read as *daiusu* were commonly used in Kirishitan literature to transcribe Deus, the Christian God.
12. Matsura, *Kasshi yawa*, *zokuhen*, 3:215–16.
13. The Ming scholar Wang Yangming (1472–1528) is known for, among other things, his emphasis on an intuitive knowledge of good and the unity of knowledge and action. These features of his teachings attracted many political activists but were criticized by others as encouraging a rash subjectivity.

14. Like others, Seizan and his neighbor seem to have assumed that Ricci, known in Japan by his Chinese name, was Chinese. However, neither of the two books mentioned were in fact authored by Ricci. The former (*Taixi shuifa*, 1612) was a collaborative project by Xu Guangqi and Sabatino de Ursis, and the latter (*Qiqi tushuo*, 1627) was by Wang Zheng and Johann Terrenz Schreck. In addition, neither work appears in the list of materials confiscated from Kenzō.
15. Matsura, *Kasshi yawa, sanpen*, 3:277.
16. Ogino Baiu (or Yaokichi, 1781–1843) was a shogunal houseman (*gokenin*) who was on friendly terms with Seizan. Mogami Tokunai (1754–1836) was a shogunal official famous for exploration of Ezochi (Hokkaido, the Kuril Islands, and Sakhalin). We have omitted the poems here.
17. Luo Rufang (1515–1588) was a member of the so-called left wing of the Wang Yangming school. He held that all people should strive to recover the "infant's heart" and its innate endowment of the knowledge of good.
18. Matsura, *Kasshi yawa, sanpen*, 3:325–27.
19. Matsura, *Kasshi yawa, sanpen*, 4:47.

13. *A BIOGRAPHY OF ŌSHIO HEIHACHIRŌ*

1. Sayo must be Sano, and Kyōya Densuke her son, Kyōya Shinsuke. Mitsugi only initiated Kinu, and both Kinu and Sano moved to Osaka at a later date.
2. Imagawa Yoshimoto (1519–1560) was a famous warrior lord of the late medieval period. He was ultimately destroyed by Oda Nobunaga (1534–1582). Ōshio did indeed claim descent from a branch of the Imagawa.
3. *Ōshio Heihachirō denki: Kinko jitsuroku* (Eisensha, 1882, 1886), ndljp/pid/1939594, National Diet Library Digital Collection, folios 7b–10a.
4. *Ōshio Heihachirō denki*, folio 35b.

APPENDIX 1. MITSUGI'S 1822 ARREST

1. *Oshioki reiruishū*, ed. Ishii Ryōsuke, 16 vols. (Meicho Shuppan, 1971–1973), 10:55–56.
2. This is Mitsugi's sometime follower Harimaya Kinoshin, who at the time of the trip was going by the name Kinuya Mitsuemon. He was sentenced to thirty days' handcuffing for his part in the incident.
3. The Rules for Deciding Judicial Matters specified that in the case of lesser crimes punishable by handcuffs, fines, or house confinement, the accused should be exempted from implementation of the sentence if he or she had been jailed sixty days or more for interrogation; *Tokugawa kinreikō*, ed. Ishii Ryōsuke, 11 vols. (Sōbunsha, 1959–1961), *bekkan*: 127. See also Hiramatsu Yoshirō, *Kinsei keiji soshōhō no kenkyū* (Sōbunsha, 1960), 754.

4. Murakami presumably served as a retainer to Lord Kujō, the head of one of the most important court noble houses.

5. In other words, a woman could not be expected to behave properly and ordinarily might be treated more leniently than a man committing the same misdeed. In this case, however, Mitsugi's misbehavior was sufficiently serious to warrant her being held to the same standard as a man.

APPENDIX 2. DISPOSITION OF THE PROSCRIBED BOOKS

1. See Itō Tasaburō, "Kinsho no kenkyū," parts 1 and 2, *Rekishi chiri* 68, no. 4 (1936): 313–46; 68, no. 5 (1936): 435–70; Peter F. Kornicki, *The Book in Japan: A Cultural History from the Beginnings to the Nineteenth Century* (Leiden: Brill, 1998), 325–31; Ōba Osamu, *Books and Boats: Sino-Japanese Relations in the Seventeenth and Eighteenth Centuries*, trans. Joshua A. Fogel (Portland, Maine: MerwinAsia, 2012), 40–68.

2. A printed transcription of the two lists as well as the 1698 list of proscribed works is included in Kōda Shigetomo, *Ōshio Heihachirō* (Tōadō Shobō, 1910; repr., Chūōkōronsha, 1977), 186–88.

3. Kornicki, *The Book in Japan*, 348–49.

APPENDIX 3. MANUSCRIPT VERSIONS OF THE KEIHAN KIRISHITAN INCIDENT DOSSIER

1. The Historiographical Institute facsimile can be viewed online at https://clioimg.hi.u-tokyo.ac.jp/viewer/list/idata/200/2019/10/1/?m=limit.

2. See Yabuta Yutaka, "Ōsaka machi bugyō to 'Keihan Kirishitan jiken'" (forthcoming). Fujiwara Arikazu has published a transcription of most of the documents from the Deliberative Council discussions; "Ōshio Heihachirō to 'jashūmon ikken,'" *Kansai Daigaku Jinken Mondai Kenkyūshitsu kiyō* 13 (1986): 231–39. Excerpts from the council's deliberations are also included in *Oshioki reiruishū*, ed. Ishii Ryōsuke, 16 vols. (Meicho Shuppan, 1971–1973), vols. 11 and 12.

3. Although the Yoshino-bon does not include the discussions by the Deliberative Council, it does contain the orders issued by the senior councillors in late 1829 regarding the sentences and other matters (documents 12 and 13). Matsudaira notes that Takai privately sent him a copy of these orders, a circumstance that indicates that Matsudaira continued to take an interest in the case's development after moving on to his new position as Kyoto governor.

4. Ōhashi Yukihiro has published a transcription of the Seishin-bon, "Shiryō shōkai: Ōsaka Kirishitan ikken (Seishin Joshi Daigaku Toshokan shozō)," *Kenkyū Kirishitan gaku* 4 (2001): 80–122.

5. The Kōda-bon ends chronologically with Takai Sanenori's reports of 1829.12.7 to the senior councillors on the carrying out of the sentences and their other directions (documents 14–17; these are not included in the Yoshino-bon). The documents translated in chapter 10, which cover subsequent developments in the incident, are taken from the Precedents of Criminal Judgments Organized by Category (*Oshioki reiruishū*). For specifics, see the introduction to part 2.

REFERENCES

The place of publication of all Japanese-language works is Tokyo unless otherwise indicated.

WORKS TRANSLATED

Judicial Records

"Jashūmon ginmisho." MS copy. Microfilm M20-10-G. Tōkyō Daigaku Hōgaku Seijigaku Kenkyūka Fuzoku Kindai Nihon Hōsei Shiryō Sentā (Meiji Shinbun Zasshi Bunko). (Yoshino-bon)

"Jashūmon ikken kakitome." MS copy. 2019–10. https://clioimg.hi.u-tokyo.ac.jp/viewer/list/idata/200/2019/10/1/?m=limit. Tōkyō Daigaku Shiryō Hensanjo. (Kōda-bon)

Ōhashi Yukihiro. "Shiryō shōkai: Ōsaka Kirishitan ikken (Seishin Joshi Daigaku Toshokan shozō)." *Kenkyū Kirishitan gaku* 4 (2001): 80–122. (Seishin-bon)

Oshioki reiruishū. Ed. Ishii Ryōsuke. 16 vols. Meicho Shuppan, 1971–1973.

Retellings

Matsura Seizan. *Kasshi yawa*. Ed. Nakamura Yukihiko and Nakano Mitsutoshi. 20 vols. Heibonsha, 1977–1983.

Ōshio Heihachirō denki: Kinko jitsuroku. Eisensha, 1882, 1886. ndljp/pid/1939594.
National Diet Library Digital Collection.
Ukiyo no arisama. Ed. Harada Tomohiko and Asakura Haruhiko. Vol. 11 of *Nihon
shomin seikatsu shiryō shūsei.* San'ichi Shobō, 1970.

WORKS CITED

Aiso Kazuhiro. *Ōshio Heihachirō shokan no kenkyū.* 3 vols. Osaka: Seibundō Shuppan, 2003.
Aizawa Seishisai. *Gyobusaku.* In *Hekijahen, Gyobusaku.* No pub., no date. ndljp/
pid/754814. National Diet Library Digital Collection.
Botsman, Daniel V. *Punishment and Power in the Making of Modern Japan.* Princeton, N.J.: Princeton University Press, 2005.
Bouchy, Anne Marie [Busshī Annu Mari]. "Inari shinkō to fugeki." In *Inari shinkō
no kenkyū,* ed. Gorai Shigeru, 171–305. Okayama: San'yō Shinbunsha, 1980.
Demura Yoshifumi and Kawasaki Masashi. "Kinsei no Gionsha no keikan to sono
shūi to no rensetsu ni kansuru kenkyū." *Doboku keikakugaku kenkyū ronbun-
shū* 21 (2004): 393–98.
Ebisawa Arimichi. *Ishin henkakuki to Kirisutokyō.* Shinseisha, 1968.
——, ed. *Nanbanji kōhaiki, Jakyō taii, Myōtei mondō, Ha Deusu.* Heibonsha, 1964.
Elison, George. *Deus Destroyed: The Image of Christianity in Early Modern Japan.*
Cambridge, Mass.: Harvard University Press, 1973.
Fujii Yoshio. *Ōsaka machi bugyō to keibatsu.* Osaka: Seibundō Shuppan, 1990.
Fujita Yūkoku. "Kōshin teisho." In *Yūkoku zenshū,* ed. Kikuchi Kenjirō, 722–24.
Yoshida Yahei, 1935.
Fujiwara Arikazu. "Ōshio Heihachirō to 'jashūmon ikken.'" *Kansai Daigaku Jinken
Mondai Kenkyūshitsu kiyō* 13 (1986): 203–39.
Gifu-ken shi: Tsūshi-hen, kinsei, jō. Gifu: Gifu-ken, 1968.
Hall, John Carey. "Japanese Feudal Law: The Tokugawa Legislation (Part IV: The
Edict in One Hundred Sections)." *Transactions of the Asiatic Society of Japan*
41, no. 5 (1913): 683–804.
Hardacre, Helen. *Shinto: A History.* New York: Oxford University Press, 2017.
Hayashi Makoto. "The Female Christian Yin-Yang Master." Trans. Elizabeth Tins-
ley. *Cahiers d'Extrême-Asie* 21 (2012): 223–39.
——. "Kinsei kōki ni okeru Tsuchimikado-ke, onmyōji." *Ningen bunka* 24 (2009):
1–12.
——. *Kinsei onmyōdō no kenkyū.* Yoshikawa Kōbunkan, 2005.
——. "Tenshukyō to onna onmyōji." *Aichi Gakuin Daigaku Bungakubu kiyō* 41
(2011): 212–20.
Hirai, Atsuko. *Government by Mourning: Death and Political Integration in Japan,
1603–1912.* Cambridge, Mass.: Harvard University Asia Center, 2014.
Hiramatsu Yoshirō. *Kinsei keiji soshōhō no kenkyū.* Sōbunsha, 1960.
Hirata Atsushi. *Shinshū shisōshi ni okeru "shinzoku nitai" ron no tenkai.* Kyoto:
Ryūkoku Gakkai, 2001.

Howell, David L. "Foreign Encounters and Informal Diplomacy in Early Modern Japan." *Journal of Japanese Studies* 40, no. 2 (2014): 295–327.

Hur, Nam-lin. *Death and Social Order in Tokugawa Japan: Buddhism, Anti-Christianity, and the Danka System.* Cambridge, Mass.: Harvard University Asia Center, 2007.

Itō Tasaburō. "Bakumatsu ni okeru Yasokyō haigeki." *Rekishi chiri* 65, no. 3 (1935): 225–64.

———. "Kinsho no kenkyū." Parts 1 and 2. *Rekishi chiri* 68, no. 4 (1936): 313–46; 68, no. 5 (1936): 435–70.

Kawaji Toshiakira. *Neifu kiji.* Vols. 2–5 of *Kawaji Toshiakira monjo.* Nihon Shiseki Kyōkai, 1932–1934.

Kikuchi Yōsuke. *Kinsei jitsuroku no kenkyū: Seichō to tenkai.* Kyūko Shoin, 2008.

Kirihara Kenshin. "Haiya to jōi: Bakumatsu shūkyō shisō ni okeru kōki Mitogaku no isō." In *Kami to hotoke no bakumatsu ishin,* ed. Iwata Mami and Kirihara Kenshin, 167–91. Kyoto: Hōzōkan, 2018.

"Kirishitan jato ikken." MS copy. 2019-1. Tōkyō Daigaku Shiryō Hensanjo.

"Kirishitan shūmon raichō jikki." MS copy dated 1783. Bunko 07 00885. Waseda Daigaku Toshokan.

Kishi Yasuko. *Kinsei no kinri to toshi kūkan.* Kyoto: Shibunkaku Shuppan, 2014.

Kōda Shigetomo. *Edo to Ōsaka.* Fuzanbō, 1934. Reprint, 1995.

———. *Ōshio Heihachirō.* Tōadō Shobō, 1910. Reprint, Chūōkōronsha, 1977.

Kornicki, Peter F. *The Book in Japan: A Cultural History from the Beginnings to the Nineteenth Century.* Leiden: Brill, 1998.

———. "Manuscript, Not Print: Scribal Culture in the Edo Period." *Journal of Japanese Studies* 32, no. 1 (2006): 23–52.

Kyōto-fuka yūkaku yuisho. In vol. 9 of *Shinsen Kyōto sōsho,* 103–64. Kyoto: Rinsen Shoten, 1986.

Legge, James, trans. *The Chinese Classics.* 5 vols. Hong Kong: Hong Kong University Press, 1960.

Leuchtenberger, Jan C. *Conquering Demons: The "Kirishitan," Japan, and the World in Early Modern Japanese Literature.* Ann Arbor: Center for Japanese Studies, University of Michigan, 2013.

Mashita Michiko. "Kinsei Ōsaka no onna namae: Hō kisei to jittai." *Josei shigaku* 10 (2000): 1–15.

Matsukane Naomi. "Keihan 'Kirishitan' ikken ni taisuru Bukkōji kyōdan no taiō." *Rekishi no hiroba: Ōtani Daigaku Nihonshi no Kai kaishi* 19 (2016): 3–16.

———. "Shiryō shōkai: Shūmon okite (kōgi yori jashūmon ofureshimeshi): Keihan Kirishitan ikken-go ni okeru Higashi Honganji gakusō no enzetsu." *Dōhō Daigaku Bukkyō Bunka Kenkyūjo kiyō* 32 (2012): 107–14.

Miki Seiichirō. "Toyokuni-sha no zōei ni kansuru ichi kōsatsu." *Nagoya Daigaku Bungakubu kenkyū ronshū shigaku* 33 (1987): 196–209.

Mito-shi shi. Vol. 2, no. 3. Mito: Mito-shi Yakusho, 1976.

Miyagi Kimiko. *Ōshio Heihachirō.* Asahi Shinbunsha, 1977.

Nakagawa Sugane. "Inari Worship in Early Modern Osaka." Trans. Andrea C. Damon. In *Osaka: The Merchants' Capital of Early Modern Japan*, ed. James L. McClain and Wakita Osamu, 180–212. Ithaca, N.Y.: Cornell University Press, 1999.

Nakai, Kate Wildman. "'Deviant Practices' and 'Strange Acts': Late Tokugawa Judicial Perspectives on Heteropraxy." Forthcoming.

Nakamura Yoshifumi. "Sekke no keishi tachi." In *Chōtei o torimaku hitobito*, ed. Takano Toshihiko, vol. 8 of *Mibunteki shūen to kinsei shakai*, 73–105. Yoshikawa Kōbunkan, 2007.

Nakano Misao. *Ōsaka ishi banzuke shūsei*. Kyoto: Shibunkaku, 1985.

——. *Ōsaka meii den*. Kyoto: Shibunkaku, 1983.

Nichirenshū jiten. Nichirenshū Shūmuin, 1981.

Nosco, Peter. "Secrecy and the Transmission of Tradition: Issues in the Study of the 'Underground' Christians." *Japanese Journal of Religious Studies* 20, no. 1 (1993): 3–29.

Ōba Osamu. *Books and Boats: Sino-Japanese Relations in the Seventeenth and Eighteenth Centuries*. Trans. Joshua A. Fogel. Portland, Maine: MerwinAsia, 2012.

Ofuregaki Kanpō shūsei. Ed. Takayanagi Shinzō and Ishii Ryōsuke. Iwanami Shoten, 1934.

Ofuregaki Tenmei shūsei. Ed. Takayanagi Shinzō and Ishii Ryōsuke. Iwanami Shoten, 1936.

Ofuregaki Tenpō shūsei. Ed. Takayanagi Shinzō and Ishii Ryōsuke. Iwanami Shoten, 1937.

Ogura Takashi. *Edo bakufu kamigata shihai kikō no kenkyū*. Hanawa Shobō, 2011.

Ōhashi Yukihiro. *Kinsei senpuku shūkyō ron: Kirishitan to kakushi nenbutsu*. Azekura Shobō, 2017.

——. *Kirishitan minshūshi no kenkyū*. Tōkyōdō Shuppan, 2001.

——. *Senpuku Kirishitan: Edo jidai no kinkyō seisaku to minshū*. Kōdansha, 2014.

Owaki Hidekazu. "Kinsei no mibun idō, nijūka to 'ninbetsu' no toriatsukai." *Nihon rekishi* 839 (2018): 21–38.

Paramore, Kiri. *Ideology and Christianity in Japan*. New York: Routledge, 2009.

Sawayanagi Masumi. "Bakumatsuki no 'Kirishitan' imēji ni tsuite: Ōshio no ran kanren shiryō ni okeru Keihan Kirishitan ikken jōhō o chūshin ni." *Kokushikan shigaku* 14 (2010): 21–49.

Seki Tamiko. "'Jashūmon ikken' ni miru danjo no shosō." In *Esunishiti, jendā kara miru Nihon no rekishi*, ed. Kuroda Hiroko and Nagano Hiroko, 200–21. Yoshikawa Kōbunkan, 2002.

"Senjutsu kakurei: Shohen." 68 vols. MS copy. 818-1/ndljp/pid/2610580. National Diet Library Digital Collection.

Shimizu Hirokazu and Shimizu Yūko, eds. *Kirishitan kankei hōsei shiryō*. Sōkyū Shuppan, 2002.

Shisei teiyō. 2 vols. Okayama: Fukutake Shoten, 1974.

"Sokkyo hen." 22 vols. MS copy. C60:73. Tōkyō Daigaku Sōgō Toshokan.

Sone Hiromi. "Josei to keibatsu." In *Mibun no naka no josei*, ed. Yabuta Yutaka and Yanagiya Keiko, vol. 4 of *Edo no hito to mibun*, 67–98. Yoshikawa Kōbunkan, 2010.

Stone, Jacqueline. "When the Lotus Went Underground: The Nichiren *Fuju fuse* Movement and the Kanbun-era Persecution." Forthcoming.

Sugimori Tetsuya. *Kinsei Kyōto no toshi to shakai.* Tōkyō Daigaku Shuppankai, 2008.

Takeuchi Makoto and Ichikawa Hiroaki. *Hitome de wakaru Edo jidai: Chizu, zukai, gurafu de miru.* Shōgakukan, 2004.

Tamamuro Fumio. *Sōshiki to danka.* Yoshikawa Kōbunkan, 1999.

Teeuwen, Mark, and Kate Wildman Nakai, eds. *Lust, Commerce, and Corruption: An Account of What I Have Seen and Heard by an Edo Samurai.* New York: Columbia University Press, 2014.

Tekagami, Tekagami shūi. Vol. 6 of *Ōsaka-shi shi shiryō.* Osaka: Ōsaka-shi Shiryō Chōsakai, 1982.

Tokugawa kinreikō. Ed. Ishii Ryōsuke. 11 vols. Sōbunsha, 1959–1961.

"Tokugawa Nariaki jūjō goji kengisho." In *Bakumatsu seiji ronshū*, vol. 56 of *Nihon shisō taikei*, 9–18. Iwanami Shoten, 1976.

Tsukada Takashi. "Early Modern Osaka *Hinin* and Population Registers." In *Japan's Household Registration System and Citizenship: Koseki, Identification and Documentation*, ed. David Chapman and Karl Jakob Krogness, 21–42. London: Routledge, 2014.

——. *Ōsaka no hinin: Kojiki, Shitennōji, korobi Kirishitan.* Chikuma Shobō, 2013.

Ujiie Mikito. *Tonosama to nezumi kozō: Rōkō Matsura Seizan no sekai.* Chūōkōron-sha, 1991.

Wakabayashi, Bob Tadashi. *Anti-Foreignism and Western Learning in Early-Modern Japan: The New Theses of 1825.* Cambridge, Mass.: Council on East Asian Studies, Harvard University, 1986.

Yabuta Yutaka. *Bushi no machi Ōsaka: "Tenka no daidokoro" no samurai tachi.* Chūōkōronsha, 2010.

——. "Ōsaka machi bugyō to 'Keihan Kirishitan jiken.'" Forthcoming.

——. "Shinmi Masamichi to Ōshio Heihachirō: 'Shinmi Masamichi nikki' ni yoru kōsatsu." In *Ōshio Heihachirō no sōgō kenkyū*, ed. Ōshio Jiken Kenkyūkai, 1–17. Osaka: Izumi Shoin, 2011.

Yamane Chiyomi. "Kirishitan kinseishi ni okeru Keihan Kirishitan ikken no igi." *Ōshio kenkyū* 19 (1985): 20–43.

Yasutaka Hiroaki. *Fumie o funda Kirishitan.* Yoshikawa Kōbunkan, 2018.

——, ed. *Hirado Matsura-ke no meihō to kinkyō seisaku: Tōei sareta daikōkai jidai to sono hate ni.* Fukuoka: Seinan Gakuin Daigaku Hakubutsukan, 2013.

Yoshida Tokutarō, ed. *Ikeda-ke rireki ryakki.* 2 vols. Okayama: Nihon Bunkyō Shuppan, 1965.

INDEX

addenda. *See* testimonies

adoption, 309n10; of sons-in-law, 85, 115, 118, 122, 128, 199, 207, 220, 255–56, 257. *See also* Hisae; Ito; Kamon; Toki (Wasa's adoptive daughter)

Aizawa Seishisai, 238, 239

Akashiya Iwa, 54

Amakusa, xvi, xviii, 299n1, 317n15. *See also* Shimabara-Amakusa uprising

austerities, water, xviii, 9, 43, 302n25; and Gunki, xxii, xxiii, 73, 93, 94; Heizō's practice of, 94, 95, 96, 165; Kinoshin's practice of, 71, 174, 193; Kinu's practice of, 6, 38, 39, 54, 64, 77–78, 160; locations of, x, xii, 305n10; Mitsugi's practice of, x, 38, 56, 59, 60, 62, 66, 67, 71, 74, 77–78, 137, 162, 163, 245, 279; Sano's practice of, xii, 8, 10, 14, 17–18, 19, 36, 37, 40, 45, 77–78, 158, 260; and Toki (Wasa's daughter), 64, 65, 66; Umon's practice of, xxiii, xxvi–xxvii, xxviii, 83, 85, 87, 164; and Wasa, 64; Yae's practice of, 20

banishment (*tsuihō*): from immediate locale (*tokorobarai*), 170, 181, 182, 205, 293; from three districts of Osaka, 170, 182, 205

Biography of Ōshio Heihachirō (Ōshio Heihachirō denki), 237, 277–82

Book of Changes. See *Yijing (Book of Changes)* divination

Buddhism, xxvi–xxviii, 165, 275; and Gunki, 91; and Heizō, 89–91; and Inari deity, 300n7; Pure Land, 304n2; Ricci on, 311n4; Shingon, 82, 164; and Umon, 81–83, 89. *See also* certification of sectarian affiliation; Dakiniten cult; Ikkō sect; priests; temple registration system; Zen Buddhism

investigators, xliv; on confraternity,
96; on Gunki's origins, 125–27; on
Kenzō, 130–31; on Kinoshin,
70–72; on Kinu, 44–48, 52; on
Mitsugi, 53, 60–61, 74, 76–79; on
other suspects, 50, 51, 65–66,
87–88, 97–98, 118–20;
preconceptions of, xxxiii, xxxv; on
Sano, 3–4, 21–24, 27–31, 32–34; on
Shōni, 103–5; on substitute image
of Lord of Heaven, 62–63
Iori (Mitsugi's husband), x, xxiii, xli,
37, 54, 55–56, 59, 62, 66, 67
Irakoya Keizō. See Umon
Iseya Kanzō. See Kanzō
Iseya Yohei (Sano's grandfather), 4
Isogawa Gonzō (Sano's father), 4–5
Ito (Wasa's adoptive daughter), x, xli,
57, 65–67, 79, 135, 193, 221; corpse
of, 226–27; death of, 154;
punishment for, 139, 171, 205
Itō Tasaburō, 287, 288
Itoya Wasa. See Wasa

Jesuits, xviii, 287, 288. See also Ricci,
Matteo
Jesus creed (Yaso). See Christianity
Jikū (priest), 169, 318n5, 320n6
Jinbei (Momijiya Jinbei; Gunki's
concubine's brother), xli, 80, 102,
123, 124–25, 199; punishment for,
175, 207
Jiren shipian. See Ten Pieces
Transcending Common Sense
jitsuroku (true accounts), 231–32, 237,
333n23
Jōsuke (Edoya Jōsuke; Koto's son), x,
xii, xliii, 43, 44–45, 192, 323n37;
punishment for, 205, 213–14
judicial system, xix, xxi; collective
responsibility in, 146, 150–51, 210;
confession in, xxxii–xxxiii, xxxiv;
and governors, xxxi–xxxii, 141–44,
146, 151, 157–68; and imperial

court, 201–2, 302n30, 313n7, 315n11,
328n7; and jurisdiction, xxxi, 52,
143, 153, 224, 302n30, 304n1,
312n15, 321n14, 328n7, 329n10;
Keihan incident's influence on,
155–56; and Osaka Magistracy,
xxix–xxx, 141, 145–48; precedents
in, 142–47, 149, 152–53, 157, 168,
172, 174, 176, 178–86, 188–89, 192,
196–97, 199, 200, 211, 212, 225,
228, 317n15, 319n12, 320n6, 321n19,
330nn22–23; review of sentences
in, xxxi–xxxii, 141–217; statute of
limitations in, 189–90, 192,
194–96, 200, 204–8, 214, 322n30,
323n44, 327nn10–11; torture in,
xxxiii, 29, 270–71, 303n33, 307n31;
types of punishments in, 314n6,
314n23, 319nn7–11; and women,
xxvi, 339n5. See also Deliberative
Council; senior councillors; specific
punishments

kabuki, 82, 234, 309n6
Kahei (Harimaya Kahei), xii, xliii,
40–42, 221; associates of, 49,
50–51, 137; charges against, 162;
and Kinu, 50–51, 161, 182; in Night
Tales, 337n1; punishment for, 170,
182, 205
Kakiya Jirobei, 70, 71
Kakunosuke (Ōshio's adoptive son),
282
Kamon (Mitsugi's adoptive son), x, xli,
74–75, 331n23, 334n19; punishment
for, 138–39, 154, 169, 171, 172, 193,
205; request for release of, 227–28,
229; State of the Floating World on,
248–49, 250
Kangiten rituals, 310n1; and Gunki,
92, 102, 107, 110; and Umon,
82–83, 87, 89, 164
Kan'in princely house, x, 301n15;
Gunki's dismissal by, 87, 101–3,

temple registration system (*continued*)
Kenzō, xliv, 201, 211, 214, 258–60,
325n66; and Kinu, xliv, 43, 134, 187,
208, 265, 336n38; and Mitsugi,
xliv, 62, 134, 187, 209, 214, 252,
273, 333n6; and relatives of
Kirishitan, 329nn13–15, 330n18;
and Sano, xliv, 18, 133, 134, 187, 208,
264–65; and Tōzō, 42–43, 134; and
Umon, xliv, 85–86, 134, 167, 187,
254–56, 333n7; and Wasa, xliv, 135,
188, 333n6
Ten Pieces Transcending Common Sense
(*Kijin jippen; Jiren shipian*; Ricci),
85, 311n4
Tenrikyō, 333n23
Teradaya Kumazō. *See* Kumazō
testimonies, xxviii, xxxii–xxxv; addenda
(*shugaki*) in, xxxiv, xxxvii–xxxviii,
60, 145, 302n21, 304n4, 305n21,
309n9, 322n29; confirmed vs.
unconfirmed, xxxii–xxxiii, xxxiv,
303n34, 320n4; reliability of,
xxxiv–xxxv; transcripts of, xxxii,
xxxiv; [unverified] suspicions (*satto*)
in, xxxiv–xxxv, 29, 30, 32, 47–48,
50, 72, 75, 76–77, 88. *See also under
particular suspects*
*Tianzhu shiyi. See True Principles of
the Lord of Heaven*
Tō, case of, 228, 331n23
Tobaya Gihei, 244, 264
Tobita execution grounds (Osaka), xii,
xv, 152, 236, 254, 337n40
Toki (Kanzō's wife), xii, xliv,
138; charges against, 159–60;
punishment for, 169, 180, 204;
relatives of, 210–11, 215, 223; and
Sano, 20–21, 24, 26–28, 31–33, 159,
160, 190, 201; testimony of, 31–33;
unverified accusations against, 32
Toki (Wasa's adoptive daughter), xli,
109, 110, 220, 306n25, 330n20; and
Lord of Heaven scroll, 79, 113; and

Mitsugi, xxiii, xxv, 54, 56, 57,
62, 64–68, 78, 138, 162, 163;
punishment for, 139, 154, 171, 193,
205; request for release of, 227,
229; temple registration of, 135
Toku (Shimaya Kiroku's wife), 22, 213
Tokugawa Ieyasu, xx
Tokugawa Nariaki, 238
Tomitaya Riemon. *See* Riemon
Tomo (Gunki's concubine), xli, 123,
124
Tora (Kawachiya Manjirō's wife), 22,
213
"Torch of Rhinoceros Horn, Draft"
(*Nensairoku kō*; Kenzō), 288,
314n7
torture. *See* judicial system: torture in
Toshimaya Tōzō. *See* Tōzō
Toyotomi Hideyoshi, 61–62, 76, 77,
238, 309n7
Tōzō (Toshimaya Tōzō; Harimaya
Tōzō; Kinu's false household head),
xii, xliii, 308n9, 321n12; charges
against, 161–62; and Kahei, 49,
50–51, 162; and Kinu, 35, 40,
42–43, 161, 279; population register
of, 42–43, 51, 137, 162, 168, 170,
181–82, 189; punishment for,
169–70, 181, 205; testimony of,
48–50; unverified accusations
against, 50
*True Account of the Coming of the
Kirishitan Sect to This Country*
(*Kirishitan shūmon raichō jikki*), xix,
xxii
True Principles of the Lord of Heaven
(*Tenshu jitsugi; Tianzhu shiyi*;
Ricci), 85, 311n4
Tsuchimikado noble house, xliii, 53,
55, 62, 188, 315n11; and yin-yang
diviners, xxiii, 135–37, 168, 301n17,
303n30, 315n12
Tsuchiya Shōni. *See* Shōni
Tsuchiya Yoshinao, 320n3, 320n4

Tsugi (Yatarō's concubine), 115, 116, 121–22, 198, 324n57; punishment for, 207, 216
Tsunehachi (Yatarō's shop manager), xlii, 122, 198, 207, 324n57
Tsutsui Masanori, 320n3

Uchiyama Hikojirō, 289, 290
Uhei (Harimaya Uhei), xliv, 16–17, 173, 189, 201, 204. *See also* Soyo
Ukiyo no arisama. See *State of the Floating World*
Umon (Fujii Umon; Irakoya Keizō), x, xi, xii, xlii; arrest of, 81; associates of, xliv, 97, 183, 253; austerities practiced by, xxiii, xxvi–xxvii, xxviii, 83, 85, 87, 164; and Buddhism, 81–83, 89; and Christianity, 85, 88, 164, 210; crucifixion of, 183, 206, 254; death of, 250; Deliberative Council on, 321n16, 322n27; and divination, 81, 83; and Gunki, xxii–xxiii, xxvii, xxviii, 82, 86, 87–89, 164, 165, 253; initiation of, xxii, 83, 87–88, 164; and Kangiten worship, 82–83; and Kenzō, 128, 129, 130, 131; landlords of, 168; local officials of, 137, 172, 188, 210; and Lord of Heaven scroll, 82–83, 88, 164; and Mitsugi, 67, 86–89, 164; as physician, 81, 85, 88; and proscribed books, xxv, 335n32; punishment for, 138, 170, 182–83, 185, 206, 319n7; relatives of, xlii, 151, 201, 210, 215, 218–19, 221, 223; in *State of the Floating World*, 232, 253–56, 335n20; temple registration of, xliv, 134, 167, 187, 254–56, 333n7; testimony of, 81–88
Uneme (Sugihara Umon), 126, 127
Urakami, xvi, xviii, 299n1, 317n15
Ursis, Sabatino de, 338n14
Uzume, 61, 63, 95–97, 165, 170, 309n6, 312n14

Wada Shūsuke, 252, 253
Wang Yangming, 274–75, 337n13, 338n17
Wang Zheng, 338n14
Wasa (Itoya Wasa), x, xi, 53–80, 87; and Christianity, 210; death of, xxv, 68; grave of, 171, 187, 209, 214–15; and Gunki, xxv, 65–66, 79, 109, 138, 197; and Kinu, 37–38, 64; and Lord of Heaven images, 78–79; and Mitsugi, xxiii, xxv, 37, 54, 56, 57, 59, 62, 64–68, 78, 138, 162, 163, 309n5; relatives of, xli, 115, 118, 151, 201, 210, 215, 218–21, 223, 313n18; temple registration of, xliv, 135, 188, 333n6. *See also* Ito; Toki (Wasa's adoptive daughter)
Wasa (Shintarō's wife), 115, 118, 120–21, 174, 198, 199, 313n16, 324n57; punishment for, 207, 216
Washinoo noble house, 75, 310n21
Watanabe Kazue. *See* Kazue
Water Margin at Tenma (Tenma suiko den), 237. See also *Biography of Ōshio Heihachirō*
waterfalls: locations of, 8, 54, 59, 69, 71, 77, 304n10; use of in water austerities, xxii, 6, 38, 60–61, 64, 66, 74, 85, 137, 158, 160, 162, 163
Western learning, 236, 274, 287, 288; in medicine, xxv, 128–30. *See also* Christianity: proscribed books on
Western powers, xvii, 232; and Christianity, xvii, xix, 237–39
women: Gunki's treatment of, xxvi–xxvii; and judicial system, xxvi, 285, 321n16, 339n5; and Meiji religious groups, 332n23; in Osaka, 40, 306n25, 307n4; and population registers, 40, 306n25, 307n4; torture of, xxxiii, 303n33. *See also particular individuals*

Xu Guangqi, 338n14